HERE'S TO CRIME

HERE'S TO CRIME

BY COURTNEY RYLEY COOPER

BOSTON
LITTLE, BROWN AND COMPANY
1937

TO

THE HONORABLE HOMER CUMMINGS

A GENTLEMAN OF VALOR

INTRODUCTION

LET's be sensible regarding this drivel that crime does not pay. The slogan was conceived by some well-meaning sentimentalist who believed the phrase would become a bogeyman to frighten little boys and girls into security against temptation. It might have accomplished its object except that the juvenile mind is so constructed that one motion picture, depicting a machine-gun murdering gangster in heroic attitudes, is sufficient to kick all the slogans in the world out the nearest window.

However, it sounded good. Generous use of it could be made to cover much sinning. The picture companies discovered this quickly. So did some of the more sensational newspapers, which speedily learned that in the repetition of this grandiose sentiment lay an opportunity to print more and bloodier crime news. The slogan, however, reached its heights in the ambitions of certain periodical purveyors who like to depict the most gory details of rape and carnage, under the holy cloak that they are displaying to all concerned the horrible lesson that "crime does not pay." Meanwhile crime continues to rake in its shekels from the mother lode of greed, avarice, and lust.

It seems rather strange, if crime does not pay, that more than three million, five hundred thousand persons should be engaged in it, thus forming by far the biggest industry in America. Motor companies, newspapers, dry goods stores, steel companies, traction and railway corporations, and all the rest of this country's business endeavors, including the corner grocery store, manage to roll up an annual income of between fifty and sixty billion dollars. To this end is used every possible advertising and sales medium. Meanwhile an absolute minimum of fifteen billion dollars is spent on crime in all its phases of profit, expense and loss.

Far fewer persons, for instance, die as a result of their crimes than die from industrial accidents. Vastly fewer are injured. Compared with the horrible totals of death and accident resulting from the use of automobiles, fatality for criminals is utterly insignificant. Some 37,500 persons died in 1936 as the result of traffic accidents, while about 110,000 were injured. While this was happening, law enforcement killed only about 1,100 persons, of whom some 200 odd were executed. Or, as a bank-robber put it: —

"It's a damn sight safer these days to kill a guy than it is to cross a street. And if a fellow does have to pass a little time away from the bright lights, I'd rather do it in a hoosegow than a hospital."

Incidentally, nobody in the criminal world "pays for crime." He "gets in trouble" or is "a loser." Only in exceptional instances is the professional lawbreaker ever punished for his infractions, crime by crime. Perhaps that needs explanation. Alvin Karpis is a good example.

This man, in ten years, from the age of sixteen to that of twenty-six, took part in the robbery of at least fifteen banks. He engaged in a minimum of three kidnappings. The murder list records his presence at numerous unlawful deaths. His intake never was published in the S.E.C. listings of notable money-makers; nevertheless, in recent years, it amounted to some sixty thousand dollars of stolen money annually. Had he been punished, one by one, for his crimes, he would have been either executed years ago, or sentenced to more than a thousand years in prison, with a casket and hearse as his only possible means of exit.

But Karpis was punished for one crime, as is the custom in America, with other prosecutions delayed until a future date. He was sentenced "to life," which means that in fifteen years he will be eligible for parole. If the usual course of events runs true to form, the witnesses to his other infractions will be scattered, forgetful, forgiving or dead. Public memory is short and criminals know it; try to remember the outstanding law violator of fifteen years ago. Therefore, if Karpis is the usual "model prisoner," other things being equal, it is possible for him to walk forth free of all charges by the time he is forty-one. Under ordinary conditions of life, his earning power would not have been more than two thousand dollars a year. He boasts that he has hidden a large part of his criminally-obtained fortune. Figure it out for yourself.

It is to display the thousand-and-one forms in which crime is being made to pay that this book is written. I hope to take the reader by the hand and lead him through the labryinths of the underworld, where the risks of the "profession" are looked upon with almost the same viewpoint as prevails with the steel-molder, the iron-worker, the railroad engineer and all other legitimate endeavors where danger to life and limb and earning power form a necessary integral of the trade in which one is engaged. There is the difference, however, that for the honest trades, this risk is a bugbear; for the criminal, and all his allies, the percentages run so small that danger is backgrounded rather than high-lighted.

Of course the public has a different idea, due greatly to the sentiment-engendered viewpoint toward "the hunted man." Thus we follow human inclinations and sympathize with the person who is caught, forgetting the victim and overlooking entirely the fellow who gets away in spite of repeated offenses. We must remember also that the law of averages demands that a person give of his time in exchange for earnings. In the workaday world this is so many hours each day spent at a desk or in labor. For the professional criminal it means, providing he is caught, so many years of imprisonment; in the end, the sum amounts to the same total.

Safety is the most necessary thing for human existence. Therefore, so you may know something about protecting yourself and your home, this volume is devoted to the why and how and wherefore of crime; how it lives and prospers. It is dedicated to the explanation of how millions of persons live upon crime and its fringes, how politics thrives and fattens upon it, how civic corruption feeds and festers through relationship with it. You should be interested in the bargain cheapness of murder, the slime of pardon, and the truth about parole.

There shall be visits to the interiors of prison, revealing little-known details of sex and homosexuality in the cell-block. We shall meet the dumb people who have made it possible for sleek Sicilians to bring about what is true white slavery; we shall even make the acquaintance of some of the madames and quite a number of the girls.

There may be much that will sound bizarre, manufactured, unbelievable; facts which seemingly describe conditions of medieval times, not those of a modern age. I am reminded of a visit last summer to the office of a Cabinet Member.

Across the big desk sat a whimsical, kindly featured man. In one hand he dawdled his pince-nez glasses. His eye twinkled and a smile creased the corners of his lips. I had been ranting for half an hour about conditions in a certain city, where at least five members of the municipal police force were married to active inmates of houses of prostitution. I had talked of graft, of money paid to district attorneys for freedom from prosecution. I had berated political set-ups by which crime thrived. And when I paused for breath, the Cabinet Officer sat for a moment in thought.

"Cooper," he said at last, "you've got a lot on your chest."

"Plenty, General."

The "General" sat for a long time looking out the window, swinging his glasses, pursing his lips. At last he rose, his spare frame towering above me.

"Then do something about it," he said; "print it. All of it. Somebody's got to do it sooner or later."

Thus the truth about a farce had its beginning. The *dramatis personae* were assembled: maundering ministers, preaching sex to fill their pulpits, puffing politicians, promising anything from pardons to protection in return for votes, excitement-hungry girls hurrying to bawdy houses that they might become a part of municipal corruption; thieves, robbers, rapists. Bank robbers, pimps, and panderers are in the cast; there are mobsters, policy men, dopesters, cannibals, race-track fixers, murderers, policemen, poisoners, and all the rest of the three-and-a-half million persons engaged in the stupendous task of rolling up the greatest crime bill in the history of the world.

Since they are all present, awaiting their cue, it might be fitting for us to pay proper homage to success. Suppose we raise our glasses in a grisly toast: —

HERE'S TO CRIME!

COURTNEY RYLEY COOPER

CONTENTS

HERE'S TO CRIME

CHAPTER ONE

JUNGLE GROWTH

IT had been several hours since Bruno Richard Hauptmann had stumbled to the stiff-armed electric chair in the tiny execution chamber at State Prison in Trenton, New Jersey. We who had seen him die were too tired for sleep; thousands of words had rolled off our typewriters into the hands of swift-working telegraphers; at last, however, it was over.

The big pressroom, set up in a prison workshop, now was merely a place of silent litter. The clatter of typewriter instruments, the rattle of telegraph "speed-bugs," the ringing of telephones, was silenced. The wire crews worked stolidly at the job of dismantling; to-morrow this place no longer would be ankle-deep in papers, nor would it be jammed with cigarette-eating newspapermen, intent upon relaying every possible detail of the death of a human being to a news-hungry public.

The floors would be clean. There would be daylight to take the place of the white-burning kliegs which had played upon us for the benefit of the newsreels while we pounded out the story of a last few steps to death. There would be whirring machinery instead of typewriters and cameras, guards instead of city editors, convicts instead of reporters. We took a last look about us, we who had lingered to send an extra "take" for the later editions. Then, in the fashion of men with jagged nerves, we went down to the Dutchman's for the relaxing influence of a seidel of Pilsener.

The subject remained Hauptmann — how he had wasted, whether or not he really had meant to walk past the chair when the guards reached out to grab him and strap him into the death seat, whether he realized what was going on, whether he really had collapsed in the death house as the guards had told us. Everything was Hauptmann — his final hours of life, his shambling entrance, his bony face and shiny, full-shaved head, his failure to make a final statement and the possible reasons therefor. But in all our conversation, wherein many an unusual fact was pointed out, one of importance was not considered. Bruno Richard Hauptmann really was an unusual criminal for these days: he remained true to one type of crime. Hauptmann's specialty in outlawry centered about the baby carriage. If every lawbreaker were like him, there would be less of an American enforcement problem.

The opposite, however, is true. America breeds ambidextrous outlaws, and thus stands apart from the rest of the world. Even in this country, there was a time when a person who pitted himself against the law did so along one special line of endeavor. He adopted a particular form of infraction in much the same fashion that a craftsman perfects himself in a given trade, to follow it the rest of his life. He was like Hauptmann, who began his march to the electric chair by specializing in robbery of women who wheeled baby carriages along German highways. To a certain degree he used the kidnapping technique even there, so frightening the woman whom he threatened that her whole thought was for her baby, thus allowing the marauder to plunder and escape without detection. For the Lindbergh kidnapping, he merely reversed the method: he took the baby and, by doing so, frightened the parents into the payment of fifty thousand dollars and eventually brought about his own death.

The Hauptmann technique in American crime would allow law enforcement to revert to the comparatively simple problems which prevailed up to the advent of Prohibition. Even in those comparatively placid days, America was the world's most lawless nation, but, at least, the underworld was an underworld and not a jungle; a person broke the law and either got caught or got away. He was not affiliated in a dozen other types of crime nor aided by an army of helpers. Moreover, he did not constitute an actual threat to the safety of a nation.

In the present days of super-crime it is almost impossible for any one to escape its results. Figures compiled by the Federal Bureau of Investigation show that it is probable that only one person out of four will live a life of sixty years without being the victim of a serious crime tantamount to robbery, assault, rape, arson, manslaughter, or murder. There are a million and a half such offenses every year. This means that the lives of seventy-five per cent. of our entire population have been or will be marred by major criminality.

A great part of this is due to the fact that our vicious criminals no longer follow the Hauptmann routine. Twenty years ago life in the underworld was entirely different from that of to-day. Pickpockets stuck to their nimble tricks, forgers remained true to their particular endeavors, safeblowers looked with scorn upon any profession other than the one for which they felt themselves best fitted. It was highly unusual in those days to find a thief who was also a counterfeiter, or a confidence man who would willingly associate with the most desperate gangsters in America.

Crime to-day, however, is a matter of many alliances and affiliations, making enforcement doubly difficult in a country where the majority of local agencies suffers from one or more of such maladies as corruption, inefficiency, lack of funds, or political dominance.

I am reminded of a luncheon in one of the big Eastern cities last winter. There were present a Federal officer, the Mayor, and a high ranking police officer. The Federal man had been talking about certain facts which had come to him concerning a racketeer whose annual "take" from this city, through race-track betting, vice, and gambling, ran into millions of dollars.

"I am informed," said the Federal officer, "that this fellow also uses extortion methods, but they are of a type which cannot be reached through Federal statutes. The case is one for the municipal police department alone. For instance, if a new night club opens and his gang believes it will be a paying investment, one of the members drops in with an offer to buy an interest at a ridiculous figure. The offer is refused. A few days later, the place is stink-bombed, waiters are beaten, and patrons frightened away. Soon afterward, the offer is renewed. This time it is accepted, and the gang thus cuts into a highly profitable investment for about ten cents on the dollar."

The Mayor squirmed.

"This is horrible," he said to his police companion. The officer was silent. The Federal man went on.

"Then, of course, there is the control of all houses of prostitution, plus a race-track betting system whereby every bookie must pay fifty dollars a day for taking bets. Another section of the gang is muscling-in on labor unions; I am told that it causes needless strikes upon which a price is set — any manufacturer who has been affected by the particular union controlled by this outfit can 'settle' his strike, not by acceding to the demands of the strikers, but by paying the controlling gang certain sums of money, ranging up to ten thousand dollars. In other words, it is an attempt at underworld control of labor through outlaw unions."

The Mayor grew red-faced. He pounded the table and whirled toward his police officer.

"Inspector," he shouted, "why haven't we learned about this before?"

The Inspector cleared his throat.

"There's a very good reason, Mr. Mayor," he answered calmly. "And I believe it is a compliment to the force. It shows that our police officers are honest. They don't mix with the underworld and, therefore, they naturally wouldn't find out stuff like this!"

I cite this instance not for its almost weird police attitude but because this particular city is rated as possessing one of the best police forces in the United States. It deserves that rating; for, as compared to other municipal outfits, it is highly efficient. In this particular case there was an unexpected denouement. A grand jury, assembled to look only into routine matters, took the bit in its teeth and appealed for a special prosecuting-investigating force to run down rumors of gang control. The Governor obeyed the demand, and appointed at its head a man whose honesty, while unimpeachable, was not of the easily soiled sort that would force the investigator to stay on the other side of the street when a crime was being committed. Within three months the granite foundations of the city had cracks in them as the result of racket revelations. Within a few months more, practically every charge made by the Federal agent had been proved and the super-racketeer was on his way to prison.

This incident in what is considered a most efficiently policed city may give you a faint idea of why you have only one chance out of four to go through life without being a victim of a major crime, why there are a quarter of a million potential murderers roaming at large with four hundred thousand potential victims who are doomed to die by murder. The illustration becomes more effective with the repetition that this police force, which was "too honest" to brush elbows with the underworld, stands near the top of a heap of forty thousand law enforcement agencies, containing one hundred and seventy thousand policemen, detectives, marshals, constables, and sheriffs. I am super-conservative in saying that more than half of these men are either inefficient, dishonest, ignorant, politically controlled, or thoroughly unaware of the requirements demanded of a first-class, present-day law enforcement agent. Further, if the fingerprints of these one hundred and seventy thousand persons could be examined and compared with the criminal identification files of the Federal Bureau of Investigation, an irreducible minimum of more than four thousand and a maximum of fifteen thousand so-called protectors of public safety would be found to have previous criminal records, ranging from larceny to murder.

It is necessary to denote these facts to explain how crime has become tangled in a jungle growth, wherein the ingredients are formed of politics, corruption, and a wide variance of infractions, the ramifications of which would overload even an honest and efficient police department. Perhaps a typical case would explain how crime grows and spreads from one man to include others in nationwide activities. First, however, there must be some historical background.

One of my memories of a wartime association with William J. Flynn, then Chief of the United States Secret Service, concerns our many conversations about counterfeiters.

Upon the walls of the Chief's New York office were the pictures of many violators of laws against the making of bogus money. Chief Flynn had some personal story to tell about each one — his art, his training as an engraver, his painstaking efforts to become a master in his "profession." Then, too, there was a large map, plentifully dotted with colored pushpins, which denoted the whereabouts of all worthwhile counterfeiters, every one corralled as it were, whether in prison or out. The Chief liked to swing his huge frame about from his desk, and, leaning back in his chair, dilate upon the futility of making imitation money.

"We've got 'em all tagged," he would say. "Every one of those fellows has his trademark. It takes years to develop a real counterfeiter; you can tell his work in a minute."

Then he would take a bundle of counterfeit bills from a desk drawer and name the maker of each by pointing out some idiosyncrasy.

"It's getting tougher every day for these fellows," he argued. "They're dying out. The ones who aren't in prison are getting old and their hands are becoming shaky — they can't do as

careful work. Counterfeiting will be a lost art in another twenty
years."

Chief Flynn long ago resigned from the Secret Service and
now is dead. His big map is gone from the wall; it could tell
little to-day, for the Chief's dream of an era in which there
would be no counterfeiting was — only a dream. True, many of
the old-timers have, one by one, vanished from the craft. There
are few zealots who give their lives to an ambition to recreate
an artistic imitation of United States money, obtaining almost
as much satisfaction from their art as from the monetary return. Those fellows were engravers first, criminals afterward.
In their place has come a new and vicious law-violator — a true
representative of the underworld with "affiliations," political
hook-ups, gangland associations, and tie-ins with the most
desperate outlaws; with the result that, instead of a counter-
feitless age, there is more bogus money in circulation to-day
than at any time since the chaotic era following the Civil
War.

All the elements of this underworld machinery can be shown
through one typical case, that of "Count" Lustig-Miller. It is a
recital of numerous complications, of much geography, and many
characters — for such is crime to-day. There are no short-cast
dramas in professional lawbreaking, no simple beginning-and-
end narratives. The trail winds from city to city and state to
state, from slums to "exclusiveness," rubbing elbows with respectability and alleged honesty. It writhes in and out of avenues
which we, as good citizens, believe to be reserved for integrity;
it shakes hands with, and sometimes fills the pockets of, persons
who are paid out of our taxes to allegedly protect our safety
and happiness. It does all this with a minimum of punishment.
Therefore, the widely varied activities of Count Lustig-Miller
must be looked upon not as a bizarre case, but as a commonplace
recital of the tangled undergrowth which is all professional
crime. There are thousands of men like Lustig-Miller in vari-

ous forms of criminal endeavor. However, since you probably never heard of this individual, perhaps it would be best to start with him from birth.

In the country of his beginnings, now Czechoslovakia, it is the custom for a bastard child to take the names of both its father and its mother. It may have been for other reasons, however, that "The Count" used two surnames; he was Lustig-Miller.

His youth was as obscure as his birth. There are evidences that he was of peasant extraction, also that he served his time as a conscript in the eternal European preparation for possible war, and that, during his period of training, he received a deep saber-cut which ran from a corner of his left eye to the middle of his left cheek, leaving a scar which was to be exceedingly useful to him in his later years.

In youth he began his career as a petty swindler, was caught and sent to prison. That was in Austria. Once out, he began to see Europe from its jails; Germany, France, Italy and other countries caught him for issuing bogus checks, for embezzlements and for swindling games which steadily assumed more magnitude.

At the outbreak of the World War, he was known throughout Central Europe as an habitual criminal, all the more dangerous because he had used the proceeds of crime for education and what is looked upon by gullible Americans as "Continental polish." He spoke five languages — always, however, with an Austrian accent. The outbreak of hostilities in Europe gave him a great opportunity. He left the Continent and made an illegal entry into America.

If Lustig-Miller had gone illegally from America into a European country, that would have been news. Here, however, it always has been ridiculously easy to beat the immigration laws. Annually enough undesirable aliens enter the United States to fill a first-class metropolis. Many of these have been "moved on" from the country of origin; the police of some

European cities use America as a dumping ground for certain types of outlaws by suggesting to them that they will have freedom from Continental prosecution if they will cross the seas. Naturally the next step is an illegal entrance into the United States.

When Lustig-Miller came here, he merely "stepped over the line" — there was not even a quota system at that time. He was a young man then. To-day, twenty-two years later, he is slight of build and somewhat stooped. The remainer of his chestnut hair, well thinned into partial baldness, is rapidly graying. He is forty-six, a smallish man less than five feet, nine inches in height. Nearly two thirds of his life has been devoted to the fact that crime can be made to pay.

Life was laid out on a silver platter when Lustig-Miller reached the United States. His proficient knowledge of languages allowed him to assume whatever nationality he chose. He also quickly became a "count," varying the country of his nobility to fit the circumstances. His saber-cut became the result in turn of a duel in France, or one in Italy, or a student affair at Heidelberg. With this as a background, he began to work in a fertile field where endeavors are founded upon what the confidence man calls "the larceny in a sucker's soul." According to The Count's story, he had smuggled into this country a marvelous machine, which, through the mere turning of a crank, could transform ordinary paper into real money. His victims, strangely enough, were often persons with a long record of church attendance and alleged high respectability. Confidence-man statistics show that the more bigoted persons are, the more eager to run some unfortunate girl out of town for having parked too amorously in Lover's Lane, the more averse to playing cards or taking a drink or dancing after Saturday midnight, the more pliable they may be to the luring tones of a man like Count Lustig as he stands by his money machine, feeding plain paper into one end and apparently scooping up real currency as it issues from the other.

In police parlance the racket is known as "the green goods game." It has been exposed to the point of boredom. Nevertheless, we repeat, for those who may drool at the mouth at the thought of a machine which makes money, there is no such contrivance. In the demonstration, the faker has "planted" the machine, which is nothing more than a wooden box and a crank, with real money. After he sells his product and makes his getaway, the contraption loses its magical power and produces nothing except the blank paper which is fed into it. Lustig-Miller sold these machines to larceny-minded "innocents" of America for more than twenty years, in one instance receiving one hundred and fifty thousand dollars. For all this, he spent not one day in a penitentiary.

There are certain cities of the United States which, at various times have had reputations as "con man centers." Los Angeles has been so listed; Miami, Orlando, and St. Petersburg, Florida, have been others. Kansas City has been lucrative, Denver a gathering-place for the swindler ever since the days when old Lou Blonger, "king of confidence men," invented the first rural hideout and there, in a home set in the midst of a cherry orchard, entertained swindlers from every part of the nation. Reno, Nevada, with its open gambling and its divorce-seekers who, in their loneliness, do not inquire deeply into the antecedents of casual acquaintances, is often fallow ground, as well as all other cities where tourists gather. Then, of course, there are Chicago and New York.

As The Count enlarged his operations, he came to know all these cities — far better than many of their residents. Lustig-Miller met crooked politicians, saloonkeepers, other con men, fixers, hide-out owners, and all the rest of the dozens of types who fatten and thrive by being the active advance men and camp followers of crime. Through these he broadened his scope until his associates included also the dangerous type of criminal: the gunman, "heister," bank-robber and professional thug. He affiliated with all; there are reasons to believe that he was the confederate of vicious offenders, not as an active plunderer, but as an advisor.

In Reno, for instance, he formed a temporary partnership with two men who later were to aid such criminals as Baby Face Nelson and John Paul Chase, the murderer of two Special Agents of the Federal Bureau of Investigation. With these two men he conducted a series of "pay-off jobs," which is another term for race-track swindles. In this game the sucker believes that, through the aid of new-found friends and tapped wires, he has won a tremendous amount of money. However, the only thing that has been tapped is himself, for when he decides to collect his new wealth he is told that the bookies will not pay off until they are assured that the sucker himself could have paid them in the event that he had lost. With cupidity in control, he draws every cent he possesses out of the bank, hands it over to his friends only to see it "lost" on another race in which everything "went wrong" and the tapped wires failed to do their duty.

The unholy trio worked this racket across the country and back to Reno again. Then The Count returned to his money machine and the enlarging of friendships. Prohibition had come; Chicago was the world center for gangdom, working without much hindrance due to political influence plus an easily bribed judiciary and police department, each subservient to Al Capone. Lustig-Miller formed an alliance, not only with Capone, but with Gus Winkeler, Bugs Moran, and many others. Soon he became a nerve center for their entire business. It was he, with others, who manufactured the bogus revenue stamps which proclaimed rotgut to be pre-war whisky when it was nothing but "bourbon"-flavored and burnt-caramel-colored alcohol, cooked in the stinking flats of thousands of members in Capone's *Unione Sicilione*. The money figure represented by the stamps thus supplied to the Capone and other mobs ran heavily into the millions. Since they cost him and his associates only the paper, ink, and effort by which they were printed, Count Lustig-Miller's crew received for them a total of about two hundred and fifty thousand dollars. Finally he was arrested. It meant little. The Count himself says flatly that he bought his way out of prosecution.

During the years which followed, if his own story is to be believed, he repeated the buying-out process some forty times. He once was confined in the same Crown Point Jail from which John Dillinger made his mysterious escape. The Count, however, departed with fewer theatrics. He was in his cell at night, gone in the morning; with nobody able to tell how it happened. Count Lustig, at a later time, blandly admitted that he paid "certain people" and that the certain people opened the door. That, sadly enough, is the explanation behind most jail-break mysteries, nor is it a costly affair. The usual escape costs an average of one hundred dollars, and many a prison door has been opened for less. The underworld must look upon John Dillinger as a sucker — that is, if the rumors are true that his escape cost eighteen hundred dollars.

The Count's own recital of how he consistently escaped punishment should be remembered by the innocent citizen whenever a criminal magically evades prosecution. There are only three ways by which an arrested person can be freed from a criminal charge. One is to prove his innocence. The other is to exert pressure, through friendship or political affiliations. The third is to use money or the ability to take advantage of ignorance or inefficiency.

Big-time offenders are quite frank about what they call "the fix." Sometimes it is money paid to a member of the law firm to which the district attorney belongs; sometimes it is a sum given to arresting officers; sometimes the bribing or frightening of witnesses, through the actions of a crooked attorney, and sometimes the purchase of freedom from political powers or through the flat buy-off of a prosecuting officer.

Discovery of such a practice causes quite a scandal in a community; nevertheless, it is widespread. For example: a group of Lustig-Miller's swindler-friends has worked the Middle West like traveling salesmen, for the last fifteen years. They center in Chicago and carry on one of the most vicious rackets in existence with the precision of a legitimate business institution. There is not an instance of one of these men having spent a day in prison for the multitudinous offenses they have committed. One reason is that each member of this mob carries twenty thousand dollars in "fall money," as it is called, sewed in the shoulder padding of his coat, to be used for whatever purpose necessary in case of a "rap," or arrest.

Count Lustig-Miller put it succinctly: —

"Everybody's got his price. Sometimes it's money. Sometimes it's friendship. Sometimes it's a good line of talk and the promise to deliver a bigger criminal. Anyway, it's a price."

The Count's record makes him an authority on the subject. In at least one instance, he not only made a dupe of the law, but turned it into an accomplice. The confederate in this case was a Texas sheriff.

This officer was one of the thousands of alleged peace-protectors of America who either have been criminals themselves or are actually in league with them while in office. Lustig-Miller, following one of the sporadic clean-ups of Prohibition days in Chicago, returned to the purveying of his beloved money machine, and traveled as far south as Texas. There in a small town he decided to sell one to the sheriff. The avaricious officer thought so well of the idea that he stole county money with which to buy the alleged baby mint. Having done this, he turned the crank and nothing came out but blank paper. So he got on the trail of the swindler.

In fiction, The Count would have gone to jail. Since, however, this is a recital of what actually can occur when crime and law enforcement meet in America, the facts are entirely different.

"Why send me to jail?" The Count asked plausibly. "I've got a better idea."

"What is it?"

"You've got access to a lot of county money. That's your part of the plan. Now comes my end. I've just met one of the greatest counterfeiters in the business. His name is Watts, William Watts, an ex-druggist who made a hobby of photo-engraving. However, he's always made small bills. I've suggested that he also go in for bigger stuff. Tens, twenties, fifties and hundred-dollar notes. That gives a selection for any purpose."

"All right," said the sheriff. "But where do I come in?"

"I'll take you in as a sort of partner. We'll have Watts make up a bunch of money. But instead of selling it in the usual way, we'll exchange it for the rest of the county funds in your custody."

The pair went to Chicago, where they were introduced by Ted Newberry, a college-graduate gangster, to a saloonkeeper who also thought so well of the idea that he furnished two real hundred-dollar bills to be used by Watts as models. Thus began a tremendous counterfeiting effort by which entirely new methods of passing bogus money by the syndicate system came into being.

Back in the old, placid days when Chief Flynn knew the name of every counterfeiter and kept track of him by colored push-pins, there was no such thing as widespread counterfeiting. It was sporadic, local. An engraver would set up his plant in a certain city. He would have his gang of assistants and money-passers, who felt fortunate if they foisted a hundred dollars' worth of "the queer" in a day. Often they did no more than make a good living. But with the entrance of syndicate methods, all that was changed.

The same system was employed as was used in the bootlegging of liquor. The factory did nothing more than turn out the money, which was sold to the jobber at about eight cents on the dollar. The jobber in turn sold it in smaller lots to a number of wholesalers at an increase in price of about a hundred per cent. and they purveyed it to retailers at another hundred per cent. increase, now bringing the cost to about thirty-five cents. Following this, the retailer put the money out, often on a commission basis, allowing another hundred per cent. profit to himself, and some thirty cents to the person who did the actual passing. Counterfeiting entered a new era.

In many instances, the activities were protected by exactly the same set-ups which had given the bootlegging business so much power in city after city. The same political-crook combinations were made available, the same police were bribed or told by higher authorities to keep their eyes closed. District attorneys shelved complaints or "forgot" to mention them to grand juries. It was not expensive. Fixing, for those in the business, is ridiculously cheap. Too much avariciousness on the part of a public official meets with universal condemnation by crookdom. Only a short time before Repeal, I stood on the street corner of a Western city with an angry rum runner.

"That lousy guy!" he exclaimed. "I goes to him, see? And I tells him my story. And he says to me, he says: 'Sorry, Jake, but the price has gone up. The newspapers are raising hell and I've got to tighten the lines. I can't do a thing for you for less than twenty-four hundred.' "

Jake snorted. "Can you imagine it?" he asked. "That lousy bastard asking twenty-four hundred dollars? Why, I knew that cheap son-of-a-bitch when he would go for a half a grand. I'll see him in hell before I'll give any twenty-four hundred bucks!"

Illusions fade so swiftly when one knows the underworld. Having been reared with a great respect for public office, it is hard for me even to-day to visualize the low type of rats which all too often crawl into seats of government. As for the "cheap son-of-a-bitch" who had offended Jake, the rum runner, he was the Governor of the State, and he wanted the twenty-four hundred dollars for turning Jake's brother out of the penitentiary.

Thus the combination of Count Lustig-Miller and Chicago gangland knew just where it could work best to gather profits from its new-found gold mine; the underworld passes along the

names of crooked officers, crooked judges, crooked governors as
traveling men exchange names in their stud books. It began distribution of money upon a true wholesale basis. Bills manufactured in Chicago were on sale on both the Pacific and Atlantic
Coasts within ten days. Lustig-Miller and other representatives
of gangland traveled about the country making contact with
syndicate after syndicate. Even children were employed on a
commission basis, as final passers of smaller bills; it is so easy
for a child to run panting into a small store, a piece of currency
wadded into a sweaty palm. There a hurried purchase is made
that "Momma wants right away." With the change, the dear
little innocent then goes to the waiting retailer who pays him
his commission and provides another bill to be passed in the
next block. Meanwhile, Lustig-Miller was engaged in big deals
with the currency of larger denominations.

He and the sheriff made several trips to Texas, ostensibly to
steal that county money. Then the sheriff dropped out of the
picture and The Count entered New York, where he affiliated
himself with Jack "Legs" Diamond and made a trip to Europe
for the announced purpose of buying tremendous amounts of
narcotics with counterfeit currency, the dope to be smuggled in
by Diamond's crew of narcotic runners and sold at the usual
morphine and heroin prices. That they were partially successful is evidenced by the fact that large sums of counterfeit
money later made their appearance in Europe. Following this,
Lustig-Miller and his associates embarked in the more dangerous business of purchasing whisky from Canadian runners
with the bogus money which Watts and his gang had manufactured.

Other members of the underworld in Chicago stole the idea,
with the result that soon the entire bootleg world seethed with
suspicions, hatreds, accusations. There were murders and reprisals; gang warfare broke out in a dozen directions. The Count
left Chicago and headed East. This was about 1933, at a time
when eighteen indictments for various sorts of counterfeiting

had been handed down by a Federal grand jury. In his travels, Lustig-Miller stopped off at Pittsburgh, Pa.

The Count was married. He had a daughter, then fifteen years old, who was being reared in a convent. Nevertheless, he loved flesh, especially if business could be mixed with pleasure. In Pittsburgh, there was an especially delectable little piece of bedroom furniture named Mae Sheible. She ran what was known as a "house of refined prostitution," at which place many of the biggest names in American business, professional, and manufacturing life had called at one time or another for blondes, brunettes, and redheads, both "straight" and "French." These girls, the pick of prostitution in the East, were catered on the call system. Mae is said to have kept a card index of size, eyes, complexion, type of disposition, weight, height, and color of hair both on the head and on more intimate portions of the body, to make sure that a platinum blonde of the reception parlor would not turn out to be a brunette in the bedroom. There were photographs in the nude and in evening dress, in case some amorous customer desired to go dancing with his evening's inamorata. Mae herself was often importuned instead of her hired girls; she was pretty, nicely shaped, a good talker, and dressed in the fashion of a sophisticated young woman who had made a fortune. But she was temporarily love-proof. Mae had a pimp named Joe, the usual worthless type of hanger-on who lives by the labor of a woman's pubic regions. However, when Count Lustig-Miller came into the picture, even Joe was shoved into the background. The Count, with his saber scar, his five languages, his Continental polish, did what millionaires had failed to do. He took Mae to bed, and between other diversions tried to sell her a money machine.

Mae was a shrewd purveyor of human flesh, but she was a sucker for a con game. At one time she seriously considered engaging in a wonderful scheme by which buttons might be made out of heavily clabbered milk. She liked the idea of a money machine, but she was more interested when Count Lustig-Miller mentioned some bonds which could "be obtained at a price." He didn't exactly say they were "hot," you understand. After all, Mae was a person of attainments, who had operated a refined call-house in Pittsburgh for some years without once having been arrested; nor had she at any time, to quote her ladylike language, received anything but the most gentlemanly treatment from the police. Anyway, Mae bought the bonds, fifteen thousand dollars' worth of them, and then squawked like a mallard duck when she discovered that they were not worth the paper they were printed upon.

This was two years ago, when Lustig-Miller was at the height of his activities, which now had extended throughout gangland. Perhaps an insight into his sinister activities can best be gained through an incident which occurred later: In running down the kidnappers of Edward G. Bremer of St. Paul, Special Agents of the Federal Bureau of Investigation arrested Volney Davis, one of the conspirators. In searching him, they discovered an almost perfect hundred-dollar counterfeit bill concealed in his hatband.

"Why carry that counterfeit bill?" they asked.

"Nothing unusual in that," Volney explained. "Those bills look swell at night, especially if a cop is in a hurry to tuck one away before somebody sees him. We use 'em to buy out if some dick or cop grabs us on a pick-up. Searching around, he's sure to come on that century note. Sometimes it doesn't help. Then again, the right line of talk and the century in the dick's mitt sends you on your way and you're out of town before he finds he's been bilked."

For the information of those officers who have found themselves possessed of such counterfeit money, let it be known that the blame should be placed on the Count Lustig-Miller gang. The bills were sold to gangdom for thirty-five dollars apiece, a petty sideline carried on as a friendly gesture toward "the boys." Practically every kidnapper, bank-robber, and vicious gangster carried one or more for use in emergency. Many still do so, and policemen should be exceptionally careful in handling money, especially at night.

However, Count Lustig-Miller had no such easy means of a getaway when the irate Mae camped on his trail for a return of her money from the fifteen-thousand-dollar swindle. (No pleasure-lady likes to be "tissue-papered" — a term which dates from the days when no really nice hustlers ever wholly stripped for action and ungentlemanly visitors sometimes took advantage of their gullibility when they were allowed to "put the money in her stocking": often the innocent thing found that when the time came to check up with the madame, her hose contained only a wad of toilet paper.) Indignant, Mae Sheible appealed to the police.

Nearly a year went by. Lustig-Miller returned to Pittsburgh; and, feeling amorous, telephoned the call house. Mae invited him out and called detectives. Joe, the pimp, appeared on the scene. Thus a grim reception committee awaited The Count.

It was not, however, an arrest. Mae did not want any publicity; she desired fifteen thousand dollars. Therefore, according to her sworn statement, an all-night conference followed, in which the detectives acted as arbiters. Mae was willing to let bygones be bygones if she got back her money. If she didn't, the detectives were to arrest The Count.

The average citizen undoubtedly will ask why The Count and Mae Sheible and Joe were not arrested. After all — here was a man who had pursued a life of crime for twenty years; here was a woman who plainly was violating the law by running a house of prostitution; here was a pimp who was living on the earnings of whoredom. Why were two city detectives willing to enter into an all-night conference designed, not to bring about punishment for a felony on the part of Count Lustig-Miller, but to hold the threat of arrest over him in order that a bawdy-house landlady might get her money? Once upon a time, I myself asked such silly questions. Repetition of such incidents dulls curiosity.

The conference was ended by Lustig-Miller's promise to repay and the passing of three hundred dollars in token money.

Then The Count went away, and in his absence Mae got in a fight with her *maquereau* when he said he caught her cheating with another man. That was fatal, for Mae had given him for safekeeping a little black book containing the names of every prominent man who owed her money for girling. Joe had taken the book home where, allegedly, it had fallen into the hands of a person who insisted she was Joe's mother. This woman was so horrified by the contents of the book that she telephoned Mae and told her that unless she forked over several thousand dollars, she'd sell the book to the newspapers. Mae told her to go to hell and sought assistance from official sources to re-obtain that book. The newspapers got hold of the story. There was a terrific front page blast which scandalized Pittsburgh, and Mae left town for New York, where after a most pleasant stay at an "exclusive" Fifth Avenue hotel, she opened another "refined house of prostitution" on East Seventy-second Street, just off "exclusive" Park Avenue.

All this jumble of events has its bearing, for in the meantime, Count Lustig-Miller, constantly threatened with arrest, had made partial restitution by giving Mae a beautiful Cadillac convertible coupe, for which he obtained two thousand dollars' credit on his refunding debt. Joe, the pimp, had gotten drunk and taken the car out, forgetting where he left it. Mae once more had sought the aid of the police. The car was found, and discovered to be a stolen vehicle, a fact not mentioned by Count Lustig-Miller. Again Mae squawked most loudly and named her betrayer. The car had been stolen in New York and transported to Pittsburgh; this made The Count an object of Federal search under the Dyer Act. It also caused Special Agents of the Federal Bureau of Investigation to look into the possibility that Mae Sheible, now in New York, might have transported girls in violation of white slavery statutes. Besides this, it gave Secret Service operatives a line on the man for whom they had been searching for nearly three years, ever since 1933 when minor counterfeiting arrests in Chicago had given them their first inkling into the activities of Watts and Lustig-Miller. They watched Mae Sheible's refined haven of prostitution. One night, practically on the doorstep, they caught Count Lustig-Miller.

According to the happy endings of fiction, the story should have stopped there, with a fade-out of stern retribution. It did nothing of the sort. Lustig-Miller viewed his arrest lightly. He had reason to do so, for in the conferences which followed he was able to persuade the Secret Service agents that he was merely an innocent adjunct of counterfeiting. Then he made a trade suggestion — he would turn up a number of plates and counterfeit money in return for freedom. A long confab followed, to decide on an intermediary who would procure these plates and money; pictures of a "big seizure of counterfeiting apparatus" always make good publicity, especially when accompanied by a story that a "tremendous ring" has been wiped out. At last the intermediary was selected. He was Dapper Don Collins, a confidence man with a police record some thirty years long — later accused of being one of Lustig-Miller's active accomplices!

If this seems a blast at a historic institution like the Secret Service, I must hastily add that such proceedings are common practice among law enforcement agencies using the older methods of apprehension and detection, and that these methods are swiftly passing into oblivion as the result of Secretary Henry Morgenthau's active interest in the rebuilding of the Secret Service.

One detail halted the pact. Dapper Don went through all the motions of mysterious contacts with unknown parties. He obtained, as mysteriously, a key to a subway luggage-locker wherein were found a number of photo-engraving plates and fifty-two thousand dollars in counterfeit money. The flaw came when it was discovered that some of the counterfeit money and the plates did not match — meaning, of course, that Count Lustig-Miller merely had turned in some worn-out paraphernalia and fifty-two thousand dollars, which would be worth nothing while the true machinery of counterfeiting remained hidden. So he was placed in the Federal Detention Building on a charge of conspiracy to counterfeit.

There he tried every dodge which had worked so successfully in former years. He wrote letters to the Chief of the Secret Service, offering in repayment for his liberty to turn over to United States authorities a Chinese smuggling ring operating off the New Jersey Coast, two counterfeiting plants in New York, the actual participants in an armored truck robbery of four hundred and twenty-seven thousand dollars in Brooklyn, an opium-smuggling ring in New York City, besides sufficient evidence to convict a United States Government official on a bribery charge connected with counterfeiting. The Secret Service viewed these offers as having the same background as the confidence game attempted in The Count's previous effort to escape punishment and refrained from falling into the trap.

Following this, The Count sought to hire attorneys who were close friends of men in the office of the United States District Attorney, hoping that their influence would liberate him. The trick failed. He sought political pressure. That did not materialize. Even Mae Sheible, through whose telephone Dapper Don Collins had made those mysterious connections with counterfeiters, could not help him, for the Federal Bureau of Investigation was hot after her on a white slavery charge. So Lustig-Miller used his last resort. He escaped from the Federal Detention Building.

The feat was accomplished by tying twelve bed sheets together, lolling back during the recreation period, then sliding down the bed sheets from the roof to the street. The physical end of a prison escape is usually the easiest part of it. What goes on before, what persons are "seen," what arrangements are made outside for the necessary getaway, what tools and weapons are slipped the prisoner during recreation hours, what guards are "fixed" to look the other way, what inefficiency of prison management is used as an assisting medium — these are the real ingredients of prison escape.

The United States Bureau of Prisons follows a grim course in the investigations which follow such a getaway as that of Lustig-Miller's. Under Sanford Bates, the Director, an implacable pursuit begins, with the aid of an investigation by John Edgar Hoover's most expert men in the Federal Bureau of Investigation. Silence closes tightly about the findings. But this is certain: if there has been inefficiency, if there has been collusion, if there has been a weak link in what is the finest prison system in the entire world, that link is removed forthwith, stern punishment descends, deeper silence follows — and men do not escape again.

Now that Lustig-Miller was out, he went back to Pittsburgh. There, magically, he found a woman to conceal him, an underworld character to bring him meals in his slatternly hide-out and a friendly soul who attempted to take him to Chicago by automobile. But as the start was made, Special Agents and Secret Service operatives closed in. About a year ago, Count Lustig-Miller was sent to a Federal prison on a sentence of twenty years out of a possible one of eighty-two years. Watts was caught and given ten years. Mae Sheible got five years as a white slaver, vainly appealing the case to higher courts. Dapper Don Collins drew six months as a contempt sentence for refusing to testify. Every one hailed what the newspapers termed "the breaking up of a tremendous counterfeiting ring." Nothing of the sort had happened. The top growth of a noxious weed had been cut off, but the roots remained undisturbed. The jobbers, wholesalers, retailers, passers, fixers, transporters, political and other helpers were not wiped out. These people had found a lucrative business. So with Watts and Lustig-Miller no longer available, they turned to other men who could supply them and business continued as usual.

The point of all this narrative, however, is not to relate the personal story of Lustig-Miller. Nor is the sole purpose to note that, granted the usual rights of parole, The Count can be free again by the time he is fifty-two years old, a retirement age at which any sensible criminal should be willing to settle down on the savings which this man must have set aside from criminal profits aggregating nearly two million dollars, and upon which he paid no income tax. The purpose of the story is to delineate the tangled morass of crime; how one gang meshes with another and one criminal threads his way through a succession of almost unbelievable events before finally being removed for a time from society; and, most important of all, to draw attention to the fact that crime cannot be wiped out until it is dragged up by the roots.

Upon reading that a giant counterfeiting ring had been wiped out, the average citizen, who heretofore had been watching all currency with eagle eyes, leaned back, relaxed — and continued to take counterfeit money. One must not forget that crime follows business lines. When the first miniature golf course developed into a rage a few years ago, everybody with a vacant lot stampeded into the business. The same is true of profitable outlawry. A few hundred persons engaged in counterfeiting until the time Lustig-Miller put it on a basis of big business; there are now thousands.

In 1935 alone, nearly four thousand persons, including The Count, were arrested for making and passing counterfeit money, and that was an increase of twenty-five per cent. over the previous year, which in turn showed an increase of thirty-three per cent. over 1932, at which time the figure was three times that of 1925, about the time Count Lustig-Miller first cast his eyes toward counterfeiting. In spite of all these arrests, which have brought about some degree of decrease, counterfeiting goes on merrily, with scores of photo-electric engraving plants working full blast, and printing done on specially imported presses which may cost up to thirty-five hundred dollars. In addition, old-fashioned engravers continue to work under political protection in the vicinity of Juarez, Mexico, and the money, which is turned out on expensive machinery, is flown over the border by airplane. In fact, the entire note-counterfeiting situation is so serious that one should examine carefully every piece of currency received.

It is true that returning prosperity has, to a great degree, slack-
ened the efforts of the counterfeiter. The Treasury Department
reports an extreme drop in counterfeiting activities from their
peak, when Count Lustig-Miller was most active. Certainly the
arrest of a man with The Count's attainments should put a dent
in the totals of any such report.

There also is some truth in the idea that by The Count's
arrest there was brought about somewhat of a cessation in
syndicate handling of bogus money on a basis of steady supply.
However, the methods which have followed are ones of true
danger. These comprise what is known as the "in and out"
system.

A counterfeiting gang sets up its plant. It manufactures bales
of money. It distributes, through the wide range of avenues
which now are available to persons in the business of manufacturing illegitimate currency, a flood of counterfeits — descending
upon business, to be undetected for a time. At last, however, the
Secret Service, upon the identification of a counterfeit as a piece
of new manufacture, broadcasts warnings.

Immediately the plant shuts down. Such passers as continue
to work, do so at their own risk — although by this time their
supply of bills has been well depleted. Time passes. The counterfeit field becomes "cool" again. Once more plants begin their
efforts — this time with new plates.

The same is true in the manufacture of bogus coins, which,
with modern machinery, can be turned out by the millions,
and in excellent imitation of real money, even to the milling
about the edges. In one arrest, a cellar full of machinery, presses,
die-stampers, power cutters, compressor machinery, and expert
mechanics to keep all this paraphernalia running, was discovered;
the output was devoted entirely to the manufacture of some five
million nickels. Only recently there has been a flood of quarters,
so well made, so expertly stamped and milled, as to be almost
undetectable; I saw five of them a short time ago in what a
politician would call the "shadow of the White House," in

Washington; an attempt was made to pass several within two blocks of the central offices of the United States Secret Service and in a restaurant which boasts that it has fed every important public official in America. In brief, gangland learned from Count Lustig-Miller that there was a huge profit in counterfeiting. However, even more important than the threat of minor inflation by counterfeit is the devious story of the various channels into which The Count's activities led him. Let us recapitulate: —

He was the associate of confidence men and crimesters from one end of America to another. He engaged in narcotic smuggling with a murderous gangster, since killed by his own kind. He purveyed to murderers and kidnappers the means of escaping arrest. He suborned public officials; he bribed, threatened and lured protectors of the peace into betraying their trust. He bought his way out of at least one jail. He engaged either in car thievery or acted for robber gangs in the disposal of their loot. He dodged punishment forty times, and then received it only through a fluke by failing to keep a bargain.

If there were only one Count Lustig-Miller, worming his way through the jungle growth of the underworld, his story would be merely an amazing recital. However, this man was not an individual, he was the representative of a type. There are thousands like him, all working upon the same principles which guided him: "Everybody's got his price."

This condition tends to support the accusation that the United States is a stupidly outrageous nation in its lackadaisical attitude toward crime in all its phases. It also shows conclusively that to combat such a situation, this country should possess a brand of law enforcement superior to anything the world ever has known. In only one segment has that been true — the thin line of some six hundred men who comprise the politically fearless, coldly efficient Federal Bureau of Investigation as built up under the driving leadership of John Edgar Hoover. From this top standard, law enforcement ranges downward by degrees to a filthy mess inhabited by a slime which passes as peace officers — men who do not dare to submit their fingerprints for comparison to guard against a possible criminal background.

It all adds up to the fact that one of the best ways to "do something" about lawbreaking would be to devote some serious attention to what should be done about the American brand of law enforcement — and that is a subject as tangled as the jungles of crime.

CHAPTER TWO

HOW DO THEY DO IT?

I HOPE it will be amazing to know that every so-called super-gangster of the Dillinger Era was able to carry on, not through courage, or resourcefulness, or daring or foolhardiness, but through the aid of one or more forms of police or political corruption. It was this protective mantle which enabled murderers and body snatchers to gain their heroic positions on the first pages as "modern Robin Hoods." Pretty Boy Floyd, for instance . . .

This man started his offensive life as a petty thief, protected against incursions of the law by the clannishness of mountain people in what is known as the "Cookson Hills territory" of Oklahoma. He was a beer-swilling, whisky-guzzling, cheap, boastful drunkard, who spent his money freely about tawdry bootleg dives, and soon surrounded himself by a crowd of admirers of a type lower in mental stature than a hog in a mud wallow. They were, however, all possessed of the power of the ballot and could swing their influence to the election or defeat of a candidate running for office.

There is nothing more acute of sight and hearing than a rural politician in search of election. Were a vote tied to its tail, he could see a lightning bug in a pea-soup fog. Floyd had a multitudinous number of relatives. In such communities as the Cookson Hills, families vote *en masse,* and in the case of Pretty Boy Floyd there was more than once a tacit understanding that immunity for Floyd was a part of the balloting bargain.

From the vicinity of home, Floyd's power over peace officers spread to many rural parts of Oklahoma. Sometimes this was brought about through the jealousy between law enforcement agencies — one so hating another as to cause a lack of coördination and coöperation. On occasions, the officers of one county refused to pass information to those of another as to the whereabouts of the outlaw when he was in a position that would have made capture easy. There also were numerous instances when a sheriff's posse started forth, avowedly to bring about the outlaw's arrest, meanwhile so heralding its approach that the only additional noise needed to make it a circus parade was that of a brass band. Beyond this, Floyd was often deliberately ignored by various rural officers and there were several towns in which he, supposedly a badly wanted man, made no more of a secret of his presence or identity than did the most respected citizen.

It requires little skill or courage to become a "modern Robin Hood" under such circumstances. Floyd's reputation grew because there were men in office who did not want to arrest him, or who were afraid, either physically or morally, to do so. The crook profited by this object lesson. He soon discovered that the same tricks — patronage, money-spending for underworld support — which had aided him in a small area would accomplish a like purpose in a larger one. As a result, Pretty Boy Floyd spent much time in several of the more populous cities of Oklahoma and southern Missouri, where he moved about freely, got drunk, and boasted of his exploits, often drinking at the same booze-joint bar as peace officers. From these surroundings, he traveled onward to metropolitan immunity.

One of his havens was Kansas City, Missouri, the underworld of which then was controlled by John Lazia, an ex-convict Italian politician of the "North Side" machine who afforded protection to criminals at a price. Johnny is since dead, murdered by some of his so-called "pals." However, his machine still prospers under the guidance of one of its charter members. Through this new leader, Kansas City remains to a degree a crime protectorate, as does every other city where, throughout the years, criminal set-ups have become heavily entrenched. In several, at the present moment, there is a tremendous ballyhoo to the effect that the "town has been cleaned up." That is pap for the sucker. In underworld parlance, the town is merely "hot," to remain so for the short life of a grand jury, or the frothing of an excited citizenship, or perhaps during a reform administration. Every city which has harbored crooks in recent years has done so for the last several decades, with only brief vacations to let the heat cool. Toledo, in my youth, was known as a haven for a certain type of bank-robber. It still possesses an underworld political hook-up which writhes like a pretzel.

Toledo also was one of Pretty Boy Floyd's hangouts. There he was protected by affiliations with what was known as "the Licavoli mob." The main members of that outfit were wiped out some time ago. Nevertheless, there are tendrils remaining, and one man who was looked upon by this gang as a great source of protection of criminals is closely affiliated with the remnants. To be blunt about it, he lives with the widow of a slain Licavoli gangster.

When he chose to leave Toledo, Floyd was well and widely known and as widely shunned by certain law enforcement officials in the outskirts of Cleveland. That was his run: from the outskirts of Cleveland to Toledo, Kansas City, and various towns of Oklahoma, using these points in the same manner that an animal would use a protected lair, from which he sallied forth on bank-robbing expeditions, often with local assistance. It was not until the Federal Bureau of Investigation got on Floyd's trail for the murder of several officers during what was known as "the Kansas City massacre" that he realized what it meant to be persistently pursued. It was this relentless chase which eventually led to his death, in spite of fervent efforts on the part of Floyd, through various friends, to "arrange a fix." On four occasions emissaries sought vainly to bring about the Federal Bureau's acceptance of Floyd's own terms of surrender. In other words, Floyd was condescending enough to offer to allow himself to be taken captive, providing he could dictate what would happen to him afterward. This perhaps, better than anything else, explains the attitude of the modern protected criminal toward law enforcement. It is indeed seldom that one ever surrenders to a local agency without first having arranged a pact of peace.

When Albert Bates, associate of Machine-gun Kelly and Harvey Bailey in the kidnapping of Charles F. Urschel of Oklahoma City, was arrested in Denver, he did not immediately display concern. The charge against him was originally that of theft from the American Railway Express. Bates was philosophic about it. Even if he couldn't "fix," it would be a "short fall," with the possibility of an early parole. For years, in and out of prison, Albert Bates had been in many tight spots. Knowing the risks of the business, he long ago had realized that it might be necessary at times to appease the citizens whom he had plundered by taking a prison sentence on his own terms.

There is no sarcasm in the foregoing sentence; the enormity of such procedures shall be proven in later chapters. When he was identified as an Urschel kidnapper, Bates speedily saw that he must work fast — even to do a favor to society by a self-chosen prison term. A conviction for the kidnapping would mean a long term in Alcatraz Prison. Bates did not want that. He hurriedly set about making plans by which he might hope to defeat justice. To this end, he smuggled a telegram out of the Denver jail, addressed to two detectives in one of the largest cities of Texas and beseeching that they come to his aid.

The telegram was not couched in those exact terms. To quote it correctly, Bates sought to telegraph the news to the detectives that he was in jail in Denver, and asked them to come to get him on an old charge of having robbed a state bank, to which he now was willing to plead guilty. The detectives, however, turned the telegram over to Federal men, thus aiding justice. That was disappointing to Bates, for this trick is counted upon as sure-fire in the underworld.

Such procedure should explain to the ignorant citizen the reason why some police agencies become unusually active in an effort to land a criminal for prosecution when he has been arrested in another city on a more serious charge. The excuse given, of course, is that the department is an implacable pursuer, that a crime was committed for which this man should be punished, and that the more serious charge can wait. This gag is worked and re-worked year after year, often accompanied by a blare of publicity which paints the law enforcement agency as a never-failing nemesis — when it, in reality, is actually aiding and abetting a dangerous criminal.

In the case of Albert Bates, had his urgent telegram accomplished its purpose, there is a possibility that an ardent effort might have been made to hurriedly take him away to answer for the Texas crime. In this event, Bates probably would have granted an interview to the newspapers in which he would have confessed that after a life of law infraction he finally had come to the realization that crime could not be made to pay; therefore he had determined to waive extradition, go back to Texas, plead guilty, and take his medicine for having robbed a bank. The catch in all this, of course, would have been the fact that in so doing, Albert Bates would have depended upon the ancient axiom that time is a criminal's best friend; that, during his model-prisoner stay in a state prison, witnesses to the Urschel kidnapping would have died, disappeared, gone out of law enforcement, or so forgotten the details as to be poor witnesses against him — thus allowing a thoroughly guilty man to "beat the rap."

Another instance of easy law violation is contained in the record of the various members of the Barker-Karpis mob of bank-robbers, kidnappers, and murderers, all of whom, at one time or another, were enabled to escape punishment through political or police aid. Naturally, since the law enforcement members I am now discussing do not dilate upon their affiliations with the underworld, it is necessary to go to the sworn confessions of the gangsters themselves.

Arthur (Doc) Barker, now serving life in Alcatraz, wrote letters to his paramour in which he asked her to get in touch with the business agents of outlaw unions — headed by Louie Alterie, who was sufficiently powerful politically in Illinois to restore to a gang doctor his license to practise even after he had served a penitentiary term for abortion.

Willie Harrison, a contact man of the same gang, was arrested in a Chicago suburb for carrying concealed weapons. The mayor of the city went his bond.

Alvin Karpis, murderous head of the gang, contributed sixty-five hundred dollars to a mayoralty campaign in an Ohio municipality, on the understanding that should his candidate be elected Alvin "would have the freedom of the city." This was at a time when Karpis was being sought both by post office inspectors and the Federal Bureau of Investigation as Public Enemy Number One. He also spent his "honeymoon" with his gun moll at a summer cottage on Lake Michigan owned by an important Chicago politician and rented by Karpis, according to the gangster's statement, with full knowledge on the part of the politician that the occupant was a dangerous criminal.

Elmer Farmer, an active member of the gang, ran a tavern in Bensenville, Illinois, where he boasted that "his connections were so good" that he was informed immediately whenever a Federal agent came to town. To prove the reliability of his informants, he correctly described the Federal agents who had visited this place in an effort to obtain evidence against Farmer. He named the dates they were in town, where they went, and how long they remained, information which could have come only from sources exceedingly close to law enforcement.

Edward C. Bartholmey, recently sentenced as a Barker-Karpis hide-out keeper, was the postmaster of Bensenville and a political power in the community. According to Edna Murray, a Barker-Karpis gun moll, he was not only a postmaster for the good citizen, but for criminals as well. It was through him that many of the Barker-Karpis crowd kept in touch with each other. In addition, he actually harbored dangerous criminals at various times, among them Volney Davis, another member of the gang, who in turn was once pardoned from the Oklahoma State Penitentiary as the result of efforts on the part of a gang-serving private detective. This individual reported that he "dispensed" two thousand dollars in obtaining the pardon, but neglected to state who received it.

Russell Gibson, a slain member of the gang, was a product of Johnny Lazia's powerful political set-up in Kansas City. He worked for Lazia's taxicab company and was protected by Lazia on various occasions when Gibson had committed crimes. He was an active worker in the Lazia political machine.

On at least five occasions, in Chicago, Cleveland, St. Paul, and Miami, members of the Barker-Karpis crowd were able to escape arrest because of "straight tips" that there was about to be a raid. On one occasion, a landlord complained to police that members of the mob were occupying a certain apartment. According to the landlord, the police answered the call, then sat about doing nothing except to inform the landlord that it was a "bum tip." Meanwhile, the Barker-Karpis gang moved out and the police raided the apartment after it had been empty for two hours.

Harry Campbell, one of the last members of the gang to be caught, owned a dog which he had bought from a source close to law enforcement. Also the sheriff of this county later admitted that he had drunk beer with Harry Campbell, but "didn't know who he was."

On at least one occasion, an important member of the gang was harbored in a suburb of Chicago by a family which consisted of the Mayor, the head of a beer syndicate, a district political leader, and the wife of the postmaster.

Three members of the gang made statements that they had "set aside" a part of the kidnap money for a former chief of police in payment of his aid to them.

"Boss" McLaughlin, a "hot money" changer for the crowd, was a Chicago politican.

Members of the gang admitted that they were "taken care of" in Reno by politically powerful gamblers when they went there to exchange the ransom money resulting from a kidnapping. These gang members also were harbored at a summer resort in Michigan run by an ex-policeman.

In a statement made at the Missouri State Penitentiary by Edna Murray, the gun moll, she said: —

"The Bremer kidnapping could not have been accomplished without the aid of two members of the St. Paul Police Department."

Harry Sawyer, a tavern keeper of St. Paul and alleged finger man in the kidnapping, boasted that he had an "in" with certain members of the St. Paul Police Department, and on at least one occasion he correctly predicted a raid upon the apartment house in which various members of the gang were living. The raid occurred — but the gang had departed.

Gladys Sawyer, the finger man's wife, accused a Cleveland police woman of offering to arrange her freedom after arrest for five hundred dollars.

Members of the mob were quite free in announcing that one of their main hangouts was a night club near Toledo. It was from this place that Dr. Joseph P. Moran, the gang doctor, is said to have been taken out and murdered by his own pals after the good doctor had gotten drunk and in a fervent speech announced that "he held this gang in the hollow of his hand." All of which is unimportant, other than as a detail of gang disloyalty. The important point is that, according to the criminals, they were harbored here with full understanding of their record and that a friendly soul to whom they looked for favors was a police officer of prominence whom they called by his first name.

These are only a few of the political and police connections which came to the surface during investigations into the activity of what has been called "the shrewdest and most dangerous crew of criminals in America." It was not delineated to "expose" any particular situation; it merely is cited as the average set-up of the average gang. Without either police or political assistance, none of the so-called public enemies of the last few years could have survived. The Federal Bureau of Investigation did no superman job in removing them; this came about solely as the result of astute investigation by men of integrity who could not be "reached." The criminal does not exist who can defeat honest and efficient law enforcement. May I enter the reminder that there are three million, five hundred thousand criminals now plying their trade in America.

Therefore it is an exceedingly dumb citizen who glows with admiration at the latest achievement of some professional criminal, exclaiming pridefully: —

"Well, whatta you know about that? He got away again. How does he do it?"

The way he does it perhaps can be explained by such facts as these: Baby Face Nelson stated quite coldly that he had a police chief on his payroll at a thousand dollars a month to give him information concerning law-enforcement activities. After he had been shot by Federal officers, he found a hide-out in the home of a small-time politician, where he died. A City Marshal acted as Machine-gun Kelly's business reference in the purchase of a car which Kelly later used for a kidnapping. It was necessary to order out the State Rangers of Arkansas in order to hold in jail Charles (Lucky) Luciano, the New York gangster, against the wishes of a sheriff, who wanted to set him free. Verne Miller, the multiple murderer, was ushered from city to city bearing letters of introduction which, in one case, put him on a golf course with city officials. Edward W. Bentz, bank-robber de luxe, more than once entertained police officials in his various summer homes and made a study of Federal jurisdiction that he might be better equipped to evade it for the sake of local jobs. According to Eddie, there was only one locality in America which bothered him: "There's a district attorney in Michigan who's got it in for me. He'd throw me in jail just for spite."

Reverting to Machine-gun Kelly: this thug one night halted in his pacing of the floor long enough to voice a deep-felt sentiment. He was being pursued by Federal agents in the Urschel kidnapping case, and he thus expressed himself to his more coldly criminal wife: —

"What a sap I've let you make out of me. Here I was, dragging in fifty grand a year knocking off those tin-can banks, with no danger of a rap that five hundred bucks couldn't square. And I let you put me in the middle where I've got Government heat smeared all over me!"

Even the Great Dillinger should shrink to his proper size when it is known that he was protected in Chicago by remnants of the Capone gang who still remain politically powerful. For those who believe that there are no remnants of the Capone mob, it might be enlightening to know that if you attended the Chicago World's Fair you probably paid tribute to them, since they possessed cleverly concealed control of at least five big concessions. John Hamilton of the Dillinger gang, dying of a police bullet in his liver, was sheltered in the back end of a Loop District sea-food cafe owned by politically strong Capone members. The "Syndicate" still operates various houses of prostitution and gambling in the vicinity of Chicago, and still owns the mayor in at least one suburb. A Capone-affiliated motor company has been selling cars uninterruptedly to thieves, gangsters, and murderers for years, often extending credit to fugitive Public Enemies. And a lawyer who had been a city prosecutor — under the regime in which Capone achieved his height of power — advised, counseled and aided John Dillinger, even to obtaining the doctor by whom his face was lifted. For that matter, if investigative reports are correct, there would have been no opportunity for Dillinger to escape from Crown Point Jail, had it not been for politics.

Femininity in public office has suffered severely because of the Dillinger escape and the fact that a woman, Lillian C. Holley, the Sheriff, was in command of the jail. Investigative reports, made under the direction of Governor McNutt of Indiana, indicate not only that Sheriff Holley was blameless, but that she made every effort to protect herself against an escape by this man. Politics, however, blocked her plans.

The report shows that, after a conference with the District Attorney, it was decided by Sheriff Holley that the Crown Point Jail was an unsafe place in which to hold a man who already had been rescued from one place of incarceration, and at the cost of a sheriff's life. Therefore, the woman planned to ask that the gangster be transferred to the safekeeping of Indiana State Prison, until such time as his case should come to trial. She was halted by a political Power.

"Now just a moment," the Power told her — it was a person more than merely acquainted with a very close friend of the Dillinger lawyer — "My advice is that a transfer to prison would be a very bad move. Election is coming on, and if you transferred Dillinger, it would be taken as a confession of weakness by a woman sheriff. I advise you to keep Dillinger right where he is."

So Dillinger was kept "right where he was" until such time as he chose to walk out. This he did without difficulty from a jail peopled by numerous persons. That the exit was not un-expected is evidenced by the fact that Dillinger's gun moll knew at exactly what street corner in Chicago to meet him the next night, having, on the morning of the escape, attended a weird celebration.

This was in the office of the Dillinger lawyer in Chicago, where reports of the escape were being received over the radio with the same enthusiasm that would be given the news of a winning side in an important football match. According to witnesses, other information also arrived by long-distance telephone, bring-ing inside stuff on what the police were doing, and especially their reports over short-wave radio. According to the witnesses, the lawyer was extremely grateful, interrupting his informer with such ejaculations as:

"Thanks, Chief. Okay, Chief. That's fine, Chief!"

Perhaps an instance in which a chief of police allegedly telephones confidential details of a crime-hunt to a super-gangster's lawyer may be classed as merely a gentlemanly gesture. In so many cases there does seem to be an overabundance of effort on the part of certain law enforcement officials to live on a basis of friendly neutrality with crime. There are few cities in America where police headquarters or large district stations are not infested with runners or hangers-on, who have no legal right whatever to use the offices of a law enforcement agency as a loafing place. In some instances, they are bail bondsmen, waiting, like buzzards, for the arrest of an ignorant unfortunate, that they may extort usurious prices for gaining the arrested man's freedom on a bond, which, should the prisoner default, would be found to be worth nothing. Practically every city has its sporadic upheavals over straw bonds, usually when some major criminal has walked out on one and not returned. There is a great deal of excitement for a while. There may even be a grand jury investigation. If the district attorney is at outs with the police department, the matter is gone into thoroughly. If they are both minions of the same political machine, the grand jury never seems quite able to get its teeth into any worth-while evidence.

Beyond the bondsmen are the jackals or equally hyena-like attorneys. The citizen, reading his paper in the morning, sees that an important criminal has been arrested upon his arrival in town. In the next line is the fact that he has refused to talk, "on advice of his attorney." Sometimes, there penetrates the reader's mind a fleeting sense of wonder that a man outside the law, a stranger to the city, should, immediately upon arrest, obtain the services of an outstandingly shrewd and unscrupulous criminal attorney. Often the explanation lies in the fact that the criminal was "wired in" to this attorney before he ever reached the town. In an equal number of cases, however, that attorney has been furnished by the very persons who dilate upon the dangerous record of the criminal — in other words the police, who have informed the lawyer's runner of the arrest, for a consideration, of course.

Sometimes this graft belongs to the desk sergeant. Again, it may be the province of the telephone operator; but more often the racket belongs to the head turnkey. Upon unfavorable publicity, there is an awful stink, and the offender even may be suspended, appealing his case to the commissioner, who in a majority of cases reinstates him for the simple reason that this service to criminals is looked upon as a legitimate, even though undercover, racket. There are so many ways in which a policeman can make "white money," as he calls it.

In large cities, it has become almost as necessary to tip the policeman as to tip the waiter. Patrolmen who act as special guards at weddings or big receptions always expect their remembrance. Roundsmen in apartment house districts where chauffeurs may wait too long parked at the curb for their employers, indulge in reprisals unless they are remembered on their birthdays and at Christmas and at New Year's. Department stores which expect large crowds at a special bargain sale know what is expected by the police detail. Sometimes when the reward does not fit desires, there is much acrimony.

Recently a big New York bank, acting as the agent for a man with a large collection of jewels, telephoned the precinct station.

The bank manager informed the captain that, inasmuch as these jewels were to be sold at public auction and a large crowd would attend, it might be wise for the police department to send some officers to guard against a hold-up. The officers were sent.

It was an auction of a private collection; and the owner, while knowing he was expected to tip the officers, was ignorant as to the proper amount. He sought the advice of the bank manager.

"Well," said that person, "after all, they are policemen. They are being paid by tax money for maintaining law and order. If they were not present at this auction and a big theft occurred, it would work a tremendous hardship on the department, to say nothing of letting a bunch of criminals get away with an easy job. Viewed from that standpoint, it seems to me that they should appreciate being informed that something is transpiring that might invite crime and therefore be in a position to prevent it. However, if you think you'd like to tip them, I should say that twenty-five dollars should be plenty. After all, they are not working overtime; they are being paid by the city for coming here, and they're probably having an easier job than they might draw otherwise."

The jewel owner followed the advice and gave the officers the twenty-five dollar tip. The next day the Sergeant dropped in at the bank and halted beside the desk of the manager.

"Say, listen," he announced. "The next time you've got a customer who's such a lousy heel that he doesn't want to slip a bunch of good fellows a century for watching his junk — just don't call us."

Whether such men are in the minority or majority, this writer frankly does not know. It must be added, also, that the honest and hard-working members of any organization cannot carry banners proclaiming the fact, and there is the ancient truth that bad news travels faster than good. However, it is a certainty that the police personnel looks each year with less disfavor upon the receipt of tips, classing them as "white money." Prohibition, however, proved that after a man has become accustomed to taking money, he asks fewer and fewer times whence it came and why it is given him, while his subservience to the giver either becomes increasingly acute or suffers from what practically amounts to an underworld dictatorship.

I quote from a recently recorded telephone conversation between an underworld character of a large Ohio city and the sheriff of a suburb in which there had been some difficulty about the opening of a new gambling joint: —

SUBJECT: Hello. How you doing?

SHERIFF: Okay. How are you feeling by this time?

SUBJECT: It ain't how I'm feeling, it's how you're feeling. What do you think about it by now?

SHERIFF: You know what I think.

SUBJECT: Listen, for God's sake, don't act like a heel. What's it get you? You can't stop that place from opening Saturday night.

SHERIFF: I can't like hell.

SUBJECT: Oh, be reasonable. That place can't stand any four-hundred-dollar payoff.

SHERIFF: That's what I said it would have to be.

SUBJECT: But the take won't stand it. I've been talking to my partner and he's willing to do the square thing. He says two hundred and fifty bucks is a hell of a load but he's willing to go for that. Seems like you —

SHERIFF: He knows what he'll have to go for.

SUBJECT: But he says four hundred bucks is highway robbery and if you don't like it you can go to hell and we'll open anyway.

SHERIFF: He will in a pig's ——— ; I'm telling you.

SUBJECT: Well, if you think you're scaring my partner, you're crazy. That guy won't take nothing off of nobody, you know that; he thinks anybody who wants to clean that joint for four centuries of graft, just for letting it run, is a lousy bastard.

SHERIFF: Who's calling me a bastard, you or him?

SUBJECT: Well, he said it, but Christ's sake, you are a lousy bastard wanting four hundred bucks to let that place open. Can't you use some sense? The joint's going to open whether you like it or not, now what do you think of that, take or no take!

SHERIFF: Yeh, and it'll close up damn quick, now what do you think of that?

SUBJECT: Like hell it will.

SHERIFF: Like hell it won't.

Thus the argument went on and on. The joint opened — and remained so, whether in defiance or upon a cash basis is not known. So many toothsome little details are missing when one gets only a part of the picture from a tapped telephone. . . .

In justice to honest, efficient law enforcement officers, it certainly is not the purpose of this book to make the flat, generalized statement that all policemen either are crooks or fail of their tasks. Rather, it is to prove a fact all too well-known in law enforcement — that the business of handling American crime in all its phases, from the time the first officer is sent to the scene of a depredation until after a man has been released from prison, is so chaotic, so desperately archaic, so inhumane in certain instances, especially where poverty is concerned, and so solicitous in others as to be farcical were it not so tragic. Of course there are honest men of law enforcement, thousands upon thousands of them. In some communities, they can prove their integrity and efficiency because they are supported by honest citizens and equally honest men in politics and public office. In others, they can only grit their teeth, perform their duties as best they can — and watch the crooks saunter by, thumbing their noses at what should and could be a most thoroughgoing police department.

There are innumerable conditions which must be changed before this country even can pretend to be law-abiding. They cannot be pointed out in one chapter; perhaps even this entire volume will be insufficient to detail the loopholes in the horrible mess we call law enforcement.

A rotten officer is like a rotten apple; he spoils the whole barrel. Often only a few key men are sufficient to undo the work of hundreds of hard-working men of integrity. Gaston Means, the master criminal now serving fifteen years for having mulcted one hundred and four thousand dollars from Evalyn Walsh McLean by the ghastly fake in which he promised to restore the Lindbergh baby, once served a total of one hundred and four days as a temporary Special Agent in the Federal Bureau of Investigation of the United States Department of Justice, in which J. Edgar Hoover then occupied a subordinate position.

That period of less than four months, in which a master crook defiled a fine organization, was nevertheless sufficient to cast a shadow over the Department of Justice for years. More than a decade of building under Mr. Hoover, during which time the Bureau has become the most efficient and trustworthy organization in the entire world, was required before the stain of one man's activities could be thoroughly eliminated.

One should keep this in mind, as this narrative of rottenness, corruption, and downright ignorance writhes forth. Moreover, one should not look so much upon the evidence of queer things done by so-called crime-chasers, as toward the conditions which instigate those actions. Perhaps, therefore, it might be a good idea to go slumming in civic government and watch the progress of crooked political control as it reaches outward to throttle the peace and dignity of an entire city.

Thus I invite you into the revelations of A Man About To Die.

CHAPTER THREE

A MAN ABOUT TO DIE

IT seemed so strange to go to the Morgue and realize that his grim prophecy had been true. Stiffened upon the drainboard, he seemed a strangely shrunken and eerie figure in his shriveled nakedness. One hand, traced by blue veins, lay at his side. The other was half-upraised, the fingers clutched tightly, and with serrations of black blood still visible in the creases about the thumb. This hand had been over his bullet-torn face, as though to shut out the horror of what finally had come to him — the thing he had told me would surely arrive, the thing at which I had laughed. Johnny the Guy had been so insistent that "they" would get him. And I had been equally positive that he was the victim of a waking nightmare. Johnny the Guy, however, knew the underworld far better than I. He should; he had been an important part of it.

As an individual, Johnny the Guy was unimportant; merely another present-day "gentleman of the rackets" killed at the instance of men who had been his pals. I have not even used his true name, largely because his case is still a matter of official investigation. The United States Government, for instance, is highly interested in why and how and by whose hand Johnny died.

It was not what Johnny was, it was the conditions he represented; you can find his type and what he stood for in almost every big city of America. For that reason alone, Johnny had his niche. Otherwise, he was merely an undersized type of rodent who did nothing for humanity while he lived and accomplished something in his death only by the accident of having used a writer for a confidant. Johnny the Guy told what few men tell — what really happens on the inside of political-gang control of our cities.

Perhaps it was because Johnny was at heart a petty person that he could not run along with the big fellows when the opportunity at last came his way. To a degree likeable, strangely eager to do a good turn in a crooked way, he might be classed as a white rat instead of the regulation sewer variety which infests the underworld. I knew him first before Prohibition days and prior to the sensational newspaper campaign which temporarily outlawed racing. He was a tout and a very poor one. Nevertheless, he was so good at finding a reason why his sure-thing decided to run backwards at the first quarter that one always got one's money's worth.

For years he had been a wanderer, but of late he had stuck close to town, making his home in a Jewish quarter. Always ready to do a favor for those who asked it, Johnny had many friends in his neighborhood. All he lacked, to make him really important, was money.

The years went by. Johnny bought an old car and used it as a jitney bus during a street railway strike. He prospered and bought others. By the early twenties, he was in a taxicab business. Within five years more he had fifteen cabs, not enough to make him a big corporation, it is true, but sufficient to provide a good living, and to permit indulgence in things which Johnny liked to do. One of these was to make a big play to the women. And he loved to be "the life of the party," at which, whatever was in his pocket went to anyone who asked for it. Fifteen taxicabs also provided the means of being a real fellow whenever there was a funeral, and when Johnny could "throw in a couple of cabs" so some of the old women might have a free ride to the cemetery. Johnny did such things because he liked to do them; yet there was lacking what might be called true generosity.

He once told me: "It makes a guy feel like a Big Shot when he walks down the street and somebody says: 'There goes Johnny the Guy; say, he was swell to my mother when the old man died!' "

In short, Johnny the Guy possessed one of the true fundamentals of the gangster, which is an overdeveloped ego taking form in acts of seeming great-heartedness. Such persons are secretly proud of sentimentalism. Al Capone possessed this trait to a marked degree; he really believed himself a public benefactor when he established soup kitchens for the poor during the early days of the depression. It probably never entered his head that the idea was generated as a mark of exhibitionism. That psychology was present in everything which Capone did: His triumphant excursions down Michigan Boulevard in his tremendous, armored car; his giant G.H.Q., maintained in a Chicago hotel, where there was as much room for loafing as there was for work; his Lucullus-like banquets for judges, police officers, and the like; his easy generosity with diamond-studded cigarette cases of platinum which he passed out so freely. Many of Capone's gifts were quite embarrassing to their recipients; they would much rather have had money which they could have tucked away in a safety deposit box, later to deny its origin. Diamond-studded platinum cigarette-cases could not be hidden; Capone passed them out to be used, and Capone was king. That was deadly to hypocrites who pretended to hate gangdom even while they were a part of it; every time that diamond-studded cigarette-case came forth, it was like flashing a brand. And if the pattern, purchased by the gross, were not recognizable, there was the inscription: —

To a Pal
From Al

Again exhibitionism — there was only one Al, only one Capone. One finds the same components in almost every outstanding hoodlum. One notorious gangster ("the Mad Dog ") liked to pretend that he was a sort of modern Haroun Al Raschid, going about O. Henry's "Bagdad on the Subway," doing deeds of kindness. A murderer of the vilest sort, even to baby killing, he could become maudlin over a gray-haired mother, and sloppily sentimental over some bum with a peg leg. He liked to pretend that his deeds of kindness were silent affairs, held close to his own heart; nevertheless, he always assured himself that some henchman was near to blat the news of his great-heartedness to the tabloids. So it goes with all of them.

Thus, Johnny the Guy possessed natural requisites for the life into which he was to be thrown. One day, after a lapse of years, I found him sleek and suave and somehow changed. His taxicab business had taken a sudden spurt. Now he had a hundred and forty cars, all new. There was a different element of authority in his manner. Many persons came to see him in his taxicab office. To all he gave a glad welcome, and there were many promises that he "would look after it." I asked the reason for his sudden affluence.

"Well, you see how it is," said Johnny the Guy. "I finally made up my mind to take over th' Tenth Ward."

"You did what?"

Johnny the Guy gestured uneasily, a shrug of the shoulders and a spread of the hands.

"Well, it's like this, you see," he began again, "I kind of got th' idea — that is, well, you know — maybe, I says to myself, I ought to go into politics."

A taxi driver, who had been on the carpet, finished making out his accident report and departed. Johnny the Guy closed his office door, meanwhile yelling to his telephone operator that he wasn't to be disturbed for nothin' by nobody. I swung a leg over the end of his desk.

"What's the lay, Johnny?" I asked. He thought a long time. Finally: —

"Well, I guess you'd say I was dealin' from the hip," he

admitted, "although you know yourself I don't touch it much, and I don't peddle none." That was not exactly what he wanted to convey. At last he blurted it. "Well, you see, we got a syndicate."

"Alky?"

"Well, that's all we're doin' now. You see it was this way," he added with that almost childlike faith which gangsters place in persons they like. "Dressed-up Eddie — you remember him — used to promote the fights here when you were with th' circus — Well, he'd been in Chicago an' New York an' he'd gotten lined up pretty well, until about a year ago when he had to go on the lam. Seems he took a fifteen-year-old kid out an' laid her, which was all right, I guess, except she belonged to a friend of Bugs Moran. So Capone said, 'What th' hell, why get a bunch of guys bumped off over a thing like that?' So Eddie lammed. Well, after he got here, naturally lookin' around for something to put himself into, he figured out a thing you'd never believe."

Johnny the Guy poked a finger in my ribs and announced: "I bet you never thought of it: This whole end of town, th' Tenth Ward, th' Twelfth, th' Ninth an' Seventh an' all along th' Lake Front — it hadn't ever been affiliated."

"Affiliated? With whom?"

"With nobody," said Johnny the Guy with increasing seriousness. "Nobody never had it. An election come along, and th' damn fools voted for anybody they pleased. So Eddie says to me, 'We'll incorporate th' Lake Shore Voters' League.' "

"What brand of politics, Johnny?"

"Oh, it's non-partisan," he announced righteously. "Like Eddie says: Suppose some stiff-neck gets control of th' Democrats, we don't want to be tied up with no Democratic Party. An' if th' same happened to th' Republicans, we wouldn't want to be Republicans, would we?"

"Certainly not," I agreed. "You want to be free, so you can go with the candidate that's willing to lay on the line."

"That's it," said Johnny the Guy. " 'Course nobody that's in politics does things for his health. It's a hell of a lot of work supportin' a guy. Anyway, Eddie had th' dough an' he was willing to spend it, so he got me to take th' Tenth Ward, an' O'Reilly th' Twelfth an' Carrolis th' Ninth an' Seventh an' Molkaeur th' Lake District an' then we started organizin'."

"For what?"

"For nothin'," answered Johnny. "Hell, everything was goin' out an' nothin' comin' in for months. I guess Eddie must have laid a hundred grand on the line before we ever made a pass at anybody. Eddie wanted to be sure where he was goin', see?"

"No, I don't see."

"Well, we were organizin', gettin' things started," Johnny the Guy explained with an air of futility. "You can't get goin' before you organize, can you?"

"Get going? Get going where?"

"Why to whoever plays ball with us."

"Tell it in umpchay language," I told him. "What did you organize?"

"The Lake Shore Voters' League."

"For what?"

"For th' good of th' people," shouted Johnny. "Like in my ward, for th' good of th' Jews, and for th' hunkies along th' Lake Shore, and th' Irish in O'Reilly's district and th' grease-balls in th' Ninth and Seventh. Now you get it?"

I had gotten it long before. One needs see a "political organization for the good of the people" put over only once in districts where there is ignorance, poverty, law infractions, and urgent need of jobs, to know all the tactics and all the ramifications.

"Must have cost Eddie plenty dough," I said.

"I'm tellin' you," agreed Johnny the Guy. "He laid out plenty. 'Course, he's gettin' some of it back now — we're all doin' pretty good. But we did a lot of work for it."

"I take it you're affiliated."

"Yeh, we hooked up on th' last election. Didn't get much out of it, only alky, an' we haven't got any exclusive on it. We ought to have at least that, for all th' work we've done."

"For the good of the people," I interjected. Johnny the Guy eyed me seriously.

"Sure," he answered.

If this conversation has been cryptic, it shall be explained, together with the psychology behind it. To a certain degree, it must be understood, the political despoiler who grows votes for market does so with a certain feeling of justification. He is not the fiction type of schemer, greedily planning to mulct a group of victims out of their birthright. He looks upon a district full of ballots in exactly the same manner that a farmer looks upon fallow ground, as something to be cultivated — at no expense to the land — for his own profit. His mentality does not waste time with the purity of the ballot, nor does he realize that he is breeding a type of degeneracy. He calculates in terms of expenditure and results. To his mind, he has done a lot of good things for a bunch of friendless people, whereupon he himself has profited, at no cost whatever to them, his price merely being their ballot cast in the direction he dictates. After all, what the hell is a vote? In return for all his labor, he has gained certain privileges for delivering these votes to persons who have wanted them. Therefore, who has lost anything, and what is all the squawk about?

Dressed-up Eddie had followed a formula. In choosing his henchmen, he had picked men who were well known in their districts and who possessed native traits of egotistical generosity. He had played upon these traits, giving them money to spend and allowing them to elevate themselves, in their opinions at least, to positions of power and largesse.

He financed the opening of Athletic Clubs. He provided for picnics and excursions on the big steamers plying the Lake, upon which tangles of maternity, paternity and progeny gained a breath of fresh air, and music of a brass band, and a bite of food, "all for nothing." There were clambakes, and free fights in the Athletic Club, the backing of district pugilists in city amateur tournaments, friendliness in time of illness, efforts to land jobs for heads of big families, letter writing, intervention for offenses both large and small wherever possible, and the spending of money where its dispensing would accomplish the most good. More than one large Italian family, plus its multitude of relatives, became the absolute slave of Eddie's machine through a few hundred dollars spent upon a decent funeral for some poverty-stricken member. To them the act was unadulterated generosity, nothing else.

All these are things which the ignorant, the poor, the down-trodden can understand. They feel that in a political leader of a certain stripe they have a friend. They know he will inter-cede when a member of the family has been arrested for drunk-enness or attempting to run a butcher knife through his next-door neighbor. In the terrible scramble for jobs, they feel that they have something which they can barter for them — their fealty to the man who works to get them the thing which puts food on their table, shoes on their feet, clothes on their back and a roof over their heads. And I believe that were society to drop its hypocritical attitude, it would admit that under the same circumstances it would do exactly what politically sub-servient districts do — obey the man who at least pretends to be their counselor, their friend, their Good Samaritan.

To such subjects, all the wonderful things which come from loyalty cost nothing, except the performance of what a good friend wants them to do on Election Day. They do not give a tinker's dam about the future of America, the uprightness of our communities, the moral right of society to rise above chicanery or crookedness. What they want is some fun out of life, a place to gather, a friend at court, a job, food on the table, a doctor in time of illness, a funeral when someone has died. With many such persons, a life ambition centers about a decent burial. It is the one time in their entire existence when they rise above the dent in society into which the misfortune of birth has thrust them. And if society really wants to wipe out the panderer, the man who feeds upon one stratum of civilization by giving a percentage of his crooked proceeds to another, if it wishes to stop elections by which persons of vicious morals come into control of police departments, or city and county and state administrations, through the delivery of solid blocks of votes which hold the balance of power in an election, let it exchange honest deeds of kindness and understanding for the sympathy-for-profit of the predatory politician.

If we are to have clean elections, then we should be able to go to the thickly settled regions of our cities with clean hands. It is all very well to sneer at the politician who has bought votes with boat rides and picnics and excursions and a thousand other forms of "free service." Nevertheless, he has given his pawns something which they otherwise would not get, and which society turns over to the all-too-often inhibited, crosspatch, sexless, unsympathetic, and coldly condescending settlement worker.

In other words, crooked politicians can be wiped out only by eliminating the conditions upon which they feed. As long as persons must live four and six to a room, with the law constantly pounding on their door to swell the arrest list for the annual police report, with a criminal charge usually resulting in conviction through the often detrimental efforts of some recent law school graduate appointed by the court as attorney for the defense, with appeals seldom granted even when a gesture is made at seeking them, with bitterness rampant, with illness and death a constant ogre — just that long will there be crooked politics. Nobody gives a damn about ideals when it is the belly which needs attention. In the last thirty years, it has been my lot to visit practically every city in the United States. I have found few where crooked political control was not synonymous with poverty and ignorance.

Thus, Dressed-up Eddie had fed upon a condition. His reward was to be "let alone" in the dispensing of bootleg liquor, with far greater profits looming in the future.

"You see," explained Johnny the Guy, "we can't branch out much until we get th' Police Department. That's bound to come, sooner or later."

In the months which followed, I had an opportunity, through the eyes of Johnny the Guy, to watch the progress of a growing political machine. The word had gone through the underworld that a 'legger who played with the Dressed-up Eddie crowd need have few troubles, with the result that many men who had worked independently now sold so-called liquor on a commission basis. Also, Eddie had availed himself of "connections" in New York and Chicago. The Chicago liquor came from Capone's distilleries in Peoria and was shipped in by freight, often as many as three carloads of it standing on the team tracks at one time awaiting unloading. Sometimes it was billed as canned tomatoes, again as furniture or catsup or groceries, and it was consigned to the Lake Shore Finance Company, which, strangely enough, had as its officers the generals of the Lake Shore Voters' League. Prohibition agents showed great acumen in arresting and prosecuting persons who were hauling in liquor by car up the so-called "Greased Trail" from the Gulf of Mexico, or from Cleveland, or down from Canada. There was a Lake Shore Trucking Company which was owned by the Lake Shore Finance Company; neither the trucking company nor the big freight cars, heavily loaded with drums of alcohol, ever were bothered. There were elements about this, however, which nettled Johnny the Guy.

"Sometimes I wonder who's got this alky business," he complained one day. "Us or them Prohi's. I never see such dough-eaters!" On another occasion he philosophized: "Ain't it the nuts? About every fourth guy in them Prohi's an ex-con, and them runnin' around sendin' up guys who never did anything but give th' people what they want."

In that attitude was much of the crime of the Prohibition era born. It was one of the things which brought about the tremendous disrespect for law in the Twenties: a feeling of unfairness or fundamental crookedness. During the years which have intervened since Repeal, the United States Government has been able to wipe out much of this sentiment. States and cities, however, remain, to a degree, under its shadow. Many of the same local law enforcement officers who took money during booze-running days are still taking it for protecting other forms of crime. Some of these men were only patrolmen in the Twenties; they are sergeants or captains to-day. And some are ex-Prohibition agents who have been kicked out of Government service that they may continue to take money in local law-enforcement jobs.

I was away from Johnny's town for a year. When I returned I found him more affluent, more powerful in his district, more able to promise votes by the thousand to whatever political party was willing to "lay on the line." He wore a headlight diamond, big enough to make the third finger of his right hand almost useless. He had bought a sixty-thousand-dollar home in which he rattled about like a shriveled peanut. His taxicab company had all the netherworld business, and his drivers made a minimum of seventy-five dollars a week, although Johnny paid them only eighteen. The rest came from tips, bootleg commissions, and cuts on the money paid to party girls.

There was hardly a hustler in town who was not eager to have her name and telephone number in Johnny's stud book on a fifty per cent. commission basis. This was quite a recommendation. Johnny was emphatic about the fact that he never would steer any guy into a tramp, or a girl who would roll a drunk, and if she ever showed up with crabs or a dose, she got run out of town. He told me all this with an air of pride which, however, could not quite erase a certain air of strain and preoccupation.

"That rather looks like you've got the Department," I suggested.

He shook his head.

"No, we ain't got th' Department yet. But that's all set for th' next election."

There seemed little joy in the statement; anticipation, it is true, but no enthusiasm.

"What's eating you, Johnny?" I asked at last.

There was a period of much fencing. Finally, he said: "Well, I'll tell you; there's some things goin' on in town here I don't like. You know — I ain't got nothin' to do with them — but it's bad for the Organization."

"What's bad?"

"A coupla guys got bumped off," he said abruptly.

The bluntness of his statement gave evidence that he did not care for further discussion. The subject was changed — returning to Dressed-up Eddie's hope for control of the Police Department.

"You see," Johnny explained, "you can't do much without th' Department. This alky thing — sure, they leave us alone on that — orders from upstairs. But almost anybody can go in th' alky racket these days if he makes a pay-off."

That, I felt sure, was what was behind "a couple of guys getting bumped off." They had made the pay-off to Prohibition and other officers, sufficient to protect them from arrest. This could not, however, eradicate competition. Under Dressed-up Eddie's veneer of geniality, there was a certain polar coldness, an element of drive, of predominant self. Eddie probably had warned these fellows and they had failed to obey him. So some of Eddie's friends had come in from Chicago or New York, — "torpedoes," in the gangster language, — and murdered the men who had persisted in infringing upon a territory where much work had been done to insure an election and thus obtain a concession.

Johnny the Guy continued: "We ain't so interested in this

alky stuff anyway. What th' hell — it's a lousy racket. But if we can get th' Department to come in, there's gamblin', an' stuff like that. Hell, that's real dough."

The election arrived, accompanied by fervent efforts along the Lake Shore — the herding of votes, the constant going from door to door where poor families were reminded to "stick to their friends" — the persons who had gotten them jobs, "fronted" for them in time of stress, given them outings, looked after their sick and their dead, and left a few dollars on the table when there was nothing in the family purse. Johnny's taxicabs worked from morning until dark "getting out the vote."

It was a type of intimidation, always carrying the reminder that the Organization might have no weight with an opposing administration. If the wayward boy of some family got into trouble, he would be forced to stay in jail unless the right crowd got in office. Other persons would lose jobs. It would be a catastrophe which would affect the health, the belly, the surety of a roof. The Lake Shore went the way the Organization wanted it to go; and its forty thousand votes, cast solidly for the gang's candidate, meant the difference between victory and defeat. Therefore, instead of merely being a block of forty thousand votes, it was "the Block," the deciding factor, the balance of power, and those who controlled it held the right to dictate their reward. Shortly afterward, there were changes in the Police Department.

It was not a tremendous shake-up, such as one would expect. It entailed, in fact, only the firing of three men and the elevation of three others who, incidentally, had been friendly with Dressed-up Eddie ever since the days when he was running prize fights. There was a new Chief, elevated from a sergeant. There was a new Chief of Detectives, brought up from a detective of the first rank. And there was a new head for the vice-auto squad, a man now Captain when once he had been merely a patrolman with an itching palm.

All three of these men had been known in the underworld as "takers." They now were in a position to become rich in a couple of years, and one more man would join them: the District Attorney, who had been placed on the ticket with "an understanding." Beyond this, however, was one more highly important ingredient. That was the knowledge that any man who got on the force, or stayed on the force, must govern his actions so that they would be pleasing to Dressed-up Eddie. That was all.

Within a month after the new city administration took office, a gambling house opened in the downtown district. It was not ostentatious; the first floor was a pool hall, and of the better grade. On the second, however, was everything from roulette to chuck-a-luck. Small buildings of sufficient depth to permit of cigar stores in front and card rooms in the rear came into demand. Slowly, as the word got about and patronage developed, other gambling joints of the larger type got under way. At last there were fully fifty, running full blast, and with as much of a chance for the sucker to win as for fleas to hate dogs. It was necessary for the house to make a percentage of at least fifty per cent. profit, due to the fact that the Organization demanded thirty-five for "letting 'em run."

Johnny the Guy became quite happy again. There were times when he left his taxicab business for a month at a stretch while he went East to see "important" people. The cause of this was something close to Johnny's heart.

"I got the horse joints and the dog track," he told me.

That was his cut for good and faithful service in the Tenth Ward. Throughout the city, in at least two hundred tiny stores, doorways, cubby-hole buildings, poolrooms and cigar stores, "horse joints" had opened, all served either by "the wire" or by a radio broadcasting company which specializes in "sporting events," over which race results came direct from the tracks. Strangely enough, no matter how small the horse joint might be, no matter if the man who ran it had, only a week before, been on Relief — for time had passed now to 1933 — one could walk into any one of them and place a bet for any amount of money he chose, even to that of a hundred thousand dollars. I shall save the explanation.

The dog track opened, with a brass band, free beer, a cut of ten per cent. on the first week's receipts to charity, and the attendance by city officials, including the Mayor, who saw in all this a "better spirit of sportsmanship and interest in dumb animals." Betting was done by bookies, with the odds changing with bewildering rapidity and with little reason therefor other than that they were dictated largely by Johnny the Guy and the small group of men "from the East" who formed his partners — a necessary obeisance to the New York and Chicago Syndicates, which feel they hold a patent on dog tracks.

Magically, slot machines began to appear in drugstores, candy stores, beer joints, poolrooms; and strangely enough, this form of endeavor was about the only one which drew concerted protest from the city's residents. That was because it was visual and reached straight into the home. When a mother gave her child a quarter with which to run to the butcher shop for twenty-five cents' worth of round steak, only to discover, after a quarrel with the meat man over short weight, that the child had been buying twenty cents' worth and playing the remaining nickel in the slot machine at the corner drugstore, she had a personal interest in making a yowl. The preachers took up the battle and spoke vaguely of "underworld influence," simply because that was self-evident. They also dilated upon gang terrorism and grew excited about the fact that gorillas and hoodlums were forcing honest, law-abiding storekeepers to install these instruments of the devil.

No doubt that has happened. Perhaps there are men who cannot sleep at night because of fear of the deadly threat of gangdom that, unless they put in slot machines, they will be beaten and their business ruined. I've just never happened to meet such victims.

True, violence does occur when two gangs collide and the

stronger one decides to put its slot machines where the other crowd's paraphernalia has been. Otherwise, the "violence" usually consists of convincing a storekeeper that the average slot machine can be regulated to pay whatever profit the traffic will stand, up to a thousand per cent., and that these profits will be split between the syndicate which owns the machines and the person who allows them on his premises. Or there may be the reminder that the fellow on the corner is going to have a "vending machine" and that he'll get all the business unless there is competition. The dire threats, the possibility of injury and gangster reprisal, usually appear as an afterthought when some hypocritical merchant seeks to explain to church people, school principals, the right kind of grand jury, or infuriated parents why he has been stealing the neighborhood's money by means of a mechanical confidence game which never was known to give the sucker an even break. As for the alibi that gangs force these on timid storekeepers, I submit the apparent fact that the one thing which gangs abhor is a "beef" from the decent element of a city. That makes the town "hot," and nobody likes that type of heat.

After the slot machines came the numbers racket, taking its plunder in every form of money from a penny to a hundred dollars, and adding new problems in arithmetic to the Syndicate's intricate existence. As Johnny the Guy explained, it all required a hell of a lot of mental bookkeeping.

"You've got to do it all on th' cuff," he said. "Everything's cash and it's cut up so many ways that a guy gets dizzy. Now with me, I get twenty-five per cent. of th' take off th' horse joints. The rest goes to Eddie."

"A good cut for him."

"Oh, no. You see he pays off out of part of it. Then there's the percentage for next election's campaign fund an' th' percentage that goes to New York."

"Where?"

"New York, to Lucky's mob. They got all th' horse joints

as far West as Kansas City. Say, I was in Lucky's place out in Westchester County when I was back East. A big swell house off th' road — somebody's estate it used to be. Nobody can't get in there unless they're in th' racket, see? Got a big switchboard there with direct wires leading to all th' race tracks. Then there's long distance stuff to all th' places he's cut in on, see? Like Cleveland an' Toledo an' Philadelphia an' Baltimore an' St. Louis an' Kansas City — he ain't in Chicago. Him and th' guy that's got th' town there, they're pals, see, and he wouldn't horn in. But Dee-troit an' St. Paul an' Minneapolis an' all that. Any bet you want to lay, that mob'll cover. That's how come a guy can walk into any of these horse joints in town an' lay down a hundred grand and have it covered right now. Then they're into Hot Springs an' Jacksonville an' Miami — oh, all around, out to th' Missouri River. So they've got to have a cut, now, ain't they?

"Then there's th' Chief of Police an' th' Chief Dick an' th' head of th' auto squad — although he don't get so much of a take. He's got tires."

"Got what?"

"Tires."

"Bootleg tires?"

Johnny shook his head.

"Hot ones. Hi-jack stuff. Maybe some joint's knocked over in Illinois for a coupla thousand tires. They ain't sold in Illinois, are they? They're peddled out around — you know. Like here in town. Th' same with hot cars — like th' mace joints that open up, pay you twenty-five dollars down on your car an' give you a sixty-day note for th' rest an' when they've bought cars for fifty-nine days, they rise up an' beat it with all th' automobiles, leavin' a lot of guys with bum notes. Well, th' head of th' auto squad's in on that. So his cut's kind of taken care of.

"Then there's th' race-track wire an' radio services that have to be paid for — a century here, a half a grand there, whatever you can knock the joints over for, dependin' on how much business they're doin'. All that's got to be cut up five or six ways, an' you got t' keep it all in your head, on account of th' income tax. Me, I'm not playin' any sucker. I'm payin' mine. But Eddie, he figures if he ever paid his he'd be owin' himself money. Eddie's handlin' plenty dough. Everything that's runnin' is bein' split up kind of like I was tellin' you. Yeah, Eddie's got heavy fur. I guess there's only two people know where he keeps his dough, me'n that babe he's been layin' up with."

"Johnny," I said for no apparent reason, "I understand this is getting to be a good town."

He looked at me queerly.

"What do you mean 'good town'?"

I laughed.

"You know what I mean. A place where guys on the lam can cool off if they pay for the protection."

Again he looked at me for a long moment.

"Yeah?" he asked, and gave no information.

After all, it was not necessary. Bank robberies were increasing in the small towns which lay within two and three hundred miles of this place on the Lake Shore. Three times, newspapers speculated upon whether certain persons of the sporting and gambling world, known to possess large sums of money, had not been "yaffled" or kidnapped and held until they had paid off ransom demands. Then, after a time, the killings started anew.

Johnny the Guy denied hotly that his crowd had anything to do with them. Eddie was a swell guy, he said, he wouldn't stand for no rough stuff. I reminded him that the apparent motives were fights over divisions of the spoils, distrust over cuts, attempts by outsiders to horn in on what was a closed corporation. Johnny's answer was only a blank denial and the sharp query as to whether I thought he would be mixed up with anything like that.

"Not of your own accord, Johnny," I said. He glanced at me swiftly.

"Sure not," came cryptically.

But the tight lines about his mouth grew more grim, the worried expression of his eyes increased. His whistling ceased — Johnny the Guy had been the worst and loudest whistler I ever had known. He even grew taciturn about his dog track, where, for the first time in his life, he could name the winner of almost any race.

Dropping in for a visit during a trip to town, I saw in Johnny the Guy a changed being. He was thin, stooped. His eyes were hollow. His hands shook. After a long time he explained with a curt: "Havin' a little trouble with Eddie. Don't amount to anything."

I did not see Johnny again until last year. One day, I got a letter. It was from Johnny, addressed from Philadelphia: —

> Well, ha ha, I guess it will be a big joak to you to here from me down here. I'm here lookin' over the Town and playing the Babes and all. Was at Atlantic City for a While but the heat was on there so I come back. Well, I just Thot I would drop you a letter to see how you were.
>
> Yrs sincerely
>
> Johnny.
>
> P.S. Could you let me have fifty? Address me as James Peterson

It was the postscript which amazed me. What had become of Johnny's horse joints, his dog track, his big diamond ring, his sixty-thousand-dollar house, his taxicab business? Why was he living under an alias? I sent him the fifty. Then, one day in Philadelphia, I looked up the address he had given me. It was a slatternly rooming house. And Johnny was in a two-by-four room, with one chair. I sat on that. Johnny hunched himself on the narrow bed.

"You see, I sold out at home," he explained.

"What became of the money?"

Johnny jerked what purported to be a smile over the brown-stained butt of a cigarette.

"They asked me whether I wanted to get paid off then or later. I figured I'd rather stall it off."

I did not understand. For a moment we sat staring at each other. Suddenly he tossed the cigarette to the floor, forgetting it — I stamped it out before the round hole in the dirty matting should grow larger. Johnny was off the bed and circling me like a caged animal, his head low in his shoulders, the fingers of both hands drumming against his chest.

"For Christ's sake!" he exclaimed. "Can't you get it? They're goin' to bump me off! Ain't you got no brains? They took everything I had, an' now they're goin' to knock me off!"

"You're crazy, Johnny." I, too, was on my feet.

"Yeah?" he asked. "I'm just so crazy I'm livin' in this dump an' hardly goin' out to eat, that's how crazy I am! I'm so crazy I blew town an' handed everything over to Eddie before three torpedoes he had brought up from St. Louis could blast th' hell out of me. An' " — he looked about him, at the four paperless walls — "I got to be lammin' it out of here, or that New York mob'll find out where I'm at."

"The New York mob? What have they to do with it?"

Johnny smiled, horribly, and spread his hands.

"Nothin'," he said. "That's a laugh, now ain't it? They ain't got nothin' to do with it. So they bump me off!"

"But why?"

Johnny dropped his shoulders in disgust.

"As a favor to Eddie; for God's sake, ain't that reason enough?"

It wasn't and I said so. For a half-hour we talked at cross-purposes. At last I asked him to start at the beginning.

"Well," he said, as he moved swiftly about his narrow room, "you see in th' paper where th' Feds walk in on Eddie's safe deposit box, don't you, an' then get an indictment against him on income taxes?"

"Yes, I saw that."

"All right. There's two people who know where that box is, ain't there? One of 'em's me. Th' other one's his dame. Well, I've always told you Eddie's gone for th' young ones. Well he started two-timin' his Babe with some sixteen-year-old punk an' she finds it out. I suppose she don't get sore. Th' hell she don't. But she don't say a word to Eddie. She just sics th' Feds on him!"

"Why didn't she tell the police about what Eddie was doing with young girls?"

Johnny the Guy glared with disgust.

"I'm sorry," I added hastily. "I forgot he had the Department. But I still don't see why he should blame you."

Johnny drew a quick breath.

"Oh, we'd been havin' trouble."

"About what?"

"Th' killin's — an' those snatches." Suddenly the dam of reticence broke. "Christ! I didn't go into no racket to murder people. I just wanted a little dough. But Eddie saw things different. First thing that happens, a lot of wrong guys begin floatin' into town with recommends from various mobs. A few come in from Chicago, an' that's all right — I figure if they've got to cool off for a while, okay. Then some more come from New York. Then there's a gang up from Hot Springs. Th' first thing I knew, they were layin' aroun' town like tarts on a hot afternoon. Big bastards, like Fur Sammons, an' Larry Doyle, an' Eddie LaRue an' that crowd. I squawked to Eddie. He couldn't see nothin' wrong in it; they were all payin' off — or they'd been billed in by Eddie's friends back East. But I told him; I said: 'Th' first thing you know, they'll be movin' in on some of your rackets.' Well, that happened. I told Eddie it was his own fault. But he couldn't see it that way, an' th' first thing I know, he goes out an' gets three or four hoods to bump a guy off, figurin' that'll be a lesson. That started it — I guess you've only got to do a job once to get used to it. That put Eddie into th' gun pocket up to his neck. He's still in it.

"There's this mob of hoods hangin' aroun', an' Eddie thinks

it's swell because he gets his take out of it when they knock off some tin-can bank an' lam back into town with th' bonds an' stuff for Eddie to shove through th' Finance Company. So when they put th' snatchin' idea up to him, he goes for it. There's Solly, the gambler. They took him for sixty grand. An' that prize fight chump from down in Texas — what's his name? Anyway, he laid him for forty. They got a couple of guys for twenty-five and thirty — Hell, by th' time th' dough was cut, nobody got much over five or six grand out of it. An' me, I'm squawkin' every minute until everybody's down on me. So when th' Feds show up, everybody puts th' finger on me, even his dame, who's coverin' up like hell. So Eddie sends down to St. Louis for a load of torpedoes. An' I got out of town."

"Well, that ought to end it," I said.

"End it?"

"Sure, you're a thousand miles away. You're out of the picture. You're not bothering anybody."

"No?" His frightened eyes surveyed me as though I did not have good sense. "I ain't botherin' nobody? When I know the whole set-up? Everything that went on? I ain't botherin' nobody? I'm botherin' 'em just so much I ain't goin' to live!"

"Johnny, you're nuts. Who's going to get you, away back here?"

"The Lucky mob."

"Why?"

"As a favor, didn't I tell you? Eddie's done plenty for them, ain't he? Do you think Eddie himself would spend a lot of dough goin' out chasin' me when he's talkin' long distance every day to New York?"

"If you mean to tell me that a certain mob is going to kill you just because you're handy . . ."

"I'm back East, ain't I?"

"Then why don't you go West?"

He smiled again, with a queerly futile expression.

"Greenie's got a mob in San Francisco. Eddie's got connections in L.A. an' Reno. O'Reilly's hooked up in Seattle an' aroun' that way. Where" — his eyes bored into me — "do I go?"

I laughed.

"You haven't turned junker?" I asked.

He pulled back his sleeves.

"You don't see no hype marks, do you?"

"Then get hold of your nerves. If you've lost out, that's one thing. But you're nuts to talk about being killed. It's idiotic, Johnny."

"Yeah?" he asked. Then: "All right, what do I do?"

"Get a job."

"Where?"

"Well, you know the taxicab business, the — "

"Sure, an' th' race game an' th' prize fight business. Everything I know is somethin' they know. Every place I go in them rackets, there's guys I know, an' they know. I suppose the word wouldn't be passed on, I suppose — "

"Now look here, Johnny," I argued. "Be sensible. You got mixed up in a lot of political corruption. You may have a different name for it, but that's what it amounted to. Then you got all tied up with ex-convicts and high-powered crooks and snatches and killings and all that. I don't say you did it, but you were mixed in on it."

"Sure, I was mixed in it. Up to my eyes. But I kept tryin' to tell Eddie — "

"I know all that. But you couldn't swing it. Eddie got down on you, and you had to lam out of town. Well, you've lammed. Now, what's the matter with forgetting everything and starting all over?"

"Where?"

Suddenly, a peculiar light shone in his eyes.

"Say, listen," he announced. "I been thinkin' a lot — maybe if I could get hold of a coupla grand, I might go down to one of these West Indies Islands an' cool off there for a coupla years;

a guy can live there for nothin' flat, they tell me. By that time, maybe things'd blow over — you know."

He was aiming at me.

"I haven't any two thousand dollars lending money, Johnny."

"No, I guess you ain't," he said hopelessly. Then: "Have you got twenty-five?"

I gave it to him, and he stood with it upon his open palm for a long time, merely looking at it. He blinked. "I wonder," he asked, "if I could sneak into a track somewhere long enough to run it up to a coupla grand without somebody seein' me?"

I laughed again. It all sounded so silly. At last we said good-by. A few days later, we met again, and the eyes of Johnny the Guy stared straight into mine, but he did not know me. It was in the Morgue, where he had been brought from a ditch which ran beside a road which led to a race track. There were two bullet holes in Johnny's face and three in his back. They told me rather forcibly that it had been I, not Johnny, who was crazy in my belief that the influence of underworld power was limited.

Who got him, I do not know. What happened in that ride of execution never will be told. Perhaps he stepped into a car, white, trembling, with guns prodding at his back. Or he may have thought that he had met friends, fellows who slapped him on the back, who told him he had been a damned fool to leave town, and that Eddie wasn't sore. Those are secrets. Johnny is dead. It happens also that by this time Eddie also is gone, dead of machine-gun bullets resultant from internecine strife. Perhaps even the men who killed Johnny are gone. And none of them is of great importance.

The prime matter is that in practically every large city where political dominance belongs to the block votes of the ignorant, this story of Johnny the Guy is being repeated and re-repeated in various degrees. Sadly enough, there are few municipalities where some type of this control does not exist; it is one of the big secrets of professional crime.

Various data regarding Johnny the Guy's underworld life and associates — under another name, of course — are to be found in the investigative reports of the Alcohol Tax Unit, the Intelligence Unit of the Treasury Department, the Narcotic Division, and the Federal Bureau of Investigation. However, despite the fact that all of these agencies were forced, at one time or another, to look into certain of the activities which resulted from the building of a crooked, local machine, in not a single case was entire jurisdiction assumed, for the very reason that the basic offense was a purely local one, to be handled only by local authorities. Since those authorities were under the command of the crooks themselves, nothing was done about it. Thus thrives the underworld, which, after all, is not a mythical, faraway thing, but something very close to us, often living in the best hotels — sitting beside us in the cocktail bars, rubbing elbows with us on the dance floor, and above all to a degree dictating our lives, our habits, and our taxes.

Someone must pay when the underworld goes into business. Unfortunately, this contributing stratum consists of a dilly-dallying and thoroughly gullible public which believes that crime does not pay.

CHAPTER FOUR

HOW TO ROB A BANK

PERHAPS there may be wonder that I did not specifically name the city in which Johnny the Guy operated. To have done so would have defeated the purpose of the narrative, segregating that municipality as a thing apart, and labeling only one city as rotten when it has so many companions equally putrid.

Again, when one hammers against local corruption as unearthed by United States Governmental investigations, the uppermost thought in the average reader's mind is that a campaign is beginning for a National Police. To one who knows Washington, and the fear which Washington holds of the American municipality, that is laughable. There is nothing which the investigative forces of the United States Government fear so much as propaganda toward the building of centralized responsibility for local law enforcement.

This writer for some twenty years has followed a policy, especially when dealing with the workings of a department, of submitting his manuscripts that they may be checked for accuracy. It is done upon the understanding that editorial opinions remain the property of the writer; if the department does not like them, that entails a difference of viewpoint which does not yield to either argument or entreaty. To the credit of the men who head the various investigative bodies, it must be said that there has not been an instance of an attempt to bias viewpoint. Suggestions for alteration have been confined to mistakes in time, date, place, name, length of servitude, circumstances surrounding arrest, misquotations in the statements of arrested or convicted persons, and matters of that sort — details which any reporter is glad to correct. References to bungling work by agents or operatives are received sorrowfully; but they are admitted. Along only one avenue is there an attempt at what might be called censorship. That is when a reference is made to the qualifications of local officers.

According to the public attitude of the United States Government, all local policemen, sheriffs, constables, marshals, justices of the peace and other agents of law enforcement are little white angels with sprigs of parsley in their hair. They are "fearless officers," or men "of wholehearted coöperation" or a "fine type of sheriff," or a "credit to the police force of their city." Never are they ignorant, stupid, coarse, third-degree artists, panhandlers, roughnecks or downright crooks.

Privately, the story is a far different one. Certainly, when there are such evidences of corruption as present themselves in the Leon Gleckman income tax case of St. Paul, where a king of bootleggers actually issued orders to the Police Department and celebrated his ransom from kidnappers by a banquet at which murderers, thugs, bootleggers and men of law enforcement sat side by side, the John Lazia case in Kansas City with its efforts at "fixing" by a dozen types of politicians, the Irving Wexler (Waxey Gordon) case in New York, with its apparent political tie-ins, both in New York and New Jersey, the Arthur (Dutch Schultz) Flegenheimer case, in which the New York Police "searched" for three years for this man without success, while he came and went about his office in the Bronx, there is ample reason for the confidential statement of Federal officers that local enforcement in many places stinks like dead fish.

In the Dutch Schultz affair, every dope seller knew where to find him. All the big men in the policy or "numbers" racket knew where to find him. A ten-year-old boy, studying a correspondence school course in detection and apprehension, could have found him, merely by "tailing" those close to him until the trail led to the wanted man. But the twenty thousand officers and men of the New York Police Department worked and worked and worked without being able to find Arthur Flegenheimer.

Again there is the unholy nausea of bribery, official connivance, bought-and-paid-for prosecutors, judges, mayors, representatives, and what not in the case of Al Capone which rests in Government archives. At least one bank was actively concerned in helping to conceal this man's income; whatever information was gained there by Treasury agents was taken, not given. Yet little of that ever has been told, except in a generalized way.

Thus goes the story — the filth which was brought into the reports of Special Agents of the Federal Bureau of Investigation by the chase of the men who brought about what is known as "the Kansas City massacre," the investigative reports of corruption concerned with the life of Alvin Karpis in Chicago, Toledo, Cleveland, Kansas City, Miami, Hot Springs (Arkansas), and other cities; the evidences of protection from official sources in the case of Thomas Robinson the kidnapper. Even the Post Office Inspection Service possesses many instances of local dominance, one of which finally led to mail robbery and multiple murder in Texas; the Narcotics Division also has its share of sickening stories. Topping it all is the muck of the Dillinger case, with the affiliated ones of Baby Face Nelson, Thomas Carroll, Homer Van Meter, John Hamilton, John Paul Chase, and others, all of whom had their pet cities in which they might roam without molestation — a trail, incidentally, which stretched from the Pacific to the Atlantic.

Even an instance so seemingly unaffiliated with the professional underworld as that of the kidnapping of young George Weyerhaeuser of Tacoma brought out innumerable instances of "affiliation," not by the actual participants, but by persons who were at first suspected and later found to be innocent of the crime. One of these was a nationally known crook, so accustomed to making his presence known in certain cities that, upon his return to a resort in the State of Washington, he invited several old law enforcement friends to dinner. The Rogues' Gallery picture of this man hung on the "Wanted" boards of innumerable police departments. The invited officers maintained a supreme position of dignified aloofness. They sent word that they were sorry they could not meet with him upon a mutual ground of companionship; they were afraid that it "would not look right." They did absolutely nothing about arresting this man, who was a fugitive from at least a dozen felony charges.

All of this material has been piled up, not as a determined endeavor to unearth it, but merely as run-of-the-mill information that is encountered in efforts to bring Federal offenders to justice. Its publication, in all details, would make a bigger shake than the San Francisco earthquake, but, if the past is a criterion, it will gather dust as a subject not to be disturbed. Officials will even deny that they possess it *en masse*. Only that part of it necessary in court trials for the conviction of an offender ever meets the light of public notice; the Government feels that this can be done without criticism. Beyond such revelations, however, local corruption must remain a closed book, shielded by a big white cloth, like a statue yet to be unveiled. Now and then, the Attorney General strikes out against it in his speeches. An even more outspoken crusader is J. Edgar Hoover, who flatly refused to work with local officials whom he found corrupt, inefficient, or publicity-mad.

One of the reasons for the Government's easy attitude is that, under the present set-up, enforcement agencies of the United States Government cannot exist without local coöperation. In many cities, this is wholehearted. In others it bears a semblance of politeness, while in additional instances, there is downright opposition.

I am reminded of the Chief of Detectives in a certain city, where more high-powered professional crimesters have hidden out than any other community of its size in America, who sent word to one of the Federal Government's biggest investigative agencies, during the search for a badly wanted robber, that as far as expecting help from him was concerned, it could go jump in the lake. Again, in a kidnapping case, the desk of J. Edgar Hoover was littered with telegrams from a police department, pledging its wholehearted coöperation. However, those same police officers were wont to gather in the room of a special writer assigned to the case by an Eastern newspaper. His brand of whisky was good — good enough, in fact, to loosen tongues. The main subject of conversation seemed to be an effort to find similes for Department of Justice Agents stronger than "son-of-a-bitch" and "bastard."

Nevertheless, even though they know they are hated in many places, Federal officers make a great display of gratitude for what they call "local coöperation." In many instances, they are sincere. There are hundreds of such bodies as those of Milwaukee, Colorado Springs, and Wichita; the heads of the New York Police Department and others give help willingly. There are more, however, who do not. Yet they are all, in Federal parlance, jolly good fellows who just love to get out and give a Washington man a lift.

Beyond the necessity to maintain a pretense of *camaraderie*, is something far more important — the life of the Federal agency. No Government bureau can afford to pick a fight with a locality. After all, the United States Government lives, not as an entity, but as the slave of the crossroads. There is nothing so outraged as the voice of a United States Senator as he rises to a point of order and delivers himself of an attack upon an investigative branch of the Government which, he insists, has resorted to the persecution of his community and the spoiling of its fair name. Bureaus live by the whim of Congress. They may plan for the future, they may have dreams of accomplishment, they may have great ideals, but if some cantankerous lawmaker who heads a vital committee decides to block their appropriation, it amounts almost to a death blow.

Senators and Congressmen come from localities. They often are elected by the same machines which take over control of city and state politics and are nervously appreciative of any desires on the part of the Boss back home. The blowing up of local corruption by official Governmental report would immediately have its repercussions in the Capital. Bureaus would be curtailed in expenditure, men lopped off, dishonesty attributed to their heads; and above all, the squawk would steam from the gilded dome of the Capitol that an American OGPU was in formation, seeking to pry into the lives of our citizens, regulate neighborhoods, emulate the Russian Secret Police.

Therefore, those who desire a National Police may as well forget it. That will never happen, unless Congress itself wills such a thing. The stink that would be revealed at home by such a move is assurance that Congress would as soon touch the subject as stick a finger in the fire. There are not twenty first-class cities in the United States which could come through a searching inquiry by a fearless, vigilant, efficient and militant investigative body, free of political interference, without at least a dozen persons of so-called prominence in each community being headed for the penitentiary.

All of this may seem to be far divorced from the heading of this chapter, which promises a dissertation on how to rob a bank. Nevertheless, there is a close affiliation. The first thing to know about bank robbery is the local set-up on law enforcement.

There was a time when I had a tremendous admiration for bank-robbers. Perhaps that came from an early worship of Jesse James and his brother Frank who, together with their comrades, the Younger Boys, tore up things considerably in the Middle West when I was a youngster. However, even a stalwart illusion like that of the courage of bank-robbers begins to fade when one learns how they do things.

The popular idea of a bank bandit is one who takes great risks, lives in constant hiding, develops a magic sense of elusiveness from law enforcement officials, and altogether is quite a fellow. That was the popular opinion of Dillinger — many persons still believe him a hero, instead of a cheap, prison-scum hoodlum, as were the numerous others whose names were in the headlines only a short time ago.

Not one of them lived up to tradition. Even Eddie Bentz, upon whom gentlemen of his own craft looked as a superman, privately admitted that he was nothing but a damned smart yegg. That he knew his business is attested by the fact that for a lifetime of crime in which he "believes he robbed a hundred banks," and during which time he was sentenced to more than thirty-three years of servitude, he actually spent only seven-and-a-half years in prison. During the terms which he was supposed to be serving but in which he was free — free on *habeas corpus*, parole, pardon, or probation, or off on good time, or escaped, or through absolute protection — there were few years indeed when his annual income did not amount to at least seventy-five thousand dollars. Yet, giving himself due credit for more brains than the average fellow, fully aware of his standing as a bank-robber de luxe, Eddie nevertheless summarized his success with a great degree of modesty.

"You've got to have help," said Eddie.

That sentence is one to remember.

Federal forces are small; there is not a bureau which is sufficiently manned to perform the labors required of it. In all cases Congress takes for granted that the man power will come from local agencies, and except for a steadily growing number of exceptions in the Federal Bureau of Investigations, that is true of all Federal enforcement bodies. They have not the men to conduct giant raids, or center huge squads in one city. Therefore, they must take the police into their confidence, often with sad results.

Recently, for instance, the Treasury Department decided upon a nationwide raid. With all its six enforcement bodies assembled, it did not possess the men necessary, since this raid was to encompass hundreds upon hundreds of cities. It therefore was necessary, upon what it believed to be a basis of strictest confidence, for numerous police departments to be given the details, that they might furnish additional men to augment the raiding squads. This information was imparted with an earnest adjuration of secrecy and with the equally earnest promise by everyone that "not a word would leak out." The result was that, twenty-four hours before the raid, there appeared in scareheads on the first page of nearly every newspaper in America, this warning to the underworld: —

TREASURY DEPARTMENT TO EMBARK ON BIG RAID

GIANT NET SPREAD FOR FEDERAL OFFENDERS

LOCAL POLICE TO AID

Then followed, in detail, every move which was to be made by the Treasury Department: how it hoped to catch the heads of narcotic rings, wipe out giant still-owners, catch opium and other types of smugglers. In other words, here was a broadcast tip for the underworld to take cover. It had come from one or several of those police departments who had promised that "not a word would leak out."

If the National Government could choose the men in local enforcement agencies with whom it desires to work, that would be different; there are plenty of honest men it could depend upon. But it must take the run of the mill, and that covers a too wide field of dishonesty, inefficiency and local conditions, which would hamstring any police department.

Therefore, the story of Eddie Bentz, the bank-robbing "impresario," is of interest because it tells, not of the distrust of Federal officers for local law enforcement, but of the faith and confidence of the criminal in such bodies as mediums of safety.

By viewing the ease with which Eddie Bentz moved about his illicit existence, and the strangely businesslike aspects of his predatory profession, one may understand for himself just why it is that Washington while it is forced to make obeisance to local agencies, would give its right arm to be able at least to summon only those law enforcement men in whom experience has shown that it can place confidence. And throughout Eddie's story it would be wise to remember that, during more than a quarter of a century of law infractions, he knew little fear or encountered no commensurate punishment until he committed a Federal offense.

It was in the afternoon of a gray day last Spring that I went to call upon Eddie and found him writing his "will." Possessions would be of little use to him where he was going; such things as his automobiles with which he had sped to and from bank robberies, his cameras with which he was an expert, his numismatic collection, his first editions which he had found as he browsed in old bookstores throughout America, were far better off in the hands of friends than lying in storage. Eddie could have no possible pleasure from them for at least seven years and possibly longer — the Federal Government is extremely chary of granting paroles to men with lifetime criminal records, and Eddie's maximum sentence is for twenty years. Eddie had made a tremendous mistake. He had "stepped over the line."

So, as he wrote his "will," Eddie and I talked of bank-robbers and bank-robbing. It was a pleasant room he occupied, high in the Federal Building in New York City, with a big, barred window which overlooked the river, a clean cot, clean floors, a table to write upon, and a chair for a visitor. Eddie said he wished he could stay here instead of where he was going. The designation was a Federal Penitentiary.

Big-shouldered, farmerish in appearance, with sparse, sandy hair, freckled features marred by a blue scar, big nose, tremendous hands, and stocky frame, Eddie Bentz did not look like a master bank-robber. Nor did he talk like one; there was so much about his conversation that was unromantic to the point of the commonplace.

"You see," said Eddie as he laid aside his "will," "you've got to take risks in any business. I can't blame anybody but myself for being here. I knew better. There isn't a fellow in the business who is better informed on Federal jurisdiction. I should have known I was stepping across the line when I knocked over that bank in Vermont. But it stuck out its face at me and I pushed it in. And here I am. You see, I'd been in the habit of robbing banks so long that I kidded myself into believing that one more wouldn't do me any harm. The same as a fellow at a bar on Saturday night: he knows damn well that the next drink is going to lay him on his face, but he takes it. Well, that's how it was."

"We were talking about how to rob a bank," I suggested. Eddie nodded and picked up his pencil, making aimless marks on the scattered paper.

"Well, if a fellow was going into the bank robbery business — which is a bad business to be in just now — " he began, "I'd say the first thing to do would be to get a place to work from. That was always my system. All the other big yeggs used it too — Keating and Holden, Frank Nash, Verne Miller, the Barker-Karpis boys, Big Homer, Harve Bailey, Baby Face Nelson — all that crowd. About the only way a fellow can really operate is to have his headquarters in some place where the police can't find you."

"Can't or won't?" I asked. Eddie grinned.

"You get it," he said. "For instance, there was St. Paul. That was good for years. And Toledo was good too. And Kansas City. Then there was Fort Worth, and Galveston and Houston, and San Antone. Oh, there's a lot of 'em. Seattle was a good town for me until things changed. You see, you've got to take that into consideration: conditions change. A fellow can't settle down in a town and build a house and raise a family and decide to rob banks out of that place for the rest of his life. Some towns are only good for a year or two. Others — well, with others, you can stick around 'em maybe for ten years before you have to lam. It all depends on the circumstances."

Those circumstances, Eddie explained, were the same ones which allow gambling to exist, the numbers racket to exert its toll, the horse joints to operate, and all the other netherworld activities to thrive as already exemplified in the tragedy of Johnny the Guy.

"Once you get planted in a town," said Eddie, "the cops from every other city in the United States can wire your location, but nothing happens. For instance, when Leon Gleckman had St. Paul, and Jack Peifer was running the Holly Hocks Inn, all a fellow had to do was to take care of Jack. In my own case, I never bothered to find out where the dough went after I saw Jack. He looked after all the details.

"Most people think of a 'right town' as some place where a yegg like myself walks in and calls up the Chief of Police and then meets him on a dark corner and gives him a wad of dough. Why, nine tenths of the time, you don't even know the Chief's name. Maybe on top of that, he's the squarest guy in the world. Now, to use Jack for an example again. Jack had certain guys staked out in the Department that were in the know. Leon Gleckman had a private detective across the street from his office that he used to relay stuff through to the Department. Between it all, if a guy paid off, he didn't have any trouble. Now that's what I mean by a place to operate. It might even be a precinct in some big town like Chicago — a precinct's like a small city, you know. Maybe if the Precinct Captain's wrong — or right — whoever is looking at it — and he's got a pal who runs a tavern, and you make it right with the tavern keeper —see how it goes? A yegg like myself doesn't care how the tavern guy works it, just so he's sure that if there's any danger, he gets word far enough in advance to let him go on the lam.

"So now, you've got a place to work. But a fellow who sells goods has to have somebody to sell them to, now doesn't he? When you're robbing banks, you're in a business. You pay so much time and trouble for a bunch of cash and securities. The cash takes care of itself; but in these days when they don't keep too much behind the counter, and with the rest under time lock and all that, a man has to think about securities. So you have to be hooked up so those will be taken care of. That's where I worked up a lot of business. I always spent a lot of time making connections for the disposal of hot bonds. The result was that other fellows in the bank-robbing business would take me in on good jobs that they had already cased, because I was big enough in the game to be able to overlook the cash when it came to a divvy and take the securities off their hands.

"It's really surprising," said Eddie, always with a business man's viewpoint upperhand, "how many people there are in the hot bond racket. A lot of fellows in the racing game — guys on the betting end, you know — will handle a few. Then there are certain brokers who will slip a bunch into their portfolio. Night clubs are lousy with hot bond shovers. Then I know a fellow who's made a specialty of doing business with bankers themselves. Some of them sell the bonds again and make a profit. Others pretend to buy them, take the money out of the deposits, put it in their own pocket, and then make the bonds a part of their portfolio. It's a good business when you figure that often a bank heister will sell out his paper at ten cents on the dollar. But the best people are the insurance companies.

"Now, there's a business," continued Eddie, making scrawls on his piece of paper, "that's going to blow up into quite a lot of smoke some of these days — the guys that insure banks. Not all of them, understand. You've always got to figure on running into a good many straight guys, and you've got to be ready for it — you know, with a quick alibi, 'all a mistake' and that sort of thing. Generally speaking, though, the insurance fellows who deal in paper are pretty well known in my business. One yegg passes the name along to another — you know how it is."

I asked for details. Eddie looked upon the explanation merely as another angle of a business.

"Well, suppose I'm an indemnity company. You're a bank. I've got you on my books for insurance against bank robbery. Along comes Eddie Doll or Old Chuck Fitzgerald, or the Gold Dust Twins, or Ripley or any of that crowd, and pushes in the bank. Say they get out of it with sixty thousand in securities.

"As I say, I'm the insurance company, with that risk on my hands. Now, which is better sense, to pay the bank sixty thousand dollars insurance money, or make a contact with the fellows who heisted the joint and talk over a deal with them? Usually, a fellow who's known as being a right guy can drive a pretty good bargain — way down around fifteen or twenty per cent., because there isn't any risk or bother about it. You don't have to change any serial numbers like you do when you're passing hot bonds out into general circulation or selling them to some shyster lawyer who's got a banker on his list who wants to buy "lifted" bonds at full price for the depositors while he puts the difference in his kick. All you do is crush the can, get the securities, beat it back to your headquarters, call the insurance guy, wait a few days until he gets authority to 'recover the bonds from underworld sources,' and get your money in cold cash, no questions asked. That's easier all the way around, and a bank-robber would rather do business that way. It's better for the insurance company, too. The right sort of guy keeps his trap shut, forgets where he got the swag, and, instead of paying out sixty thousand dollars in insurance money, settles his risk for ten thousand or fifteen thousand, returns the lost property to the bank, and everybody's satisfied."

"Of course," I interjected, "that's suborning a felony."

"Sure," answered Eddie, "if you want to look at it that way. But it's convenient. I used to do it a lot. It made things a lot easier in my business and it saved the insurance companies money. So what the hell?"

With his twisted mentality, the bank-robber saw nothing wrong in that. That such a system made fences and consorts out of certain insurance representatives, to say nothing of actually stimulating bank robbery by creating an easy market for the loot, did not concern him. He proceeded with the details of his business.

"Now, the most important things are out of the way. You've got a place where you can cool off and not be disturbed. You've got a market for your goods. The next thing is to get a bank. To do that, you've got to case a jug. Old Harve Bailey, I guess, had as much money as anybody in the bank-robbing business. Why, he was in the racket as far back as 1922, when he and Chi Slim and Big Fitz and Jim Ripley and that gang robbed the United States Mint out in Denver, and peddled the currency at a percentage to a young fellow in Minnesota who used it to build up a fortune — legitimate, too, and he's highly respected. Anyway, Harve made a lot of money. It was a bad year if he didn't gross a hundred thousand. A lot of it's put away now, and he's out in Alcatraz on a life sentence for the Urschel kidnapping, but the way we figure, damned few fellows ever serve life. But what I was getting at — With all his money, and all his connections with the Capone mob which protected him around Chicago, and his two farms, still the one thing Harve Bailey really loved to do was to case a jug. Why, when the first days of spring would come, you'd find Old Harve out making the towns four and five hundred miles from Chicago, like a traveling salesman, just casing jugs.

"There's another point — you never want to rob a bank any where near the place where you cool off. Pick a town three or four hundred miles away, at least — hell, it's nothing these days to make a run like that. You can crush a can in the morning and be back home by night, with any kind of driving luck. I was a lot like Harve. I loved to case jugs. I guess there isn't a bank in this country that amounts to anything that I haven't looked over.

"You see, it's a lot like playing solitaire. You drive past the bank a few times and size up the surroundings, whether there are good getaway streets, whether the bank's got a squawker on the outside, whether there's a traffic cop on the corner; John Dillinger used to like to strike up a conversation with cops and ask them if Dillinger had been seen in the vicinity. Everybody thought that was great stuff and called the cops chumps. People ought to give the cops a better break than that. The average guy in brass buttons is a pretty decent fellow, trying to do his best. And a lot of 'em are honest. But I leave it to you. Did you ever meet Dillinger?"

"I don't know."

"There you are. Maybe you did meet him. A lot of people met him, and didn't ever know it. A lot of people have met me and thought I was a swell guy. I've played golf on every big course in America and with some of the best people. They didn't know I was a yegg; I'd get on the good side of the professional, tell him I was a district manager for the American Telephone and Telegraph Company or the Western Union — whatever popped into my head — and bull him into letting me play the course. Then I'd strike up a conversation with somebody around the first tee and we'd go around together. I didn't know who he was and he didn't know who I was.

"Well, it's the same with the cops. This idea that people have about cops carrying crooks' pictures around with them so they can study the features is a lot of apcray. There are a few with camera eyes, like Dad Bruce out in Colorado Springs and fellows like him, but that about ends it. Why, the pictures of just the professionals would make a book so big you'd have to load it on a truck. Sure, if there's been a bad murder in a town and every cop's on his toes, he'll memorize a face. But that's about the limit; you can't expect fellows to have motion picture memories. In all the time I was operating, I never bothered about anybody picking me off unless he looked at me twice. I'd talk to cops, play cards with cops, ask directions from cops and never worry. I went to cabarets and dance places and big hotels just like anybody else. Even if a person looked me over it never feazed me. Of course, if he looked twice that was time for me

to lam, because then I knew he was thinking he'd seen me somewhere before and was trying to place me.

"Just figure it out for yourself. You're a writer. Do you give
a damn what some other writer out in San Francisco is doing
unless you're personally concerned? It's the same with cops.
They've all got their local problems and what is somebody
else's headache is none of their business until something bobs up
to make it so. Now, if the Department is right, and some other
department sends on the picture of some badly wanted man
who is supposed to be in this particular city, why, of course,
they'll make a special effort on it. But you can't expect cops to
spend all their time studying crook faces. They'd go screwy.
It would be like counting the stars.

"So, if a fellow stays away from running in a groove, and
doesn't get drunk, and observes traffic laws, and doesn't get in
a jam with women or pick fights, and generally conducts himself decently, he doesn't worry about being picked up. Therefore, when you're casing a jug, you act like anybody else. Maybe
you meet the bank manager and hand him a line about intending to go in business in the neighborhood and open a good
account. Maybe you'll throw out a few hints that you've heard
the bank wasn't too solid, and half the time the guy will take
you on a personal tour of inspection to show you what a swell
lay-out he's got.

"Now, during all this time, you're studying the bank. You
see how many wickets there are, where the officers sit, how
old the watchman is, and where he usually stands, and all that
sort of thing. You can figure out what kind of fellows are at
the wicket, whether they're young and foolish, or men with
families who'll think twice before they'll get hurt saving the
bank's cash, when they know it's insured.

"There's one thing that I always watched for when I was
casing a jug. I was always careful to see that there wasn't a
woman or an old man stuck off somewhere, up high at a place
which couldn't be reached easy by a stairway, and where there

was a telephone. Nobody in the business ever worries about a squawker — you know, those horns or bells that are rung outside to give the good citizens the news that the bank is being robbed. All that does is to tip off the outside guards of the heister crew that some employee has stepped on the button. But when there's an employee like a telephone operator, or an old, coolheaded bookkeeper, stuck away off somewhere at a place where a guy can't throw a gun on him, and where he can look down on everything — that's the kind of a bank not to rob. Why, he can telephone news of the robbery without anybody knowing it, and the first thing a yegg knows, the whole block is lousy with harness bulls. The minute the sirens begin screeching, your outside man or car driver gets excited and warms up his engine, or yells, or does something that gives the tip-off. Then he's either surrounded or gets scared and makes a getaway, leaving the gang to try to commandeer machines and lam it as best they can. That's bad, because it isn't long then until the shooting starts.

"Keep away from that kind of banks. I've often wondered why more banks aren't set up that way. But if they all did that, it would put some bankers in a hell of a hole. I used to get some nice business now and then out of bankers who'd gotten to spending the house dough. They'd start the playboy stuff and get to laying molls around night clubs. It wasn't long until they'd hook up with somebody in the heisting business, maybe through a moll that they'd told their troubles to when they were all boozed up. Well, several times it has led to me robbing banks to order — you know, taking a lot of stuff that was insured anyway from some place where it was all laid out for me. Then the bank guy would report that the loss included enough to cover what he had stolen, and that straightened out all his defalcations.

"But I was talking how to rob a bank. After I'd cased the jug, and figured on just where I would put my men, then I'd go to the Public Library. I'd look up the bank's last quarterly statement and make allowances for changes in the security and cash position. Generally a fellow can figure within five or ten thousand dollars of what the bank actually has — of course, some yeggs use finger men, but I never found it necessary.

"Now that's done. You know all about the jug. The next thing is to run the roads. There's the real fun of bank-robbing — running the roads. Old Harve used to love it. I've seen him run roads when he had no intention of ever knocking over a can. Same with a lot of others.

"You start out from your cooling-off joint, and make a circuitous route out of town, sort of feeling your way by the back roads to the place where you're going to rob the bank. Maybe you'll go over the route five or six times, maybe you'll spend a half-day on eight or ten miles of ticklish territory. The job is to pick out the cat, the unused roads which will lead you in a straight line, but keep you away from cities and away from the main highway, for at least a hundred miles from the robbery. When a bank robbery happens, everybody who has witnessed it usually notices which way the robbery car starts away. So, as the cops arrive, the bystanders all point and yell 'They went that way!' — and of course the cops, having to think fast, decide that they headed out on Highway 41 for Tonsilville. Well, the game — and it's really a game — is to look like you're going one direction when you're really going another. You start North from the bank on the main street. Then you turn West, and maybe North again, and maybe get back to the main stem again before you switch East, swing around a block, and go South and West again before really heading for where you want to go.

"It's quite a trick, because you've got to make every move exactly right. So as you run the roads, you make a 'run and gets,' which is a getaway chart with signals on it — just like the old Blue Books we used before roads were marked. Remember? 'Mile 5 and one tenth, turn right at old church, go straight eight miles, cross wooden bridge,' and all that? The result is that there's no way for cops to chase you because they don't know where you're going, and you wouldn't either if it wasn't for that 'run and gets.' Besides, if they do hit your trail you've got the advantage, because you've run the roads and know exactly what speed they'll stand in every kind of weather. That's why cops' cars go into the ditch and the bandit cars keep right on their way just when it seemed the law was about to get 'em. The heisters had slowed down; they knew what the road would stand. The cops didn't."

"And then what happens — after you've run the roads? You get your gang?"

Eddie looked out of the big window.

"Well, you don't get your gang exactly. You tie up with 'em. Like I would figure certain men would be the right ones for a certain job. I'd write to a tavern keeper in Calumet and tell him to ask Ripley to get in touch with me. Then I'd drop a note to Eddie Doll at a place where he got his mail in Chicago, or to Big Fitz in care of a friend of his who ran a night club, and so on. Or maybe, we'd correspond through the personal want-ad columns in newspapers — about half of the professionals do their letter-writing that way. You know: 'George: Come home. Mother is dying.' You see, it's code. Finally, when we'd get together, well we'd pick our day and rob the bank."

"What happens, when you rob the bank?"

"Nothing. You just walk in and rob it."

"But — "

"Oh, there's a few details. Myself and the other inside men used to stall around in a parked automobile, maybe loaded with toys, like we were salesmen. Of course, since I'd cased the jug, I knew the janitor by sight. As soon as we saw him come down the street, we'd go over, edge up and put our guns to his back as he was unlocking the door, and walk in behind him. Then as the rest of the personnel came along, we'd make 'em lie face down on the floor. It's usually easy to find out which guy has the keys to the vault. So you just yank him to his feet and make him open up and shove the stuff in a sack, and that's about all."

"Except the shooting."

Eddie assumed a hurt expression.

"I've been robbing banks for twenty years and I never shot anybody yet," he said. "Only the hoodlums do that, the fellows who haven't cased their jug right. Dillinger and bums like that. Even when you walk in on a bank full of people, you don't need to shoot if you've got your men placed right. As for getting the money, you use the surprise element. Here's a teller all bent over, with a wet thumb, counting dough. He looks up, into a gun. He's speechless. You tell him to hand it over and he hands it. No," added Eddie, "a good bank-robbery shouldn't take more than five minutes if it's done right. But, of course, there are bums in every business. Even I turned out a lot dumber than I thought I was."

I knew that story. It concerned Verna, a seventeen-year-old girl with whom Eddie had fallen in love. Clothes crazy, pleasure mad, Verna had run away from her home in south Wisconsin with this man. She had believed it would be wonderful to be the moll of a bank-robber, to have all the money which one possibly could use, to ride in big cars, to dance and drink and carouse. She loved Eddie's show-off life far more than she loved Eddie; after all, he was more than twice her age.

With Eddie the attitude was different. This farmerish-appearing man with a love for reading, for amateur photography, for philosophy, and masquerade by which he indulged for long stretches in seeming respectability, was, to a degree, the simple person he appeared to be. He realized that he had taken a young life and twisted it into crookedness. They lived together for a time; then Eddie insisted that they be married. It all seemed rather silly to Verna, but she agreed. Then Eddie announced that he intended to quit the bank-robbery "business."

"I've always felt I could make good in a legitimate racket," he said.

Little was left of the cash which had streamed through his hands. He had buried bonds in plenty but was then afraid to cash them. There was enough money, however, to buy a home in a New England city and to start a novelty factory, one of the main products of which was leaden toys. The factory was begun. Eddie Bentz, bank-robber, went on the road, a traveling salesman, to sell his product.

"Things were tough," said Eddie as he recounted the story. "You know, conditions and all that. I couldn't get the business and I felt it was dangerous to cash the bonds I've got hidden. But I had faith in the racket. I figured that if I had just a little more capital I could make a go of it. I'd gone crazy about putting the proposition over, I let myself forget the one rule I'd always followed: never to step over the line — that is, never to do anything that would start the Feds after me. There was a bank in Vermont that was a push-over. And damned if I didn't go and rob it, to get that extra capital, without stopping to be sure I wasn't going over the line. Sure enough, it was a National Bank.

"Well, doing a Federal job is different from doing a local one. When you pull a local job, it's like standing on a stepladder, jumping over a fence and then pulling the ladder after you so the next guy can't follow. Once you're out of town you're fairly safe, unless somebody stools on you. A city hasn't got all the money in the world like the Federal Government. It hasn't got men sprinkled all the way across the country who look on America as being no larger than an ordinary city, the way they telephone back and forth or swoop here and there in airplanes.

"A city has to work with the tools it's got. It can't keep up active touch with every other city in the United States. It does what it can, if it's honest, which a lot of them are not." He grinned. "I ought to know. But if it's honest, it gets out circulars, and sends a Wanted notice to the Identification Division of the Federal Bureau of Investigation — in case you're picked up somewhere else and your fingerprints are sent in there — and it assigns a couple of men to the case, who write letters around and follow tips as best they can. But those men can't run all over the United States after a man: the appropriations won't stand it. A couple of trips and the City Council begins to raise hell.

"Of course, a lot of cities work together. But then there are a lot of other towns where everybody's sore at everybody else, or where there is a bunch of wrong guys in the Department who wouldn't turn up a guy for murdering his grandmother. It's damned expensive for a city to chase a gang. Usually it doesn't result in much. Besides if a bunch of burglaries happen in town and the papers begin to raise hell about a crime wave, everybody is pulled off of everything else and put on that and the bank robbery is forgotten.

"But these Feds keep on coming. When one man looks for a fellow, everybody looks for him, whether it's Secret Service, Alky Unit, Narcotics, Post Office, Treasury or the G guys. You see, they've got offices everywhere and they're all in touch with each other. It's just as easy for a guy in New York to work on a tip that's been handed him by a fellow in San Francisco as it is for a city cop to look up something on his beat that's been told him by a pal three blocks away. So when I saw my picture in a Boston newspaper as having been identified by the G men as the robber of the Caledonia National Bank, I took it on the lam."

There was a moment of silence.

Then I said: "I think I know the rest of that story, Eddie. After that, you couldn't give Verna all the things she wanted. You couldn't go dancing or live at big hotels or buy her swell clothes. So you began to have trouble and finally split up."

Eddie sat for a moment in thought.

Finally he said: "No, it wasn't exactly that way. You see, I thought a lot of Verna. I still do. I love her better than anything in the world. And I didn't want her to be a moll. That's why I tried to stop robbing banks.

"So when all this came along and we began having disagreements, I sat down and had a talk with her. 'Look here, Verna,'

I said, 'you're young. Only twenty now. I'm forty-five. If I go up for a stretch, it'll be all right. I've made a swell living out of heisting banks, and I've had you, and altogether, I guess I've gotten my money's worth. But you're just a kid. Nowadays, the Feds make it tough for anybody who hangs out with criminals. If you stick with me they can send you up on a harboring charge. I wouldn't want that.

" 'I tell you what you do,' I said. 'You pack up and go home. I'll wait awhile and then write you a letter and tell you where I am. Then you can call the Feds and give them the address, and they can pick me up and' " — he hesitated — " 'and you'll get the credit.' "

That was hard for Eddie Bentz to think about — the fact that Verna had turned him in.

At last, I said: "Eddie, do you remember one time when you criticized my last book — told me that I shouldn't publish so much about the methods used by the Federal Bureau of Investigation?"

"Sure," said Eddie. "I remembered all that when I was on the lam. How they look up everything about you. I even changed my brand of cigarettes every two weeks, so they couldn't trace me through my fags."

"And yet you did the one thing that turned you up: If you wrote her that letter, Verna never received it. She pretty well proved that she's had her lesson, so she wasn't prosecuted. But all she could tell was the address of a place where you lived together a long time ago, and where you left some furniture. The mistake you made, Eddie, was to send a truck after that stuff and have it moved to Brooklyn, where they caught you. Verna didn't tell. She didn't know. You caught yourself. The G men trailed that truck."

Eddie grinned.

"Verna didn't tell, eh?" He was silent a moment, the true gangster, turning over in his mind the thought that perhaps Verna did get that letter, that she remained true to underworld

precepts, that she had lied to protect him. He rubbed his hands
— big hands, horny ones, like those of a hard-working farmer.
"Say, that's swell, isn't it? Say now, that's swell."

He resumed the writing of his "will." I feel sure that he
made some changes in it — to the greater benefit of Verna.

CHAPTER FIVE

PARTNERS IN LOOT

THERE was a time when this writer would have hesitated to reveal the details of the "bank robbery business" as set forth by such an authority as Mr. Edward Wilheim Bentz. Great changes have come about, however, and to-day the chronicle of bank robbery is one which to a great extent represents a fading field of endeavor. All this proves that crime, even when bulwarked by hide-outs, protected by the underworld, and perpetrated by the best brains, can easily be eradicated when the attack is made by agencies which have no hampering factors of politics, dishonesty, or inefficiency. Three years ago, bank robbery was the most lucrative of depredatory crimes. It was a heritage of rich tradition, descending with increasing popularity from the days of the James Boys, the Daltons, and other bandits who have taken their place in the folklore of the Middle West.

Thirty-six months is a short time in which to cripple an ancient and highly specialized profession, especially when the true campaign has been, in reality, confined to less than half that time. Nevertheless, where there once were nearly two hundred bank robberies a year, there are now less than fifty, with insurance rates going downward, and steadily fewer towns where it is necessary to support the local police by Vigilante Committees recruited from the merchants of the city. It all came about in quite a simple way. The pursuit of bank-robbers, through a natural sequence of events, departed from the province of local law enforcement agencies into those of a Governmental body, the Federal Bureau of Investigation.

Until three years ago, it was not even a Federal offense to rob a Federal bank. If a cashier absconded with funds, or an embezzlement occurred, that infraction was within Governmental jurisdiction. But if a gang of bandits, slaughtering everyone in sight, descended upon a bank, that was a matter wholly for local pursuit and prosecution. The result was that, in one state alone, the bank robberies in a single year amounted to nearly a hundred, with fifty as an average.

Never was there a better chance for comparison between local and Federal law enforcement than was afforded during the era of bank robbery, now ending. The most spectacular and brainy men of crime formed the predatory personnel, most of these being practically immune from adequate punishment. This is not to be taken as a statement that the police did nothing about bank robbery. In fact, they worked hard; the victims were influential, particularly as regarded pressure upon newspapers, with the result that even lethargic law-enforcement agencies were goaded into extraordinary efforts.

However, they were hampered by many difficulties. In the first place, there was the bank-robbery system, which demanded that its perpetrators never remain in the jurisdiction where they committed the crime. To descend upon a state, pull their job and move across the line as swiftly as possible into a haven where they felt they were protected was the formula of professional plunderers, and they reaped a hundred fortunes from it. The specialists of this era were like members of a fraternity; they knew associates in every part of America. Corresponding by code through the personal columns of newspapers, by long-distance telephone, by telegraph, or by mail, they could obtain partners needed for any type of job. As Eddie Bentz explained, there were no such things as staple gangs; when a person had "cased" a job, he got the men he wanted and proceeded to his task. There were perhaps fifty leaders, such as Harvey Bailey, Frank Nash, Eddie Doll, James Ripley, Eddie Bentz, Charles Fitzgerald, Baby Face Nelson, Verne Miller, Barker-Karpis and their type. I have not included John Dillinger. He was made by headlines, not by accomplishment. He took the credit for the brains of other members of his gang: Baby Face Nelson, John Hamilton, Homer Van Meter, Charles Makley, and Harry Pierpont. These were the men who knew bank robbery. John Dillinger knew how to shoot a person in the back, how to squawk his head off at paying underworld prices for liquor, women, and protection, and how to get sloppily drunk on beer, but he did not know how to lead a gang of bank-robbers. In fact, the underworld gives John Dillinger credit for only one thing: through the fact that he was such a bungler and wanton killer, the profession dropped from its status of the most lucrative of violent crimes to its present low estate where only kidnapping excels it as a risky business.

The Dillinger gang was too ready on the trigger. Shooting was almost a certain adjunct when this particular crowd robbed a bank. During his brief career, John Dillinger himself was wounded, John Hamilton shot several times, Baby Face Nelson nearly frightened into the jitters because a bullet struck his bullet-proof vest, Homer Van Meter wounded, and lesser members grazed by bullets, while policemen and innocent bystanders formed an extensive mortuary list. This came at a time when America was hypersensitive about violent crime, because of the ravages of kidnapping. So the cry went up that the Federal Government should do something about it.

At another time, Congress might have called this the usurpation of local powers which were not local powers at all, but purely Governmental ones, due to the fact that practically every bank in the United States is now a depository of Federal funds, a member of the Federal Reserve system, or operating under Federal Deposit Insurance. This makes them, to a degree, Government property, to be protected as such.

Localities had failed so utterly to protect themselves against the raids of wandering bands of marauders that they were glad to be relieved of the task. They actually sought relief, and the political pressure that otherwise might have been placed on Congress to vote against the bill, was missing. So the Government took the job and bank-hold-up insurance started downward.

Regarding insurance, the estimable Mr. Bentz cast many aspersions upon some of its practices, and with much justification. There have been numerous instances, especially in the last few years, of collusion between insurance companies and law violators, not only in bank robbery, but in other forms of depredation as well, particularly those of large thefts of jewels. The onus rests in general upon the representatives of the various companies, rather than upon the management; over-zealousness accounts for some of it. In other instances, however, there is evidence which points to orders from above. For all of this collusion, there is an amount of mitigation in that there have been times when certain companies felt they could not depend upon law enforcement agencies either to bring about the detection, apprehension and punishment of culprits, or to obey the desires of society in the recovery of loot. Thus an attempt was made to convert two wrongs into a right.

Perhaps insurance men become somewhat desperate when they survey conditions such as the following, brought out during the interrogation of a Middle-Western bank-robber by an attorney for a large indemnity company.

ATTORNEY: Now, if it is agreeable with you, perhaps it would be best to relate the whole story, including the robbery or burglary of the bank and your actions and expenditures after its occurrence, up to the present time.

CONVICT: Well, on the morning of March Eighteenth, we got into the bank by forcing the porter to let us go in with him and, as the rest of the force came on duty, we locked them up in a room in the bank. Then we found out when the time lock on the vault was supposed to open. We had nearly an hour to kill, so we got behind the counter and

pretended to be clerks, so that passers-by would not know
there was anything wrong. The time lock went off at nine
fifteen, and we forced the manager to open up the vault.
Then we tied him up and the porter with him, put the
money in a satchel we had brought along, and left the
bank.

Therein lies the reason why the real professionals of the craft
believed Dillinger a two-spot. True craftsmen have robbed banks
for a quarter of a century without loss of life and with the
firing of few shots. All in a few months, Dillinger's trigger-itch
"threw the whole profession into bad repute." However, to return to the inquiry: —

ATTORNEY: Then what did you do?

CONVICT: We split up the money.

ATTORNEY: Share and share alike?

CONVICT: Yes. My end of it was about five thousand
dollars.

ATTORNEY: What did you do with your share?

CONVICT: I didn't do anything with it. I didn't have a
chance to.

ATTORNEY: I don't understand.

CONVICT: Well, after we split the take, I came into
town here with my money in the satchel. I blew around
town a little and spent a few dollars and I think a fellow I
knew stooled on me. Anyway, the day after I got here,
two detectives came to my room in the hotel. They threw
a couple of guns down on me and walked in. After they'd
cuffed me, one of the dicks stood over me in a corner of
the room while the other fanned my stuff. He got into
the bag and found the money.

ATTORNEY: Then what happened?

CONVICT: Well, of course I had known these two dicks
before, and we got to talking. You know, just talking, about

what jobs I had been in and all that. One of them asked me
if I wanted an attorney, and I said "Sure." Then the other
found this dough in my bag and began to count it. You see,
it isn't always customary; but, with a lot of dicks, when they
walk in on you and find you with kale in your kick, they
generally take what they want, especially if it's currency
they are pretty sure can't be traced.

So I began to put up an awful beef. That's about all I
could do, because I was in a spot. I didn't intend to plead
guilty, and so how was I going to make a squawk that
they'd taken a lot of money away from me? Anyway, a
crook's got the dirty end of the stick any time he tries that;
you can't prove it and what the hell. So about all you can
do is beef your way back into whatever you can salvage.
So I asked these guys, "What the hell, give a fellow a break,
leave me enough to pay my attorney." They said sure they'd
do that and they'd furnish the attorney, the best guy in
town.

There was about four thousand four hundred in the bag.
The dicks took all of it, and made a deal with me to take
one thousand of it to a lawyer in the Fidelity Building, for
him and his partner to act as my attorneys. They kept the
rest — anyway, I guess they did, because I haven't heard
from it since.

ATTORNEY: You have a receipt here for one hundred
and sixty-five dollars.

CONVICT: Did you say one hundred and sixty-five? That
ought to be two hundred and sixty-five.

ATTORNEY: The sum is one hundred sixty-five. Where
did this receipt come from?

CONVICT: That was the receipt given me by the desk
sergeant after they searched me at police headquarters. The
dicks had overlooked my billfold. There was two hundred
and sixty-five dollars in it. I didn't look at the receipt —
I guess I'm a century out.

ATTORNEY: In other words, the desk sergeant took two hundred and sixty-five dollars of your money and gave you a receipt for one hundred and sixty-five?

CONVICT: It looks that way.

ATTORNEY: Were there any other financial dealings?

CONVICT: Well, there was one with my attorney.

ATTORNEY: Then they got you the lawyer.

CONVICT: You mean the dicks? Sure they got me the lawyer. They're usually pretty square that way; if they say they'll do it, they do it.

ATTORNEY: And this lawyer came to see you at police headquarters?

CONVICT: Down at the jail. He wanted more money.

ATTORNEY: For what?

CONVICT: Well, he'd had some expenses, and then he said he needed some more money to make a fix with.

ATTORNEY: Did he say whom he was going to fix?

CONVICT: No, he didn't say, but from what happened —

ATTORNEY: I'd rather hear just what you know. How much did you give him?

CONVICT: I gave him an assignment for one thousand, five hundred and sixty-five dollars and my car.

ATTORNEY: This was some money you had on the outside?

CONVICT: Yes, a friend of mine had it stached in his cellar, in a fruit jar.

ATTORNEY: The money, you mean?

CONVICT: Yes. The car was out at Belden.

ATTORNEY: Were there any other dealings?

CONVICT: There was a little one with the jailer.

ATTORNEY: What was that?

CONVICT: Nothing much. I was on the third tier and found that my brother was in jail, on the second. So I gave the jailer an order for one hundred dollars to move me down into the cell next to my brother.

ATTORNEY: And these are all the financial dealings you have had with the Police Department in this city?

CONVICT: Yes. That's all.

ATTORNEY: One more point. You intimated that you knew where the money went which your lawyer said was for a "fix"? What caused you to draw the conclusion that it went to a certain place?

CONVICT: I was allowed to cop a plea.

ATTORNEY: You mean you were given the right to plead guilty to a lesser crime than the one with which you were charged?

CONVICT: That's right. They had me up for armed robbery. You can get jerked to Jesus for armed robbery in this state. They let me plead to breaking and entering.

ATTORNEY: What was your sentence?

CONVICT: Two years. I'm up for parole now.

ATTORNEY: That is all. Thank you.

There was a strange sequel to this conversation. The two detectives accused by this convict of having robbed him of thousands of dollars which, in turn, had been stolen from a bank, now are dead. They fell before a blaze of gunfire as they attempted to block the freedom of an escaping prisoner. Their names now stand on the Honor Roll of the Police Department and are commemorated each Memorial Day as those of heroes to be emulated. Because of this fact the demand for a grand jury investigation planned by the insurance company on the basis of the above testimony never was made.

Perhaps I used the wrong word when I described the act of these detectives as robbery. It is not looked upon as such "in the profession." The strange relationship between the journeymen crimesters and local law-enforcement agents is too often purely that of a game — winners take all. Therefore, the confiscation of money by arresting officers is regarded with a certain degree of philosophy. After all, the money never truly

belonged to the crooks. They stole it, and in losing it to marauding detectives were merely fleeced of something they never had.
Further, they believe that it is far better that such money be
taken by officers who, indebted to a degree, often perform commensurate favors, than that due process of law should deprive
them of all benefits by returning the swag to its proper owners.
If a census could be made of all revolvers and other firearms,
feminine wearing apparel, jewelry, automobiles, and safe-deposit
money which has traveled from the hands of criminals into those
of law-enforcement officers, the sum would reach heavily into
the millions of dollars. Here, indeed, does crime pay.

Most of these transactions are classed as "legitimate." If a
prisoner possesses a mink coat which he desires to sell to some
officer for one fiftieth of its worth, the transfer is regarded merely
as one of buying and selling. Applications often are made to
heads of departments who call themselves honest, by arresting
officers desiring to buy a prisoner's automobile. That the car was
obtained with the fruits of law violation, and that the purchase
of a two-thousand dollar car for one hundred and fifty dollars
may, to a degree, stultify a properly unbiased attitude when the
officer reaches the witness stand, are not considered. The viewpoint is almost unanimously the following: —

"Well, the guy was in jail, wasn't he? The car wasn't doing
him any good. He needed money for his defense, so he was willing
to sell the bus cheap. I bought it. What's wrong about a trade
like that?"

In warfare between nations, this would constitute a law violation known as "trading with the enemy." Present-day crime conditions virtually constitute a war between society and the underworld, where there should be no visiting between the trenches.
There are few law enforcement bodies, however, which hold
that view.

But to return to the subject of bank robbery . . .

The status of the professional yegg, or bank-robber, until a
very short time ago, was this: He was elusive regarding state

lines, thus throwing innumerable obstacles in the path of the honest police department which desired to pursue him. He traveled from one end of the country to the other, making the cost of local pursuit prohibitive, especially if the robbery had occurred in some small town or county seat. He usually operated from some city where the police-political-crime set-up was sufficiently rotten to allow him sanctuary.

Beyond this there was in his favor the cheapness of freedom through money-weakened testimony, fixed cases, and the ever-present facilities prevalent at many police stations whereby one might obtain the services of certain attorneys who know their way around. Had there not been graft, inefficiency, ignorance of proper law-enforcement methods, and absolute crookedness in enough communities of America to make the situation an exceedingly dangerous one, there would have been no need for such a prison as Alcatraz Island. Practically every man now confined there was for years a consistent and persistent violator of local and state laws before he turned to the breaking of Federal ones. Had there been the proper pursuit, the proper adjudication of their cases, and the proper punishment, they all would have been executed or incarcerated for life in state institutions, long ago, and thus removed from the habitual life of crime which finally led them to become desperate Federal offenders and therefore necessitated the building of an escape-proof prison for mad dogs. Perhaps the story of a man called Dutch Normandale will illustrate the course by which offenders finally reach Federal prosecution.

He was arrested by police eighty-one times on charges of misdemeanor. He was charged in state courts with petty larceny, assault and battery, wounding less than mayhem; and twice accused of assault, beating and wounding, in one of which cases he was sentenced to sixty days' imprisonment. He was charged with disturbing the peace, with manslaughter, with shooting with intent to kill, and three times with grand larceny. He was accused of willful shooting, reckless driving, the use of mutilated license plates, malicious mischief, and assault to rape. Twice he was held for robbery and eight times for assault and robbery. This entire conglomeration of charges was rolled up in less than ten years, followed by release in practically every instance, either by the cases being nol-prossed, appealed, dismissed, or by a verdict of not guilty. The few times which resulted in conviction brought sentences totaling about eleven years, but there is no indication that he served even a fairly generous portion of that time. So, at last, having run the gamut of municipal and state infractions, he held up and robbed a United States mail truck, was caught, convicted, and sent to Atlanta Prison.

There is something stinkingly wrong with all branches of law enforcement which allow a man to dance through the entanglement of more than one hundred arrests, all within a few years. And there was something horribly wrong with the type of enforcement in regard to bank robberies when a wave of kidnapping swept America a few years ago.

Under the so-called Lindbergh Law the job of cleaning up the "snatch" racket was given into the hands of the Federal Bureau of Investigation. The pursuit of these renegades brought about some interesting information.

Practically all had begun life as petty offenders in small towns where they had committed from one to ten infractions before receiving adequate punishment. By the time enforcement really clamped down, they had gained the belief, and for good reason, that they could defy the law and get away with it. Following this, they had been consistently paroled or pardoned due to local influence.

The record of nearly every member of the kidnap bands also showed either an association in or an affiliation with various bootleg rings, which, of course, were enabled to exist through bribery or political protection. Thus, to a degree, society itself was to blame for a condition which made men contemptuous of enforcement. Long records of success in the game of cops and robbers was the factor which caused men — and women —

to believe they could hold human beings for ransom and avoid punishment. When they found they could not do so, kidnapping stopped, which again proves our point.

So much for the causes of kidnapping, which, after all, are no different from the causes of petty larceny, booze selling or murder. The Federal Bureau of Investigation began its highly successful campaign against body snatchers, and within a short time discovered another highly important fact: every major member of the various gangs had graduated into this form of crime from that of bank robbery. Therefore, the Bureau found itself doing a double job; in removing kidnappers, it also was eliminating some of the most aristocratic members of the bank-looting craft.

The first authority given to a Federal agency to proceed against bank-robbers was approved by the President in May of 1934. It then applied only to National Banks and members of the Federal Reserve System — Congress later gave the protection of Federal Deposit Insurance banks into the same hands.

The Bureau of Investigation went at its job in a businesslike way. It assembled all possible information about known bank-robbers. It made a collection of their "monikers" or nicknames. It collected information concerning their friends and contacts. It "broke down" their fingerprints from the composite ones of the Henry System to single prints, so that should a latent or accidental print be found at the scene of a robbery, it could be identified at once. By the use of Wirephoto, it is now possible for Washington to make a positive identification from any large city within comparatively few minutes. The Bureau also collected all possible data on the *modus operandi* of bank-robbers, and issued forms to banks for use in case of robbery in which there were outstanding characteristics, mannerisms, types of speech, walk or carriage. Thus the witnesses to a bank holdup could set down on paper every peculiarity they had noted about the bandits while their memory was still fresh.

Beyond this, however, there was a most important ingredient.

It was the fact that the Federal Bureau of Investigation really and earnestly and honestly set out to catch bank-robbers and then, having caught them, to convict them. Within twenty-four months, two hundred and thirty-four important yeggs had felt the results. One hundred and sixty-two of these were prosecuted in Federal Court, drawing three life sentences, one indeterminate term, and two thousand, six hundred and seventy-nine years of imprisonment. Seventy-two cases went to state courts — cases, however, in which work had been done by the Bureau and in which Special Agents testified. They drew eleven life sentences, one death, and six hundred and eight years in actual, suspended, and probationary sentences, plus fifteen indeterminate sentences. There would be more incisiveness to the fact that state courts imposed all those life sentences were it not for the face that the average time spent by a "lifer" in a state prison is less than ten years!

Nevertheless, bank robbery took a decided slump. At this writing there are few unsolved bank robberies and not more than fifty expert bank-robbers are at large. All the rest are dead or in prison, and a strongly entrenched heritage of crime is becoming a lost art. Many of the old-timers who still remain outside penitentiary walls have quit the business. Yet no magic was used whatever — only the desire to clean out a dangerous crew of violators, plus invulnerability against "approach" or fixing, whether monetary or political. Incidentally, some of the cases into which this Bureau delved revealed thoroughly unholy situations. There was, for instance, the robbery of the St. Charles National Bank, at St. Charles, Illinois, near Chicago.

When employees of this bank entered it for work one morning in January 1936, they found four masked and armed men awaiting them. The robbers bound and gagged their victims, forced them to lie on the floor, compelled the assistant cashier to open the vault, and departed with fourteen thousand, one hundred and forty-eight dollars and sixty cents. The case was one for the Federal Bureau of Investigation.

It is an investigative rule to "start close to home," especially when there are evidences of apparent magic on the part of the perpetrators. The four robbers evidently had gained entrance to the bank building by using a key. It therefore became a plain duty for Special Agents to check up on the actions, financial position, and other backgrounds in the lives of those employees trusted with a key to the front door. One of these was the merchant policeman, a former member of the regular St. Charles force, and now paid by businessmen to be an extra safeguard for their premises. Special Agents discovered that he had been seen in his garage a few days before the robbery, comparing guns with an ex-convict.

That called for investigation into the ex-convict; and it was learned that he had a Chicago record. Coöperation was entered into with the Chicago Police Department. Special Agents and police learned that one of the convict's hangouts was a tavern, run by a former deputy-sheriff. When they reached the place, it was closed.

"You see," the former deputy-sheriff explained at his home. "I've been thinking about running for State Representative. Well, there's been a pretty bad class of fellows hanging out around my place, so I thought I'd better close it up and get rid of them in case anybody started throwing mud in the campaign and accused me of not running a first-class dump."

That explanation did not satisfy. They kept the ex-deputy-sheriff under surveillance. He admitted that several bank robbers had been in his place on the night before the St. Charles affair. He named them. They were arrested and confessed, not only to the robbery, but to the fact that the whole job had been planned during many meetings in the former deputy-sheriff's tavern and that following the hold-up they had brought a part of their arsenal to the ex-officer's home to be disposed of. It consisted of eight pistols, five shotguns, and two rifles, which the obliging ex-deputy had planned on dumping in the river — for which favor, plus the use of his tavern as a hide-out, he had received two hundred and fifty dollars in loot.

It was found that the merchant policeman also was an obliging soul. He had furnished the bank-door key from which the bank-robbers had made a duplicate. And there was one more homey little touch to the robbery: —

Special Agents learned that the town of St. Charles depended greatly upon a Vigilante Committee to back up the local police in case of outstanding criminal activity. One of the very alert members of this Vigilante Committee was a florist. To better carry on his duties as a Vigilante member, the florist had been deputized as a special deputy-sheriff. The bank's alarm bell rang in his office and he was quite a fellow except for one small item. The head of the robber crew named him as the finger man of the whole affair; he had been so eager to learn the set-up of the bank that he had offered flowers at half-price to certain employees of the institution that he might have better opportunity to talk about banks, banking, the amount of money on hand, and protective devices used. In his house were found five pistols and a collection of rifles, some of which he insisted were necessary for his work as a Vigilante.

Thus, it is easy to see why Federal forces look over their ground with exceeding care before they confide their secrets to local authorities. After all, a merchant policeman wears a uniform and is supposed to be an upholder of the law. Under ordinary circumstances, one naturally would feel safe in confiding in a deputy-sheriff and ardent member of a Vigilante Committee. And a former deputy-sheriff, so filled with the desire to serve his people that he plans to be a candidate for the office of State Representative, would — in fiction, at least — be quite a fellow.

Unhappily, however, the state of law violation in America is a state of fact, not fiction. The wise enforcement officer is he who uses as much care in selecting his confidants as he does in chasing criminals. Otherwise, he may never get the man he's after.

CHAPTER SIX

THE FRUITS OF THEFT

EVERY time the clock ticks off a minute and a half, there is a robbery, burglary, hold-up, theft, or embezzlement somewhere in the United States. The machine of crime churns on tirelessly for this type of infraction; homes are burglarized or armories broken into for United States Army guns and ammunition with which to equip the underworld; there is a multiplicity of stick-ups and jewel robberies; banks and other institutions are looted by trusted employes as well as by heisters; cars are stolen — on and on the list travels into an aggregate money cost so great that no one ever has been able accurately to estimate its totals.

Often the robbers are caught and punished; the looting, however, does not decrease. There are always more robbers to take the place of those who have been started away for prison; always recruits, outward bound from prison, to fill the ranks and keep the business churning. All this is due, not to the robbers themselves, but to persons who seldom feel the hand of a policeman on their shoulder, and who often go through life without a conviction. They form the army of fences or receivers of stolen goods. Without them, thievery could not exist.

Speaking of plunder, there is a fine point of underworld delineation regarding those who deal in loot. When John Edgar Hoover and his Special Agents were returning Alvin Karpis, the multiple murderer-kidnapper and bank-robber, from his capture in New Orleans to his place of trial in St. Paul, Mr. Hoover made a grave error in etiquette. They were eight thousand feet in the air, in a chartered airplane, fighting thick, bumpy weather and the danger of fierce storms which at any time might bring about a forced landing and a chance for escape by this self-confessed thug, who, incidentally, was quite frank about the fact that he intended to get away if given the slightest opportunity. The mind of Alvin Karpis was centered on that eventuality. He also dwelt on the determination that he would delay matters in St. Paul as long as possible, before taking the medicine of conviction which he knew was certain.

"As long as I can stay out of Alcatraz," he said, "I will have a chance to escape. And if there's a chance, I'll take it."

In spite of these mental weights, including, of course, the knowledge that his life otherwise was a matter of doom, Mr. Alvin Karpis immediately rose to a point of social order. Mr. Hoover had called him a hoodlum.

"I'm no hood!" he snapped, his cruel mouth tightening. "And I don't like to be called a hood. I'm a thief."

"As far as I'm concerned, you're a hoodlum," answered the practical John Edgar Hoover. Karpis shrugged.

"But you don't understand," he explained magnanimously. "I was offered a job as a hoodlum and I turned it down cold."

Mr. Hoover merely looked out at the scudding clouds. He and his men do not possess that delightful spirit of camaraderie which demands that they regard all captured criminals, especially those of wide reputation, with the awe and respect which so many other law enforcement agencies bestow upon them. No one ever sees a picture of a delighted group of Special Agents posed affectionately about a super-gangster. The Federal Bureau of Investigation believes in eliminating its Dillingers, not hugging them; and the same goes for United States District Attorneys. Therefore, Mr. Hoover was not heavily disturbed by his breach of etiquette. Karpis, however, was accustomed to more deference.

"You see," he explained, "a thief is anybody who gets out and works for his living — like robbing a bank, or breaking into a place and stealing stuff, or kidnapping somebody. He really gives some effort to it. A hoodlum is a pretty lousy sort of scum. He works for gangsters, and bumps guys off after they have been put on the spot. Why, after I'd made my rep, some of the Chicago Syndicate wanted me to go to work for them as a hood — you know, handling a machine gun. They offered me two hundred and fifty dollars a week and all the protection I needed. I was on the lam at the time and not able to work at my regular line. But I wouldn't consider it. 'I'm a thief,' I said, 'I'm no lousy hoodlum.' "

John Edgar Hoover looked him over, from his paunch-jowled face to his almost effeminate feet.

"From my standpoint, you're still a hoodlum," he answered.

This incident is not recited to accuse Mr. Hoover of impoliteness; he is one of the most gentlemanly persons I ever met. However, in certain viewpoints concerning criminals he lacks the finesse and true admiration shown by some of our more considerate law-enforcement agents, prosecuting attorneys, and citizens at large, who believe it only proper to bask in the reflected glory of a widely publicized gangster. Since there is no Emily Post of the underworld, I recite this correction so that persons who like to be photographed with thugs and murderers may know the correct manner in which to address them. Call them thieves, not hoodlums. After all, hoodlums are nothing but lousy scum. And so are thieves, as far as this writer is concerned.

And so are fences — perhaps a filthier type than the men they support. One reason for this is the fact that through the peculiar manner in which they operate, they sooner or later make unwitting accomplices of even the most law-abiding citizens. There are indeed few adult persons in the entire population of the United States, including all law enforcement agents, who have not been victimized into acting as aides to crime by becoming the final recipients of stolen goods.

The American love of a bargain enables the fence to exist.

Because of this, it is entirely possible for the meat that is on our table, the butter which covers our bread, the eggs which form our breakfast, the tires which we obtain at "Selling Out" prices, the automobiles we drive, the clothes we wear, the layettes which adorn our babies, the furnishings which complete our homes, the engagement and wedding rings by which we enter a marital state, the birthday presents we buy, and even the greeting cards which we send at Christmas and New Year's — all to be stolen goods. We often smoke stolen cigarettes and stolen cigars. Canned goods, unless bought at a store of known legitimacy, can be stolen. The bonds with which we fortify ourselves against old age often reach our safety-deposit boxes through the hands of hood — sorry, thieves, and their scummy consorts, the fences. There is hardly an item of use in our daily life which cannot and has not been handled by the dregs of the underworld.

It is a fallacy to believe that a thief steals because he cannot resist the temptation of possession. In cases of kleptomania this may be true, but much alleged kleptomania is due to the easy way in which a long name rolls off the tongue rather than to a widespread psychosis. Mainly thievery is carried on as a business in which a stock in trade may be obtained for the taking, plus a certain amount of preparation and experience. After this, it is not put to personal use, but is sold, at wholesale, to illicitly established marts of trade. In the main, these distributors are the fences, who often have designated the places to be robbed, and picked the men best fitted to rob them.

Beyond this, there is a vast retail business which reaches its zenith with the shoplifter. Her plea that she simply could not resist stealing is belied by the fact that practically every chorus girl's dressing room, every circus lot and boarding house where live circus and carnival and other types of show people, every gathering place of extra-people in the motion pictures, almost every whore and call-house, as well as every apartment of "party girls" — in fact, every concentration place for women is, in many instances, on the regular route of shoplifters and other peddlers of stolen goods. From them one may obtain — at cut prices — such articles as gloves, furs, costume and sometimes real jewelry, silk hose, underwear, piece goods, hats, socks, and on occasions dresses and suits and overcoats.

At times, the booster or shoplifter may pose as a representative for small factories, thus explaining why she will vend gloves or stockings to-day while to-morrow her stock may consist of hats, brilliants or perfume. In too many cases, however, she frankly admits that the goods are stolen, and supplies the name of the store as a guarantee of their value. Often the buyer seeks information as to whether the merchandise has been boosted not as a guide to conscience, but as a means of allowing her to gauge better when, where, and in what associations to wear her bargain with safety. I quote from an investigative report arising from a surveillance of a group of night-club chorus girls suspected of having gangster affiliations: —

At 7:45 a woman referred to as Nina came into the girls' room, with a display of sweaters, stockings, purses, hats, gloves, etc., and said they had been "snitched"; the girls bought several articles of clothing. Wilma purchasing a new hat. Nina is a shoplifter who sells stolen articles of women's wear to the various night club hostesses.

Again: —

At 8:30 o'clock, a girl with a dog came in and said she had a lot of gloves and other wearing apparel which she had gotten from a "lifter."

Then Nina came back with some "gorgeous perfume" which she got at Saks. It was ten-dollar perfume, she said, but she offered it for three dollars. Nina was in a loquacious mood that night. She talked of her husband Ralph and of the girls who worked for her as disposers of the various articles which she accumulated in her voluminous, pocket-filled skirts during her daily grind as a booster. She invited the girls to come up to the house sometime for a square meal. It seems that a booster must observe the same proprieties toward customers as anyone else in the merchandising business.

It is as cut-and-dried as that. When one knows chorines, show-folk, hangers-on around certain types of pool halls, horse joints, gambling halls, barber shops, sporting clubs, training camps, hang-outs for pugilists, night club performers and hostesses, whore-ladies, procurers, pimps, and the like, it is as polite to refer to the "heat" on wearing apparel, bonds, or jewelry as it is to talk about the weather. The business of shoving stolen property has become so widespread that vendors often gauge their prices by the standing of the business establishment from which it is stolen. A dozen pipes lifted from Dunhill's have their same relative value in the world of shoplifting as they do in a display window on Fifth Avenue. Vendors of stolen goods take great pride in the showing of advertised brands.

Thus, the butter which comes to your table as the result of a cut rate on a widely known brand, may have been hijacked, and the driver of the truck murdered or kidnapped. In an instance unearthed by the Federal Bureau of Investigation which has jurisdiction in matters of theft from interstate shipments, the proprietor of a commission house, allegedly a place of legitimate business for more than a score of years, was found to be the associate and confederate of one of the most desperate gangs of dairy products hi-jackers in the Middle West. Incidentally, in that case, evidence was produced to the effect that the criminal efforts of this gang possessed the cooperation of several highway policemen who sometimes demanded as much as one thousand dollars per job for looking the other way. In another case, the commodity was canned soup and vegetables, stolen from trucks operating from big canneries, and rebranded with fake labels produced in underworld printing shops. This brand held its place in the affections of thousands of consumers. Sold at a rate far below the prices of other canneries, it was marketed through a chain of gangster-owned stores. In the same fashion, activities of Special Agents revealed a chain of tire stores, operating in a Middle Western state, owned by the head of a hi-jacking crew and run solely as a means by which to dispose of the loot of highway robberies.

The important consideration in these hi-jacking activities is that commission merchants, tire stores, grocer shops and other merchandisers could not sell stolen goods unless consumers bought them. That this is done innocently is taken for granted; this reveals, however, two structural weaknesses in the prevention of crime. One is the thoughtless cupidity aroused by goods greatly underpriced. The other is that public patronage enriches the professional fence and to a degree protects him. There are always the alibis of ignorance, previous good record, lack of intention — the fence has many excuses, plus the lack of drama so necessary for stern punishment. Charles Dickens, the novelist, has convicted more fences than most law enforcement agencies combined. It is doubtful, however, if all the Fagins since the days of Oliver Twist have rolled up a dollar aggregate of illicit trade equal to that of the jewel fences of America for a single year. One case will illustrate: —

For eight years, Federal forces, plus municipal, railroad and private detective agencies, pursued a will-o'-the-wisp, named William Malcolm Ritchey. They had learned his name through tracing the identity of a hotel dweller in whose room had been found the rifled trunk of a jewelry salesman. Beyond this they possessed nothing except a constantly growing list of robberies. In every case, the description of the thief fitted that of William Malcolm Ritchey.

His system was clever. Ritchey himself was a sort of detective. When he determined upon a robbery, he set out to learn everything possible about his victim, invariably a traveling salesman for a large jewelry house. With the victim's habits established, his route ascertained, his daily actions catalogued by careful shadowing, Ritchey would wait until the salesman sent his trunk to a railroad station for checking to the next town. Almost immediately, Ritchey himself would check a trunk. Then, after a short time, he would return to the station, show his check, and state a desire to open his trunk to obtain something which he had packed inadvertently. Once inside the baggage room, he would work swiftly, switching the trunk checks so that the one which had been on his baggage was now on that of the salesman, while the jewelry man's check would call for the trunk which Ritchey had owned. He even entered a baggage car and stole a trunk by this means while a train was traveling between Philadelphia and Maryland.

At last Ritchey was captured by St. Louis police who recognized him through pictures printed in the *Fugitive's Bulletin,* a monthly thief-catching publication of the United States Department of Justice. He pleaded guilty and was sentenced to five years, which point is not important. The interesting part of this man's career is that, in his eight years of activity, he is known to have stolen jewelry valued at more than a half-million dollars, regarding the disposal of which he would give no information. Free again in a few years, Ritchey may desire to resume his old occupation, and a thief cannot work without a means of disposal. The code of self-preservation demands the protection of a fence.

There is no evidence that any appreciable part of the stolen gems and adornments has been recovered. In one instance, more than two hundred watches were taken. At another time, hundred of diamonds, pearls, and other jewels were stolen to disappear beyond trace. Yet it is almost certain that the trinkets eventually reached the possession of honest persons, and it is within the range of possibility that some of the very concerns which endured loss again bought and sold their own jewels without realizing the fact. This, of course, entails an explanation of how the jewel fence works. That best can come through the story of a three-hundred-thousand-dollar robbery in a Southern resort in which were involved some fifteen hundred pearls.

First, however, it must be explained that the handling of

stolen goods in these advanced days of crime is a highly organized business, with ramifications which may be nationwide. The fruits of a Chicago robbery may be disposed of on the Pacific Coast; the loot of a Seattle jewelry-store hold-up may be dispensed in a half-dozen cities of the East by traveling men who, themselves, may be the innocent tools of a crooked "importer."

The jewel thief, of course, knows exactly where to go, or he would not be in the racket. Often his work is suggested by the fence who has "cased the job" and learned exactly what is to be stolen, following this work by making arrangements for delivery to a second fence, masquerading as an honest gem broker, when, as, and if the robbery is accomplished. At times, there are numerous contacts to be made, with one man who specializes in diamonds, another who sells pearls, a third perhaps who goes in for "colored stuff," as rubies, emeralds, and other colored stones are called. Then, of course, there are the arrangements to be made for the disposal of the settings as old gold.

Therefore, once the actual robbery is accomplished, the job really begins, an intricate affair of memos and commissions which may extend half across America. Sometimes the thief is paid outright for his work. At other times, he may not get his money until the stolen jewels are at last in the hands of an innocent purchaser, ranging all the way from the heavy gravy Daddy who buys a bracelet for a hot chorine to the ardent young man aflame with the righteous glow of purchasing an engagement ring. A return to the subject of the stolen pearls becomes necessary as a means of explanation.

When the resort robbery finally was traced down, its ultimate trail did not lead to some filthy den of crime, but to the stores of legitimate jewelers on Fifth Avenue, New York. Here necklaces were found which had been placed for sale on a commission basis by other legitimate houses; which, in turn, had received them on memo from allegedly legitimate brokers or importers. Even then the evidence was highly circumstantial, inasmuch as not one of the necklaces or collections of pearls matched the original stolen property. In all likelihood, each collection of gems contained the fruit of a dozen robberies at various points across the length and breadth of America. This had been accomplished by what is known as the "breaking up" process. In a workshop of crime, they had been unstrung, to be jumbled with pearls stolen from New Orleans, others from Chicago or Detroit, or Cleveland or Kansas City or San Francisco. The clasps and other identifying possibilities had gone into old gold. Out of the conglomerate collection, new strings had been fashioned, new clusters, new bracelets and necklaces and tiaras until no one collection contained more than a few pearls from any original string. Fiction to the contrary, present day thieves are not highly tempted by unusually large and widely romanticized stones; they prefer a type which can be matched by thousands of others of a like weight, color, and flawlessness. Thus, once out of a setting and mingled with other stones, such gems are lost to identification. Because of this, jewel thieves can be sent to prison interminably, but as long as the manufacturing fences exist, gem insurance will remain high.

There is a widespread belief that every thief treads a beaten path to a pawnshop, there to rid himself of his loot. The truth is that most pawnbrokers shy from the rewards of theft like a skittish filly from a barking dog. Pawnshops long ago became the first line of investigation in the field of law enforcement. Records must be kept of purchases, and a pawnbroker with a memory so short that he fails to identify a pawner of goods soon becomes an object of intense police activity. In fact, the pawnshop serves more often as the first step toward a penitentiary than as a means of rewarding crimes. Detectives make the rounds daily, checking upon reports which are filed at police headquarters of goods received. Gun numbers are checked, often resulting in the first clues which lead to the arrest and conviction of burglars and murderers. The Sign of the Three Balls is a lure only to the amateur, the petty thief, and the man desperate enough to take long chances. Who then are the fences? Often they are persons supposed to be the best friends of law and order.

No matter how often fiction detectives solve crimes by clue and deduction, the backbone of law enforcement rests upon that old standby of Scotland Yard: "from information received." Detectives of practically every large city are allowed expense accounts from which to pay for information that will lead to the arrest of wanted men, the name of the informant remaining secret. In addition to the stool pigeon who sells information is the one who squeals on his pals to keep his own carcass out of jail, often committing crimes in immunity because he is a good tipster. This last-named person often is an important cog in the disposal of immense amounts of stolen property. If the incentive is sufficiently high, he will turn up his own thieves, either bargaining with police for a light sentence, if the chase is hot, or willfully betraying them to keep his "in" since new thieves are easy to obtain.

It is regrettably true that such men exist in every large city. In places of loose law enforcement, the police know the men's occupation but ignore it because their tips mean an appeased public. In flagrant cases there is not even this redeeming feature. The fence is a politician, or pays politicians, and the police get orders to lay off.

One of the biggest fences of stolen cars arrested within recent years was a man who ran the most popular parking lot in town. He was a member of civic organizations and so important in fraternal orders that he engineered the acceptance of a number of other crooks, much to the later discomfiture of his Lodge brothers. The biggest shover of hot bonds in the Middle West, now a cell-block resident, was a widely known road contractor. A New York private detective of wide reputation, later sentenced for perjury, revealed a surprising acquaintanceship among the professional merchants of stolen jewels. One of these fences, when arrested, was found to spend much of his time on Jeweler's Row in New York and was known there as a supposedly honest business man. The trail of hot money, resultant from kidnappings, revealed the fact that this money was changed into "fresh dough" through the operations of politicians, doctors, lawyers, cigar-store keepers, night club owners, race-track bookmakers, farmers, manicure girls, merchants, whisky dealers, garage owners, and even an air pilot who made his principal livelihood by flying gangsters and didn't care whose money he took. There are cases in which detectives and policemen have fattened through a lucrative business consisting of partnerships in shops which dealt exclusively in the fruits of thievery. The greatest source of stolen goods is that resulting from the bankruptcy racket.

The method is easily explained. A crook hires a crooked auditor to make a false statement concerning the financial status of his company. Upon this financial statement, listing assets and accounts outstanding which do not exist, he buys a bill of goods on credit, selling it off at reduced prices to merchants who are willing to ask no questions if the price is right. The proceeds of these sales go into the private pocket of the crook instead of into the business. Bills become due. Creditors press for payment and find no assets. The business is thrown into bankruptcy, presumably merely another concern which has failed through mismanagement or bad business. During the depression, business failures throughout the United States often ran into the high hundreds every week. It is impossible to compute the number of these that were fraudulent — undramatic robberies, to be exact — in which thousands upon thousands of dollars in merchandise were stolen from legitimate factories and wholesalers and resold at bootleg prices to further complicate a deflation process already sufficiently serious without the addition of criminality.

This sort of thing goes on incessantly. Its prevalence is proved by the wide ramification apparent in the case of some thirty-three New York gangsters who really put their hearts into wholesale robbery and the disposal of stolen property.

Here was criminality upon a true business basis. The group of thirty-three was split into three divisions, each with its specific duties. One was composed of certified public accountants devoted to ferreting out possible fields of activity. In auditing the books of a legitimate business, to use an example, they would find that this firm was in financial difficulties. Immediately they would report to the businessmen of the group, or the second division, whose job it was to argue the owners into allowing them to take over the institution and "pull it out of the hole." Previous to this time, of course, the business had possessed a fair rating and had merited credit. As soon as the gangsters moved in, this rating swiftly went upward. Instead of presenting a true picture of conditions as they existed, the crooked accountants painted the status of the almost defunct company as one to appeal to any manufacturer. Thus it was possible to buy huge bills of goods on a long term basis. Then the third division of racketeers swung into action.

These were the fences, nearly a dozen of them, operating what appeared to be legitimate brokerage houses, warehouses, and even retail stores. Since the combined gang had its hands in a variety of enterprises, there must be an equal number of wholesaling and retailing outlets. These included the high-powered activities of a paper company, a rayon concern, a storage and warehouse firm, several grocery corporations, a transatlantic trading corporation and two neighborhood store chains designed to place the fruits of robbery straight into the hands of the consumer.

Beyond this there were sales companies which acted as clearinghouses for the main places of business, and through which tremendous bills of goods were diverted to the dozen or so fences upon forged bills of sale, fake invoices, contracts with firms which never existed and receipts from concerns, the backgrounds of which existed only in the imagination of the gangsters. Clothing, silks, trunks, groceries, brooms, anything and everything which could be purchased in carload lots, from kitchen ranges to automobile tires, were flooded into circulation. At the time of investigation by the Federal Bureau of Investigation, legitimate manufacturers had been robbed of more than a half-million dollars and merchants had suffered to an even greater extent, through crooked competition. The investigation was a long and costly one; Special Agents worked for months, at last to present their evidence in court and stop the frauds.

It is in the field of stolen bonds, however, that the fence comes into his own. Any person who, these days, buys bonds which do not bear the backing of legitimate concerns, is taking a long chance. The changing of serial numbers has become a highly specialized business. The trail of crookedness which the hot bond travels leads into the offices of shyster attorneys, snake-like bankers, night club proprietors, outlaw brokers, and is an exceedingly slimy one. Nevertheless, the pretense of respectability is highly important. I quote from a confession: —

I was in the Chicago office of an ex-Congressman regarding an estate which his real estate and mortgage company controls when I was introduced to two men who wanted to buy some bonds or mortgages to bolster the financial condition of an insurance company. I made inquiry about town to ascertain if I could obtain any bonds that would answer this purpose. In a few days a man called on me with a list of bonds and I referred him to my lawyer. He gave the lawyer a list, which was the inventory of a number of bonds stolen in a Connecticut bank robbery. We made a date to meet at my attorney's office and the next day, we were all there, when the bonds were delivered by a man who said he was a practising physician.

Perhaps that will give a rough idea of the course sometimes taken by the fruits of a bank or vault robbery. Like other fences, these men hide in no dark alleys. They have offices, they stay at good hotels, they often parade as honest men — representatives of real estate companies, mortgage companies, and the like. And all too often, they come from the ranks of those persons so dearly beloved by the American sucker, the night club owner.

Just why night club proprietors should have been sainted by Repeal is somewhat beyond my understanding. Many of them now pay a license to the State for the privilege of selling liquor when once they paid off the precinct captain. Fundamentally these are the same men that they were before. They wear the same kind of dinner jackets — just a little too tight in the shoulders, a little too smooth over the chest; style has dictated a Dubonnet carnation in the lapel instead of a white one; otherwise they remain sartorially as well as morally unchanged.

A number of them still belong to a phase of America which is unalterably and fixedly linked with the underworld. They still know more fags, fruiters, prostitutes, fixers, crooks, wrong guys, yeggs, framers, con men, badger game women, high and low class whores, blackmailers, queer money shovers, gangsters, louse politicians, and slimy racketeers than any other class of persons existent. In instances, they either belong to or are front men for the controlling syndicate of the city, just as they were members or fronters for the old bootlegging commands. Such persons exist as barnacles upon society, often employing cappers, drunk-rolling hostesses, gambling shillabers, and other forms of crookedness that would be called crime if discovered on a carnival lot.

In many instances, they act as tip-off and finger men for blackmail artists, preying upon business men who have committed indiscretions. In one large city, there is actually a night club which caters to blackmailers; there they themselves become suckers on money they have "yipped" from other suckers by the "shakedown" route; the conversation regarding the racket in all its phases is quite casual. One looks about and says, admiringly: —

"Oh, there's Philadelphia Charlie. Spending dough like quicksilver — usually money's mucilage in that guy's pocket. He made a big knockover last week — fifty grand on the badger game."

There are night clubs which still serve as post offices for

crooks. Their proprietors still act, look, think, and live crook-edness. Jack Peifer was a good example of the type; a jolly good soul, was he: always friendly; always willing to stop at a table and chat a minute. Never upstage — democratic, you know — Why, after you'd been to his place a couple of times — he ran the Holly Hocks — it was just like you'd been going there forever. And if you had a favorite piece you wanted played — all you had to do was to tell Jack.

The unfeeling United States Government, not possessing the strain of hero worship necessary to the adulation of night club operators, yanked Jack Peifer into Federal Court. There it pro-duced evidence which proved that this dressed-up rat had been the go-between for practically every high-powered crook who had visited his city in the last six years. Hot bonds streamed through his hands into those of persons who would change serial numbers, arrange contacts with crooked bankers, inno-cent purchasers, or those "desiring to improve the financial status of their company." He could be depended upon to wash the illegal proceeds of a kidnapping. If a gangster sought con-tact with the rest of his mob, Jack did the job for him. He was accused of being a pay-off man between the underworld and the police.

I mention Mr. Peifer because he was the epitome of genial, democratic, well-liked, generous, kindly and crooked night club operators, and also because he was typical of many of his kind in nearly every large city of the United States. To a de-gree, many such persons have social standing. Debutantes love to be invited to broadcast from their microphones. Sucker so-ciety women, horsing to get their names in the paper, vie for the table nearest the door, which somehow or other gives them social standing.

Jack was such a swell fellow that, upon his arrest, the col-umnist of a newspaper of wide circulation got out his asbestos paper, inked his typewriter with fulminate of mercury, anointed his brain with brimstone, and let loose a columnar blast against the United States Government that would have burned down Babylon. Jack, however, failed to live up to the ballyhoo. He heard himself convicted of the charges against him, he received a sentence of thirty years in a Federal penitentiary, and he then shocked all his worshipers by confessing his guilt through a medium of a poison pill which removed him from the county jail in a dead wagon.

Thus the list of fences and shovers rolls on, even to the unearthing by the Federal Bureau of Investigation of what was known as the Little Stock Exchange, a group of hot bond purveyors operating in conjunction with bank thieves who are known to have stolen at least two million dollars in securities. These bonds were sold in many parts of the world. The important point is that, sooner or later, there was only one ultimate end for them. That was in the hands of the innocent purchaser.

Of all fields for stolen-goods operatives, however, the biggest is automobile thievery. Here the thefts run to an annual value of nearly eighty million dollars. A part of this is due to casual theft. Other losses come about through "borrowed" cars taken by joyriders. But the main body of depredation is the result of well-organized auto theft rings, such as that of Gabriel Vigorito of Brooklyn, New York, who owned an "auto exchange," and conducted an exporting business, and thereby shipped so many stolen cars to Europe that the used-car business of the Continent was threatened with extinction.

Other fences and heads of theft rings approach the business from a different angle. Some, through the connivance of crooked garages and machine shops, steal only high-priced cars, and within a few hours so change their appearance that the owner could not possibly recognize them. In this business, the "numbers changer" is a skilled workman; he draws high wages for altering the motor serial numbers in such an expert manner that the substitutions are invisible, sometimes, to microscopic inspection. Only by the application of acids, which bring out the original numbers through restoring the primary abrasions made in the steel, can the true number be ascertained.

Beyond this, in many machine shops which make a business of "handling hot shorts," the cars are received from the clouters or thieves and denuded of every piece of equipment they possess. Fenders, clock, dynamo, fan — everything is taken off, sorted and sometimes reconditioned, passing from their hands into those of cut-rate equipment stores which run their legitimate rivals into bankruptcy. And the queer angle about the whole racket is that everyone concerned in it, except the clouters themselves, look upon themselves as honest, normal American workmen. The mechanics, in their own estimation, have only taken apart cars about which they have asked no questions. The cut-rate dealers have done no more than sell parts which they have bought cheaply.

As for the aids to stealing, it is practically impossible to protect a car against theft. "Shapes" or duplicate keys to newly sold cars are often peddled by crooked minor employes of automobile sales companies, who obtain the keys to new cars as they come from the factory, have duplicates made and then, as the car is sold, furnish to car thieves the "shape" plus the name and address of the purchaser. Even this person regards himself as only indulging in a little trickery, nothing crooked, you understand; it is the thief who clouts the car, not the man who sells him a key. The crooked operators of parking lots operate in the same fashion. After the owner has driven his car on the lot, leaving his key in the ignition, as required, the lot owner or an employee abstracts it and takes it across the street to a key duplicator who doesn't earn a dime by any other means in a week of holidays. Yet he also regards himself as honest.

Such precautions as duplicate keys are taken only when a prospective victim locks the doors of his car. Otherwise the clouter merely reaches under the dash and re-aligns the ignition wires. For that matter, no home is absolutely safe against the professional who wants to get in. By cutting a small hole in a pane of glass, a professional can reach in and outwit any window lock. Many fancy door-locks can be removed simply by cutting around the outlines of the buried metal with a heavy sharp knife. A burglar's jimmy will make almost any door look sick. Burglar alarms can suffer through cut wires. As for so-called locks which presumably cannot be opened except with the key made for them, I was amazed recently to see a fifteen-year-old boy who, with one key, easily opened numerous locks.

"Just a master key," he explained.

"So? Where did you get it?"

"Oh, I didn't get it. I made it."

"Where?"

"In high school. I go to Manual Training, you know. Another kid showed me how to turn it out in the machine shop."

Here the average person may be constrained to inquire as to what opportunity there may be to escape the thief. The answer comes partly in the story of a man named Alexander Runion, the head of an automobile theft ring which stole cars in Cincinnati and hid them in the vicinity of Manchester, Kentucky. Federal Special Agents and members of the Kentucky State Highway Patrol coöperated in attempting to solve the case, in which some sixty-eight cars eventually were recovered.

Runion was a powerful gangster. He had many "connections." He also was able to persuade so many persons that he possessed tremendous political and official aid that out of more than a score of victims who could have identified him, only two were not afraid to do so. More than that, a County Sheriff, undoubtedly filled with eagerness to protect Mr. Runion's lily-white reputation, so resented the activities of the Highway Police that he jailed one of the State Patrolmen on a charge of breaking and entering a garage, thus forcing the Governor to call out the State Militia as an aid to law enforcement. It must have pained the Sheriff considerably when the well-protected Mr.

Runion pleaded guilty on four counts and got twenty years in a Federal penitentiary.

Thieves have invaded even that supposedly safe protectorate wherein one depends upon the watchfulness of canine protectors. One of the truly big-paying occupations in the vicinity of large cities is the theft of thoroughbred dogs.

If one is familiar with the dog shops of exceptionally large cities, one may wonder at the difficulty which often is encountered when an effort is made to obtain a pedigree upon a recently purchased animal. Or one may receive the necessary paper, only to find it forged, and the dog shop, upon investigation, out of business. Or a sire is revealed as fathering hundreds of puppies. The reason, of course, is that the purchaser of a puppy from this particular dog shop has unwittingly bought the offspring of a stolen animal.

The suburbs of such large cities are havens for this type of thief, and perhaps a part of the story can best be told through the experience of a friend who lost his dog and refused to sit at home and merely wait for him to return.

This man, the associate editor of one of America's largest magazines, lived in a suburb of New York. Early one rainy morning, he turned out his Boston bulldog for a run and waited in vain for its return. Investigating, he found the front gate open and the dog gone.

That was unusual. The dog was several years old and highly trained. He had no proclivities of the usual runaway. He was not in the habit of following strangers, nor could he be fed by a chance person, thus being lured away. He had been schooled against invitations into automobiles. Moreover, the owner now remembered that he had heard the dog bark, as if challenging someone, only suddenly to desist. This had not been investigated, because the dog was in the habit of barking at passersby. Now, however, with the gate open and the dog gone, there seemed every reason to believe that he had been stolen. The accomplishment of this was a mystery.

On the chance that the dog had strayed away, the editor offered a reward in want-ad columns, steadily raising the amount
until it reached one hundred dollars. There was no reply. Therefore, he attempted to trail whatever person had wanted his dog
so badly that he had engaged in theft. His discoveries were disillusioning. There had been no desire for a canine companion.
The theft had been cruel, crafty and cold-blooded. It had been
accomplished by one of many men engaged in the business of
stealing dogs.

All this my friend pieced together from information gained
from many sources. Officers of the A.S.P.C.A., for instance,
revealed that dog thieves often "case" a canine before stealing,
apply for a license for an animal of that description, obtain the
necessary tag, and have it in readiness to place on the dog the
moment he is stolen. This is especially true if the animal is a
fine specimen, desired for breeding purposes. Necessary proof
of ownership might halt such stealing, they said, but for some
strange reason legislatures did not seem extremely eager to put
through the law.

Perhaps one reason for lack of such action is that legislatures
may look upon it as trivial. On the other hand, failure to grant
protection to dog owners may have a more sinister meaning.
Quite possibly necessary protective legislation has been held up
at the behest of the filthiest type of crooks in existence — those
men who make a business of stealing pets, plus certain confederates who get rich through the killing of dogs. All this points
to a racket which requires a rather lengthy explanation.

It is more than likely that when my friend's dog barked that
rainy morning, he did so at the approach of a man who opened
the gate, stood there a moment, then slowly moved away, as
though he had mistaken the number of the house. The dog,
following natural instincts, had rushed to the gate, hesitated
there, sniffing. Then he had done something against which he
had been trained. He had followed this man away, without any
apparent invitation on the part of the thief.

Explanation discards any element of mystery. The hundreds of dog thieves who operate in the suburbs of big cities like New York choose the times of early morning and late night for their activities. Particularly they like rainy weather, as this not only precludes the presence of the owner, but, through the dampness of the air, heightens the odor of bitch scent with which they have soaked the cuffs of their trousers. Animal instinct being what it is, even the most thoroughly trained dog will follow any person heavily laden with the scent of a female in heat. Thus the dog thief has an eternal alibi, especially if he is "fixed" either with the police or with the district attorney. If caught, he produces the excuse that the dog followed him of its own volition, that he thought it lost and therefore was about to do a humanitarian thing by taking it home with him. That this procedure was induced by the bitch scent which smeared the thief's trousers does not interest a "fixed" official. The thief goes free.

Once out of sight, the dog is lured into an automobile. Thieves specialize in Bostons, cocker spaniels, and Scotties, due to the difficulty of identification of these three breeds. Big dogs are prey only when being sold to dog pounds for killing purposes.

The editor's advertisement brought no result for the reason that professional dog thieves never answer want ads, no matter how high the reward. They are in a business, with hundreds of dog shops and hideaway "puppy-raisers" as their fences, and where they have a steady market for stolen animals of apparent good breeding at $10 a head. The grief of dog-owners means nothing. Far better, from a professional standpoint, that thieves continue in business with their fences than that they yield to the temptation to return a stolen dog, even for a high reward, thus risking identification and possible prosecution — if the District Attorney doesn't happen to be a "right guy."

There is no place in the world where there is such a heavy market for dogs as in New York City. And indeed, there are few cities where there is so much crookedness in many pet shops, so much evasion, so many evidences of cruelty and rottenness.

I have seen shops where practically every dog was burning with the fever of distemper, and where the owners took no precautions for the segregation of animals with infectious diseases, meanwhile prattling of their love for animals as they passed these germ-ridden canines out to trustful buyers. I have seen numerous shops where the purveyors of "one and two year old dogs" were not even able to "remember" the names of the pets they pretended to know so well, summoning ones from imagination to which the dogs refused to answer.

There are shops which open for a week, sell hundreds of puppies, promise pedigrees "within ten days"; then, overnight, fold up and abandon the premises. There are others in which forgery of pedigrees goes on merrily until detection, this being followed by vacancy within twenty-four hours, inasmuch as the storeroom has been rented upon a day-to-day basis. There are other shops which have as their stud one dog and several females, all pedigreed, and which seem more gifted with progeny than a flock of rabbits. Every puppy which goes through this shop is registered to this group of dogs, even though the bitches may be so old as to have been sterile for several years. In other words, these shops use registered dogs for "fronts" — meanwhile handling the puppies of stolen dogs as sent them from perhaps a half-hundred hide-outs.

Even the best of shops often are the victims of the activities of dog thieves, receiving puppies in good faith only to find that pedigrees are not forthcoming. This, in itself, affords a blind for the whole crooked stolen-dog business, which, incidentally, in New York alone, amounts to far more than a million dollars annually. Because the honest shops can prove that they have accepted dogs in good faith, all shops, whether or not they be fences or "drops" for numerous thieves, can escape detection in the same manner.

In such shops, no dog is more than "one or two years old." Partly this is because the crooked shopkeepers have no idea of the age of the animal. Further, a year-old dog is the usual goal of a person wishing to buy a pet past the danger age of disease. Usually such pets are sold on the basis that "someone was going away and just had to get rid of his pet." If the dog is five or six years old, and has a few gray whiskers, the shopkeeper may admit the possibility that he "may be a little more than eighteen months in age." In the infrequent event of identification of a canine as stolen, there is the alibi: "We took him in good faith. We didn't know he was stolen. We thought the man was his owner. He told us the same story we told you. How were we to know that nice-looking gentleman was a thief?"

It is a business, carried on with extreme craftiness. But even in its worst aspects, it is not half as filthy as that of numerous dog-pound keepers.

The next time you notice an extremely hot fight between two men of political affiliation for the job of dog catcher or pound keeper, it might be interesting to learn for yourself just what this office has paid its incumbents in previous administrations. This will be particularly true if the struggle occurs in heavily populated suburbs of big cities, where there are many villages, each adjacent to each other, and if the job pays upon the fee basis.

Dog-pound keepers have been known to operate in conjunction with dog thieves such as previously described. This becomes true, however, only when the regular market has been glutted and the fences refuse further shipments of animals at ten dollars a head. Then the dog thief reaches his lowest level, and throws in with the pound-keeper or dog catcher.

Since such dogs have been duly licensed, it is impossible for the crooked dog-catcher to send out his men and cart the animals away to the lethal chamber. He often is paid a fee of two dollars for every dog he kills, and being the low-lifed, filthy crook which he sometimes is shown to be, he is not above getting dogs by any means whatever. Therefore, he, instead of the crooked dog-shop owner, becomes the fence. He has the alibi that no owner has appeared during the time in which dogs usually are held before being put to death. The explanation of this is simple. The dog, with numerous others, probably was stolen some fifty miles away and transported to this dog-pound, thus obviating any chance for its real owners to discover its whereabouts. Even had the owners appeared, there would have been no record of such a dog in the pound. So the pound keeper kills a dog for which someone sorrows, thereby getting two dollars. The thief has received a dollar for his share. Sometimes the racket does not even stop there.

Dog catchers have been found to operate upon the syndicate system, shipping their kills to each other. Suppose, for instance, that five villages surround a big city. They are under separate governments, even though their boundaries may crowd each other. Instances have been discovered wherein rings of pound keepers have kept the bodies of executed dogs moving from one town to another until they reached the point of putridity, each pound-keeper making his collection. Perhaps that requires explanation.

Pound keeper A kills twenty dogs. He presents them for inspection and is thereupon credited with forty dollars. Meanwhile Pound keepers B, C, D, and E also have each killed twenty dogs and have been granted their fees. Now begins a series of transshipments. The twenty dogs, which Pound keeper A has killed, go to Pound keeper B in the next village, again to be counted and credited, while the dead dogs of other pounds continue the rotation. Thus, while each pound keeper has, in reality, killed only twenty dogs, each has been credited on a municipality's books with the death of a hundred canines. It therefore is easy to see why the price to dog thieves often is raised to two and even three dollars apiece if there is a dearth of unlicensed animals.

It was discovered a year or so ago that a string of pound keepers in a certain county had finished the year with incomes ranging from twenty-five thousand dollars to thirty thousand dollars. Inasmuch as there had been numerous thefts, public interest in such mammoth earnings became intense. An investigation was demanded. The District Attorney's office was furnished with what seemed incontrovertible evidence that these men not only had been acting as the fences for stolen dogs, but had been piling up illegitimate profits as the result of the transshipment of bodies and the padding of accounts.

The District Attorney delved and delved and delved into the activities of his fellow politicians. The more he delved the farther away from court the case seemed to get. After a time, the usual thing happened. Public interest, dulled by the passage of time, began to lag. The investigation went into a pigeonhole dedicated to forgotten things — and there remained.

My friend never found his dog. In that he had the company of thousands of other pet owners, as well as persons throughout America who every minute and a half, discover thefts, call the police, wait for something to happen — and wait, all too often, in vain.

CHAPTER SEVEN

FIRST AIDS TO CRIME

PERHAPS this is the place to reiterate the fact that law enforcement as a whole is far from crooked. Fundamentally, the average police force in America wants to be honest, and the average one could purge itself in a few months under the proper, unhampered guidance. If this statement seems to be out of juxtaposition with instances cited, it must be remembered that law enforcement is the one agency, above all others, which must enter into no truce with crime in any form or in any segment. If there are ten thousand policemen on a force and fifty of them are dishonest, then the whole organization must suffer. If the entire personnel is upright, with the exception of the Chief or the Commissioner, then there may as well be no police force. And if the officers and men are straight, but subservient to crooked political influences, the situation becomes more grave, in that honest men are being suborned into aids to crime.

Again, there is the possible argument that, if conditions are as black as they are painted, why are there so many arrests, why do the courts grind on, why are there courts and judges and district attorneys, why are there crowded prisons and why does the news of the electric chair continue to occupy the first page? The answer to that can be given in a few paragraphs.

Once upon a time there were six young boys. They were tough, there is no doubt about that. They were criminally-minded. And they also were poor, which is among the greatest of American crimes. The most ruthless, and the most successful, prosecutor who ever stalked into any court of this country is

Poverty. Once an indictment crackles in his bony hands, you may be sure that Justice will prevail. The court-appointed nitwit, just out of law school, will stammer and halt in this, perhaps his first appearance before an august judge and jury. If the defendant insists that he can prove an alibi by obtaining witnesses from another city, Poverty grins eerily, and asks where in hell he'll get the money to bring them into court. If a juryman winks a one-hundred-dollar wink, it meets only a blank stare. Here is Justice, with her eyes blinded, her sword upraised, and her virtue undefiled. Justice must have been the first gold digger; she has such a long and unbroken record for never having been raped by a poor man.

These six boys were poor. Again it must be remembered that they also were tough. They wanted money and did not care how they got it. They held up a subway station employee and killed him. For that they deserved to die, since it is the law. And since Poverty helped in the prosecution, you may be sure they were sentenced to the chair. In fact, the judge said: —

"Unpleasant as is the duty of sentencing men to death, I feel that it would be a good thing if every prisoner in our near-by jail were here to hear these sentences. The fate of these men is dramatic proof that crime does not pay."

Therein lies the burden of this book. Crime does not pay those who seek so hard to make it remunerative — who are the poor. Crime pays only such persons as those about whom I write — the professional crimesters; the ones whose miraculous escapes from punishment lead simpletons like those six youths into believing they can get away with it.

Beyond pointing out the injustice of convicting Poverty while freeing Influence, and of fumbling for some answer to why law enforcement proceeds so admirably against persons unsupported by financial or political or business influence, and so poorly against others, this book has few premises. The great army of our convicts are the casuals of crime, the drifters, the bits of chaff and straw and waste which circle about a whirlpool until at last they are sucked in. Anyone who can invent a term which will separate them from the professional will perform an heroic deed in social service. They are a part of crime, it is true, a highly important and serious part of crime; they are the seeds from which jungle-like growth can and does grow, but until the jungle sprouts they are not Crime itself. The representatives of that antisocial order of the jungle would have had many a belly-laugh had they heard that stern sentence of death with its challenge to the underworld. These young fellows belonged to no such protected aristocracy as theirs; they were merely six tough punks who had killed because they believed law enforcement to be so futile that almost anyone could take human life and not pay for the deed. They had been so amateurish that they had spent their loot of forty dollars in nickels about the very neighborhood in which they had lived. They had been bereft of the benefits of *habeas corpus*, high-powered attorneys, delays, missing witnesses, interested district leaders, and all the other habiliments of protection with which any shrewd lawyer can surround a client of sufficient funds. Moreover, the fools had confessed their crime — which is against every rule of professionalism.

It is easier to catch small fish than big ones. The same rule holds good for crime, and it is the small fry who provide the major portion of our prison fodder. They form the grist of the law enforcement mill. And after a time, they become big fish also.

Professional criminals may die at the hands of law officials, made trigger-quick by the belief that they receive little support from the courts, but they do not die by execution. If, out of the approximate two hundred gray-featured men and women who stagger to the chair or the rope each year, there are five persons of influence or wealth, then indeed Justice is working overtime. In fact, I cannot remember a truly affiliated desperado who has died by execution since Gerald Chapman — and he did so only after a prison escape in which yardlights were mysteriously extinguished, ropes appeared as though they had been pulled out of a hat, and turret and wall guards displayed the greatest inability to shoot at a fleeing figure ever exhibited under one canvas.

True, local figures have died, such as Raymond Hamilton in Texas, but even they have been few in number. Others have been sentenced to death, with earnest pleas of "interested persons" bringing about commutation, with the result that they now are awaiting pardon or parole. True crimesters regard the electric chair as having been built for suckers. Fellows with brains may be put into the death house, where they can watch the casuals of crime travel on to the last waltz, but it is only a visit until "somebody can get to the Governor." And, of course, execution never even threatens the thousands of persons in the behind-the-scenes army of supporters who, like a movie star's cast, make it possible for these professionals to gain their reputation as supermen.

I remember a certain grim morning in November of 1934. All the previous night, the newsboys had pounded up and down Pennsylvania Avenue in Washington, shouting the news that Baby Face Nelson had added the lives of two more law enforcement officials to his string of murders. The victims were Special Agents of the Federal Bureau of Investigation who had given their clean, useful lives that they might wipe out the slimy one of Nelson — who had been paroled, allowed to escape, gently dealt with, and protected by everything from crooked garage men to renegade law-enforcement officials. One of these Special Agents, Herman B. Hollis, — young, ambitious, and the father of a family, — had worked day and night for months in the efforts of the Bureau to rid the Midwest of its affliction of gangsters. The other, Inspector Samuel Cowley, was, in addition to a great law enforcement officer, a teacher of a Mormon Sunday School; he lived the kind of life that should be lived by a man who honestly wants to teach clean thoughts to a bunch of youngsters. It was he who commanded the campaign against John Dillinger. He was head of what is known as "the Special Squad," the "trouble shooters" of the Federal Bureau of Investigation, composed of what might be called Super G Men. He, for instance, signed the contract with Anna Sage, the so-called Woman in Red, for the delivery of Dillinger at a price, and it is to him that J. Edgar Hoover gives full credit for the elimination of the Midwest outlaw. Sam Cowley, incidentally, never endorsed a razor blade nor did he advise young men, via the comic pages, how to catch criminals by eating a certain brand of breakfast foods.

The deaths of Hollis and Cowley had made it a bitter morning in the headquarters of the F.B.I. At his flag-flanked desk, in the tremendous room which forms the nerve center of the Bureau's activities, sat the Director — talking quickly, yet calmly, as Special Agents in Charge reported over the long distance telephone from all parts of the United States. A deadly hunt was on for the companion of Baby Face, a Pacific Coast product of protected bootlegging known as John Paul Chase, who was to remain at liberty only a short time before being sent to Alcatraz Prison under life sentence.

The Director was haggard. Not for a moment, since the teletype had clicked out its deadly news the night before, had he relaxed from his task of directing a nationwide man hunt. Even beyond fatigue was the weight of sadness; Mr. Hoover knows every man in his organization, not as mere functionaries, but as co-fellows in a hard and dangerous occupation. He had been accustomed, day after day, to hearing the quiet voice of Sam Cowley, coming over these telephones from here and there about the country: —

"We're making progress, Boss. We've got a line on these fellows — sooner or later we'll get 'em."

But now Sam Cowley was dead; and Herman Hollis was dead — both torn from life by the stuttering fire of underworld automatics. At last, in a cessation of the stream of investigative calls, Mr. Hoover rubbed his tired eyes, and turned for a moment in answer to my questions.

"Of course, I'm bitter, Ryley," he said slowly. "But strangely enough I am not so bitter at the men who actually killed Hollis and Sam. They were the instruments of a system. It's the rats who hide behind such men as Baby Face Nelson who provide the real threat — the fellows who pretend they're honest, but who are even more rotten and filthy than the gangsters themselves: lawyers, and doctors, and hide-out owners; renegade politicians, fellows in law enforcement who forget their oaths, judges who release murderers on probation for no apparent reason, sob-sisters who work night and day to change prison bars into putty. They're the ones who killed Hollis and Sam. Baby Face Nelson merely pulled the trigger."

It has been only a few months more than two years since Baby Face died in the "Battle of East Barrington, Illinois." It was possible for the Government to track down and convict a number of his aides; men and women who had given this kill-crazy desperado assistance and succor, who harbored him, bought machine guns for him, furnished him fake license plates, gave him food and shelter that he might escape the law, tipped him off with information concerning the activities of enforcement officials and otherwise aided him into believing that he was so far above punishment that he could actually joke about the number of officers he had murdered. They were all sent to jail or prison and, as this is written, they are all out again, their puny sentences served and the way cleared for them to again become first aids to professional crime.

There was the old ex-safeblower, a tall scarecrow of a figure who posed as a highly honest member of society in a Pacific Coast city. He managed the town's hospital, presumably for the service of citizens, but really as a hide-out where gangsters could be treated for bullet wounds and gangster's women could be operated upon to remove the ravaging results of the venereal diseases with which practically all are afflicted. He is free again.

Then there was the garage man in Reno, who actually endangered the lives of Special Agents by revealing to the Baby Face gang the tag numbers of the Federal men's cars. He is back from his short sentence, like the gambler and political figure who also assisted the murderers.

The wife who ran with her murderous husband from one end of the country to another, using their baby as a camouflage, is out on parole. So are a dozen others. Perhaps they "have learned their lesson." Perhaps their names will not again appear in the crime news. Such miracles have happened.

With the exception of a few persons who delayed incarceration by long legal fights and appeals, there is not a gun moll, underworld helper, ammunition buyer, hide-out owner, crooked license-tag purveyor, tipster, hide-out finder, or face and finger-tip changer convicted during the drive on the Dillinger and allied gangs of a few years ago who has not finished his or her brief jail or prison sentence, been paroled, or been allowed probation. To this statement there are two exceptions: the women of Alvin Karpis and Harry Campbell. Prison days are over for the others — unless they again team up with high-powered crooks, to provide hang-outs and hide-outs, to act as post offices for the underworld, and to form the foundations without which professional crime cannot live. Yet the law regards them as "mere adjuncts."

There are no statutes which can truly reach such persons. State enforcement does nothing about it whatever; unless police can actually fasten upon them a charge of conspiracy in the commission of the main crime, the usual district attorney dismisses for lack of evidence. Gun molls are rarely held by police other than for questioning. Only the Federal Government attempts punishment; and even then it is hampered by probation-inclined judges, and an absence of adequate laws.

It is almost impossible to receive more than a most minor term in prison for providing a backbone to crime. You may do almost everything except the actual infraction, and be charged

only with "harboring" — which, upon conviction and imprisonment, less good time, pardon, or parole, rarely brings more than
a few months of actual servitude. To aid crime by providing its
sinews is a highly lucrative business. Hide-out keepers sometimes demand two hundred dollars a day from extra-hot fugi-
tives.

Consider, for instance, the case against Louis P. Piquett, attorney for John Dillinger. He testified that he had helped to
keep this man in hiding, that he had advised him how to escape
officers, that he arranged for a hide-out in which he could be
concealed, that, through his efforts, a facial operation had been
performed on the bandit and an effort made to eradicate his
finger-tip patterns. All this, he said, was within his rights as an
attorney, because Dillinger was his client and he was attempting
to stave off arrest until he could "fix" a charge of murder which
hung over the man. Moreover, the judge ruled that an attorney
can assist his client in ways which an ordinary man might regard
as devious and still be within his rights, due to the fact that a
lawyer and his client have certain confidential relations. If that
is so, there should be some new rules. There should be nothing
confidential about crime, and the sooner the Bar Associations
realize it, just that much sooner will lawyers and judges regain
some of the repute which the last ten years has cost them.

A queerly clannish bunch, this group of men called attorneys.
To the main body, one must grant honesty. Nevertheless, they
see little that is incumbent upon them in the cleaning up of
their profession. Privately, they admit many transgressions by
renegade members. Publicly, many feel that they must stall,
evade, twist, turn, squirm, and actually lie to cover up what
everybody knows is a canker sore of crime. To this end, they surround their members with every protection but a barbed-wire
fence. The disbarment of an attorney, no matter how foul his
reputation, is almost equal to a cataclysm. Again Piquett is an
example.

The Federal Government finally got him, and, after having

fought the case all the way to the Supreme Court of the United States, made valid the puny sentence which he had received. This was done by proving that he had performed the same services for another bank-robber that he had given Dillinger — the exception being that the second hoodlum was not his client. After all this was over, he was disbarred from practice.

Previously, however, there had been charge after charge against Piquett. He was accused of graft, he was accused of being a go-between for the underworld and police of Chicago, where he was powerful politically, having once served as Prosecutor for Cook County. It was charged that he was a fixer for streetwalkers in the Morals Court. His general reputation was that of a pal of gangsters. He was a trickster. He was accused of having sold fake securities in Wisconsin. Former city employes alleged that he took money from them on the promise to restore their jobs to them, and failed to do so. Yet with all this as a background, it was necessary for the Federal Government to move against the man and convict him, before the bulwarks by which attorneys have surrounded themselves could be torn down and this crook disbarred from practice in Illinois. The citation, in part, is illuminating: —

That Louis Piquett was found guilty in the United States District Court for the Northern District of Illinois, June 6, 1935, upon the charge of conspiracy to harbor Homer Van Meter, and was sentenced to two years in the Federal penitentiary and to pay a fine of $10,000, that this conviction denotes a lack of good moral character, and tends to bring the courts of justice into disrepute and contempt; that the board recommended that the respondent be disbarred and his name stricken from the rolls of attorneys for the State of Illinois.

Ambiguous as legal phraseology must be to allow many of the dimmer lights of the profession to make a living, it does seem that the Grievance Committee might have been a bit more horrified at the things which Piquett did, rather than at the fact that he was convicted of having done them. Unconsciously, however, here is displayed a rule all too often followed in the legal profession; it is not what you do, but what you are caught doing. When lawyers awaken to the fact that they themselves should possess the necessary vigilance to determine whether or not a man is a proper person to serve as an officer of the court, the profession will resume an air of cleanliness.

The legal profession, wittingly or unwittingly, has done more to clog courts, to delay prosecution, to open prison doors, to surround criminals with legal and statutory safeguards, and to stultify justice, than any other single medium in our criminal history. One has only to look at the record of a man named Charles J. Fitzgerald to realize just how much a person can get away with when he possesses the necessary money with which to pay fees and thereby find representatives who "know the right people."

Mr. Charles J. Fitzgerald, alias Charles Morgan, alias W. M. Funk, alias Charles H. Lowe, alias J. C. Hammond, alias Frank West, alias J. C. Adams, alias "Chi" Slim, alias Big Charley, alias Long Charley, alias Slim Williams, alias Daniel Mathias, alias D. M. Logan, alias Charles Jordan, alias "Big Ben," and other monikers, served a term previous to 1898 in the State Reformatory at Hutchinson, Kansas. Since that time, he has been arrested in practically every state in America, and charged with everything from the unlawful transportation of explosives to the blowing of safes; the Federal Government recently sent him to Alcatraz Prison for life as a kidnapper. Previous to this final misfortune, however, with few exceptions, his record shows a continuous display of such notations as the following: —

As J. C. Adams, arrested Dallas, Texas, April 1909, charged with safe burglary. Released. After release, it was discovered that he was one of gang who blew safe and vault at Buffalo, Texas, April 13, '09. Also blew safe at Frankston, Texas.

It is one of the tricks of a professional criminal to get hold of an attorney at once, either to obtain release on bond or by *habeas corpus.* Charlie knew his lawyers. Charlie remained free, with few intervals, for more than forty years, during which time he was continuously engaged in a life of predatory crime. And yet there are judges who believe in themselves when they intone heavily from the bench, as they sentence six punks to death: —

"Crime does not pay!"

It paid Dr. William H. Loeser several thousand dollars. Dr. Loeser was a parole violator on a narcotic charge from Leavenworth. He is the man who performed the facial operation on Dillinger. He also mutilated the finger tips of a confidence man known as William Mead, for whom Post Office Inspectors had been searching for years. At last, Mead was arrested in Northampton, Massachusetts, under the alias of Carter.

The arresting officer saw that the suspect's finger tips had been altered. His true name was not known. The only charge upon which he was being held was that of false registration of an automobile, and a bail of two hundred dollars had been set. Frantically, the Sergeant of Police in Northampton telephoned about the country in an effort to effect an identification before the arrested man could furnish bond. No police department was aware of any charges against a person named Carter. Yet the Sergeant felt sure he held a dangerous criminal.

This was a case in which identification must be effected almost immediately. There was no time to send the man's fingerprints to Washington, inasmuch as it was almost certain that some shyster would appear shortly with bond money. The Sergeant called the Boston office of the Federal Bureau of Investigation. A Special Agent, upon going to the jail, examined the man's finger tips. It was plain that they had been mutilated, either by caustics or a knife. There is no law upon which a man can be held because he possesses mutilated finger tips — lawyers see that laws all lean the other way. While the Special Agent worked as desperately against time as the Sergeant to effect an identification, a runner for an attorney with a heavy gangster practice arrived with the bail and demanded immediate release. William Mead, who had fleeced victims from one end of America to another, walked free from Northampton Police Station on the promise, of course, that he would return for trial. Northampton is still waiting. Mead, after a further chase and the expenditure of thousands of dollars of law enforcement money furnished by tax payers, finally was caught by Bureau Agents and turned over to the Post Office Department. Dr. Loeser, who had made this man's escape possible, suffered only a return to Leavenworth for violation of his parole. As for the attorney "with a heavy gangster practice," it is possible that he did not know the identity of his client. Yet he was willing to risk two hundred dollars in cash — of somebody's money — on Mead's freedom. That the prisoner did not return for trial would indicate that this money was Mr. Mead's, and that the attorney might have given the police some valuable information. Perhaps that attorney lived in the safety of a viewpoint such as was described in a speech by Homer Cummings: —

Frequently prosecutors have gained information concerning an attorney which would warrant suspension or disbarment. A prominent and able state's attorney recently stated his willingness to coöperate with the Bar Association in this matter, but added that no request ever had been made of him for such information.

Thus the aides to crime go blissfully unpunished, unless they violate the rules of their own kind. The various taverns wherein gathered members of the Dillinger crew, the Barker-Karpis mob, Baby Face Nelson, and all the rest of that putrid clan, remain open and continue to form the hangouts for a dozen types of lawbreakers. At least one of the resorts has traveled into the keeping of the second generation, the founder having died and his son carrying on the good work. Another, run by an ex-convict who is known to every high-powered crook in the country, oper-- ates just as it operated when this place was a gathering spot for the Keating-Holden gang of train-robbers, back in the twenties

— never having closed, except for repairs. It must not be presupposed, however, that these supporters of crime are always of the lower strata. There was a certain priest who believed it his duty to be eternally near gangsters, going hunting with them or attending chicken fights, or generally joining in on their fun, for the good influence he might exert. Eddie Bentz, being the businesslike soul that he is, put a different construction upon these activities.

"Father tipped me off a couple of times. I used to take him out on a job once in a while."

Then there was Big Bill, the contractor of Hackensack, New Jersey. Everybody knew Big Bill and his bluff ways; he was called Bergen County's millionaire ex-milkman. He had standing in his community. The County Prosecutor's office used his taxis and contracting equipment. Captured contraband was dispensed of through his warehouses. As he was an influential, substantial citizen, county officers often confided to him just what plans they were making to proceed against bootleggers and the like. Big Bill was quite a fellow. Then one day, some gangsters, who didn't believe in social standing, shot him down.

Racketeering gangsters do not, as a rule, kill quiet, inoffensive citizens. Police proceeded upon the theory that Big Bill must have done something to offend the gentlemen of death. They dug into his record and found that for six years he had been an underworld fixer — bribing policemen, using trickery to detour contraband whisky out of his warehouses and back into the hands of booze-runners, and making himself generally useful. But at last he had promised to make the proper arrangements by which a large distillery could run, and for that had received eight thousand dollars with which he was to pay "the proper persons." Instead, he had kept the money. There had been a raid — and gangdom had felt very angry about it. So Big Bill had died.

In the same vein, there was some local sympathy in Indiana not so long ago for George Barrett, a bootlegger car-thief who was convicted and hanged for murdering a Special Agent of the

Federal Bureau of Investigation. A former Kentucky mountaineer, this man had shot and killed his own mother, and he
had beaten his sister to death, an act which resulted in such feeble
prosecution that the jury disagreed when Barrett pleaded self-
defense. The mountaineer was brought to trial again, and the
prosecution was such that the judge threatened the prosecuting
attorney with contempt of court. Nevertheless the weakness
continued; the defendant was freed, and straightway became a
bodyguard for the Commonwealth Attorney who had just finished prosecuting him. Thus, in after years, when Special Agent
Nelson B. Klein of the F. B. I. started on Barrett's trail as an
offender against the Dyer Act, the mountaineer depended upon
his political influence to aid him. It did. A hanger-on about
Police Headquarters came on the run to notify him that Special
Agents and police were about to attempt to take him into
custody.

Of course, there are grounds for wonder as to exactly why a
police hanger-on should be able to learn that George Barrett was
to be arrested. But such things do happen, and the hanger-on
brought his message in plenty of time for George Barrett to be
waiting for the agents, gun in hand. He began shooting. The
Special Agent fell mortally wounded. For that, there was no
weak county prosecution. No frustrated judge felt it necessary
to admonish the prosecution. No hints of political affiliations were
made. No job of bodyguard awaited George Barrett when the
trial was over. There was, instead, the United States Marshal
into whose custody he was given that he might be hanged. And
hanged he was.

Thus, a few times a year, professional criminals actually meet
the same fate as crime casuals and poverty-ridden accidentals
of law infraction. However, nothing seems to have happened
to the willing news-carrier, who, like an underworld Paul Revere,
sped out from Police Headquarters that he might warn this outlaw and allow him to prepare himself for murder.

Such examples could go on endlessly. Perhaps, however, the

story can best be told through the life of one man and his accomplishments. May I therefore introduce a pleasant rapist, known as William Harrison.

Willie was a good fellow — everybody said so — it was anything for a laugh with Willie. His record started in 1926, when he first was listed as a liquor runner in Calumet City, Indiana. Then, for a few years, he ran a tavern, frequented by businessmen, by politicians, and by hoodlums.

He was a great golf player — an expert, in fact. He often played with Al Capone and his brother Ralph, and other members of the Syndicate. Another partner was W. W. O'Brien, a Chicago lawyer, who, after years of affiliation with the gangster element, finally came to the attention of the Chicago Bar Association and last July was stricken from the rolls of Illinois attorneys. This was on a charge that he had received four hundred dollars from an Italian woman on the promise that he would have her husband's fingerprints removed from the State's Attorney's office, and another two hundred dollars to free her son from prison, he doing nothing about either. It seems rather unfair to disbar Mr. O'Brien for a petty thing like this, when for years he had represented the murderous Capone Syndicate which, through attorneys, accomplished some remarkably devious achievements.

While Willie Harrison was closely connected with all the heads of the Chicago Syndicate, he really was not a member. Willie was friendly with everybody, even the Mayor of a nearby town, who also was an active member of the Capone outfit. He was merely a good fellow of the type the gang liked to have around — to send down South to run a dog track, or start a tavern in a resort town where they had gained part control. Inadvertently, however, in 1933, Willie Harrison, who had a reputation for never believing a girl when she said "no," tried to rape one whose affiliations were as strong as his. So to escape the charge against him, he turned to the protection of gangdom. He knew nearly every big hoodlum in the business.

The Barker-Karpis mob was at its height. Willie Harrison became its contact man. He arranged hotel hide-outs. He lugged the women about. When the rest of the gang was away robbing a bank or kidnapping someone, Willie could always be depended upon to show the girls a good time.

Having been a booze-dispenser in various parts of the country, he knew other tavern and night club owners whose viewpoints were the same as his. Therefore, in the gang's movements about the country, it always depended upon Willie to stir up a good night spot where it could drink, pick up women, gamble, get drunk, and be safe. Willie's contacts were so excellent that several of these night club introductions led to police affiliations by which the gang remained in various cities for months at a time.

Willie, however, had one fault. He liked to talk. With a big cigar angled from a corner of his mouth, his hat slanted over one eye, his clothing a bit too jaunty to please the usually conservatively dressed crimester, Willie, in spite of his jokes, his dirty stories, and his ability as a procurer, became something of an impediment. There were times when gang members believed they could trace the activities of law enforcement agencies to Willie's loose-jawed habit of standing around bars and taverns and night clubs and, in the parlance, "belching his guts." By this time, the Barker-Karpis mob was hotly pursued by the Government. Under such circumstances, nobody likes to be burdened with a "blab-mouth." So, they decided to kill Willie.

This gang had lived because of Willie Harrison. He had brought tips of police activities, gained through his vast number of acquaintances. It had been he who had found them a haven after St. Paul had become too hot for safety; again, when Special Agents had begun to close in, it had been Willie Harrison who had stirred up contacts in Miami, through which the gang not only found safety, but met the persons through whom they were able to wash a part of the two hundred thousand dollars resultant from the kidnapping of Edward G. Bremer. But gangdom has one quality which might well be emulated by the more decent strata of society. It enforces its laws. Willie Harrison had turned blab-mouth. So Willie Harrison must die.

A part of the gang returned with Willie to some of its old haunts near Chicago. Then, on a night in January a year ago, a bunch of the boys took Willie out for a little ride. There was nothing of the motion pictures about it — no scowling, no guns in the back, no thin-shouldered "hoods" with upturned coat collars and low-visored caps. This was a crowd of good fellows, out for a little trip in the night air; and they had a surprise for Willie. It seemed, they said, that some of the Bremer ransom money was hidden in a deserted barn in the vicinity of Ontario-ville, Illinois. They'd all go there — dig up the "furs," as money is sometimes called in gangdom — and then put on a whale of a party. Meanwhile, did Willie know any new stories?

Willie did. Willie told them as they rode along. Everybody laughed like hell. Then they jumbled Willie into the old barn, shot him to death in a concerted blaze of gunfire, soaked his body with inflammables, sat his sprawling form upon a rafter, tipped back his gory head, jerked open his mouth, poured gasoline down his throat, and then set him and the barn afire. On the following day the charred outline of an apparently un-identifiable torso was found in the smoldering embers. The only possible identifying item was a wrist watch and a gold link bracelet which lay beside the body.

The Sheriff tried in vain to identify that watch. Jobbers were circularized without result. Microscopic examination was re-sorted to, which resulted in finding a jeweler's repair number, C-633, which had been scratched on the inside of the case. The Sheriff advertised these facts in a jeweler's magazine. It brought nothing.

Meanwhile, the Federal Bureau of Investigation had heard underworld rumors that Willie Harrison would blab no longer. Therefore, the thirty-seven field offices of the organization had been watchful for all unidentified male bodies. The Chicago office received reports of the finding of a charred torso near Ontarioville, plus the fact that a wrist watch also had been recovered. In its investigations the Bureau long ago had learned that Willie Harrison was addicted to a wrist watch, attached to a chain-link bracelet. A Special Agent was assigned to the case. He got the watch from the Sheriff's office. Then he hurried for the old stamping grounds of Willie Harrison, around Calumet and Hammond, Indiana.

Up one street and down the other he went in these two towns, displaying the watch and its repair number and asking at each place if the timepiece ever had been seen there. No one could give a clue.

Every shop listed in the telephone directory was exhausted, but the Special Agent did not give up hope. He became a repair shop detective, seeking out by word of mouth the addresses of any part-time watch repairers, any tinkers' or fix-it shops, where Willie Harrison might have taken his timepiece. Again the list was gone through. Finally the Special Agent heard of a little shop on a side street, run by a man whose name began with C. The Federal man glanced at the repair number, C-633, and hurried for the place. Was this his mark?

The man in the little shop looked carefully at the watch. He consulted his repair order book. He nodded.

"Yes, I repaired this watch. It needed a new mainspring."

"Is the name listed?"

The repair man smiled.

"Yes," he said. "It was a friend of mine. Funny sort of fellow, always laughing and bragging. Full of jokes and all that. His name was Willie Harrison."

So a case was marked closed in the files of the Federal Bureau of Investigation as being that of at least one aide to crime who had received something more than the usual judicial slap on the wrist:

"It is the sentence of this court that you remain on a year's probation. And may this be a lesson to you!"

CHAPTER EIGHT

ODDS AGAINST THE SUCKER

IT had been a stifling day in Washington, with the temperature at 106°, and the Potomac Valley steaming humidity which made the city all but unbearable. On the way to my hotel for the momentary respite of an afternoon shower, I asked the taxi driver: —

"How about a rate for this evening? To drive me out somewhere in the country for dinner, then a good long ride on the chance that the city will cool off by ten o'clock or so."

We had stopped at a red light. He grinned at me over a shoulder.

"Say, Pal, if you'd put that up to me yesterday, I'd have fell on your neck. I ain't interested to-day."

"Well, I suppose it isn't much fun, sticking at a wheel on a hot day."

"I wasn't thinkin' about that. You see, I was broke yesterday. But I'm in the dough to-day."

"Pick a winner?"

"I hit the numbers. And I mean I hit the numbers. I hit 'em for three grand."

I gasped.

"Three thousand dollars?"

"Sounds good, don't it? Boy, I needed that dough. I mean I needed it. And what do you think? The guy says to me, 'Larry,' he says, 'I don't take no ten per cent. commission on that win. It's all yours.' How's that for a square guy?" the driver asked. "Ain't he all right?"

"You were a regular customer; is that it?"

"I'll say I was; three years."

"Did you win often?"

We were now talking, regardless of traffic, the driver proceeding more by instinct than by the use of his faculties.

"Can you imagine it? This is the first time I ever knocked that game over. Three years I stuck to it, thinking every day, I'd make a killing. That's leaving out Sundays, of course. And I never hit it once until to-day. But I'll say this about them numbers guys; a lot of people say they won't pay you if you do win. Say, my friend handed me out the dough — just like that. All in twenty-dollar bills — it made a roll as big as your neck. Never a squawk" — he now was driving with one hand, the other being used for gesticulation — "not a cheep, and the guy don't take no commission; he's got a right to chisel ten per cent. Not a penny he takes. Is that a right guy!"

"Of course, you became pretty good friends in three years."

"Oh, sure. I've been one of his real customers. I always knew where I could find him if things got a little hot. You know, every now and then there's a yelp in the papers about all the dough these numbers guys are makin', so the police chase 'em around a bit. Maybe then the runners 'll have to work out of alleys, and the writers pretend they've closed up, except to fellows they know. There wasn't a day I couldn't buy a ticket — that's how much they trusted me. And when I win, they pay me like that."

I had been doing some mental computation. The numbers pay on a basis of six hundred to one, less ten per cent. commission to the man who sells the ticket, unless he is a magnanimous soul like my taxi driver's friend. Therefore, to have won three thousand dollars, the driver must have bet five.

"Was that your usual bet?" I asked.

"Never slipped once. Not once in three years," he added proudly.

"Thirty dollars a week? You don't make that much driving a taxi?"

"Hell no. On short jerks around this town you're lucky if you clear ten or twelve. But you see, I own my cab. I ain't got anybody else in with me. Result, I can work twenty-four hours if I have to. And say, I've had to. Lots of times I've gone without eating, but I've always put up that five bucks every morning. Then again, I've borrowed until they wasn't a driver in Washington that wouldn't run when they seen me coming. Then I'd go after it any way I could get it.

"There were the women, for instance. The heat's on strong here on hustlers; guess you know that. Still they got to live, now don't they? If there ain't anything doing in town, you'll find 'em propositionin' drivers to get 'em out to the joints in the country where maybe they can pick up a customer. Most of the drivers'll haul 'em for a lay; not me. I'd say, 'Baby, you might be the best hose since the Queen of Sheba, but I ain't interested. I got to have dough.'

"So, I'd make a deal to take 'em where they wanted to go. I'd wait for 'em an' bring 'em back if they didn't make connections. But if they grabbed a pick-up, they were to bull the guy into using my cab. Besides they'd give me my percentage of what they made off him, including my end of what they rolled him for, if they was that kind. Some of these dames are good that way — you know, see a drunk who's tryin' to get out of a place but can't stand up. Then they rush up and pretend to be a friend and help him to get outside, frisking him on the way. Then they leave him at the door and make for my cab and we hit for another joint. Well, I got half of that; a lot of cabbies don't like that kind of money; neither do I, maybe, but when you're desperate, you're desperate, and I'd made up my mind to beat the numbers.

"Then, of course, there's an awful lot of legitimate dames — ones that don't do anything but stay with a guy, one way or another. And I'll say this for all of 'em: there hasn't been one of 'em that's made a deal with me, but what she stuck to it. They're square that way. They don't want a bad name among the cabbies. They got too much to lose."

"So, one way or another, you got the five dollars a day."

"I'll say I did. You know, a bottle of liquor here and there, or pick up a stranger at the Union Station and run up forty cents on him instead of twenty getting him to a hotel. Besides that, I guess I've got more private hustlers on my stud-list — you know, girls working for the Government and just doing it now and then for a little dress money — than any other cabbie in Washington. I'd made up my mind to beat the numbers, and," — he shook his head savagely, — "by God, I beat 'em."

"Sure of that?" I asked.

We were in a traffic tangle; nevertheless he turned his head.

"I got three thousand bucks out of it!"

"Yes, but for three years, six days a week, you had been putting thirty dollars a week into the pot. Three years means one hundred and fifty-six weeks. Thirty times a hundred and fifty-six is four thousand, six hundred and eighty which you spent in order to get back three thousand dollars."

The taxi swerved.

"Christ!" the driver exclaimed. "You sure of that?"

I made the multiplication on a piece of paper and handed it to him. He clasped it in a grimy hand against the wheel, staring at it betimes as he started and stopped, stopped and started in obedience to Washington's jittery traffic signals. There was no comment for many blocks.

At last he grinned sheepishly, pulled at his cap, and said: "Yeh, I guess you're right. But they say when a guy's luck changes, he sure gets hot. Maybe I'll win the damn thing now three or four times running."

Therein, he expressed a phase of psychology upon which is founded the biggest profits ever known to the underworld. This comes through the wave of public gambling which has been gaining force ever since the beginning of the depression. The figures are amazing.

In cities which have conducted thorough, impartial investigations, it has been found that the totals in this new racket are far beyond the amounts spent even in the wildest days of Prohibition and bootlegging. The amount per capita is, in fact, at least seventy-five dollars a year, placed on bets, which means that much of it is turnover. That is not the amount wagered by each person who gambles, but it is the result of dividing the total sums by the aggregate of every man, woman and child in the city. There are comparatively few towns in America above a population of three thousand in which slot machines, punchboards, horse joints, the numbers, bolita, or some other form of lottery does not flourish. Therefore, assuming that all rural districts are free from the taint of gambling, — which they are not, — a gross population of about eighty million persons is dallying with six billion dollars in winnings and losings, of which all but about a billion goes through the hands of the underworld — where much, of course, remains.

A half-billion dollars of the "legitimate" gambling money goes to fairs, carnivals, county race meets, charities, and a number of small games of chance which are affiliated in no way with organized syndicates. The other half-billion is bet through legitimate channels on the races. Last year, for instance, Massachusetts' racegoers backed their hunches thirty-five million dollars' worth; Kentucky let go of about eleven million; Florida guessed about twenty-five million dollars' worth; California, always seeking to better its rival, took more than thirty million to and from the race tracks; while Michigan, Texas, Oregon, West Virginia, South Dakota, Nebraska, Nevada, Rhode Island, Louisiana, Maryland, Illinois, and other race-loving states contributed something like a hundred and ten million. This money was wagered in places where pari-mutuel betting is permitted and where it is possible accurately to gauge the amounts risked. Incidentally, it might be interesting to know that in one New

England district, where nearly a half-million dollars poured into races, in a single month, the majority of persons in the area were on relief.

Besides the pari-mutuel betting must be considered the bookie system of betting in New York, where, it is estimated, nearly three hundred million dollars were wagered.

This, according to the average man's belief, is all the money which went into racing, either through bookie or pari-mutuel systems. However, there was another "system" which made no reports, and which handled more money than all the race tracks combined. That was gangdom.

There was a time when the usual representative of crookdom who fell into the police net, felt it incumbent upon him to pretend some legitimate occupation. To-day, however, he settles the matter by stating that he is a "betting commissioner."

If he is a legitimate bookie he is, of course, entitled to be considered free from gangster affiliations — except, of course, for the fifty-dollars-a-day tax which so many of them are forced to pay on threat of getting their heads bashed in by the remaining members of Charles (Lucky) Luciano's gang. If, however, he runs a horse joint, which operates through any of the seven or eight big gangs which have split major control of the United States between them, he is a gang commissioner instead of a betting commissioner.

When you drop in at the corner cigar store and lay a two-dollar bet on the fifth race at Bowie, you may believe that this money by some magical means reaches the pari-mutuel machines at that race track and becomes an actual part of the betting money from which you are paid — minus, of course, the "service charge" which the horse joint may tack on for handling your bet. But, as Johnny the Guy once explained: —

"Now just why should th' boys give th' pari-mutuels a cut out of their dough? They're a pari-mutuel themselves. Think it over.

"Here's a bunch of guys that have practically got th' United

States in their mitt when it comes t' race-track gambling. They're tied up with every city that amounts to anythin', by long distance 'phone. If there's a hundred horse joints controlled by a syndicate in a town, do you think they're goin' to give a part of their take to Bowie or Havre de Grace?

"Pari-mutuel race tracks operate on a 'kitty' basis. They figure out what it costs for th' race meeting — how much is paid out in purses, how much it costs to hand out all th' passes that th' cops, th' City Hall, and th' State House wants, how much for dinners for politicians, how much for th' lobby that has to keep its eyes open all th' time to keep some apsay from introducin' an anti-racin' bill, how much for salaries, imported dicks from other cities to watch for pickpockets, an' all that sort of thing — an' take a percentage out of th' pari-mutuel. It's just like a poker kitty in a gamblin' hall.

"Now, if th' syndicates send in their money to be bet pari-mutuel, what are they doin'? They're contributin' to th' kitty, ain't they? Ain't th' answer simple? If pari-mutuels make enough money to keep big tracks runnin', doesn't it stand to reason that the same sort o' system would pay off th' same percentage to a big outfit which takes in money from all parts of th' country, an' pays it out again, without havin' to own a race track?

"So th' syndicates are really big pari-mutuels, except of course for tracks that have bookies. Th' money floods in from a hundred thousand horse joints around th' country. Th' syndicate has wires to every track, or gets its dope through th' News Service or th' radio, just like th' horse joints. It doesn't even need to bother at figurin' odds — th' tracks all do that. So when a race is run, every little horse joint pays off accordin' to what the pari-mutuels have paid, minus what chiselin' is done. Out of what's left, th' horse joint guy pays his expenses, whatever th' wire service is knockin' him down for, an' what th' syndicate takes. You'll hear a lot of these racin' officials squawkin' their heads off about how they're tryin' to stop ticker and radio service out of their tracks to th' horse joints. They say they're doin' it to keep gangsters from gettin' a foothold in th' racin' business. Maybe some of 'em are — there are a lot of white guys in racin'. But there's also a lot of 'em who are tryin' to stop it because it's cuttin' into profits. A lot of tracks ain't payin' hundred-per-cent. dividends like they used to. As for th' other bets, th' syndicates work th' bookie stuff just th' same as th' guys at th' tracks, win or lose."

Beyond Johnny the Guy's dissertation there have been other evidences of gangster activities at the tracks. The Narcotic Division of the Treasury Department contains many cases in its files pertaining to the doping of race horses. Its agents must be ever alert, through the saliva test, to prevent the needling of equine contestants. Practically every case ties up more or less closely with the activities of syndicates which deal in women, gambling, loan shark activities — and dope.

That the syndicates at least attempt to "handle" many races is evidenced by the number of jockeys who constantly are being admonished, fined, or suspended, in spite of the fact that race-track men, like lawyers, while admitting privately that conditions are rotten, would jump in the river before they would tell the truth to the public and make a real attempt to clean up conditions.

Theoretically the racing business is in the hands of capable stewards. Actually, however, it is controlled by a small group of undersized men of terrific power, the jockeys, the vast majority of whom are eager for only one thing: the winning of races. Nevertheless, there is the same element of human greed in jockeys as in other humans. Instances have developed in which riders can be "reached." While it is true that no rider can win races at will, there is no horse on earth which can win a race when his jockey has decided otherwise, nor when the trainer has given the word at the last moment that perhaps Auto Inn better be given the air to-day. Even a crooked jockey, unless he has seen enough money to make him rebellious, seldom violates training orders. Racketeers make their money at times by furnishing the carefully placed wise money which is on a winning horse at heavy odds. In the aggregate, however, they win through the horse which loses. It is far safer to bet against a horse which simply cannot seem to get going, than it is to endure the dangers of detection when an equine ice wagon suddenly becomes endowed with cocaine and the speed of Mercury. This recently became more apparent than ever in gangland attempts at a Maryland track to force certain horses to run badly by placing pieces of sponge in their nostrils, thus making it difficult for the racers to breathe.

It never seems to enter the heads of some racing stewards that among rough riding jockeys who crowd other horses, who pocket them, who cross the field, or who even may reach out and grab the reins of an opposing boy, one might perform this violation with some other thought in mind than a fevered desire to win a race. Even the fact that such a jockey might be riding a horse which couldn't win a turtle race apparently implies nothing but overzealousness. Yet it has happened that the gangsters, who virtually fatten from racing, have paid jockeys not to win and not to lose, but to cause the favorite to lose. If all jockeys are straight, it is because they are all either sainted or angels; certainly there is little of really stern discipline to aid them in avoiding temptation.

The jockey who is permanently "set down" becomes front page news, and there have been few stories of that type. The usual penalty for rough riding, for tricks at starting, or for unsatisfactory rides is rarely more than a suspension for the remainder of the meeting. Even the use of narcotics, until recently, brought only such slaps on the wrist as a suspension for sixty days. The reason is that jockeys are employed by wealthy men whose horses are necessary to the tracks, plus the fact that there are comparatively few jockeys, which brings the circle around to its completion. Because there is a dearth of little men who can ride, the ones who can do about as they please. It is rare that a big meeting proceeds to its conclusion with less than twenty admonishments, fines, and suspensions. That the jockey thinks little of such penalties is evidenced by the fact that he often attempts the very same tricks in the same track before the same stewards almost as soon as the penalty has been paid.

To beat the races, one must outguess gangsterism, divine the condition of the horse, the private feelings and morals of the jockey, and the ambitions of other riders. Beyond that, one must be able to read the owner's mind, the trainer's mind, the minds of various stable hands and hangers-on who, that morning, may have received a new shipment of narcotics. And if you do all this and keep at it long enough, the kitty will get you anyway, so what's the use?

This writer has spent the best part of his life in an atmosphere which included the tracks, gambling halls, gamblers, carnivals, merchandising wheels and every conceivable game of chance which exists. There is not a single one of them which cannot be "gimmicked" or "gaffed," so that the beating of it is an impossibility.

That includes everything from roulette wheels to the three nigger babies for which you get cigars — if you can knock them down. Transparent dice can be, and are, loaded.

As for cards, I have sat for hours with gamblers, as they dealt and redealt the deck, meanwhile admonishing me: "Now lean closer. Watch my hands. Could you see me when I did it?"

Not that they were giving an exhibition. They wanted a stooge, who would watch the movements of their swiftly flying hands and attempt to detect a false movement as they dealt seconds, thirds, and even fifths and sixths. A card shark rarely "deals from the bottom." Rather, he deals "down in the deck," holding out the cards he wants for himself at the top and giving other players the ones which lie beneath. This he does by being able to move the hold-out cards backward and forward so swiftly that the movement cannot be detected, until such time, of course, as he decides to deal these cards to himself.

Even the canes at which you throw a curtain ring can be gimmicked. So can all other games of chance, even to the amiable slot machine in the corner candy store. There is nothing in the world as crooked as a slot machine — unless it was an ex-convict named Paul Stanley, who received the attention of the Federal Bureau of Investigation about a year ago.

A complaint came from the Sheriff at Cairo, Illinois, that a man had entered roadhouses in various near-by towns, showed a badge announcing him to be a Federal Officer, and then confiscated the slot machines.

In each case, he had introduced himself as Officer Green, in the Government service. Through the aid of local officers, the ex-convict was caught, and sentenced to serve three years in Leavenworth prison — not because he took the slot machines, which he was selling to another syndicate, but because he impersonated a Federal officer.

The machinery of a slot machine is so intricate, so cleverly devised, that it can be set to bring in almost any profit desired. Perhaps the best evidence of the machines' capabilities arose in a recent case in the Midwest.

Some muddle-headed judge decided that if a person knew exactly what the machine was going to pay on the next play, it could not be classed as a gambling device. Almost immediately slot machines appeared which gave that information. There was a small aperture at the top into which either a zero or a number appeared with each play. Authorities were surprised to see that slot machine play became heavier than ever. The suckers had decided that if the machine was to pay nothing on the next whirl, then the one following certainly would be a big winner.

All this proves that gimmicks and gaffs could be explained forever without in the slightest affecting the person with the gambling itch. Perhaps, then, the fact that gambling in any form denotes something far more important than the loss of money is of interest.

Look about you in your town. If there are slot machines,
if there are horse joints, if there are roll-down games, or pin-
ball games which once were called "bagatelle"; if there are
punchboards, — and there never was a punchboard which paid
out more than about half what the customers put into it, — if
there are back rooms to cigar stores, if the numbers racket
flourishes, or if there is concerted gambling in any form whatever, then someone or some body of persons in your city or county
administration is crooked.

There can be no other interpretation. Either the District
Attorney's office is crooked, or the Mayor's office is crooked, or
the police are crooked, or the Sheriff is crooked, or they all are
under the domination of crooked political power. It is not possible for gambling to exist without freedom from interference by
the authorities, and that freedom is usually paid for in one form
or another.

This fact is so apparent that during a recent attempt to keep
the foothold which they had gained through some weird workings of a legislature, slot machine operators in Florida put on a
propaganda campaign. Their machines had been licensed by the
State; citizens were trying to beat that law. The main plaint
of the operators, on placards and in letters, was this: —

It is necessary in areas where slot machines are not legal to pay a
minimum of 20 per cent. in graft to local officials for allowing these
machines to operate. Is it not better for these machines to be legal than
that local officials should receive these bribes?

It is surprising how much protection may be obtained for
twenty or thirty per cent. of the take. A gambling house flourished in a suburb of a large Ohio city, controlled by a crowd of
politically affiliated racketeers who "had the town." It became
necessary for the District Attorney to ask that a warrant be served
there, and this warrant was handed to the Sheriff. The Sheriff
refused to act.

In this particular gambling house, Pretty Boy Floyd had received shelter. Alvin Karpis was a visitor and player as well as Fred Hunter, his partner in crime during his last days of freedom. Harry Campbell, another member of the Karpis gang, had frequented the place. Other gangsters had worked there as lookouts, guards, game-keepers.

The place, in this regard, was little different from any of the thousands of other gambling houses which flourish throughout America. They are hangouts for professional criminals, and are widely used as hide-outs. Practically every big kidnapper and bank-robber of recent years has worked at times in gambling houses, either as a dealer or in some other vital position. By so doing, they have had at least the indirect protection of the police, who, either having been paid or having received orders not to molest the place, of course molest no one within it. That was the status of the "club" in question. The Sheriff or someone who controlled him was getting part of the take.

Having failed to obtain the serving of his warrant, the District Attorney turned to the Commissioner of Police in a large city of the county.

"I wish you could do something out there at that club," he begged. "I want to put it out of business."

"What can I do?" the Commissioner asked. "It's outside my jurisdiction."

The District Attorney smiled.

"There are ways, you know," he said. "Any citizen, observing a violation of the law, can make an arrest."

The Commissioner nodded. Then he went downstairs to the police wardroom. A platoon of officers were going off duty.

"Gentlemen," he said. "There is a gambling place outside the city of which all of you are aware. You know that at various times it has harbored some of the most notorious criminals in America. You also must be aware of the fact that you have no jurisdiction beyond the city limits. However, I would like to know how many of you desire to volunteer as citizens to go out there, and, witnessing a violation of the law, attempt to do something about it."

The club in question was so well guarded against attack by other gangsters that it possessed, among other things, a machine gun on its roof. For a time there was a hint of armed resistance. But the sight of twenty policemen, marching toward a gambling house door for other purposes than a friendly visit, is not pleasant to contemplate. The doors were opened. Then they were closed again. The club passed out of existence. But within a month, while the Sheriff looked the other way, another club opened, with the same personnel and management, only a short distance away.

Thus gambling lives and thrives through protection. Slot machines are handled by syndicates, often operating a thousand miles from New York, Chicago, and other cities, which form their headquarters. Gambling houses as far away as Florida have their New York and Chicago angles, in that gangsters of those cities "own a piece of them." It must gall Al Capone, out in Alcatraz, to know that what he regarded as a petty thing now is a business which flourishes throughout America with an annual turnover of some five billion dollars. Capone's chagrin must be especially severe when he realizes that it was this petty sideline and not his main business of quenching the Midwest's thirst, which sent him to prison.

The technical evasion upon which Capone was convicted was that he failed to pay his income tax for six years on a total sum of $1,055,365.07, practically none of which was liquor money. Most of it had come from the profits of a single gambling hall, the Hawthorne Smoke Shop, in Cicero, Illinois, plus bookmaking profits from the Hawthorne Race Track, and affiliations with bookmakers throughout the country. Thus again Capone takes his place as a pioneer, in that, as a leader of gangdom, he brought into being the system which was to furnish a haven for his kind when Repeal apparently robbed it of the means of a crooked livelihood.

However, at the time the Hawthorne Smoke Shop opened for business, Capone regarded it only as "a good little money-maker." He and his gang had "taken over" the city of Cicero at an election. They used it partly as a headquarters, partly to provide "drops" for liquor and beer, from which they could be distributed to thirsty Chicago and points South and West, and partly for another venture: that of the first Syndicate-controlled bawdy houses.

In the main, all this was endured by Cicero. Al Capone had only two weapons: he bought and he killed. Of the two, he preferred the former. It was so much simpler, and there was no necessity of going unshaven for days or of sending a huge wreath with the streamer: "FROM AL."

Through purchase, he added a number of merchants and citizens to his list of legislators, Congressmen, State Senators, prosecutors, mayors, chiefs of police, city councilmen, ward committeemen, precinct captains, tip-taking policemen, and judges of municipal and state courts. To the merchants, he "threw his trade," and when one considers that in his hey-day Al Capone ate from gold plates, ordered suits in lots of twenty at one hundred and thirty-five dollars apiece not only for himself but for his associates and bodyguards, that his grocery bill was often a thousand dollars a week, and that there were few evenings when he did not invite at least twenty dinner guests, one may understand that Al Capone's trade was something to be sought after.

As for private citizens, he paid off mortgages, put in new sidewalks, contributed heavily to charities, and appealed generally to the larceny in the soul; most of us do not care about the origin of money, as long as we know the police are not eyeing our possession of it. Or, as an interior decorator who specializes in fifty- and sixty-thousand-dollar jobs for gambling houses, recently put it:

"I hate to do business with these rats. It's a crime, the way they fleece the public. It's all horribly revolting to me, not that

I'm against gambling, but against the type of human vultures who run the business. So, whenever I take a job, I make them pay me fifty per cent. down before I ever make a move, and the other fifty per cent. the minute my work is completed."

Upon this basis, hundreds of persons in Cicero "reviled" Capone, while thousands looked upon him as "a Modern Robin Hood." However, there was one group of property owners and citizens with whom he could not get together. This was late in 1929.

This group forced the Sheriff's office and police to make a raid upon the Hawthorne. That was an exciting day. The entire second floor, which was given over to roulette, blackjack tables, dice games, and "the Cage" or "chuckaluck," was dismantled and the equipment carried away, while Scarface Al stormed about in his fifty-dollar Sulka pajamas and even resorted to pleading, that some of his equipment might be saved.

There were free-for-alls and slugging, in which gangsters assaulted the citizens who led the raid, so intimidating them that they failed to appear for prosecution. However, during that raid, Al Capone had admitted to these men that he was the owner of the place, an important fact which was to link up with a piece of evidence found several years before, and forgotten.

That piece of evidence had been the usual little black book, which had been taken by police during a raid in 1926 when Capone was sought for the murder of Assistant State's Attorney W. H. McSwiggen. It had gone to the State's Attorney's office and from there to the Chicago office of the Intelligence Unit of the Treasury Department, where it had been filed with a number of unimportant papers, inasmuch as there was no tax case against Capone at the time. There it gathered dust for four years.

During all this time, Capone was making millions. There never has been a correct estimate on the amount of money which he garnered, and there is no way to determine how much of it now is being used by the various members of his gang who continue to operate in half a dozen cities of America. There are still Capone Syndicate dog tracks, Capone Syndicate night clubs, Capone Syndicate automobile salesrooms, Capone Syndicate money in distilleries under dummy names, Capone Syndicate horse joints and bookie joints and houses of prostitution, of which the Big Fellow has his piece, while sentimentalists weep over the fact that, out in Alcatraz, he is supposed to have written a mother song.

Investigators never have been able to get at this money. Neither were they able to find his Prohibition profits. The Big Fellow had no staple auditing system, he had no bank accounts in his own name, he bought no property as Al Capone and kept no safety deposit boxes which could be traced. But he did salt his money, and much of it is still salted. There is every probability that he never would have reached a Federal prison had it not been for that little black book and the insistence of one man, Herbert Hoover. When he became President, he was determined that the United States should do what local law enforcement had failed to do — remove Al Capone as a symbol of the underworld. To that end he prodded his various departments constantly. There must be some way, he insisted, to dig into the gang-overlord's Federal violations and through them, send him to prison.

The Prohibition Unit gave its usual imitation of the three Chinese monkeys: it saw, it heard, and said nothing. Its thousands of agents could not find the evidence by which to convict Mr. Capone. Meanwhile, automobile after automobile bearing tags which had been issued to Prohibition agents was observed to draw up in front of Mr. Capone's various headquarters in the Hawthorne, the Lexington, and the Metropole, while the owners of those tags strolled up to Mr. Capone's rooms, there to remain long enough to extend an itching mitt.

Since the Prohibition forces could gain no evidence, the President turned his pressure upon the Treasury Department. Elmer

Irey, head of the Intelligence Unit, was allowed free headway.
But there were many difficulties.

There were reports which had been made and jacketed; they
had gotten nowhere. There had been suggestions that Capone be
allowed to compromise his tax case; they had been turned down.
Matters seemed at an impasse. Then, in 1930, Chief Irey made
a sudden switch in the investigating personnel. He sent to Chicago one of his best Special Agents, Frank J. Wilson, recently
made Chief of United States Secret Service.

In the White House, the President asked for special reports
and got them. A short time after Mr. Wilson got on the job,
there was news of extreme importance. In digging into the various files in the Chicago office, Wilson had discovered that little
black book. It was established to be the "ledger" of the man
who handled financial transactions for the Hawthorne Smoke
House.

Special Agents hunted down this man, found him in Florida,
and persuaded him to talk. Other witnesses gave unwilling testimony. For the first time, a part of Capone's financial dealings
came to light, and by their figures prophesied the fortunes which
awaited Prohibition gangsters with the coming of Repeal.

In 1924, for instance, according to the little black book, the
Hawthorne Smoke Shop banked by devious means $300,250.94,
all of which was profit, inasmuch as bills were paid in cash.
Capone's share was forty-one per cent. or $123,102.89. By 1925,
the Big Fellow had increased his holdings to fifty-two per cent.,
due no doubt to the split-up, among various members, of the
thirty-six per cent. share held by Dion O'Banion, who had been
killed in his flower shop. Another partner also was listed. It
was: —

Cicero Town Officials for graft and protection. . . . 20 per cent.

The receipts for two years were all which the little black book
contained. The income for four other years, under which Capone
was prosecuted, was computed by running down the deposits

made by Capone men who were plainly affiliated with the gambling and slot machines. In one year Capone's share ran to a quarter of a million dollars. That may give a faint idea why to-day there is more money invested in gambling paraphernalia than at any time in history, not even excepting those good old days of the California and Colorado gold rushes.

It also is the reason why, now and then, one sees the story of a mayor being beaten up by members of the underworld or a state representative being shot. Perhaps they hadn't played ball as the Syndicate thought they should do, or had refused to allow gangster-controlled games in areas under their jurisdiction. There is, in the history of the Capone case, even a murder plot against influential servants of the United States Government.

The President, receiving reports of progress at every Cabinet meeting, one morning heard some disconcerting news. This was in November, 1930, and until this time there had been much favorable information. Witnesses were being hidden against the efforts of Capone to intimidate them; one had even been sent to South America, there to await the day when the Big Fellow could be brought to trial. Others were under guard. Jack Guzik, one of the financial men, had been tried and convicted of income tax evasion, the testimony regarding him also having come from revelations brought about through the little black book. With every evidence of progress, the President had issued orders that the drive be carried on with even greater intensity. The Chief of the Intelligence Unit was making frequent trips to Chicago to heighten the enthusiasm of his men. Then had come the amazing information that Capone, fearful at last that he would be caught and convicted, had decided to end Governmental activities. He had imported five gunmen from New York, with orders to murder the United States Attorney, the Special Agent in Charge, the Investigator for the State's Attorney's Office, and Special Agent Frank Wilson. This information had come directly from Wilson. And Wilson was not the type of man to send in idle rumors.

The Government did the thing by which it has gained the respect of gangdom. The very men whom Capone had marked for death were started upon an active chase for Capone himself, to bring him in, together with his imported gunmen. The State's Attorney's Office was notified, as it was necessary to procure the aid of a number of Cook County detectives for raids to be made and resistance to be given to what, in effect, amounted to an armed threat against the power of Federal law enforcement. But Capone could not be found, and it was learned that his five imported gunmen had been sent hurriedly back to New York. Mr. Capone had received full information of all the plans of the United States Government's counteroffense through a Cook County detective — who had been paid by the Big Fellow for his information.

Perhaps that is only so much narrative, except that it should remind you again of the surface eagerness of the Government to coöperate with local officials and to reveal the real reason why, privately, the Government wishes it could at least, choose its men. After all, when even a person who plots a mass murder can own his messenger boys in local enforcement, it is not pleasant for the intended victim.

Again, all this might be ancient history except for one highly important point. Where there was once only the Hawthorne Smoke Shop, sometimes known as "The Ship" or "The Subway," there are now thousands of such places, not only in the vicinity of large cities, but even extending into municipalities of forty and fifty thousand population. The "take," in many an instance, exceeds, by far, the modest one of the Smoke Shop. High-powered methods have been introduced to force the amount of play into the bigger brackets. The feminine touch has been added.

All that requires a chapter of its own.

CHAPTER NINE

THE HOSTESS RACKET

EACH night, here, there, everywhere throughout the United States, hundreds of thousands of girls and women primp with thoughts of profit and prepare for labors of solicitation.

They run the gamut of age and appearance, from the excited youngster eager for adventure, to the pre-aged hag, stagnated by every possible experience that can befall a woman. They are girls from the country, girls from mill towns, girls from farming communities, girls from steel centers, girls from department stores, girls from drab or mediocre homes. They are girls who farm the children of early marriages out to caretakers that they may feed, clothe, and shelter them by what happens during the night. They are girls of good backgrounds whose derelictions have led to broken family ties and additions to the lengthy police rolls of missing persons.

However, in spite of varied beginnings, they all have two things in common as they dab their lips, pluck their brows, enamel their nails, and paw for the mascara. Sisters of the evening dress, the returns of their night depend entirely upon how successful they may be at making sex pay. And almost invariably the surroundings in which they seek their wages of "sin" will be at least next door to crime, if not locked tight in its arms.

How many girls and women there are who make a nightly living by providing "companionship to lonely men" cannot be computed. There is no census, no "hostess association" to gather statistics, and little general knowledge of the working methods of a great army of women described so expressively by the underworld as "tease gals."

The average hostess is exactly that. She may tell her mother that she is merely a taxi-dancer. Another may explain her presence in a tavern by saying she is merely another type of waitress. Still another may silence parental fears — if the parents are so unusual as to be concerned over her source of income — by insisting that her work in a night club is merely that of entertaining lonely gentlemen who desire a companion at the table, someone to whom they can talk as they eat. But the underlying truth is that she is there to arouse the sex instincts of men and, by so doing, increase their money-spending desires. The Anti-Saloon statisticians estimate that fully a million girls are employed in the United States as barmaids. This writer, having had opportunity over a period of years to observe the dour enthusiasm with which the Anti-Saloon League exaggerates anything which will serve its purpose, believes these figures to be as grossly in error as the Anti-Saloon League's belief in Prohibition. However, there can be no doubt that barmaids, "shillabers," "cappers," hostesses and all other forms of feminine association with liquor number fully a million. The taxi-dancer is far more interested in selling drinks than she is in selling dances — not to promote the use of Demon Rum, but because she gets a percentage on the drinks and also a part of the six dollars an hour which the house charges a man for sitting out dances with a hostess. A girl capper for a gambling house sells liquor because she also gets a cut on everything the sucker loses when he gets drunk enough to become reckless. But more important than the selling of liquor is the purveying of the proximity of sex.

There is no misguiding of innocence about the vast percentage of "tease workers." Ninety per cent. of all places which use feminine attractiveness as an aid to business do so upon a definite basis of understanding. Sometimes the orders are given by insinuation, leaving to the discretion of the girl the amount of money she earns by sex promotion. With syndicates, however, there is no beating about the bush. A girl knows what she is supposed to do. If she does not do it, she is fired and that's an end of it. Perhaps the girls themselves — or at least, a digest of carefully garnered information from them — can best explain. The girl of the "tease" dance hall reveals: —

"Sure, I know what I'm here for. I'm here to make a fellow believe that he's going to be able to take me out after a while and get me up to his room. I'm supposed to let him feel me just enough to get excited. My orders are to call him 'honey' and 'darling.' I'm not supposed to kick if the customer's hand moves down under the table and feels my leg. I'm supposed to tell him that if he'll stick around until three o'clock, and buy tickets for all the dances, maybe I'll sneak up to his room with him and pay him back for being so nice to me. It's up to me to do as I please about that. I'm free after three o'clock."

The microphone travels on to the girl in a night club, and frankness engendered by many conservations: —

"We get a percentage on all the drinks that are sold any customer we're with. It's up to us to kid the customers into buying as many as they can hold. Of course, we mustn't make a show of ourselves, and we're supposed to know what to do to keep a customer from being rowdy. It's all right, late at night, when other people are drunk, if he loves us up, and puts the heat on. Until that time, we're supposed to limit him to feels under the table and maybe locking legs a little. Our hours are from ten o'clock at night until four o'clock in the morning. We're docked if we show up late. We're not allowed to leave the place with anybody, not even at quitting time; if we want to meet them around the corner, we do it, although the management doesn't like it: we might go crazy over some fellow and stop coming here. We're supposed to wear as sheer clothes as possible, cut low enough in the front to show our breasts when we bend over, and to bare our backs down to the waist line. We're not allowed to drink anything but what they call 'coasters,' which couldn't get anybody drunk. If we want a real drink, we have

to sneak it. And if we get plastered, we're fired. We're supposed
to get the customer high, not ourselves."

From the night club to a cocktail room, and again a basis
of understanding makes for frank conversation: —

"Sure, the management figures we're tarts. But what is the
management going to do about it? They've opened up these
places to both men and women and you can't have a morality
test for customers. As long as a woman conducts herself all
right, it helps business for girls like us to be around. We're
well dressed. We're quiet. We don't actually do any soliciting
— that is, we don't wink at men, or ogle them, or anything
like that. You can do plenty with just an understanding smile.
So men who are looking for what they want come in here, buy
a few drinks, pick their girl; and, when they leave, they walk
slowly down the street. We pay our checks about the same
time and meet them on the corner. It's a lot more convenient
than ordinary streetwalking — and it's nicer, since you don't
have to beg a man to come stay with you, and you don't get in
trouble with the police, and it sells drinks. So everybody's
satisfied."

And there was a private conversation with a bartender: —

"Well, I'll tell you the reason we moved from that other
dump. It was too far from the hotel district. You see, you've got
to go where the business is. What the hell does the boss care
about selling drinks to this fellow and that fellow when he can
concentrate his business? Get what I mean?

"You know what the boss was before he went into the booze
racket. He was a lousy pimp. And he still is, as far as I'm concerned; changed his racket a little, that's all. He still knows
every clip girl in town and he still lives off them, only the
method's different.

"I guess the boss has got a hundred dames working for him,
all damn good-looking and smart as hell and all of them clippers. Well, they hang out in pairs around hotel lobbies. That
gives the sucker his pick of two babes instead of one. Besides this,

it's a stall in case the house dick can't be fixed — although that
doesn't happen so often. Two dames sitting together have always got the alibi that they just dropped in to wait for a friend.

"Anyway, they're there. Along comes the sucker, in town
overnight and out for a time. He sits down in an opposite chair
and the first thing he knows, he gets an eyeful of legs. You
know, a dame doesn't have to put on a burlesque show to give
a guy a good idea what she's got — not if she's smart. At first
they won't let him think that they even know he's on earth.
But at last, one of 'em gives him the glad eye and there's a
pick-up.

"Now, he's hooked with two dames. One of them's hot for
him. The other isn't. The warm babe has got her arm locked in
his and she's rubbing up to him as they leave the hotel. He
knows that if he can get rid of the other dame, he can lay this
one as easy as falling out a window. So he asks his girl how in
hell they're going to ditch the friend.

"She doesn't know. They were going to a picture show together, she says. But maybe if they walk back toward the apartment where the kid lives, they might be able to park her there.
So they start to walk. The girl that's going to be ditched puts
up a hell of a squawk. She wants to go to that picture show and
her pal promised to go with her. The other girl tells her not
to be a short sport, and she says sure, she doesn't want to do that.
Then, all of a sudden, she gets thirsty, and where she happens
to feel that way is right in front of this joint.

"By this time, the other girl has apparently gone for the guy
like a load of potatoes. She's all snuggled up to him, with one
hand under his coat, and her fingers working through his vest
buttons, to tickle his chest. He's burning up. So when the cold
dame says she wants something to drink, he says hell yes, he'll
buy her a drink; he's willing to buy her a flock of drinks since
she's said she wants to be a good fellow and leave 'em to their
fun. So they all come in here. The dames get just enough booze
in their glasses to be able to stall the guy that they're drinking

— the rest of it's ginger ale or water. The guy gets a double shot. The first thing you know, he's drunk. Then the dames begin buying wine on him. The score usually runs from thirty to a hundred bucks — whatever we think he'll stand. The babes get twenty or twenty-five per cent. commission. The guy never gets his lay; hell, he's lucky if they don't stall him into a taxi-cab, roll him for the rest of his dough, and leave him waiting outside some joint while they pretend to go to the toilet and sneak out the back door."

From the barroom, the story of the hostess racket progresses to a one-room-and-kitchenette apartment on the first floor of a brownstone front. There are two chairs, an aged phonograph, a bare, waxed floor. Nowhere is there a couch or anything else upon which one can recline. In the window is a Neon light which announces: "Dancing Lessons."

If one goes there frequently enough and is sufficiently shrewd at interrogation, the running story will piece itself into the following: —

"No, you've got this place wrong. You can't take a girl to bed here. I'm strictly decent. Of course I know there are places that advertise like this merely as a front for prostitution, but this isn't one of them. I just give dancing lessons. The police come here every day and look me over, because there's been an awful drive on white slavery here and they're on the lookout. But there isn't anything of that kind here; there isn't any place where a person could lie down, even if they wanted to. Girls like me don't want to. We're not that kind.

"I work for a syndicate that's got two or three hundred of these places scattered through town. I don't know who runs the syndicate. I think the same people run it that have been interested in those bawdy houses; I don't know. Several of the girls have wanted to make more money and they've spoken to the collectors and they've gotten jobs for them all with madames.

"The hours here are from ten o'clock in the morning until ten o'clock at night — that keeps it decent and the police don't kick. The reason I've got that kitchenette and dining table is because I cook my meals here. A girl's not supposed to leave, once she gets here.

"The charge is three dollars a lesson. You get a half-hour for a lesson. If you just want a dancing lesson, you can get that. If you want me to shake it for you, I'll shake it. A lot of my customers like shaking. You can't get it in any dance hall in town on account of police regulations. But here, of course, a policeman has to ring the bell first, and it only takes a second to switch from shaking to regular dancing. I can throw it up to you real nice if you want it. A lot of my customers would rather come here than go to one of the regular bawdy houses. In the first place, I'm not a chippy. And there isn't any danger of catching a disease, is there, if you get what you want by keeping all your clothes on and just rubbing against a girl. And I don't know what you're doing, do I? You know, I've got an idea but I don't know just exactly what's happening. So I'm not anything like a whore, am I? And it's so much safer for both of us."

Recently there has been an extension of this technique, reaching into some dance halls.

The mayor of a Chicago suburb was tried on a charge of malfeasance in office for allegedly permitting such dances. He was acquitted. Thirty days passed. The place ran full blast again — in appearance, merely a suburban dance hall, but in reality a public rendition of the one-room, brownstone-front apartment. One girl, aided by several drinks, was quite frank about her job: —

"Why call me a chippy? I never had my clothes off with a man in my life. Sure we rub 'em up. That's our orders. Either we shake it or get fired. When the men get you over against the wall, and really finish up on you, we call that the Limit. The management doesn't let us wear panties, and the only reason we wear bras is because one of the girl's mothers threatened to sue the management because a drunk had pinched the girl's titty until it was bruised terrible. Huh? Oh, I don't know that it's so bad working here. I worked in a tavern for a while, serving drinks. I never knew whether men came in there for drinks or to feel my leg when I served 'em in the booth. Only I get more money here; men like shake places. I get fifty per cent. of what I earn; sometimes if you get three or four old fellows in a night, you really make money. The young one's aren't so good. They go too quick."

The trail of the hostess travels on, into a supposed night club — merely such to the average patron, but leading, by broad stairways and deep carpeting shielded by heavy draperies, to an increasing air of brooding quiet. Here the subdued music of the night club has faded; the clink of dishes and silverware passing into nothingness. Finally there is a door which tosses back memories to the twenties, with a little sliding window, set heavily in steel. And the press of a button, bringing into view the glowering eyes of a man who pretends not to know the hostess with a sucker in tow; the door swings open into a gambling hall, brewing with luxury. If one comes to know the accompanying girl well enough, there is the casually amazing confession:

"All of us girls have different systems. That is, they are different except that we all make the men believe we're going to give him something he wants. The more he wants it the easier it is to make him lose his money. We get a percentage, you know.

"Some of the girls try to shame their customers into playing. That makes them gamble because they believe that if the girl thinks they are cheap-skates, they'll run out on them and not take them home to bed with them after they're off work. It all begins and ends in that, you know; the gambling's all incidental. If a person is really crazy about gambling, he doesn't want a girl around to distract him. The others have to be wheedled into it, and that's why the place has us girls. There are a lot of girls who work the same way I do. I get a gentleman a little tight and make him think I want him as badly as he wants me. When he gets to propositioning me to sneak out of the place with him, I suggest we come up here and gamble while I try to think of a way I can take him home with me without losing my job. I rub against him a lot when he's playing, and keep him hot. When he comes back at me about sneaking out, I whisper to him that I've thought of a way. If he should happen to make a big winning, I tell him the management will be darned glad to get rid of him before he breaks the bank, and ease us both out. It always works, especially if he's a little drunk; and he plays until he's broke. Then it isn't my fault if I can't go out with him, is it?"

If these statements seem too glibly given, it must be understood that they are summaries, not individual statements, and that they come from interviews with more than two thousand girls of dance halls, night clubs, gambling joints, cocktail bars, taverns, roadside "Dine and Dance" places, barbecue stands with "hostesses," and every other form of endeavor where proprietors, often under syndicate control, depend for a large part of their profits upon what is nothing more or less than mental prostitution. It is a type of feminine confidence game, racket-born, racket-encouraged, racket-extended, in which a woman is not averse to allowing a man to express sexual desire for her, and in which she pretends to be as eager as he, thereby inveigling him into the spending of money. In greater or lesser degree, the condition exists from one end of the country to the other; in some places it may take the mild form of mere jovial association. In others the gamut is run to the use of knockout drops or the "rolling" of drunken victims, picking of pockets, catch-as-catch-can prostitution, blackmailing, and a dozen forms of robbery, all brought about by hostess solicitation.

Of course there must be exceptions. That is what makes the entire business so beset with trickery, crookedness, invitation to bribery of public officials, and deceiving to the general public. If the whole hostess business could be justly assailed, the evils of it could be wiped out. But there are decorous places and decorous hostesses; all cannot be classed as bad. Moreover, the racket is mercurial in the extreme, what obtains one day may present itself in absolutely opposite fashion the next. Evidence can be gathered only by the most astute work. The policeman in uniform who attempts to inspect a crooked dance hall has little chance of success.

The most ribald of "tease" taxi joints can be transformed into a place of greatest sedateness, all in an instant. All that is needed is a warning. Instantly, strangle holds are broken, men's hands are raised from buttocks, abdomens which an instant before squirmed against each other are withdrawn to a decorous distance; a jumble of sex becomes the abode of pleasantly polite association. There is no dance hall that operates upon the booth system, or that permits the "shake," which can also be entered directly from the street. One usually must go up a flight of stairs, there to be stopped by the girl at the ticket window, then by the she-pirate in the cloakroom, and after that one must pass the inspection of a dinner-jacketed lookout at the door. At any instant of this time, a bell need only tinkle beside the chair of an inside watcher. Immediately he flashes the signal that everything "be on the up and up." A wriggling mass of humanity becomes a respectable dancing hall, and a syndicate has another laugh up its sleeve.

Again it must be stated that there are numerous dance halls which are properly conducted. There are cities which maintain rigid inspection. There are others which demand that it be possible to look in upon dancers without going through a routine which would serve as warning. In many places booths are barred. Beyond this, there are independent dance hall owners, night club owners, dancing academy owners, tavern keepers and other proprietors who hire female companions with express instructions that they be there merely as feminine ornamentation and not as persons to emphasize sex. But for every one of these, there are a score who engage girls with but one idea in mind. That is the purveying of drinks, or dances, or communion in the darkness of booths, or the heightening of the gambling instinct by emphasis on sex. In the words of J. Edgar Hoover, Director of the Federal Bureau of Investigation, the hostess racket is one of the worst and most degraded forms of crooked chiseling in America.

The entire hostess set-up of to-day, especially in its relationship to crime, is an outgrowth of Prohibition days, and of syndicate management of speakeasies. In the early twenties, it was discovered that men would drink more if they had women to prompt them to do so. Speakeasies introduced the café hostess, usually a prostitute, young or passable in spite of age, who would arise from the depths of a speakeasy and come to a table when a lone man walked in. At first only the lowest of dives used such persons; then they advanced to drinking places a few steps above. They never invaded the more sedate speakeasies, just as they never have invaded the more sedate night clubs of the present day. With Repeal, they entered into a new era of activity.

Now, in many cities, certain night clubs actually advertise that you can summon a girl to your table, merely by a nod. Such clubs are usually under the management of the syndicate which is politically protected in that city, and such advertisements amount to little more or less than public invitation to play at the game of "tease" with the inevitable "25 — Beautiful Hostesses — 25!"

Viewed in its essentials, all this is little more than a return to ancient devices which the average person regards as quite abhorrent when he reads of them in the olden days of the West. In other words, the present-day hostess is nothing in the world but an up-to-date dance-hall girl, of the same type which "worked the boxes" in the honky-tonks of Denver or San Francisco. She wears present-day clothing and she has present-day ideas; she rides in an automobile instead of an open-necked hack. Instead of wearing short, fluffy dresses which show her legs, she wears the more amorously clinging silk and prefers to show her back. Beyond that there is little difference.

There were good girls who worked as dance-hall girls in the old days. They didn't make as much money as the others, but they kept their virtue, whatever that was worth. There are good girls working to-day as hostesses; but it is doubtful, under the present standards of morals, if as many of them are as miserly concerning their hymens. The old-time girls got a commission on all the drinks they sold, and a percentage on the losses which they brought about for some drunken miner at the gambling tables. There are no more drunken miners, so the present-day business comes from drunken playboys of all trades and professions; the commissions remain the same. The old-time girl often worked in a place where there were convenient rooms near by, equipped with a bed, a washpan, and other necessities. The same conditions can be found to-day, with the addition of running water. Present-day night clubs are sometimes conveniently located on the first floor of assignation hotels. The old girls were limited as to their hours of freedom. So are the new ones. The old ones were advertised on placards or on throw-aways, tossed about the various saloons. The new type is advertised in rotagravure, and in give-aways to be found in hotel rooms. And to-day's girls aren't as tough under the wings as the ones of olden times.

Of two thousand or more girls interviewed in a cross-country tour, few were more than twenty years of age. Many were seventeen. All were perfectly aware of what they were doing and accepted it: the entire two thousand could be summed up in the psychology of a girl who had testified at the trial of a "shake" hall proprietor charged with permitting lascivious dances.

The newspapers had depicted her as a slave of a "gilded dance palace," forced by a brutal manager to dance according to his likes or walk the streets, searching for a job in vain. As it happened, she already had a job, which was that of working at odd times in a lingerie shop. She was holding on to it until she could decide where she could make the most money, in the shop or in a "love-booth" joint.

This girl was nineteen. Her father and mother had been divorced when she was a child — rather, as she put it, they had stopped living together. She had two sisters. One of them had married the manager of a grocery store, the other was working in Chicago. She had been working in such places as this since she was sixteen.

In her conversation there was none of that note which appeared in the newspapers when she supposedly told of "her dread life in a vice den." The better the ability to paint femininity as recoiling from the advances of men, to picture girls as panting in their struggle for virtue, weeping out their eyes at the thought of being forced to adopt a life of sin — the better the ability of a reporter for this sort of sobby untruth, the oftener he is assigned to beats where things are happening. This girl was typical of thousands one may meet in night clubs, in taverns, dance halls, hostess joints — hard yet queerly soft, sophisticated, yet as naïve as the kid she was, and above all philosophical. If this was the way to make a living, well, this was the way to make a living. That she might be working for the Syndicate which continued to carry on for one of America's most publicized lawbreakers during his incarceration in prison, brought merely the polite rejoinder: —

"Yeah?"

Nowhere is this attitude toward a syndicate more casual than that of the girl who works in a combined night club and gambling hall. During the last year, this combination has increased a thousandfold; beginning in the vicinity of Chicago, it now is spreading until there is hardly a city which does not possess, either within its boundaries, or in adjacent outlying territory, from one to a hundred places which are equipped with every sort of gambling device, and with the girls whose job it is to see that men play for stakes. America is on the worst gambling spree in history; the mixing of night club entertainment with games of chance plus the feminine angle is a recent development. Gambling has moved up in life since the old days of Al Capone and the Hawthorne Smoke Shop. It has become much more decorative. But it remains, to a large degree, in the hands of gangsters.

There are thousands of persons who patronize some night clubs without the slightest knowledge that they are going to gambling joints. The downstairs is in the old tradition; it may be one of those places too snooty even to possess "25 — Beautiful Hostesses — 25." It may have the best orchestra in town. It may be quiet and "refined," and observe all the proprieties. It may be such a place as one I know which has the society element of a certain big city by the tail — society not knowing, of course, that its proprietor and his whole family were so tough that they once were run out of a Midwestern city. It may be the type of spot sought by persons who desire to get their names in the gossip columns as having been seen there. Nevertheless, in many instances, it may possess a second floor devoted to every possible kind of gambling equipment and where there is practically no limit on the play. There is hardly one of these, in the large cities of the United States, or in the suburbs, which is not showing a profit of at least a quarter of a million dollars a year. And there is not one of them which, in some degree, is not paying for protection. If less than a half-billion dollars annually is being spent on this type of forgetfulness by law enforcement, then, indeed, prices have fallen.

When one talks to the hostess in such a place as this, he realizes how wise the young brain can become, how clearly aligned along thoughts which at least condone criminality. The usual calm, self-possessed hostess of nineteen may not know the terms of the gambler. She may not be able to recognize a "drop-case" or a "flat-joint" if she meets them on the street, and she may think that a "store" is a place where goods are sold and a "high pitch" something concerning baseball. But despite this lack of technical knowledge, she knows more about being a true "shill-laber," or steerer of suckers, than any professional capper in the business. This is mainly due to the fact that she uses a weapon which male cappers do not possess. Her prime job is first to muddle the head of the victim with thoughts of sex. After that her methods may be shrewd or crude; it matters little if she has been able to achieve her first goal. And if one approaches the subject carefully, she will tell all about her job, and with a certain degree of pride. Nor is that attitude confined to the girl in the gambling hall. The average hostess has little time to talk about herself, especially when her dealings are mostly with men who are bent on convincing her that their wives are invalids.

Certainly it is not possible to go out and ask any given number of women a set of questions and expect revealing answers. It is possible, however, through the careful and painstaking building up of a status of common understanding with taxi-owners, tavern keepers, bartenders, dance-hall owners and the like, to obtain a like basis with the women with whom they run. In a tour of countrywide interrogation, there were casual conversations, highly interesting ones, many differences in speech and mannerisms. But one theme ran throughout the entire route, from coast to coast. That was the proximity of crime.

Every girl knew someone who had "been in trouble." Sometimes it was a member of the family, sometimes it was the "boy friend," sometimes it was a girl with whom this hostess had worked. Crime eternally poked its head into the conversation. There was an inherent hatred for policemen, unless the officer happened to be a bedfellow. There was an abiding philosophy of defeatism, which did not exactly show on the surface, but which took form in a certain air of resignation, as though this girl had wanted much and received little; she did not differentiate between wanting and discerning. And in too many cases, the crime was even closer: the girl herself had a record, even though it never had been written up on a police blotter.

There are so many ways in which youthful femininity can engage in crimes, which all too often never reach the attention of law enforcement. One finds this especially true in such places as Florida, where women, reaching the dregs, become the "hostesses" at what are known as "jukin' joints." If you never before have heard the name, it is a Negro term, originally designed to describe a gathering at which everyone gets drunk, dances wildly, and usually gets in a fight. The popularity of this form of amusement caused whites to copy it; "jukin' joints" now exist by the hundred, with the coarser touches which the white person can give to anything adapted from the Negro race.

In the "jukin' joints" there is, of course, the prime requisite of liquor. The joint itself may be merely a thatched shed or ramshackle building in which the music comes by radio. Once the dancing and drunkenness has started, the "hostesses" move in. In taking this name, they become inimical to the true member of the hostess racket. They do not tease. They offer, and consummation may often be obtained for as low as twenty-five cents.

The same is true in many instances where "dine and dance" pavilions are operated in conjunction with tourist camps. This form of hostelry should be made the subject of rigid investigations. Often poorly run, rarely policed, badly supervised, many tourist camps are merely houses of assignation and cater to little else. If there were enough tourists to accommodate the hundreds of camps which cluster about every large city, then indeed traffic would become congested. All take tourists, of course. Likewise, many are not at all averse to the patronage of customers — too often boys and girls — who come there for sexual or drinking purposes only.

I drove out of a western city one night last summer with a Sheriff, and a chief of police. Presumably we were merely headed for a ride, but a short distance out of town the Sheriff wheeled his car down a side road and stopped before a tavern.

Music blared from within. Through the half-open door we could see a struggling mass of young couples on the dance floor, legs entwined, hands on buttocks, bodies pressed tightly together. Many "tongued" each other as they danced, lips clasped in a light suction.

Outside the door were three young people beside an automobile. One, a fifteen-year-old girl, was vomiting; two boys, both sodden drunk, were holding her head.

The Sheriff called a Deputy from the door.

"You haven't been able to keep many out?" he asked.

The Deputy shook his head.

"No, I show 'em my star and tell 'em to go home. But that's all the good it does, and the proprietor laughs at me."

The Sheriff shrugged. I learned then that he had been trying for months to close this place. "Astute" lawyers and most profound courts had prevented him. All he could do was station a deputy at the door to beg youngsters and others not to enter. That accomplished little and kids continued to get drunk. Tourist camps, incidentally, were not far away. Even while we watched, a young pair, thoroughly drunk, announced their intentions, entered their car, and careened away for a night without registration, in a "tourist camp." This scene is repeated thousands of times over throughout the United States each night.

Beyond this, the files of the Federal Bureau of Investigation reflect that every super-gangster pursued by this organization within recent years has used tourist camps as havens against arrest. Baby Face Nelson used them. Dillinger used them. The Barker-Karpis crowd used them. Machine-gun Kelly and his crooked wife hid out in them. White slavers look upon them with favor, as they do upon many of the "Dine and Dance" pavilions which cluster about the outskirts of the city.

For those who wonder why there should be such concentrations of this type of hostess-purveying establishment beyond municipal limits, the explanation is the same as in the case of the outlying gambling hall — it often is easier to "fix" public officials in a rural than in an urban district. There are fewer persons to "grease." The rewards are great. Sheriffs, elected only for two years, see in that space of time an opportunity to get rich, merely by "letting a few places run." They feel a degree of safety in that the patrons are from the city; therefore they believe there will be little objection from the voters of the

county. It was this psychology which allowed a New England
constable to enter a certain "Dine and Dance" inn upon many
occasions during his tenure in office, without once noticing anything to arouse official curiosity.

State Police found an entirely different condition.

There had been complaints that the "hostesses" here were not
all they pretended to be. The officers went to the inn, and found
nothing until one noticed a ridge under the rug. He rolled back
the floor covering, and, by so doing, uncovered a trap door.
Opening this, he discovered two girls hiding in a small aperture
beneath the floor. Questioned, they admitted that they were not
truly hostesses, but prostitutes, having been brought here across
state lines.

The case was turned over to the Federal Bureau of Investigation. Before the inquiry was finished, a syndicate was unearthed
which had shipped girls from place to place in New Jersey,
New York, Pennsylvania, Connecticut, and Vermont, with earnings running into the neighborhood of three million dollars a
year. There were procuresses who advertised for "waitresses"
to go out of town. Upon receiving answers to these ads, the
madames would drive to the homes of the girls, interview them
as to their qualifications, survey them from a standpoint of
saleability and then inform them that this was not exactly a
waitress's job, but more like that of a hostess.

If it was established that the girl was willing to be a hostess in
the true sense of the word, with emphasis of course, on sex, it
was not a difficult matter to carry the conversation further and
dilate upon how much more money could be made by truly
selling sex instead of merely using it for teasing purposes. Thirty-
three persons, all principals in the racket, were brought into
court, and many convicted. The interesting phase, however, is
that, of hundreds of girls who were interviewed by procuresses,
not one made an official report that an attempt had been made to
inveigle her into prostitution. Moreover, many accepted the prof-
fered jobs.

One learns, in talking to vast numbers of girls in the hostess racket, how easy it is to step from this status into criminality. One hears in the course of conversation the stories of hostesses who went into what is known as the "parked car racket," wherein a number of girls working with young hoodlums conspire to be picked up by motoring Romeos and taken to Lover's Lane, where, shortly after they have moved from the front to the back seat, robbers appear. A variation exists with men, dressed as policemen or who are actually policemen, threatening arrest and consequent publicity unless money is paid for silence.

The extent of this blackmail racket can only be conjectured; there are no figures. One hears little of it, except from the lips of a girl as she bends over her drink: —

"Oh, Mamie? She isn't working here any more. She threw in with Louise and those other girls in the parked car racket."

Likewise there are no figures on the thousands of business men who are followed home after a night out, during which time, loquacious from liquor, they have told their entire history to the starry-eyed hostess who has not objected to a hand on her thigh. There is a different story to follow — one brought about through the action of shyster lawyers, who represent some mysterious client who wants to tell the man's wife about what her husband has been doing on his nights out.

There is the house detective racket, in which a hotel detective — who all too often is not a detective at all, but merely a piece of human scum — discovers, by prearrangement of course, that a guest, teetering from liquor, has sneaked a girl into his room. That the little tart has worked this racket for months and perhaps years with this same detective; that she, in fact, may be his woman, is not known to the guest, of course. He only sees the shield of authority. He only knows that he can be disgraced by the news reaching the business world that he has been thrown out of a hotel for having with him a woman not his wife. So he pays for silence. It is a variation of the hundred forms of badger game: blackmail, thieving, robbing and hi-jacking methods entered into by many of the hundreds of thousands of feminine "teasers" who each night preen and primp for sex solicitation.

They do not regard themselves as criminals, not even as harpies. In some ways they are strangely naïve, queerly pliable, almost childish in their wants. They wish they could go to Hollywood. They'd love a trip to New York. Or they have a friend who was a beauty parlor operator and who's been to Seattle and back. Then she married a gambler who traveled all over the country. It must be wonderful to go places and see things and have all the money you want and buy clothes and have automobiles . . .

If you care to spend your time that way, you'll hear this over and over and over again. You'll hear it in night clubs, you'll get it from hard-boiled hussies who'd roll you for a two-spot, you'll listen to it in dance halls, from the girl who waits on you in beer taverns, from the waitress in a peg joint, from the girl out of the floor show; and if you know crime and where it feeds, it will not be at all humorous. For it is out of the ranks of persons such as I have mentioned in this chapter, those in whom sex has been exaggerated into one of the big thoughts of life, those to whom clothes are a fetish, to whom escape from sordid surroundings is paramount, that there come the most dangerous criminals in all our annals. They are the gun molls.

CHAPTER TEN

HUSSIES IN HIDING

THERE are several ingredients which one finds in almost every female companion of crime. She is an inveterate reader of motion picture magazines, and those dealing heavily with romance. She has been either a manicure girl, a taxi-dancer, a waitress, a hostess, or a night club entertainer. Her background often shows either a home life that was broken by divorce when she was a child, or a lack of moral fiber on the part of parents, or conditions which made for a lack of home discipline. In a number of instances, she is revealed as having been married in her teens and the mother of a child within a year, this being followed quickly by divorce or separation.

Almost invariably she has taken for granted the fact that the man with whom she agrees to consort is in some illegitimate line of endeavor. As invariably, she does not care, as long as he has money to spend upon her. Evasion of the law she looks upon as glamorous, exciting. Invariably also, either she or her consort has venereal disease which both soon share. And only in rare cases is she more than twenty-three years old.

To persons who do not understand how wholeheartedly the gun moll enters into a criminal life, her existence is usually conducive to the deepest sympathy. One looks at the background: lack of home, sordid surroundings, eagerness for sparkle and glamour, a love of adventure, — whereupon the wells of compassion become exceedingly well filled.

However, it must be remembered that for every such girl there are hundreds of thousands of others of even more unfortunate backgrounds who either have possessed the fortitude to endure their surroundings, or through hard work, faith and determination, have been able to exchange them for better surrounding conditions. One prime requisite of a gun moll is an adversity to work, to confining hours, to discipline. She wants to do only that which pleases her; if she could be a star in Hollywood, she would not be a gun moll — provided, of course, that there was no continued effort, no discipline, no hard-and-fast rules or prescribed working hours necessary to stardom.

Perhaps the best diagnosis of a gun moll is that she is a woman who wants what she has done nothing to deserve. She desires leisure without knowing what to do with it; she yearns for Paris clothing without having studied the requisites of hats and shoes and gloves which harmonize with the dress. She craves jewelery only as jewelery and not as a part of an ensemble. She wants unlimited amounts of money for little other purpose than squandering. As compared to the male criminal, she is to a large degree parasitical; nevertheless she is of extreme importance in that she often performs the acts which allow her consort not only to commit his law infractions, but to remain free from capture while doing so.

Perhaps it would be well to trace the lives of a few of the molls who have figured in the crime news of recent years. In one or two cases, only their aliases shall be used. They have recently finished sentences imposed upon them for having harbored dangerous criminals. If the unusual has happened and they have been reformed by imprisonment, it would be unfair to describe them under their true names, to the use of which they undoubtedly have returned.

Therefore, as a beginning, there was Pat, the red-haired woman of John Hamilton, a member of the Dillinger gang.

This woman had been born in 1903, the second daughter of a locomotive inspector, living in Arkansas. Her mother and father were highly righteous persons, sincere churchgoers in fact. But there was something wrong with the girls — Pat, and her sister Opal (a name which also is an alias).

They resented the discipline of a restricted family. They were heavily supplied with the sex urge. Both were selfish. Both wanted more than life had given them. Both rebelled against parental guidance. Both liked to sneak away with boys for purposes best known to them.

The father's work took him from home a great deal. The mother, while highly respectable, seemed to possess little interest in what went on about her, gaining most of her pleasure through following the roaming life of her husband or by visiting among her relatives. Though she believed in discipline for her children, it was sporadic, perhaps ill-conceived. The girls did as they pleased.

By the time Pat was ten years old, the family had lived in Arkansas, Oklahoma, Texas, and finally had moved to Philadelphia. Grade school education had been obtained for the children on the hit-or-miss system, a detriment, however, which failed to react unfavorably upon Pat. Abnormally alert, she had been graduated from a Philadelphia high school and had managed to attend a university for a semester by the age of fifteen. Education was again interrupted when the family returned to Oklahoma. There Pat met a railroad fireman, and became infatuated with him. This was shortly after the death of her father in 1919; she was married while still fifteen. She was a mother within a year.

A short time later, Opal married or pretended to do so. The husband said he was a tailor, but his criminal record shows that within two years of his marriage he was sentenced to prison on a larceny charge, having been previously convicted and fined for the same type of offense. Inasmuch as Opal and Pat were inseparables, it seems that it was Opal who brought crime into the family, and that Pat was willing to share it.

Pat and her husband had quarreled. She accused him, evidently with good cause, of running with other women. Finally, came divorce. Pat went to work in an Oklahoma drugstore until she had earned enough money to go East, taking her child with her. Then, again working in a pharmacy, she took lessons in specialty-dancing. Her ambition was to work in night clubs. She got her wish, as the type of dancing which she had learned was done mostly with the hips.

It is interesting to note the devotion which gang mothers believe they hold for their children or for close relatives, comparing this with what they do or fail to do for the future of these persons. If one were to take Pat's story at face value, her sole concern was for her daughter. It was because of her child, so she said, that she decided to come East and take lessons as a dancer. It was because of her child that she, according to her own viewpoint, followed a straight and narrow path for years. Queerly enough, this path did not preclude getting drunk, or going to bed with some chance friend of the night spots; the woman, in reviewing her life, seemed to believe that in avoiding criminality for a time she had followed an impeccable course.

She worked in Philadelphia and New York, for the sake of her child. She went to Chicago for the same purpose, boarding the daughter for a while and then performing what appears, to this writer, to be an ultimate service: she sent the girl to live with Pat's sister, whose husband, by this time, was rapidly progressing upon a trail of robbery, larceny, bank robbery and other crimes which finally were to make him a Dillinger gangster and at last lead to his incarceration for life, as a murderer!

As for Pat, she continued to shake it up about the night spots until she met a member of a widely known orchestra who played the trumpet by night and robbed banks by day. They were married. The trumpet-playing burglar essayed a post office robbery, was caught and was sentenced to fifteen years in Federal Prison. Pat went to the home of her sister to recover from this blow. There she met a friend of her brother-in-law.

It was one of his bank-robbing, murderous pals. Pat almost immediately became his sweetheart. He also belonged to the Dillinger crew, but was caught early in the pursuit and sent to Indiana State Prison.

Pat now had become a true gangster's moll. There had been no point in her career, other than during the early days of her marriage, when she was not headed inevitably for the life she assumed. Even while she ran with her second criminal mate, she was visiting her former crook husband in Leavenworth Penitentiary, assuring him that she lived only for him and was working for his release. Perhaps she was, for this type of woman possesses primeval ideas concerning her relationship to the male.

"What the hell?" a gang moll once asked me. "Just because my man can't get anything in stir is no reason why I should put on tin pants. I'm human. What hurt does it do if I go out and stay with a friend now and then? I love my man just as much and I'm not taking anything away from him. There'll be plenty left when he gets home again, and ain't I working my damned neck off to get him out of the pen? Haven't I already put up two thousand dollars to that god-damned lawyer toward a parole? If my man thinks I'm going to pass out all my dough to get him out and then sit in a strait jacket while I'm doing it, he's crazy. I'm giving him everything I've got, ain't I?"

This was the viewpoint. If a woman works and schemes toward her man's release, if she can enter into sexual relationship with a guard or warden to that end, if she can become the woman of a lawyer and thus pay in sex instead of money for his efforts toward a parole, she regards it as an action of acumen. Thus what might be called restricted prostitution serves all necessary purposes, leaving money to be spent for important things like clothes or drinking.

Therefore, with her daughter living in the home of a vicious criminal, herself the consort of two men who had just been sent to prison, Pat continued in her night club life, eschewing marriage as a delusion and taking men for the pleasures of the moment. At last Pat met a "nice young man" in a Chicago night club. That was her description of him. He was John Dillinger and Pat introduced him to one of her co-entertainers. Then Dillinger returned the favor. He brought forward his lieutenant, John Hamilton, for Pat. According to Pat, they "entered into an agreement."

She did not love him. Apparently he had no claim upon her, other than that he was a man possessed of sex, and what she felt was glamour. He told her he was a bond salesman, and if she believed it, then indeed she had learned nothing by being the wife of a post office robber and the woman of a murderer. The agreement was that she would leave her life for his. This agreement continued almost throughout the entire life of the Dillinger gang.

They depended upon this woman. She was as invulnerable to the questioning of law enforcement agents as a stone to water. Otherwise she was jovial, heavily addicted to beer and maundering over her ambitions for her child, nevertheless coldly alert to dangers, a cop-hater, and a woman valued for her "hunches."

The gang obeyed her sudden commands to "get moving," seemingly for no cause. She believed these "hunches" to be psychic; they were, in truth, only the workings of a subconscious mind long attuned to the actions of criminals and police. This, coupled with her feminine intuitive qualities, gave warning when there was a threat of danger. Perhaps it was an inflection in the voice of a landlady, told by police to keep a close watch on new roomers until a raiding squad could arrive; perhaps a sharpness of glance in someone who looked the gang over in an apartment house hallway and thus involuntarily signaled the fact that memory of newspaper photographs had been vaguely awakened. In one case, it was merely a short delay in the return of her gangster pals after a visit to town.

Pat, her consort, and another member of the gang had driven to Nashville, Tennessee, following a police tip which had allowed them to leave a St. Paul hideout only a short time before the arrival of a raiding squad. As usual with gangs when they are "on the lam," they were staying at a tourist camp on the outskirts of the city. The men went into town to buy groceries, planning to remain away about an hour.

The men made their purchases and then desired some soft drinks. Inasmuch as they were carrying a Thompson sub-machine gun in the car, they decided on curb service. They drove to the front of a drugstore, honked for the soda-jerker and gave their order. Meanwhile, their trained eyes told them of something unusual in the vicinity.

Across the street were two young men whose every attention was centered upon the drugstore. They interested the gangsters.

"Those guys are planning a heist," said one of them. "Let's stay and watch it."

Thus, in grandstand seats as it were, the two high-powered crimesters settled themselves for what they thought would be an interesting sight — the robbery of a store by a pair of amateurs. They forgot their promise to return to Pat within an hour; dawdling their drinks, they waited, minute after minute, while the two potential robbers started toward the store, drew back, started again and once more were delayed by a stream of customers whose presence might interfere with a swiftly executed job. Suddenly, they turned in flight. A police siren had sounded only a block away. Someone else beside the crimesters had noticed their unusual actions and reported to headquarters. Now, Pat's friends found themselves in a predicament.

"Stick it out," one of them suggested. "The cops won't think of looking us over."

Calmly, they sipped at their drinks as a squad car raced to the drugstore. Suddenly, however, they stiffened. A patrolman was rushing straight for them.

"Seen anything of a couple of fellows who were trying to rob this store?" the policeman asked.

The crimesters shook their heads.

"No. Haven't noticed anybody."

Perhaps it was their tone which aroused the officer's curiosity.

"Who are you fellows?"

They gave fake names. The officer was not satisfied.

"Got any credentials?"

Now they were in danger. One of the gangsters shifted quickly, swinging the sub-machine gun upward until it covered the officer.

"Here's our credentials," he snapped. "Now get the hell out of here and back into that car."

The command was obeyed with such alacrity that the officer stumbled and sprawled on his own running board in making his objective. Both cars wheeled away at the same time, in opposite directions.

The gangsters took no pride in the fright they had given the police. They had been "jumped up"; as soon as the officers could reach a telephone, they knew, squad cars would be searching the city, sufficiently equipped to give battle to desperate men, armed with a machine gun. The crimesters raced for the tourist camp, and as they swung to their cottage, brakes screeching, there was Pat, awaiting them on the little veranda with all bags packed. The car did little more than pause. The gangsters and the woman were loaded and out of town almost before the hunt for them could be organized.

"I just got a hunch," Pat explained. "So I thought I would pack up and be ready for trouble."

Her hunch, of course, had come about through the slight delay in the return of her criminal pals. When one's nerves are constantly attuned to the dangers of pursuit, seconds can seem like minutes and minutes like hours. The gangsters had

not been more than ten or fifteen minutes late; that had been
sufficient warning to Pat.

It was because of such achievements that the woman came
to be known as "Sergeant Pat" in the Dillinger organization.
She could be trusted to find hideouts; the gang so confided in
her that she often was sent to various underworld contacts to
collect money which had been left "on deposit" there; she was
the gang's liaison agent, its emissary. Often, when hotly pursued, the male members would ask her advice regarding tactics
to be employed in defeating the plans of law enforcement
agencies. She also was the gang nurse.

In one instance, Dillinger brought John Hamilton to her, so
badly wounded that death seemed inevitable. Then Dillinger
departed; Hamilton wounded was of little use to him; Hamilton dead meant nothing. In fact, when Hamilton finally was
killed, Dillinger himself superintended the burial of the body
in a gravel pit, and, before a spadeful of earth could be thrown
upon the body, said farewell by sprinkling canful after canful
of lye upon the face and hands of his former friend, to prevent
identification and thus preclude any possibility that the discovery of Hamilton's corpse might lead to his own capture.

The case in which Pat acted as a nurse was on a previous
occasion. Following a bank robbery in South Bend, Indiana,
in which a policeman had been killed, Dillinger came to her
room.

"Where's John?" she asked.

"Down in the car," answered Dillinger. "Shot up. Seven
slugs in him."

Pat became solicitous.

"We've got to do something for him."

"Sure you have. I can't stay. I've got a date to meet the rest
of the gang in Tucson."

The "date," as it developed, was merely one of the rowdy
parties which finally attracted so much attention that they led

to Dillinger's capture — the one preceding his break from the Crown Point jail. Perhaps it was such cold-blooded selfishness as this that brought about Dillinger's disrepute in the underworld. He did not even linger to assure himself that his pal might live; he merely turned him over to Pat and left her to care for him as best she could.

From hoodlum hangout to hoodlum hangout she went in Chicago, at last to find a haven in the home of the wife of a convict. There she lugged the wounded Hamilton, dragging him into the house after darkness. Following this she continued a search for a criminal doctor; at last, toward midnight, obtaining Dr. Joseph P. Moran, an ex-abortionist. His fee was fifty-one hundred dollars, paid by the gang. The convict's wife demanded a hundred dollars a day for providing the hideout, which was paid. After a time, Pat rented an apartment, and, following a quarrel with the drunken, inefficient Dr. Moran, dispensed with his services and nursed Hamilton back to health.

For such actions she was captured, tried and convicted in the general clean-up of the Dillinger gang. After serving a short sentence in a woman's reformatory, she now is free. So is her sister, who also served a sentence for having harbored her murderer husband. As for the child whose future so concerned Pat, it is presumed that she is again with her mother. What will happen to either or both is for the future to decide.

Gangsters' molls preach constantly about their love for their children; meanwhile they do exactly the things which may handicap those children forever. Instead of realizing that the lives they lead, the associates with whom they surround themselves, the men with whom they run, the constant talk of robbery, murder, adultery and pursuit, cannot help exerting a detrimental influence upon the child, they believe that they fulfill the highest form of mother love in wanting their children always close to them.

There was the son of Edna Murray, a woman even more vicious than Pat. Only a slight difference exists in the parental

backgrounds of these women. After a childhood spent on a
Kansas farm, the girl Edna moved to Cardin, Oklahoma, where
her father worked in the zinc mines and her mother ran a
boarding house. There were five children, two girls and three
boys. The male members of the family apparently have kept
within the law; both the girls were gun molls, as they were in
Pat's family.

Both sneaked out to meet boys. Edna's friend had Indian
blood in him; the father forbade them to "go together" — so
they defied the parental discipline and were married, remaining
in this state long enough for Edna to become pregnant. Then
she came home with her unborn child.

She remained there until the baby was born; shortly afterward, she left home and went to Sapulpa, there to work in a
restaurant. The child remained with its grandmother.

The restaurant was a counter joint. A gangling youth sprad-
dled himself on a stool one day and began "his line." It is marvelous how some waitresses can be determining whether they
will spend half the night in the back seat of a parked automobile with some young fellow and still are able to keep
their minds on serving meals to a string of customers. Edna
Murray decided in favor of this young stranger. They followed the usual course of parked automobiles and haystacks
for a time; finally they sought the thrill of disrobing. To do
this, it was necessary that the young man go to Edna Murray's
room. There police arrested him as Volney Davis, a murderer.
But on the way to police headquarters, he knocked down one
policeman, dodged the bullets of the other, and escaped. Within
ten minutes, he telephoned Edna to meet him.

It is at such a point that the psychology of persons who naturally are law-abiding and those who are congenitally criminal
sharply divides, with the result that it is almost impossible
for one to understand the other. The good person believes that
any woman who shares the life of a murderer either must be
driven to it by circumstances, or be so wildly in love that she

is blinded beyond reasoning. Therefore, her actions are looked upon with commiseration, sympathy, mitigation.

The truth is that the average gun moll becomes such almost with a shrug of the shoulders. There is already built up in her mind a certain resentment against the law and a distinct admiration for those who live against it. Edna Murray did not hesitate; she sneaked out of her room, watching carefully lest she be shadowed by the police. She met Davis near the Public Library, heard from his own lips that he was accused of murder, and, with that queer sense of the theatrical which exists in all feminine consorts of crime, promised to be his woman forever. Within two days they were dodging police together. Within twenty-four hours more, she was the active agent who allowed Davis to escape a detective who was on his trail. Then, event of events, Volney Davis, the murderer, drove Edna Murray home to visit her baby.

The same strain runs through all such persons. If they feed their children, if they dress them well, even with crooked money, if they are vociferous about their affection, then nothing else matters. They may parade murderers before them; they may plan robberies, even indulge in sexual intercourse, in the same room with a child old enough to know what is going on, and these are excusable. Is not their love so great for this baby that they cannot bear to allow it out of their sight? Thus are they not the best of mothers? There is not a gun moll who will confess that in any way has her life been detrimental to that of her child.

This is not an effort to detail the life of Edna Murray. Volney Davis was caught and sent to prison, presumably for life. Edna worked and saved and struggled to pay lawyers' fees, but she put no padlock on her sexual activities. Soon she was cohabiting with a robber known as Diamond Joe. Their home was a perfect nest of criminality; crooks of all sorts hung out there. And to that home, Edna Murray brought, with great delight, her baby boy.

Well, to get rid of Diamond Joe, he finally killed a policeman and was executed for it after a daring escape from prison.
Edna Murray protested her continued love for Volney Davis.
But she slept with a man named Jack Murray, a hold-up artist,
with whom she finally went into the highways as a co-worker.
Her son was living with her when she was caught by the police
and sent to prison on a twenty-five year sentence as a highway robber. "The Kissing Bandit," they called her. Edna Murray, with a show of the theatrical, always offered a victim a
kiss after she had held him up at the point of a revolver and
taken every cent he possessed.

The woman went to Missouri Penitentiary. She escaped. In
this regard, it is always well to remember J. Edgar Hoover's
admonition to those who believe that prison escapes come about
magically: —

A person cannot escape from prison except through malfeasance or
nonfeasance in office.

Edna Murray escaped. She was found in a Chicago house of
prostitution and brought back to prison. Again she escaped.
By this time she was a user of narcotics, weakened through
venereal disease, and had been the consort of two murderers
and a hold-up man. But she must have her son with her. So
the boy, now nearly grown, left the place where he had been
cared for during her imprisonments and again joined his mother.
Incidentally, Volney Davis got out, about this time, and he
and Edna again became crimester and gun moll. They continued
this relationship until Federal agents closed in on them as
conspirators in the kidnapping of Edward G. Bremer.

During the years of this last love-feast of Davis and Edna
Murray, they associated with the Dillinger gang, the Keating
and Holden mob of bank robbers, the Eddie Doll group of
crimesters, and the Barker-Karpis gang of cutthroats, murderers, and kidnappers. The crime record shows that Edna had
her son with her almost constantly. And in her cell at Jefferson

City Penitentiary, to which she has been returned to serve out the remainder of her twenty-five year sentence, Edna Murray says sorrowfully: —

"The one thing I miss is my boy. I always have tried to be a good mother to him."

The same sort of story goes on endlessly. Mrs. Baby Face Nelson often carried her young son with her as a camouflage to deceive police who sought her husband. Again there was the psychology of the law-abiding against that of the law-evading. Policemen felt sure that no mother, even though she were a gangster's wife, would subject her child to criminal associations and temptations. Therefore they did not search cars containing a man, a woman, and a little child. The woman of Verne Miller, the multiple killer who shot down four officers in Kansas City, had her daughter with her when she lived as Miller's consort in a house which fairly bulged with crime. However, did she not cause the little girl to receive dancing lessons, and did not a whole crowd of gangsters once attend a school entertainment at which she spoke a piece — just to be sure that she got the prize? Kathryn Kelly, the brains of the Urschel kidnapping and the nagging, cruel, domineering wife of henpecked Machine-gun Kelly, could talk for hours about her great love for her little daughter by the first of her three marriages. But Kathryn's love took the form of filling her home with prostitutes, burglars, drunken parties, of her being the wife of a bootlegger and then a kidnapper, and of often getting pie-eyed drunk as a good example of what a first-class mother should be.

It is in a gun moll's blood to look at the world through entirely different eyes from those of true motherhood. First, she has not the fear of crime which attacks the average mother; she is a part of crime. Even if it results in imprisonment, innate resentment against the law remains and she is not horrified by the thought that her child may become the companion of evil associates. Her concern begins and ends with her own dominating motives, which are a show of finery, a feeling of luxury without effort, and the association with people who are judged by her wholly in relation to what they have meant to her or have done for her. If John Dillinger killed seven men and returned home with his clothing caked with their blood, but, at the same time, brought home a five-carat diamond for his momentary *innamorata,* then whatever he might have done to obtain this gem would be forgotten in his sweetness, his thoughtfulness, his kindness and gentleness toward his gun moll. It might be well to think over these characteristics in case you are ever one of a jury which tries a gun moll. It may aid you in arguing with some fool who believes her sweet and kind and misled and beautiful. Incidentally, the evidence that a woman on trial had gonorrhea or syphilis would do more to convict a gun moll — especially if she were pretty — than the oratory of a dozen district attorneys. I have found, through many years of court attendance, that the conviction or acquittal of a woman by twelve good men and true is largely dependent upon how many times she has been mentally raped by the jury.

Perhaps the letter of a gun moll to a rat of a husband will give a deeper insight. This girl was one of three sisters, all of whom, with their eyes wide open, became concubines of crime. Her name was Dolores Delaney; and when she was seventeen she was hanging around night clubs, where she was looked upon by habitués as a girl who would "go for a fellow she liked." The rodent-eyed Alvin Karpis flirted with her. In a matter of days, they were living together.

He deserted her, when she was pregnant, as he escaped Atlantic City police during a raid which, to my mind, leaves much for explanation.

Karpis knew exactly where to go in Atlantic City, and carried a letter of introduction when he sought his hotel. There were strange delays in the raid, during which Karpis and a male companion escaped, leaving their women behind. The police reports of the escape picture a battle in which machine gun bullets flew like hail. Alvin Karpis, after his arrest in New Orleans, said casually: "Oh, I guess we shot a couple of times in the air. The cops fired a few times but the bullets didn't come anywhere near us. One hit my girl in the leg."

So take it as a desperate battle, or reserve it for contemplation. In one case Karpis got away through sheer desperation and of course could not take his pregnant woman with him. Viewed from another angle, he plainly deserted his wounded woman. The other woman was so sure she had been deliberately left behind in a most cowardly and ungentlemanly manner that she became a government witness. Dolores Delaney, however, remains the true gun moll. Here is the letter she wrote from her place of incarceration, in Milan Prison for Women, to her beloved murderer-consort while he rested in St. Paul County Jail on the way to Alcatraz Island. Her boy was apparently left in charge of Karpis' parents; she evidently received reports from them about his "welfare."

My Darling Ray,

I am just filled to the brim with things I want to say to you but somehow I can't seem to put them down on paper. I have been sitting here for over an hour trying to find the words to let you know how I feel but all I can say is that I love you, honey, more than anything or anyone in the world. It doesn't matter what has happened or what is to be — I'll always feel the same. Remember how you used to tell me it was just puppy love and I'd get over it — you were so very wrong, darling, for I won't — ever. Instead of that I seem to love you more each day and I didn't think that was possible.

I don't know whether you will be allowed to answer this or even if you will want to — but, ah, sweetheart, won't you, please, write me just a few short lines as soon as you can and let me know what you are going to do. If there was only something I could do for you. I would gladly take your place if I could.

I would have written as soon as I could but I didn't get permission until now.

Darling, if you need any money won't you let me know, *please?*
I still have all the jewelry you bought me. I don't know how much
I could get for it but if it would help I'd be so happy to do at least
that much for you.

Honey, if only you could see that boy of ours — he is getting to
look more like you every day and I just prayed that he would. I named
him Raymond Alvin Karpavicz for you. Your Mother and Father adore
him and no one could be better to him than they are. They are wonderful to me, too, and I hope I can repay them someday for all
they've done for me.

I must stop now, darling, but remember that I am always only
your

own loving

DOLORES.

Perhaps it is all very well for a gun moll to forgive her
crooked paramour for having deserted her, pregnant and
wounded. It may be proper for her to desire to do anything
possible for him — even to yielding up the jewels which he
had bought her with money obtained from murdered or kidnapped victims. No doubt, it also is extremely proper in the
mind of that gun moll to desire that the illegitimately conceived fruit of her womb resemble his notorious father as much
as possible, that he bear the same name — and perhaps grow up
to be a murderer like his illustrious daddy. Those who have
sympathized so deeply with gun molls might spend an hour
or so in perusal of this hard-nosed woman's letter and try to
find, somewhere within it, anything that even resembles a decent
mother's honest desire that her son become a worth-while addition to the nation's population.

The warped viewpoint of the Dolores Delaneys of criminality
may be gauged by the fact that, in addition to his other failures,
Alvin Karpis had truly forgotten all concern for his paramour.
As a result his transgressions included the spending of eight
thousand dollars on a Middle West prostitute of whom he had
become enamored, of having lavished gifts on another in a

house of prostitution in Toledo, and further of establishing himself as a gentleman of niceties by sending flowers to a third one while she was confined in a hospital as the result of an operation necessitated by venereal disease. However, I hope the reader has not forgotten one characteristic of the criminal, upon which much stress was placed in earlier chapters. Ego rules constantly. Alvin Karpis was now on the front pages of every newspaper as Public Enemy Number One, so dangerous that even the Director of the Federal Bureau of Investigtation had risked his life to bring about his capture. No gun moll ever existed who could withstand the urge to get in on such a carnival of publicity.

Nor are gun molls the only offenders. If I appear to be giving special emphasis to the fact that the average gangster and the average gangster's moll are rotten with gonorrhea and syphilis, this is done with thorough deliberation. It seems to be the only way in which the tinsel can be stripped from these filthy beings, the pedestal torn from beneath them; I have seen supposedly respectable women, the wives of supposedly respectable men, hanging about a jail like gawkers around a Hollywood first night that they might sigh with pleasure at the sight of some publicized criminal. Meanwhile, the offenders for whom these allegedly sensible and respectable persons were showing such adulation were so rotten with open sores of syphilis as to constitute a menace to the health of any person who touched them.

Check the entire list, one after another; one finds the same history. Even Wilbur Underhill, worshiped by many a sapient Midwest boy as "the Tri-State Terror," laid aside a gonorrhea syringe to pick up a machine gun when officers closed in on him for the battle which resulted in his death. Pretty Boy Floyd, who liked to be photographed with his baby boy, narrowly missed capture on several occasions when the pain of his diseases drove him to doctors. John Dillinger had gonorrhea. Connie Morris, the consort of Fred Hunter, who was the partner of Alvin Karpis during his last days of freedom, was more of a hospital case from venereal disease than a law enforcement one when she was arrested in the raid which netted Karpis, who also bears the urethral scars of gonorrhea. The records of one of the biggest clinics in the world contain the aliases of dozens upon dozens of gang women who, under assumed personalities, have been patients there as the result of too much sex life.

In case, however, a more personal glimpse is needed into the viewpoint, the actions, the thoughts and conversation of the average gun moll, there is herewith transcribed a surveillance record, obtained through Dictograph by investigative officers in Chicago during the pursuit of Frank Nash, an escaped prisoner.

These beautiful females were Gladys and Carolyn, one a cigarette girl from a night club, the other a hostess. Gladys had been known to associate with bank robber friends of Nash; hence, in the hope that her conversation might lead to some hint of the escaped man's whereabouts, she was placed under surveillance. The officers in the next room obtained what might be coarsely termed "an earful."

One morning at four-thirty, after night club work was over, the girls, who evidently had recently joined forces, began to get personal.

CAROLYN: Say, Glad, what's your full name?

GLADYS: Gladys Loretta Margaret — and you know my last. What's yours?

CAROLYN: Carolyn Agnes Francisco, but I've shortened the last to Frances.

A girl named Violet arrived. For a time they all talked about various persons who evidently were wanted by law enforcement agents. Then there was general conversation about getting money from men. Several widely known criminals were mentioned. Violet called a speak-easy and asked for a notorious labor head and racketeer, said by the underworld to protect criminals, even to the extent of placing them in various gangs, all through his political power. That seemed to be all for the night.

The next afternoon, a man who called himself "Jay" came into the room: —

JAY: Say, you girls know Gano — I knew him when he was in jail in Waukegan, Illinois.

GLADYS: Oh, you did? Oh, I've got some pictures to show you. (*She showed Jay the photographs, adding:*) You remember the Wop that got kidnapped for two hundred thousand dollars? Well, my friend, the one in this picture, got one hundred and four thousand. He's the lookout for the man who's running for mayor back home.

Where that nominee lived was not divulged. Gang molls have a habit of being loquacious and secretive at the same time. Certain it is, however, that if he was elected the underworld had a good time, ruled as it was by a man whose "lookout" was a kidnapper. There was nothing more of interest that day, but on the following night Gladys grew confidential.

GLADYS: I howl every time I think of that night at Ball's place. Ball's a bad egg, and Eddy who runs around with him carries a gun all the time. Carolyn and I had been drunk one night and he pulled it on me. If I had been sober, I would have been scared. He just stood there and pointed it at me. I told him if he shot I would have some of my friends drill him.

That was all for a while, until Eddy himself came in, evidently with his gun safely in its holster. The subject turned to that of the best district in which to live in Chicago. Eddy objected, it seemed, to the place where the girls had established their residence.

EDDY: Don't you know this used to be Armour Avenue, the toughest section in Chicago? Even now, they got more junkers (narcotic addicts), wrong guys, whorehouses, than anywhere else in town.

CAROLYN: Well, we know too many people south, and we won't live north, and you couldn't hire me to live west.

Eddy stayed until five o'clock in the morning, when another man entered, conversed awhile, and left with Eddy. After they were gone, Gladys dilated upon what wonderful men they were. Eddy was the head of a union and made so much money he couldn't spend it. Smitty, his pal, owned a "swell-joint" night club, in which persons were forced to wear dinner jackets and evening clothes. Eddy and she went out there one night, all dressed up, but two men followed them and Eddy thought there was going to be a stick-up; and Smitty, in his swell-joint night club, so Gladys said, was nervous as hell. Following this, the innocent little girls went to bed and the next morning left their rooms to be absent for several days. At last they returned in the bright sun and at ten o'clock the telephone rang. Gladys answered very sleepily.

GLADYS: Hello — say, what do you mean, why can't I sleep another hour or two? I've been up all night. I don't want to be bothered. I drank beer until eight-thirty o'clock this morning.

Evidently, however, at this moment, the man at the other end of the wire said magic words. Gladys immediately changed her act.

GLADYS: Who is this? Couldn't you tell I was joking? Well, who then? Friends of mine? O.K. I'll be there in half an hour. (*The conversation ended; Gladys turned to her sleeping friend.*) Babe! wake up and get dressed and come with me, I just know there is some trouble. Maybe it's the gang from St. Paul; they want to see me.

Out they went, to be pleasurably disappointed. It was merely two men who had awakened with a desire to spend the rest of the morning in bed — with feminine companionship. At one o'clock Gladys returned, convoyed by two males, called Jim and Joe. One was the former president of a large taxicab company. The other was an old pal.

JIM: You look just the same as the last time I saw you, Glad.
GLADYS: Yep, I'm just the same, only about two pounds heavier, than when I came in from the Lake. (*The Lake was a nice place; she had occupied a cottage there with her bank-robber sweetheart.*) I had

a swell time there. Oh no, I'm different. I've got a cut over one eye. Some fellow hit me over the head with a gin bottle. I don't know why; I wasn't talking out of turn or anything.

But to get on. The next day Carolyn and Gladys discussed matters closer to their hearts.

CAROLYN: Buddy kept playing with his gun last night. Damn foolish to carry one unless a person has some reason.

GLADYS: Yes, persons shouldn't have guns. Something always happens when there's a gun around. But some people do have a reason for carrying one. Bill (her bank-robbing paramour) always carries one, but he's got a reason.

CAROLYN: Yes, so I heard. What was it, bank robbery?

GLADYS: No.

CAROLYN: Well, what was it?

GLADYS: What do you know about it?

CAROLYN: Well, I heard he was a bank robber; that he was wanted in Nebraska, North Dakota, Minnesota, and Chicago.

GLADYS: Yes, he's a big shot. He was in the pen once, but he was too smart for them. Say, don't you tell anybody about this. How did you hear about it, anyway?

CAROLYN: Oh, I had heard it before.

GLADYS: Who told you?

CAROLYN: I'll tell you sometime.

GLADYS: Well, he's smart; they'll never take him alive. He's a good shot with a gun and he sure can handle his mob.

CAROLYN: Guys that get away with that stuff are just lucky.

GLADYS: Oh, I don't know. He's the sweetest thing. I boss him around. Say, I even make him wash my stockings.

CAROLYN: Where is he now?

GLADYS: I wish I knew. I'm so worried about him. The son of a bitch didn't even send me a Valentine.

The conversation took a different turn for a time, Gladys talking somewhat heatedly concerning a most annoying incident which had occurred in the night club where she was then employed. It seemed that she had been sitting at a table with three police officers and that one of them, being no gentleman, had called her a "gigolette." From her general conversation it appeared that Gladys had no objection to being known as a "hustler," but for anybody to call her a "gigolette" was too much. So she had left the night club in a huff and that had made Jerry, the manager, sore, since she had insulted three police officers, and there was hell to pay all around.

To get off the subject, they turned to a discussion of the horror which some girls seem to have of being raped. Neither Gladys nor Carolyn could exactly understand that psychology. As a testimonial to the false modesty with which some girls seem to burden themselves Gladys intimated that her first sexual intercourse had come when she was about ten years old and that she hadn't found anything about it to scare anybody. Here, however, the conversation swerved temporarily. Jay, who it now developed was the hotel dentist, entered the room, and after indulging in the usual social amenities, asked abruptly: —

JAY: Say, I've been meaning to ask you. How's that dose of clap of yours getting along? The one you caught last summer.

GLADYS: Oh, it was doing fine until a little while ago. Then it broke out again.

JAY: Well, you're not going to do it any good laying around with fellows all the time.

CAROLYN (*laughing loudly*): No, and she isn't doing the fellows any good either.

JAY: You ought to be going to a doctor.

GLADYS: Hell, I am going to a doctor.

That ended that. Jay remembered that he had to meet a friend, and that he wanted to bring him up to meet the girls. They thought that would be fine. So out went Jay, and when he returned, he brought his friend with him. The man was a policeman.

In fiction, and in the movies, the advent of a policeman into the room of a gun moll would indeed be a Tragic Situation. There would be drama in the raw: the cold, clear eye of the law enforcement officer centered upon this woman of the demimonde, the parrying of the female for the protection of her beloved gunman. Fortunately for Gladys, there was no such high drama. Jay had brought some liquor. They had drinks. The policeman grew talkative.

The conversation which followed contained the views of the policeman that there wasn't any court where fixing couldn't be done, if a person had the right sort of contacts. There were a lot of the judges who took dough, but then there were a lot also who couldn't be reached that way. A fellow had to know somebody who really knew the judge, who could get next to him or who had something on him. Gladys came in with the announcement that there were plenty of these guys on the bench that a person could get something on. The policeman dilated upon the art of "fixing," not only in court, but at the time of arrest. Then, dropping this matter as having been fully discussed, everybody turned in for a good old-fashioned chat on how much fun it was for a bunch of men and women to strip down to the nude and, to quote the dialogue, "just go to it."

After an elevating evening, Jay and his friend of law enforcement departed, allowing Gladys and Carolyn to resume their conversation. For a time it concerned only how generous or stingy men were in times of sexual excitement, and how Gladys once got forty dollars from a sixty-four-year-old efficiency expert during a convention. From this they went into an evaluation of the various night clubs as places in which to pick up men who would spend money readily. They discussed, with some horror, the fact that a girl who was "playing the tables" at one club, sneaked out of there and under an assumed name solicited business at the club in which they worked (thus perhaps violating union rules). This brought up night clubs in general, with the result that they took for their subject a certain Chicago rendezvous which catered only to moral perverts, the affirmative stating that it was a lot of fun to go there and watch the nances and Lesbians, the negative insisting that she couldn't get any kick out of it, that she liked her friends old-fashioned. Then, finally, Gladys unburdened her soul of the beautiful story of why she loved Bill the bank robber.

"It was when I was working there at the Club in St. Paul," she said. "I was peddling ciggies. Well, one night, Bill came in there and I'd never seen him before, and of course, I walked up to his table and asked him if he wanted any cigars or cigarettes. Maybe he was drunk, I don't know, but anyway, it made him sore as hell for me to come over there talking out of turn to him and he swung in and cussed the hell out of me. Of course, I wasn't going to stand for that, even if he was a patron of the club, and so I gave it right back to him. Well, Bill just kept on swearing at me — I mean he swore at me.

"And all of a sudden — it was the funniest thing — there was another man sitting at a table a little ways off; a great big fellow, he must have weighed two hundred pounds, he was so tall; he must have been six feet four inches. Well, when he heard Bill cussing me out and all that he got up and came over to the table where Bill was swearing and sonsabitching around, and told Bill that he shouldn't talk to me like that.

"Bill didn't take it off of him for a minute. He jumped up and pulled his gun and shot this Buttinsky in the leg, and then there was hell to pay. Of course, Bill was on the lam then, and it was an awful brave thing for him to do, because if he had gotten pinched, they might have taken his prints away from him and found out who he was. But he was so mad he didn't think of that and just pulled out his gun and shot the big bastard. Well, I didn't want to see Bill in bad, so I told him to lam, and then not wanting the cops to pick me up and ask me a lot of questions and all that, I lammed with him. So that was how it all started."

CAROLYN: Then what happened?

GLADYS: Oh, nothing. Bill paid the guy's hospital bill and then got the fix going and there wasn't anything more to it, except that Bill and I got to going together. Bill's the first real beau I ever had.

CAROLYN: Oh, you've had more.
GLADYS: Not that I've been crazy about.
CAROLYN: You've lived with other men.
GLADYS: Yes, but I didn't love them.
CAROLYN: How many?
GLADYS: Only six.

Perhaps this is the place to leave Carolyn, twenty years old, and Gladys who, at twenty-two, was living with her seventh man, a bank robber. The conversations of this sweet young pair, the ideals, the general trend of thought, the ambitions, are typical ones: a gun moll thinks crime and sex, sex and crime; loves it and lives it. I have tried, throughout investigations into numerous cases, to find even one instance of the romance, the fealty, the honesty of high purposes attributed to these females by imaginative romanticists, and I have failed. In fact, I have found them to be nothing but a selfish, law-hating, piglike crew of filthy-minded sluts, and the sooner they are so regarded by the general public, the sooner will the professional criminal lose one of his most valuable allies.

CHAPTER ELEVEN

SOLDIERS IN SLIME

IT was during my early days as a newspaper reporter that a flood of propaganda began to sweep America against what then was known as "The Scarlet Woman."

There had been honest beginnings to the campaign, but these motives had become strangely warped. For years there had been an interstate and international traffic in women. Prostitutes from Europe were shipped in large numbers to America, and here distributed to lumber camps in then comparatively pioneer districts. Proprietors of dance halls in Western mining camps sent to Chicago or Kansas City or St. Louis for new girls as casually as a storekeeper to-day would send in an order for merchandise. Invariably, the main profits went to the shippers and not to the women who formed the objects of their exploitation. There were many instances — as there are instances to-day — of women who alleged that they had been forced through various methods, to become inmates of bawdyhouses. Thus, there was extremely good reason, as there is now good reason, to attack those who brought about such conditions. Since there were no laws by which to govern such practices, exploitation was widespread. Therefore, there is every evidence that the first persons who began an outcry against what soon came to be known as "white slavery" did so with the honest purpose of bringing about stringent regulation of segregated districts, and supervision over those who had been thrust by circumstance or the devices of procurers into a life of prostitution.

The accomplishment of such a program would have been a marvelous achievement. Had the originators of the "white slave crusade" followed a carefully prepared plan of procedures there might have been fewer headaches for the future. The commercializing of vice for the profit of exploiters might have been wiped out. Rigid medical and moral supervision might have come about, plus coöperative Federal and State prosecution of a severe nature against anyone who forced a female, by any means whatever, to become a prostitute.

There might have emerged clean, well-policed, highly segregated districts, operating under the efficient supervision of non-political boards of public health and morals. The earnings of women might have been carefully guarded for their benefit and protection. There might have been laws, rigidly enforced, for the national registration of prostitutes, with fingerprint identifications, cards of identity, and medical inspection. There might also have been the establishment of hospitals designed especially for the treatment of venereal diseases, plus stringent control of all physicians who cater to patients suffering from such maladies. Provisions like the latter would have forced to the wall a perfect army of conscienceless charlatans, fakers, and medical criminals who for years have thrived, and continue to do so, upon the most horrible of practices in the so-called treatment of venereal diseases. Here is a branch of medicine, outlawed by the ethical members of the medical fraternity, in which worse crimes, viewed from a moral standpoint, are committed than ever could be charged to all the Dillingers and Pretty Boy Floyds on record.

Once a sufferer from syphilis or gonorrhea gets into the hands of a crooked doctor, he places his entire future in that man's hands. Perhaps the story of one such practitioner, as told to me during the long hours of a desperate night, will give an insight into the viewpoints and money-making possibilities which lay within the reach of this racketeer.

It was during some labor troubles in a Western city that I

was assigned to spend the night with an armed group of imported strikebreakers, hired to protect the property of a manufacturing plant. The city had been red with carnage for three days; there had been riots and fights, firing by troops and strikebreakers; only the night before, this group with whom I now was quartered had killed three persons.

The National Guard had been called into action, for the safety of non-belligerents and as patrols against looters. Communists and other radicals had hurried into the city to foment trouble wherever possible. The "importing" of strikebreakers brought into the state by private detective agencies, and consisting largely of the scum of existence, had given excuse to racketeering labor exploiters whereby they might arouse the worst instincts of the befuddled workers upon whom they preyed. Store windows were being smashed, streetcars overturned, trucks held up, and drivers beaten; all in a few days, the city had gone mad with hatreds. Such men as formed this little factory guard (all proudly heralded by their private detective impresario as killers) had become a major object of venom.

All night long the sirens had screamed, coming closer, then fading into the distance, as riot cars, ambulances and automobiles filled with Guardsmen in full fighting array, roared to scenes of disturbances. The telephone had jangled at intervals, bringing rumor after rumor, all fakes, — that a mob was forming to march upon the plant, that men with dynamite bombs were to sneak into the alleys and blow up the building, that sharpshooters with long-range rifles were taking positions from which they could snipe at us. During all this time, the man in command, an undersized, sharp-featured little fellow, moved quietly about, changing the position of his killers, re-aligning the guards to more strategic points, or moving a nervous man from front-line position deeper toward the rear. A strangely calm person, this commander of killers. Toward morning, we fell into conversation. I asked if it were true that he had slain two of the three persons listed on the death toll of the previous night.

"Sure," he answered bluntly, "I bumped 'em off."

"Doesn't a thing like that ever bother you?"

He stared.

"Hell. Why should it? That's what we're here for. Either they bump us off or we bump them off. What the hell?"

One instinctively wonders, when talking to a cold-blooded killer, what his antecedents may have been, what motivation might have brought him into a casually brutal business. I inquired into his past.

"I was a doctor," he said.

Unfortunately, this writer always has possessed an illusionary brain, in spite of constant disillusionment. This answer was appetizing to the imagination. Perhaps here was a man who once had held high dreams for his future in an honorable profession. Perhaps he had written a wrong prescription, thus bringing death to a patient and ruining his future. Perhaps he had failed in a major operation, and then, his nerve gone . . .

"Christ!" he broke in. "A fellow finds himself in funny places, now doesn't he? I had a swell racket down in Memphis. I was a clap doctor. But a guy finally ran me out of town with a gun. I got into this business — had to make a living. Now that I'm in it, maybe it's cleaner than what I came from."

As the hours passed, he reminisced upon his "racket."

"I had a swell layout," he said, "right on a main corner, with eight windows and an electric sign. A fellow in trouble couldn't miss it. And I never missed a sucker. I figured on every man who came to my office being worth from fifty bucks to five thousand, maybe more. Trouble with me was I spent more dough than I made. I guess anybody does who has it rolling in so fast he thinks there's no end to it."

His was the true psychology of the racketeer — to get money, by any means whatever, and to obtain almost his entire reward by the fleeting feel of it as it streamed through his fingers. One sentence had struck me as peculiar.

"Do you mean that every man who came to you had gonorrhea?"

"After I got through examining him he did!" There was a glint in his eye — the same sort that I have seen in the eyes of confidence men, circus grifters, pickpockets, when they speak of their victims. I asked for explanation.

"Hell," he announced. "There's as much clap (gonorrhea) caught in a crook's office as there is from women. Look here," he warmed to thoughts of the past. "Suppose a person has any kind of urethral inflammation. Every man knows such a thing can happen and still not be clap. So he comes to my office.

"Now, I used to go on the assumption that anybody who was smart enough to recognize the kind of disease I treated was smart enough to know that maybe he didn't have what he was afraid he had. So I'd pretend that he shouldn't worry until we'd had a thorough check-up. Tell him about how fellows got scared for no reason at all. The only way to be sure was to make a microscopical examination.

"Then I'd get all fixed up with the gadgets of the racket, white coat, rubber gloves and all that, and take a smear on a glass slide. I'd let the sucker think he saw every move I made. But just when I'd go to the microscope to examine the slide, I'd discover that my oil-of-cedar bottle — used it, you know, to aid enlargement — was on a shelf in another part of the office. Naturally, by this time, the patient was a little worried and not paying too much attention to what I was doing. I'd walk away from him, plainly carrying that slide in my right hand. On the shelf where I kept the bottle would be another slide that I knew was full of bugs because I had taken them from an acute case. When I got the bottle, I switched slides and came back with what he thought was the original smear in my right hand, just as it had been when I left him. Then I'd make the examination.

" 'Sorry,' I'd say, 'I guess you're just unlucky.' Then I'd get out a g-u book, show him pictures of microscopical enlarge-

ments in gonorrhea cases, especially regarding the bacilli gono-
coccus, bacilli Friedlander, pneumococcus and staphylococcus
that so often go together. I'd be sure to point out how the
gonococci look just like coffee beans, laid out in pairs, with the
flat sides to each other. Then I'd tell him to take a look through
the microscope. He'd look, and that would be enough. He'd ask
me how much it would cost to cure him up.

"Instead of answering him, I'd privately press a button which
rang a bell in my private office, and excuse myself to 'answer the
phone.' Of course what I did then was to examine his real
smear on another microscope and determine whether he really
was infected. If he was not, and he looked like a guy who
couldn't stand much pressure, I'd guarantee to cure him in
three weeks for fifty bucks. But if he seemed to be ready dough,
I'd hand him a line about how his trouble really couldn't be
fixed up in less than six weeks and not even then if complications set in. Usually I'd hook him on a sort of sliding scale
proposition, and then give him a 'treatment.' If he was worth
dough, and really had clap, I'd just give him inflammatory
injections to be sure of complications. If he didn't have it, I'd
inject him with a culture, and make damn certain he was going
to get it."

The announcement was as brutal as that, and with a certain
amount of reminiscent pride. For some weirdly unexplainable
reason, there are few quacks who do not look upon venereal
disease as being excruciatingly funny.

"After that," I suggested, "you'd have the sucker nailed."

"Sure," answered the little killer. "I was certain to be in the
dough one way or another. Then, of course, every time the
patient came to see me, I'd ask him questions. Ask him where
he thought he caught this dose and who from. If he was mad
enough, he'd tell. Usually he thought he got it from a whore
or some cheap tart or charity pushover. But every once in a while
a patient, mad as hell, mind you, would let it out that he'd
been laying some married woman. Then it was up to me to find

out if she had money. If she did, and this was a case where I'd faked clap, I'd tip off a private dick who worked with me and he would see that the dame paid what we figured it was worth to keep her husband from finding out that she'd been laying another man. If it was an honest case of disease, and the patient had caught it from a rich widow or divorcée, the pickings were even easier, because there's no woman who wants that information peddled around.

"There's a million ways to cash in on clap or syph. They're a mint. There's the patient himself; get him scared enough and drag his case out long enough and you can get every dime he ever had. Even after you've cured him up, you've got it on him for the rest of his life — especially if you read in the paper that he's going to be married. You don't even appear in the picture, of course. You work in cahoots with a private dick who does the blackmailing. The trouble with me was that my partner — the dick — was a loud-mouth bastard. He used to get drunk and blab all around town how he made his dough and who was in with him. Well, there was a hot-headed young fellow that I'd scored for about eight thousand dollars, and he went crazy and came down to my office and took three shots at me. My dick friend got me to a hospital and kept the story away from the newspapers. But I knew my skin wasn't worth a dime if I stayed in business. So I took it on the lam." He fingered the gun in his belt as sirens screamed again, and police cars roared past in the break of dawn, which soon was to end my vigil. "And now I'm in a different profession. . . ."

"Maybe it isn't so different," he added after a time. "Here you bump 'em off sudden. In that other business it just takes longer — half the guys in the clap and syph racket don't know the first thing about really curing a tough case — and don't give a damn."

It must not be concluded that this writer's accusations against the buzzards of the "Men's Diseases" racket are predicated upon a specific instance. There is no fraud so fiercely attacked on every possible occasion by the American Medical Association as the practices of criminal quacks who pretend miraculous cures with high regard for their own pocketbooks and little consideration for the patient. Such activities have largely eliminated the old "shows" once widely used by "Men's Diseases" quacks in which victims often were obtained through mental suggestion engendered by displays of wax figures depicting various stages of gonorrhea, syphilis and other ailments. Nevertheless, more elusive and less spectacular, the "clap and syph" racketeer continues to exist. The very secrecy of venereal disease protects him to a large degree in that his patients, no matter how grossly deceived, how viciously blackmailed or injured through malpractice, often are either ignorant of the cause of their woes or fear the publicity resultant from complaints against the men who have swindled them. And even when honorable men of the medical profession make martyrs of themselves in an effort toward unlicensing crooked practitioners, they often find the renegade entrenched behind a stone wall erected by powerful politics.

If it is possible for ex-convict doctors, such as Dr. Joseph P. Moran, of the Barker-Karpis crew of kidnappers, to have their license to practise restored after they have served penitentiary terms for death through abortion, it is even easier for men in the "clap and syph racket" to protect themselves through the same working of political machinery. There have been numerous instances in which medical men, convicted of everything from abortion murder to the selling of narcotics, have resumed practice within a few months following release from prison. The records of these men usually show a close affiliation with some one "wired in to the Board."

The same is true of the "clap and syph racket." One finds these men highly interested in politics — especially that of municipality, county, and state. They often contribute to campaign funds. They take care of "the boys," without charge, when one of them suffers because of a social error with a woman. They are great friends of district leaders and ward heelers and party committeemen. They use the privacy of their offices as propaganda posts for the election of men who they feel sure will favor them in case of a campaign against quacks. They do this because they know that in many cases, without the active aid of political protectors, they would not be able to exist. In numerous cities they are banded together in whole-sale lots, one protecting another.

Look about you in cities of political cheapness, or where reg-ulation, of medical boards or of police departments, is lax. You will find that the "Diseases of Men" doctors often are congre-gated in areas adjacent to railroad stations, bus stations, room-ing houses, districts in which prostitution is protected, and where travelers come and go in large numbers. The natural in-clination is to believe that they are here because patients may be near by. That is partly true, but there is a greater and more fundamental cause. This is the fact that they must be within easy reach when their army of steerers, cappers, shillabers, and sap-herders have a sucker in tow, and want to get him to the office in a hurry, there to become the victim of a ghastly farce.

The bus and railroad station, the hotel lobby, the motion picture show which operates on a "grind" basis and where men drop in merely to pass time; the tavern, the beer joint where men may loaf — all these are active fields for the shillaber, or steerer, for "good old Doc."

Their method is simple. They engage a near-by companion in conversation, especially if his appearance denotes him to be from rural districts, or if he gives evidence of protracted drink-ing. Some time is devoted to the establishment of confidence. This done, the shillaber supposedly begins to unburden his heart in talk of moral derelictions in which he carefully sounds out his companion concerning any possible time when he too may have strayed from the straight path.

At discreet intervals, the capper has spoken vaguely of "good old Doc," and "the finest doctor in the world," and "the fellow who really saved my life," whom he intends to visit in a few minutes, having come to town for this purpose. He dilates upon general aches and pains, and seems highly surprised to learn that his companion has something of the same symptoms, usually no more than those which occur from constipation, acidosis, or a dozen other thoroughly common ailments.

If the victim has any blotches on his skin they come in for sharp, but supposedly surreptitious, scrutiny. Always there is the build-up of the "good doctor" as a soul of honesty, of endeavor, of professional high-mindedness. Without ever having seen the physician, the victim becomes imbued with a subconsciously high regard for him. That is the moment to strike. The shillaber looks at the clock:

"You've got a little time on your hands," he says. "What say you take a stroll down the block with me?"

Here is the reason for the easy accessibility of the "good" doctor's office. It is only a short walk; a victim is passing time. Soon he finds himself in the faker's presence, watching his new friend as he takes treatment, listening to the oft-repeated rote of the racketeer and his confederate as they dilate upon symptoms, all of which stir curiosity in the victim's mind.

Again it is time to strike. The shillaber says:

"Doc, I wish you'd do me a favor. I know you won't charge anything for it unless you find something. My friend here seems to be bothered about the same way I was when I first came here. Mind looking him over?"

If the patient has not been sufficiently sold, there is another campaign upon the basis that every man should be examined at least once every six months, and that this service on the part of the doctor is without charge. How often have you innocently stared at those emblazoned signs —

CONSULTATION ABSOLUTELY FREE!

Certainly, this is no accusation that every quack who so advertises is a racketeer. However, it is a fact that every racketeer who operates upon the basis just described, does so with a free

examination as the bait with which he lures his victims. The
sucker is examined. When he leaves town, he is an entirely different man mentally from the person who, only a short time
before, was passing a few hours between trains or buses in a
station, lobby, grind-show or tavern. He carries with him the
ghastly belief that in some manner, innocently or otherwise, he
has become a victim of syphilis. Already, he may have had his
first injection of Salvarsan or some fake which the racketeer
calls "606," with the smiling prediction of the good doctor
that after another injection or so plus two years of intra-
muscular hypodermics of mercury or salts of bismuth, he will
be just as good as new.

Such fakery is all the more tragic when the tremendous scope
of syphilis is recognized, especially concerning its phases of
wholly innocent contractability. Back in the days when crusad-
ers against white slavery made their way about the country,
the subject of syphilis was an unmentionable subject — even now
it is only emerging from an age-old covering of darkness. If it
was referred to at all, it was in hushed tones under such names
as "French disease," or "city disease" or "private disease."
The fact that about fifty per cent. of it came from prostitution,
or through clandestine cohabitation, while the remainder was
communicated through the drinking cup, towels, kissing games,
and a hundred other innocent forms of contact, could not be
made understandable, because the disease itself, like prostitution, was a subject too naughty for clearly conceived thought.
The whole problem must be approached from an attitude of
hypocrisy. There are yet remaining too many persons who believe that cohabitation, legitimate or illegitimate, should never
be mentioned and that diseases resulting directly or indirectly
therefrom should be hidden under the coal in the cellar. A
cause of crime, disease, unhappiness, illness, death, and insanity,
greater than anything heretofore mentioned in this book, is
hypocrisy and inability on the part of the average person to
boldly face any public problem of any sort.

However, no matter whether one faces or evades the facts, the reality remains that America rapidly is becoming a syphilitic nation. If such an announcement seems sensational, if the findings of the United States Public Health Service, of research by the Health Department of the City of New York and the observations of such men as Dr. T. A. Gonzales, Acting Chief Medical Examiner for New York City, based upon thousands of autopsies, many of them in criminal cases, seem far removed from your own smug community, it might be well to look about you in the town which forms your home. Consult genito-urinary men, and note their well-filled offices. Ask the heart specialist why so many young persons are dying from arterial ailments affecting the heart, brought about, not through "the speed of our modern age" as we like to think, but because of complications resultant from acquired or inherited syphilis. Talk to psychiatrists, keepers of asylums for the insane. Obtain statistics from hospitals which reveal epidemics of venereal diseases in high schools, some brought about through lax morals, a greater number caused by innocent inoculation. Make inquiries of judges who are of sufficient mental alertness to divine that a person accused of annoying women or flirting with young girls, or of having committed rape, may be more of a hospital case than a punitive one. Such actions often are symptoms of the early stages of paresis, a result of syphilis commonly called "softening of the brain."

In New York City, it is estimated that there are nearly four hundred thousand cases of syphilis in active, latent, or inherited form, thus making sufferers of fully five per cent. of the population. To confuse the picture, only about one case in nine is of record. Private doctors have been enlisted in an effort to reveal the true extent of a widespread scourge.

The disease leads to insanity in several forms. It can cause blindness. It may bring about death through spinal afflictions. It is the factor which converts stalwart men into pitiful, shambling figures, crippled through locomotor ataxia. The disease is growing nationally at the rate of more than a half-million new cases every year. Writing in the *Survey Graphic*, Surgeon General Thomas Parran of the United States Public Health Service traces to this disease ten per cent. of all insanity, eighteen per cent. of all disease of the heart and blood vessels, and innumerable deaths of the newly born. Beyond this are bad teeth, bad vision, loss of hair, and a hundred and one imitations of other disease which syphilis assumes in its later stages. The scourge is so prevalent and spreading so rapidly that any man or woman who marries without first submitting to a Wassermann test to determine the absence or presence of syphilis is committing not only an indiscretion but a moral crime against the person beloved and against the future of any child who may result of the union.

The same vile history is true in less vicious measure of gonorrhea, with its attendant threat of death in extreme cases from rheumatic complications, through the necessity of horrible operations for women, prostatic infections for men also sometimes necessitating dangerous operations, and always the haunting danger of blindness, both for the victim and for children born of infected women. A rarely-occurring bugbear of childbirth, especially in rural districts where delivery is not always attended by the safeguards which a hospital can throw about a newly born infant, is that of gonorrheal ophthalmia. Fully a third of the blind persons who beg on our streets, swell our relief rolls, and crowd our institutions there to pitifully fumble at the weaving of baskets or the making of brooms, can trace their affliction, in some fashion or another, to gonorrhea or syphilis.

There can be no greater service on the part of those who seek to clean up their cities than a searching inquiry into the practices and working methods of medical quacks who prey upon those afflicted with so-called "social diseases," remembering always that there are men sufficiently degraded to make good their diagnoses by the actual inoculation of their victims. This is no haphazard charge; the "clap and syph racket" is known to everyone experienced in those twilight zones of the underworld occupied by the professional grifter and chiseler, whether he is a steerer for a gambling game, a capper for a whorehouse, or a shillaber for a confidence man. Like all other rackets it is worked upon a percentage basis; professional runners and shillabers engage in it with the same lack of concern for their victim that a lead-sheep has when it lures a flock into the killing sheds of a packing house.

All such things might now be of the past had the original ideas behind the onslaughts against white slavery followed a well-planned program. However, it was not possible to pursue any course regarding prostitution in an orderly fashion, the rewards were too great for charlatans and professional reformers and disgraces to the altar, who soon had gathered about them an honest, but gullibly meddlesome, group of innocents, the effects of whose endeavors still are to be found in dozens of cities where vice and crime have been united as a vicious part of gangsterism, where bribery is rampant, disease equally so, and — where there are just as many "white slaves" as ever.

All that requires a later and more detailed explanation. Gullibility helped greatly to bring it about, just as prudishness has for years allowed disease to smolder and spread until it now assumes an alarming status. Much of this trouble comes from the attitude of the pulpit that the wages of sin is death and that one must not talk openly of the dread instruments by which the end is achieved. Beyond this, the interference of the pulpit in problems demanding solution through clear, scientifically balanced approach, instead of through the haphazardness of emotion, has opened wide the doors of law-evasion to the craftiness of criminality.

To the pulpit, for instance, must be charged much of the super-sentimentalism and gullibility which politics has used so effectively in its breakdown of the parole system. This is not merely the conclusion of the writer; it is a repetition of what scores of thinking ministers and priests themselves have told me. There are few crooks indeed who do not deliberately look to the pulpit as one of their great friends in escaping punishment for law infraction. It sums up, in convict language, to this:—

"Get the sky-rider on your side. What the hell does it cost you to bull the guy that you're suddenly all full of God and goodness? Ask for a Bible. You got to have readin' matter anyway. Hand a line to the first sucker who comes along lookin' for lost sheep. The minute you get him interested, you've got a front guy — someone to step out and argue for you. Ain't that something?"

This may be painfully disillusioning to hundreds of ministers who believe that they have been saving souls when in truth they merely have been the innocent means of lowering parole barriers, and bringing about pardons and commutations to hardened offenders. Or, to put it in the words of a ministerial friend:

"We're too gullible. We're too innocent. We gauge the thoughts of other persons by our own thoughts, which, in the main, are good thoughts. We want to feel that there is good in the world and that there is nothing so bad but what it can be remedied — especially if that bad thing be a man's soul. So, we accept dishonesty for truth, when we should be more suspicious, more alert, more aware that a crook will use a minister or priest to his own ends as readily as he will use anyone else. I know that we have brought about many pardons and paroles and commutations when we should have stood aside and allowed the law to take its own course. And we have interfered in too many cases where proper punishment was needed instead of the freedom given a prisoner at our request. We have done it with the best intentions in the world. But," he smiled, "what is it they say about the pavements of Hades?"

Beyond this, the gullible minister has been made an active assistant to crime in countless cases. Prisoners look upon him as an ideal way in which to smuggle letters from penitentiaries;

many of these have contained plans for escape. In a recent case, an innocent minister, violating prison rules simply because a convict asked him to do so, became the means by which queer money was smuggled from a prison counterfeiting plant to outside confederates. In the case of one dangerous impostor, ministerial trust was so aroused, that the man of God actually lied to Special Agents of the Federal Bureau of Investigation in stating that he did not know of the whereabouts of this fugitive. Again, in the Lindbergh case, a mistrial was nearly caused by a trusting man of the Gospel who believed he possessed a confession. The case history of practically every recidivist is somewhere high-spotted by association with a minister who believed the crook's stories of reform, when in truth the preacher merely was being used as a cover against the law, a bulwark against prosecution, and an easy avenue toward freedom. It is a certainty that the present low status of parole administration in many states never would have reached its truly degraded depths had it not been for the readiness of the pulpit and its followers to believe that any person who professed a desire toward a better life really deserved it. (Since disease has been a partial subject of this chapter, it might be noted that at least one out of every twelve paroled convicts comes forth from prison with communicable gonorrhea or syphilis.)

Political mishandling of crime problems has been fostered through playing upon the inexperience of men whose knowledge of the seamy side of life has been almost wholly neglected. No one can learn the intricacies of crime in a theological institute. No one can learn the truth about a crook by his own self-serving statements. The pulpit, all too often, has placed ready credence in such plaints. So have social workers; I have the word of one altruistic woman of great riches, who, in a lifetime of effort, has been able to truly reform only one major criminal from a total of more than two hundred.

Politics always seeks an alibi. In parole and easy freedom, especially by grafting governors, the sucker in the case has been the minister. Some preacher always can be found to "front" for a convict who "wants to reform." Nor does he know that perhaps he is being made the victim of a bribe-taking official, whose actions are thoroughly covered by a notation upon official records: "Released to Reverend Brown."

As for the muddling of the problem of white slavery, it was the result of a combination of chicanery and gullibility. Certainly the exploiting of women was something which should have been discussed from the pulpit. However, immediately that discussion began, charlatans appeared like locust-clouds, not to seek an answer to what, after all, was a sociological problem, not to attack the source of rottenness, but to avail themselves of a far more lucrative avenue of effort — the use of the pulpit as a money-making device. The preaching of lascivious discourses under the guise of an attack upon white slavery became almost a racket. Soon enough, the whole foundation of the true fight disappeared. Instead of a determined drive against the sources of prostitution, the panderers, the procurers, the pimps, and other persons who fattened upon prostitution, the battle veered to one in which every effort was concentrated upon prostitution itself. Even when, at last, the Mann Act was passed, designating as a Federal offense the transportation of women from state to state for purposes of commercialized vice, the bill was so muddled in its language that it brought about one of the worst eras of blackmailing in American history.

This happened because reformers, so-called, had centered their interest not upon the cause of prostitution, but the act of it. To-day, the Mann Act stands as a law which must be mal-administered in order that justice may be done. Were it to be truly enforced, the jails of America could not hold its victims, for any man and woman not husband and wife who cross state lines and thereafter cohabit are technically guilty of a felony. The legislative mind had become so confused at the time of the passage of the Mann Act, so excited, that even the normal sexual acts of a man and woman who truly loved each other, yet were not married, must be confined to one state, lest they constitute a penitentiary offense.

The reformers did it, pretending righteousness while they pandered to every gross instinct of the tremendous audiences which everywhere received them. There was little reward in coldly and efficiently attacking the exploiters of women. So they built these exploiters up from cheap, rodentlike imitations of men into passionate ogres, and then, by a meticulous description of carnal attacks, provided highly sought aphrodisiacs in the pictures they painted, not of the white slaver's activities, but of the reactions of the persons upon whom he preyed.

It was not good theater to depict these victims as prostitutes; far better to trace their downward course, from the moment when they, — innocent, beautiful and young, — were raped by some villain and thereupon descended into a threat against every married woman in America.

By these methods, they appealed to every sadist, and there were thousands who reveled in the stories of attack, of rape, of lust. They pandered to degenerates. They whetted the appetites of the repressed. And they gathered to their aid gullible ministers by the hundreds who also felt that they must preach upon this terrible subject and forewarn their flocks against the danger of the Scarlet Woman.

And so, instead of keeping prostitution where it belonged, apart, segregated, there to be surrounded with the proper safeguards, both for inmates and society, they scattered it. All idea of social service was forgotten in a blather of emotion out of which the prostitute emerged, not as a person to be treated clinically and sociologically, but to be reviled, hunted, dispersed — and eventually to end where she is to-day, under the protection of criminal-manned syndicates which bribe city administrations and police departments and own their women as a farmer owns his cattle.

CHAPTER TWELVE

LADIES IN PARLOR A

I REMEMBER most vividly a most ardent laborer in the White Slavery Vineyard who called himself by some such name as "the Reverend Divine Dr. Hope," and whose formula was standard for many of his type. He used the camp-meeting method and his main recipe was to trace the white slave from her days of girlish innocence through the time, when, in an unguarded moment, she met a white slaver. This fiend incarnate was of a sort thoroughly at variance from the true procurer or panderer.

The true type often accomplishes his aim through his attitude of weakness, preying upon feminine sympathy to such a point that he is able to inveigle his victim into going on the streets for his benefit. Sometimes the whore-maker may be of the slick-haired variety, vowing eternal love, promising a hundred things including marriage "just as soon as we get a little money." Or, he may be a man who sufficiently establishes himself as a brute in the mind of a woman with whom he lives, for her either to fear his beatings and therefore earn money for him by the oldest method, or for her to do so with the incessant hope that some really lovable paramour will come along who is big enough and tough enough to knock hell out of the bum with whom she is afflicted and bear her away to a new life.

The Reverend Dr. Hope's white slaver was none of these persons. This Horrible Example wandered through life like a marauding monster, snatching innocents from the very apron strings of their horrified mothers, kidnapping them, bearing them away in his arms, locking them in dank dungeons and foul dens. Moreover, he was a sort of magician. Once he had wreaked his carnal passion upon this frail flower, he inoculated her with a terrible desire to get even with all mankind. This foul fiend had wrecked her virtue, the hate which seared her heart therefore changed her into a vengeful vampire, bent upon a career as a destroyer of men.

Through these methods, fakers like the Reverend Divine Dr. Hope were able to paint a most lascivious picture and, at the same time, to draw the moral lesson that all girls were potential victims for plotting men who would tear off the fair one's clothes, rape her, and, through some weird sort of Svengali control, be able to transform her almost immediately into a she-menace to marriage. Thereby he aroused passion in youth, desire in the repressed, and, what was far worse, an abiding hatred in the heart of every woman who wanted to hold her husband. This hatred took form in wild forays, in which prostitutes were hunted like beasts in some cities, and which have brought about, in our life of to-day, a concealed business which nets millions upon millions for crooked politics and gangster-controlled bawdyhouses.

To all the Reverend Divine Dr. Hopes and their gullible followers may we give thanks for such blessings. I remember him quite starkly — the old faker. My assignment card often demanded that I cover his camp meetings, especially when the placards announced that on this night he would preach upon that subject of such intense interest: "WHAT OF THE FALLEN WOMAN?"

Looking back upon those meetings, I doubt if five per cent. of the entire assemblage viewed the great pastor's sermon as the depiction of a problem to be solved by society in a scientific, humane fashion. In that five per cent. I do not include the Reverend Divine Dr. Hope. I have met too many of his hypocritical kind, filling churches and pocketbooks and at the same time pandering to a love of publicity by tirades against what

they choose to call "the Mary Magdalenes." As for the hot spot
of the Divine's excoriation, I remember it almost word for
word: —

"And then, this fiend in human form, his lust paramount,
takes this child of innocence into his den of iniquity. I can see
him now, his eyes gleaming with the brutal passion, his horrible
hands outstretched toward her beautiful, fair young form.
He strips her clothing from her, revealing the soft, pink flesh
of her innocent body to his lecherous eyes. He creeps upon
her, forcing her to his will, this monster who will turn her
into a vile creature of the brothels, dressed in abbreviated skirts,
with her hair cut short, and without the unmentionables with
which her limbs should be clothed — and soon, my dear friends,
sweet, innocent virtue is transformed into a painted Jezebel,
luring men to hell."

It has been thirty years since the Reverend Divine made his
flaming way about the country. During that time, spent almost
constantly in an atmosphere of murder, courtroom, police stations, and other surroundings which permitted easy inquiry
into the personal history of prostitutes, I have never encountered
an absolutely authenticated case in which a hitherto innocent
girl was seized, carried away by force, robbed of her clothes
and her virtue, then, all in a few days, transformed into a
prostitute who continued her profession in spite of opportunity
to escape. More specifically, I never have encountered one who
could even qualify in any one of these details, much less all of
them. Nor do I know anyone who ever saw such a being. No
doubt, such persons exist; I speak only of personal knowledge.

It would seem, however, that if there is white slavery there
should be white slaves. There are, of course, thousands of women
who might have led some other sort of life had it not been for
men, or women, even to close relatives, who led them into a
degrading existence. However, the white slave as a cringing,
innocent, wholly reluctant young thing, fighting for her virtue,
willing to die for her honor, a pawn for the lecherous assaults

of passion-mad men — I am now using reformers' language —
all that simply does not and cannot exist.

There is a very good reason. Commercialized prostitution
is a business, and always has been. It is regarded as such by
madams, procurers, pimps, refined, respectable church members who rent their rundown property for use as bawdyhouses,
and bribe-taking policemen of the type who have brought about
the saying "as vile as a vice cop." Abortionists, restaurant keepers, lingerie shops and the like, look upon their trade as legitimate. Druggists who live in respectable neighborhoods and belong to the "Everybody Sing" type of luncheon clubs, and who
have a weird ability to spot a district wherein prostitution thrives,
see no harm in fattening upon bawdyhouse money. Nor do
taxi men, who often get a heavy percentage of a girl's earnings
for providing her customers.

Nice, fine doctors with nice, fine wives and children, sleek
and well-fed and well-dressed and housed upon the money
obtained by bleeding chippies of their bedroom earnings through
dragged-out, designedly inefficient treatment of venereal diseases look upon their earnings with the same calm viewpoint
as a seller of Bibles. Even the girls regard their occupation as
a business, the difficulties of which must be endured with
something of the same resignation with which a miner faces
silicosis, a bridge-worker daily looks down toward his possible
place of death, and a gangster fears the bullet of the policeman he cannot bribe. Never once, throughout the many years
in which I have talked upon a basis of thorough understanding
with thousands of prostitutes, procurers, madams and other
adjuncts of the business, have I ever heard white slavery referred to in a serious vein. Yet in spite of all that, it exists —
horrible, filthy, vicious. I repeat, however, that I have never
met one of the Reverend Divine's virginal white slaves.

I have, however, met many Reverend Divine Dr. Hopes. I
have encountered them in raiding squads in the red light districts, so intent upon looking at the legs of prostitutes that

they tripped over the furniture. I have seen them ranting up and down the crib lines of Western cities, driving women before them like cattle, not caring where they went, not giving a thought that they were spreading prostitution into respectable neighborhoods and laying the foundations by which it might become a paying investment for gangsterism.

I have seen them — in large and small churches — as they painted word pictures of debauchery and lechery, of lust and passion and sexuality, to an audience which drooled at every word; and as they covered this horrible hypocrisy by the demand that all such women be driven from the highways and the byways, that our youth be safe and our children undefiled. And I have seen those same women driven into the same block as the minister, even into the same apartment house, there to bribe janitors, corrupt elevator boys, and the cops on the beat, that they might carry on their traffic under the very nose of the man who fought so hard to make sex safe for everybody.

On the other side of the fence, I have questioned many women regarding the means and causes by which they came to be, in the parlance, turned out. The average story simmers down to the tragically simple explanation:

"Oh, I don't know. I was out of a job and my clothes were about down to the last rag. I got to running around with a guy. He said to me one day: 'Hell, what's the use of you being a charity piece all your life? Why don't you make some dough out of it?' So I did and I've been keeping that guy ever since."

These few sentences tell, to a large measure, the story of a great part of prostitution. There are few girls in the business who have not met at least one of those Four Horsemen of white slavery: Vanity, Moral Weakness, Adversity, and Love. These are the real procurers, without their aid no pimp could live.

Quite true, even if it sounds contrary to previous statements, there have been innumerable instances of compulsory prostitution in which women, enforced for one reason or another, have

sold their bodies and passed over the proceeds to their husbands, their sweethearts or their pimps. There have been numerous cases of unkindness and brutality.

All these were such that the men involved seemingly deserved to get much longer penitentiary sentences than they
received. Perhaps those longer terms would have been meted
out, except for the fact that in almost every instance the girl
herself played a more or less willing part in the beginnings of the
fortune which befell her. That is not meant as mitigation for
the acts of white slavers. It is merely confirmation of my statement that for thirty years I have looked in vain for the type of
black-bearded man who seizes a young, wholly innocent young
girl in his hairy arms, bears her away to be made a captive of
vice and, perhaps, to be starved or beaten into submission until at last she gaily announces that she will answer the landlady's call for the ladies to show up in Parlor A, then beg, cajole
and entice some highly selective man, surrounded by feminine
besiegers, to come up stairs and have a good time with her.
The whole thing does not make sense.

Again there must be the reminder that prostitution is a business. More than that, it is a business built wholly upon the
alleged purveying of pleasure. There may be old maids and
jealous wives and imaginative nit-wits who believe that all
men are such brutes that they would pay for the company of a
weeping, oppressed and recently assaulted child of innocence.
And there is a certain percentage of such men. Almost any police
reporter of wide experience knows the names of dozens upon
dozens of supposedly respectable citizens who sneak into
houses, bearing with them requisites of perversion which include
everything from specially made whips for flagellation to caged
pigeons from which the heads will be torn at the proper moment.
Such perverts readily might be highly interested in a novelty
like a weeping young girl, provided there was no danger for
them in her association. Such persons, however, are exceedingly
eager that there shall not be the slightest possibility of the invasion

of their secrecy and that of their acts. They ordinarily obtain this protection by payments of extra money and with full understanding on the part of their feminine co-workers that, once out of the house, they are forgotten. They want the association of no one who might, in a moment of revulsion, kick, scream and yell loudly enough to attract passers-by.

So even the lowest forms of human existence do not care to take part in the so-called "breaking-in of a white slave." No way ever has been found to so gag or make dumb any compulsory victim of prostitution that she cannot tell her story to some person who will help her. The lower in social stratum her merchandised lovers may be, the quicker they will respond to any plea for aid. A hunkie from railroad construction or from a lumber camp, or a ditchdigger or a hobo, has no social position to lose. He doesn't care if his name gets in the papers. It won't affect his business. And his fellow hypocrites in his lodge or luncheon club or church will not look upon him with scorn, meanwhile wondering if that's the girl they had last Tuesday night.

Beyond this, a powerful protector for the reformer's innocent virgin would be the super-maudlinity of the average whore. One may hear more cheap mother-doggerel and more mawkish sentiment, may witness more idiotic hokum in the parlors of bawdyhouses than in all the picture shows of America. Hustlers are eternally dragging home sick cats, mangy dogs, moulting canary birds and bargain goldfish, simply "because they felt sorry for them." There is a saying in the underworld: "As soft as a whore-lady's heart."

It is rather unlikely that a young girl, a virgin, kidnapped from the streets and held captive against her will and pleadings, would long remain as such in a house of prostitution where there were other inmates. The average experienced whore will stand for many personal indignities. She will and can be framed by police. Her clothes are often taken from her to prevent escape with some new lover or pimp. She is systematically robbed.

She is a sucker for every sort of a con game that exists. But let imposition be visited upon someone or something which she believes to be friendless or helpless and she will fight like a tigress.

Beyond all this, there have been few white slave cases in which an attempt was made to go into conditions which existed before the girl was put into prostitution. There is the crime, there is the evidence, and there is the conviction — *ergo,* everything upon which evidence has been given has been true in its most stark form, and the evil has been eliminated. If a girl testifies in court that she was held by guards, that she was threatened, that she was beaten and tortured, no thought seemingly is given to the fact that this girl may be striving desperately to hold what vestiges of self-respect may remain to her. Even though it be granted that she was beaten, that she was held captive, that she was forced by threats or physical fear to give herself to men, a logical viewpoint would be that there was some other compelling motive — some inducement which began it all, some willingness on her part to at least skirt the edges of prostitution, and some great cause which underlay even these structural weaknesses. It is granted that there have been a few individual cases where the "captured" girl was truly virtuous. In such instances almost the first man to whom she appealed became her knight errant, and not only saved her but became a witness against her defamer.

Every true story, however, brings hundreds that are untrue, perhaps mercifully so. The girl who tells such stories is making a valiant fight for the future. Her occupation and identity revealed by a raid or investigation, she naturally is faced with the necessity of going home. It is to her credit that she tries to save herself in the eyes of her parents. Beyond this, she must return to the old town, to the sneers of the cruel and inhuman, the eyebrow-lifting of so-called Christian women, the viciousness of the respectable. Far better that she should do so with a court's unvoiced benediction upon her fable, which did not affect the verdict, than that she should be branded by him an inordinate and incorrigible hussy. At least it gives her a chance, and a chance is worth taking.

Newspapers print the dramatic side of any story, often forgetting the sordid details which would mar the drama of a good yarn. Hence the typical case of a "white slave" known only in the records as Lucy is of interest. It must be taken for granted that the man in the case was a first-class, deckle-edged skunk. The accounts of this trial made him a fiend incarnate, which he probably would have been if he had thought he could get away with it. And he had the aid of other villains — conditions and causations upon which every procurer depends. Therefore, I introduce Lucy, a seventeen-year-old girl, discovered weeping and truly forlorn, in the alley of an Eastern city.

The police found her, a frail, dejected figure. They questioned her.

Finally she blurted: "My boy friend beat me up."

Then came her story of having been forced into the streets to supply the wants of the man who had promised to marry her, a twenty-year-old bootlegger-pimp, who was not only living upon the illicit fruit of this young girl's work, but that of several others, for all of whom he had been the compelling force in their adopting of prostitution.

In each of the cases of the several girls who worked for this man, there had been a considerable period of cohabitation between the girl and the man before prostitution ever was mentioned. Further, in one case, this white slaver had promised to marry a girl with whom upon numerous occasions he had engaged in sexual intercourse. He had sent for her to come to him, whereupon he had intended to put her on the streets. However, when she arrived, she found him in bed with another girl, became angry, and went home. That girl had sense enough, and moral courage enough, to do the right thing, and no man could have made a prostitute of her.

Another girl said that the man had promised to marry her, but had evaded the issue. Nevertheless, while time went on and on, she made no attempt to leave him; in fact, she took him to her sister's home, pretending that they really were married. She was not tongue-tied when she saw her sister; she could have found aid there. Instead, she continued to do what she had been doing, which was walking the streets for this man, because of the fact that one of white slavery's Four Horsemen dictated it — she was in love with him.

The man got what he deserved, which was four years in a Federal prison as the result of prosecution by the Federal Bureau of Investigation under Mann Act charges. Possibly he should have received a more severe sentence, especially in view of the fact that he had also put seventeen-year-old Lucy on the streets. However, there were some mitigating circumstances:

Lucy's mother was dead. She lived with her father, who allowed her so much leeway that at fifteen she had met this man, had engaged several times with him in sexual intercourse, then had lived with him. He later took her into another state where she went on the street for him. Finally they returned home for Christmas, intending to stay there. But she left home and returned to her former fields of prostitution — this time as a streetwalker for her own benefit. The pair later met. The pimp demanded some money. She refused to give it to him. He hit her on the head with a beer bottle, and she told the police — not because he had lured her from home, not because he had made a prostitute of her, not because he had failed in his offer of marriage, but *because he had hit her with a bottle.*

Therefore, to solve the problem of such girls as Lucy, one must go behind the panderer and the procurer. One wonders, for instance, whether or not the agencies which are supposed to look after the fortunes of luckless children were functioning in the city in which this girl lived. One wonders what sort of police protection existed in the "joints" this pair visited when first they met, the dance halls, the barbecue dumps, and all the other hangouts and hideouts of youth. One wonders what sort of mental cesspool was possessed by her father, that he would allow his fifteen-year-old daughter to wander sufficiently to be a pick-up for the first fellow who came along, and then become his bedmate and his whore, working the streets to put money in his pocket.

These are the real white slavers — such facts as the foregoing. These are the Four Horsemen, riding to the aid of every slick-haired rat who lives by the labors of a woman's body. Yet, I doubt if the father blames himself. The system of education in that town sees nothing that it neglected. The police dismiss the matter by saying that "you can't do anything with these kids." The dance hall proprietors and the hamburger booth-joints continue to flourish without a thought that they may have played a part in the degradation of a child.

The main trouble about all the jumble of white slavery mis-information is that there are too many men — and a number of women — who would curl up and die if it ever became pub-licly known that they ever had passed the doors of a house of prostitution. Having once been a crime reporter, with my main sources of information the fifty or sixty bawdyhouse land-ladies of a large city, I have been admitted by the back doors too many times not to know the names and social position of the male and female "folks from up on the hill" who had de-cided to go "hopping" that night and had sneaked down to Anna's house, where they bought out the place and locked the doors.

Thus, I realize that the persons who really know prostitution at first hand are afraid to talk about it. The average vice or morals squad cops who are entrusted with the enforcement of local laws concerning prostitution all too often are sleeping with the landlady, or have a girl in the house, or are such double-crossers that a girl would not trust them with a used deck of cards. As for Federal men, a landlady would bite out her tongue rather than talk to one of those fellows; a slip might mean a jolt in prison on richly deserved Mann Act charges.

Thus the whole subject is left to a comparatively few sources of information. There is the Captain of Police, or the District Attorney, who, following a raid, and upon questioning the inmates, hears not the real story, but the one which the girl wants believed at home. When Special Agents of the Federal Bureau of Investigation or men like Thomas E. Dewey of New York attempt to dig into syndicate white slavery, they find themselves confronted by stubborn and recalcitrant witnesses whose volubility has been thoroughly devitalized by the realization that if they talk they will become material witnesses against gangland. There are the professional reformers who are in it for the money. Then there are the gullible ministers and their more gullible flocks who believe every word that a reformer tells them. Added altogether, the total spells nothing of the general picture. Only once in a while does true information leak out, such as a hand-written "code of ethics" discovered by Special Agents in an investigation into a white slavery ring operating between Cleveland and New York. Here indeed is a Lexicon of Prostitution. Evidently written by the head procurer for this gang it gives an excellent picture of the cold-blooded, businesslike attitude held toward the racket by those who look upon girls "in the hustling profession" with the same eyes of appraisal held by persons who buy and sell cattle for market. Likewise, since one does not go from door to door interviewing prospects for prostitution, it is implied that applicants go out and look for a job like any other feminine worker. Therefore, it would seem that a large body of our prostitutes regard the life in almost as detached a manner as the flesh-purveyors who hire them. Here is the code for "interviewing," as used by one large syndicate. It is bizarre evidence.

In Choosing a Girl.

One should consider:

Meet for a conversation and judge personality, youth, beauty, health. (Cheerful, pleasant, willing, sociable? Judge characteristics, disposition, and temperament.)

COHABITING: Passionate or cold? Real or pretended? (Weigh intellect, sexual vigor, recommendations and references. Ask age, size, weight, facial expression, and if real blonde or brunette.)

GENERAL APPEARANCE: Take note of form, general, and breast, legs, buttocks and abdomen. Tall or short? Slender or heavy? Ankles slender? Tapering calves? Full thighs? Developed breasts?

SKIN: Smooth or rough? White or otherwise? Pores large or small?

CARRIAGE: Poise? Gait? Movement? Gestures? High or low arch? Foot large or small?

ANY NOTICEABLE DEFECT: In teeth, tone, limp, bowlegs, bad breath, etc.

HABITS: Language? Quiet? Secret? Reliable?

DRINKS: This is to be judged by whether or not the house desiring a girl serves drinks. Some object, others request it.

TYPE OF RELATION: Natural? French? Permit French? Accept an all-night man? Be present at an exhibition? Or take part in one?

PIMPS: Inquire if she keeps a pimp and if so how often she wants to see him. What race? Does she support others?

ACQUAINTANCESHIP: Know friends? Callers? Special Police?

WORK: Where has she worked, when, what? What experience gained under proper guidance? Former police registration and where?

EARNINGS: Figure what her approximate earnings will be for the house. Get real name and address. Also business name. Judge her manner of pre-approach, approach, reception, and dismissal of patrons.

Regarding other phases of cold-bloodedness, there have been outstanding examples which should cause active efforts to ensure their not happening again. In certain cases, whoremakers have adopted female children from various institutions and reared them by the dozen from childhood in surroundings and habits which included every sort of depravity, including cohabitation with the male foster-parent. Then, at an early age, the girls have been put on the streets to contribute a share of their earnings in repayment for their rearing. It is sickening and disgusting that such things should be. Nevertheless, they have happened and will continue to happen until society strikes at the source — which is the loosely run, poorly administered, po-

litically corrupt handling of many private and state institutions for the young. In most parts of the United States, precautions to assure decent, clean, crime-free parentage for adoptees
seemingly never has been considered. Not only much prostitution
can be traced to this cause, but a tremendous amount of crime.
Perhaps it would be well not to endow every mealy-mouthed
applicant for a baby with the angel-desire of sacred motherhood.
Beyond this, the sale of a girl's virtue by parents before she is
independent is not unusual.

An investigator sat one night last winter in a certain Minnesota bawdy house, talking to the landlady. The police had
told him the town was as "clean as a whistle." Newspapermen
had intimated otherwise and later won a Pulitzer prize by
proving it. There is no magic about efficient investigation. One
needs no false mustache, or even an assumed name. One simply
loafs around a few pool-halls and drinking places, meets bartenders or tavern-maids or dance-hall hostesses or taxicab drivers,
buys drinks, talks their language and asks questions. Whereupon,
if he looks "right," he learns from them what every policeman
already knows, which is the names and addresses of every bawdyhouse and gambling house in town. There is nothing very secret
about vice or gambling; it cannot exist without word-of-mouth
publicity. Likewise, there are few prostitutes, keepers of call
houses, bawdyhouse landladies, or even streetwalkers who have
managed to exist without paying off either the cop on the beat,
his active superior, or someone higher up.

Therefore, to learn all about this city's vice in one evening
was no task whatever. The investigator simply chose a wise
taxicab driver, who saw in him some ready money, and asked
to be taken to "some spots." So, it happened that after a time
he was buying a drink for the landlady of a bawdyhouse, described (after later raids) as possessing "twenty-two voluptuous girls."

The conversation on police fixing, political-gangster protection, house rules, and all that sort of thing, came about as casually as talk about the weather — perhaps more so, since there had not yet been any snow, and Minneapolis in the winter without snow is hardly worth discussing. The landlady was youngish, pert, and extremely proud of her business. All her girls were under twenty, she said, and every one of them was an "all round girl," which meant that no matter what type of pervert might enter the place, no matter what sort of circus or exhibition was desired, it could be arranged with as many as five and six eager young participants from among the "twenty-two voluptuous girls," at a maximum cost of ten to thirty dollars. All that was passed over with a wave of the hand, as it were; so many places are that way these days. What really counted was the high ideals of Cherry for her girls, many of whom, she confided, "were highly refined" and came "from awfully good homes."

"No customer can ever say," said Cherry as she sipped her wine, "that they ever came into this place and got bummed to death by girls chiseling cigarettes. I won't stand for it. There's nothing that takes a gentleman's mind off of what he came for quicker than to have a gang of these new-fashioned little chippies ganging him for ciggies. And if you'll notice" — she glanced appraisingly out at what was called "the traffic," carried on to the accompaniment of the incessantly ringing doorbell and a constant shifting of couples from the various parlors into bedrooms, which extended into the next building — "you'll see that none of my girls do much drinking. I don't fake the customers that they're buying a girl a drink when it's only ginger ale instead of whisky, or plain water if they order gin. I let the girls have a little wine and that's all right. But there's no drunkenness, and when a girl gets through work she can go home as clean as when she left there."

"You've got a big place here," the investigator suggested.

"Oh, yes. And I keep it clean."

"Cost much?"

"My rent, you mean?"

The investigator indicated an itching palm.

"Oh, that? Well, it varies. Sometimes it's plenty, depending on how much the Bunch needs, or whether it's around Christmas or — you know. Usually a hundred a month lets me out. Of course the syndicate handles that — there's a little syndicate here, you know. It's tied up with St. Paul, Sioux City, and a few more towns. The Jew's got the town here; he pays off, I don't bother, except about seeing him. No, all that's easy enough." She sighed. "But you see, I do a lot of hiring for the Jew. The girls are all right. It's t! ose goddam mothers that get my goat."

"The who?"

"The mothers. The girls' mothers. They've always got something on their chest. I won't hire a girl unless I know her mother; I'm not going to have some little chippy getting sore at me and running out and saying she's been white-slaved. Either their mothers know all about it, or they just don't work." She shook her head. "What a bunch of bitches!" she exclaimed. "Can you imagine it; getting sore as hell, because I insist on these girls only working twenty-five days a month?"

It would be less degrading if Cherry could be described as an unusual example of the present-day Syndicate landlady. Unfortunately, however, she has many counterparts.

Another cause of white slavery is listed in many outmoded investigative reports as "marriage to exploiters." At one time that was true, nearly every prostitute had at one time been married. To-day, however, they often come straight from high school. The age limit on prostitution has gone down; a girl of twenty-two is old and of deep experience. As for other causes, there are procurers and panderers by the thousand. There are men who have inoculated girls with venereal diseases to make them afraid to go home and thus force them to obey them. This, however, usually happens when a man wants a woman to go on the street for him, and she usually does it.

A pimp is a strange creature. but a pimp's woman is stranger.

The explanation is even more weird, usually summing up to this: "Well, when you come right down to it, we really don't know any men. We see fellows for a little while and we don't give a damn about them. How are you going to get interested in anybody when there's twenty or thirty of them, maybe in a night? Now, when I was a manicure girl, it was different. I'd talk to my customers about different things — but here, there's only one subject and all the men are usually in a hurry to get to bed, and then in a bigger hurry to get out of the place before somebody sees them. So, even if a man's a steady caller, he hardly ever tells you anything about himself, and if he can't tell you anything about himself, how can he talk? Now, in the barber shop, I really was interested in my customers. They'd talk about their business, or their family and all that. But here, a girl really gets lonely. So if some fellow comes along and makes a play for a girl, it sort of flatters her, now doesn't it? What I mean, it isn't the same kind of a line you get from your regular customers; all you see of them after a half hour or so is their face in the mirror when they are being sure their tie looks just like it did when they came in. So, finally, some fellow comes along that's kind of nice and spends what money he's got on you; oh, I don't know, he's sort of weak, and you get to mothering him, and he's always kind of half-sick, or maybe the bastard's just lazy; I don't know. Did you ever hear Helen Morgan sing that song 'My Bill'? Well, that's it. So the first thing you know, you're giving the big bum money and working your tail off for him, but you kind of don't mind it."

Thus a girl will go out on the streets in fair weather and foul for "Her Bill." That is why she supports him, feeds him, clothes him, endures hell for him, and in practically every case where there has been procuring, where a panderer has lured some girl into prostitution through promises of good wages, good times, pretty clothes or even marriage, one finds that this could not have been done with a feminine person who possessed the necessary moral foundation to resist even the slightest of temptations.

This is said in no sense of mitigation for the procurer or panderer; as far as I am concerned they can all be emasculated and then boiled in oil. But it does point out that criminal prosecutions, the building of more crime by viewing prostitution as one to be coped with by policemen and judges and juries, will no more affect the problem than rain on a tile roof.

Why is it, for instance, that procurers flourish in coal-mining towns where there is muck and grime and drunkenness; where there are slatternly homes, dirty, muddy streets, gaunt, gray outlooks, and home life which would not even recognize itself if called by name?

It must be dismissed as a fairy tale that white slavers grab their victims by the hair of the head, drag them away, dress them in gaudy gowns and, by some big-third-act of the old time mellerdrama, hypnotize them into bedizened females who hurry forward, like hounds on the chase, whenever the Madame calls out in her practised tones: "Ladies in Parlor A!"

Rather, the procurer works with his Four Horsemen of Vanity, Moral Weakness, Adversity, and Love ever at his elbow. He cares not at all about stealing a girl's virtue, except perhaps as a personal adventure. He is in a business, and the prerequisite of business is the pursuit of money. Therefore, his task is not that of breaking hymens, but of seeking those who have obligingly had this fleeting trademark already effaced. Nor is this difficult.

If one knows prostitutes, one knows above all else that they run to a certain type. It is not the hard-bitten, vicious, coldly-calculating character with which Inexperience paints the so-called "Fallen Sister"; the adamantine quality usually comes into being after the hardening influences of a thoroughly disillusioning life have beaten out every remaining vestige of faith and belief; then existence becomes a cutthroat affair, and men merely so many bags of momentary passion to be taken, like Coney Island waffles, while they're hot. The potential prostitute is an entirely different being.

First of all, she must be the type of girl who will believe that the moon is not made of green cheese, but camembert. She must be sickened with her surroundings, either through genuine revulsion, or though some supersensitive ego which makes her long for things to which her rearing, her mental capacity, her general ability, strength of purpose, and ideals do not entitle her. She must be a chaser of rainbows. She must be easy to look at, — in the practical sense, — the sort of girl who does not raise her nose when she is ogled. She must possess very little common sense. I have known procurers who could walk along the streets of a town and spot unerringly the girls whom he wanted and whom he later got.

There is no mysterious ability to it, no hypnotism, no magical formula. Candidates run to certain definite symptoms: constant looking in the mirror — evidence of a certain amount of the narcissus complex; eagerness for male association — faces which denote not only an inability to voice the negative but little desire to do so; a certain air of gaudy finery about the mode of dress, even when more fitting clothing can be afforded. There is a love for loading on jewelry, the novelty type being preferred to the genuine, an inordinate fondness for silk; a self-worship, taking form in devotion to every cheap fad of dress, foot, and fingernail adornment, or movie press-agented hairdress and wave. Such a girl can be told she resembles even opposite types of the screen, and be vain enough to believe it. Above all, she must be fairly well-known around the poolhalls, the cigar store, and the drugstore, as a pushover.

Given these potentialities, it is only necessary for a procurer to paint a picture which places her in her motion picture dreams of plenty of money, all the clothes in the world and a good time. Often he need not even do that.

Perhaps the girl is fed up at home. Perhaps her mother is a slattern, the house a pigpen, and her father a drunken boor. There are thousands of such cases, and in most of them there are few girls who have not expressed themselves as much happier walking the streets than enduring what is so often called "the sanctity of home and mother."

Therefore, perhaps it isn't the procurer who is wholly to blame. Perhaps it is haphazard education, which, in too many communities, is in the hands of politicians and shot through with graft. Perhaps those social workers who pay more attention to being nasty-tempered than they do to remedying glaring conditions directly under their noses might bear their share of the onus of white slavery. Perhaps those corporations whose directors look upon municipal beauty, proper amusement, playgrounds and happiness as evidences of Communism, should shoulder some of the responsibility. And perhaps society itself, which regards the prostitute as a criminal instead of an evidence of something distinctly wrong with our social structure, might refrain for a time from sneers at these unfortunates and regard itself for what it is: a white slaver, *par excellence.*

Perhaps, too, something might be done about parents — the idiotic, blind, selfish type of parents, who refuse to see that white is white and black is black, who seemingly have forgotten all the filth which had filtered into their minds by the time they were twelve or fourteen years old and pretend to believe that such things passed out of existence with the disappearing generation. Perhaps if the super-blind type of mothers and fathers were thrown in jail for pretending to believe that their sons or daughters were merely engaged in harmless petting until two and three o'clock in the morning, they might bestir themselves and discover that their dear bashful children possessed such innocent playthings as lipsticks or oversized pencil eraser holders or vanity case "cigarettes" which concealed contraceptives; that certain types of rubber goods other than automobile tires can be purchased at any filling station which is highly popular with the youth of the town, and that there is more than one high-school in America where various types of sexual reward, from masturbation to perversion, are demanded by certain boys and freely given by certain girls in return for bids to picture shows, dances, and proms. Perhaps they might become more interested in the sexual effects of marihuana, which will be discussed more fully in another chapter, and which finds one of its great fields of distribution in the vicinity of high school buildings. Perhaps if they discovered all these things, perhaps if it was revealed to them that since the beginning of "the Era of Youth" the sale of rubber contraceptives in one large factory alone has increased by seven thousand per cent., they still would continue to close their eyes, to evade responsibility for kindly, common-sense home discipline, to smile blandly and say: —

"Oh, yes, indeed. Conditions must be terrible. But you see, our Beatrice is different."

CHAPTER THIRTEEN

SEX AND THE SYNDICATE

THE Queen was in her boudoir, not eating bread and honey, but taking a slug of gin now and then as she made up for the evening. Thereby she presented a strange picture.

Once upon a time, this big room with its Louis XV furniture and a certain air of delicate dignity, had mirrored the activities of a rich and influential family. Even now there were vestiges of their reign: a few oil paintings and brocaded silks which remained of the original wall coverings; a silken bell-pull hung at the head of the Queen's canopied bed. Only the carpetings were new and garishly out of harmony. The Queen was not of the family which once had made this home a gathering place for the society of one of America's largest cities.

Back in the days when the Queen's visitor had been a tow-headed youngster, taking his first deliberate step from the place of newspaper beginnings toward that mirage of all writers, New York, he often had passed this place with the proper awe which a cub reporter should give a Sanctum of Society. Once he even had rung its doorbell and asked the stiff-necked butler a question regarding the Europe-bound intent of the Great Family which lived there. The place then had been a massive, stone structure of a design of the 'nineties, with ivy clinging to its walls, gates of wrought iron, and an atmosphere of the unapproachable about its wide, smooth grounds and curving driveways. It was the abode of Money and of Society and of Privacy.

The ivy still clung to the walls, weathered now by the passage of more than a quarter of a century. The wrought-iron gates remained, even though they did creak a bit wearily upon their hinges. And there was a man at them, just as there always had been a man on guard back in those cub reporter days. Where the inner blaze of lights had been discreetly shielded by well-pulled shades in the old days, there still remained that attitude of the aloof, the set-apart.

With that, all similarity ended.

No shiny victorias, drawn by spanking, bob-tailed horses, now shimmered along the curving driveway, under the porte-cochère, and onward to the big stables. Automobiles had taken their place, but they were not of the sleek, heavily cushioned variety. They were taxicabs, which drove up with a big rush, halted at the driveway gates until the outside guard could look them over, then slid into the darkness, there to discharge passengers, and either depart or wait, depending upon the type of fare. Society long ago had abdicated this place, with the decline of the neighborhood, asking no questions of those who bought the house and its furnishings. The purchaser had been the Syndicate.

The guard would accompany each caller to the door, himself ringing the bell and waiting until a Negro maid had answered. After that, he returned, either to the big iron gates, or to the group of chatting taxicab drivers in the shadows of the unlit stables. Everything seemed so active out here, and yet so gloomy.

Neighboring houses were black with emptiness, a condition brought about, it seemed, not so much from a lack of tenants as from decay and general disuse. Windows were paneless, verandas sagged; the snow had not been cleaned from the walks, which, in several cases, paralleled rotting fences.

A first glance from the taxi window, upon the cab's rounding the corner, had centered upon the general dishabille of the surroundings. The driver had explained: —

"Well, the way the Syndicate figures, it's cheaper to let a few old places that are already run down just lay empty rather than try to fix them up and rent them. The Syndicate can usually square things with the assessor's office to cut down the taxes, so they don't amount to much. And without anybody in the houses close to you, there's not much danger of a squawk that might cost a lot of dough, especially to a joint like the Queen's."

Strangely enough, there had been as great a change in the Queen as there had been in this neighborhood. In other days she had run a two-dollar house down on the Row, a place far different from this establishment which the underworld knew as "the Mansion." Life for the Queen was quite different now.

In those olden days, the cop on the beat dropped in at Thanksgiving, Christmas, and New Year's for a glass of eggnogg, and this he did quite openly, for he owed the Queen nothing, just as the Queen was not in his debt. In fact, the Queen had no debts in those days. Once a month she sallied forth in a hired hack and went down to the City Hall, where she planked down two hundred dollars license money. Otherwise, her only outpourings were to the constant bell-ringing of charity solicitors and for the bribing, by heavy contributions, of workers for a certain soul-saving organization — who, if the nightly disbursements were not regarded as sufficient, would gather in heavy numbers before the Queen's establishment and sing at the tops of their voices: "WHERE IS MY WA-A-NDERING-G-G . . . BOY TO——NIGHT?"

In those days, the clanging bell of the hoodlum wagon, known on the Row as "the Bitch Buggy," was a serious affair. There would be no bail bondsmen, employed by Sicilian or Jewish racketeers to appear miraculously and provide instant freedom, at a price, whenever a girl was arrested. If a caller got full of fighting whisky, resisting the efforts of the girls or landlady to put him to bed or put him out, the Queen called the cops. If a pimp became obstreperous, the Queen also called the cops, probably with no more exertion than leaning out of the door and yelling down the block. If some bank robber got full of beer and boastfulness, displaying the money he had just obtained by crashing a can, the Queen adorned herself with her feather boa, announced that she thought she'd get a breath of fresh air — and again called the cops. Either she did this or she lost her license.

However, it is not to be understood that the Queen, even then, was in a high-minded business. There was almost a total lack of true antisepis, there were barrel-houses and saloons near by, there was drunkenness and lechery. However, there was less bribery, there were periodical clean-ups, there was as good or as bad supervision as the citizenship demanded.

The houses were closely watched, not so much for evidences of moral laxness, or even for peccadillos concerning the selling of liquor or observance of closing hours, as for the presence of criminals. Police then worked on the French system of *cherchez la femme,* and like French police, took it for granted that sooner or later a fugitive would somewhere seek a house of prostitution. In that they were eminently correct, as is evidenced by information gathered by the Federal Bureau of Investigation into the activities of all recent high-powered criminals. Practically every one of them, at one time or another, was hidden by prostitutes or Syndicate bawdyhouse keepers.

In the old days, there was little such hiding. The police used the power of the license to make every landlady an informer. Beyond all this, vice was set apart, by itself. It did not live in the next apartment.

Indeed, times had changed for the Queen, since those old days on the Row. Perhaps the best way to visualize it would be to go into the Queen's boudoir and watch life flow by.

The Mansion was a bustling place that night. The maid and the housekeeper came and went in and out of the big room wherein the Queen sat at her make-up table, her hand-mirror held to the light as she traced eyebrows with a pencil where eyebrows long ago had ceased to be. She was dressed in flowing crepe de chine, was the Queen; the fluffiness of it emphasized the girth which years of late hours and gin had heaped upon her. Meanwhile, however, as she beaded her lashes and shaped her lips, she kept a chary blue eye upon four bottles — one of gin, one of rye, one of bourbon and one of Scotch — which sat on a small table near by and from which the Negro maid poured drinks into small, thick-bottomed glasses, then hurried forth with them to the orders of various parlors and rooms. There was much movement in the halls, something like the switching of cars in a freight yard, one party being held until others were safely out of sight behind the closed double doors of old-time parlors. Then, of course, there was the constant entrance and exit of girls, like clerks hurrying to the cashier's wicket, as they gave money to the somewhat overdressed housekeeper and then waited to receive the implements of cleanliness and antisepsis without which they could not proceed to their duties. The Queen pursed her lips, an action which ruffled her wattles considerably.

"It's all business now," she said. "Nothing social about it any more." She sighed heavily. "Chats like this come seldom. Ho-hum." Then, with a turn of the head. "Walda!" she ordered of the housekeeper. "That last taxi driver — did he get his cut?"

"Yessum," said Walda. "Don't ever worry about those fellows."

"I don't worry. I just don't want to be bothered by him coming back and trying to two-time me." She shook her head. "Everything's chisel in this business. It isn't like it used to be when I was on the Row. If there were fifty paying customers, that meant a hundred dollars, all money. Now, you've got to get what the traffic will bear — and keep books in your head while you're doing it." She had been fumbling some currency. "Oh, driver!" she called as a cabby passed, accompanying his fare on the way home, "let me give you my card! So you'll know the place."

The driver sidled into the room and she wadded the money in his outstretched, grimy hand. He grinned, glancing quickly toward the receding form of his fare, now anxious to reach the front door.

"Thanks. I'll keep this card," came loudly. "Might want to come this way again."

He winked heavily; he had been bringing patrons here for months. The byplay was merely to prevent the customer from knowing that of every five dollars he had spent in the place, two was paid the driver as a commission for having brought him here. Prostitution, in these days of so-called "hiding," cannot exist without taxi drivers. The cabby departed. The Queen returned to the shaping of her lips.

"Yeh," she went on, "it's all percentage."

"What of it?" asked the Queen's visitor. "You're making lots of money."

"Me?" she asked. "I'm on a percentage, just the same as the taxi drivers and the girls. You don't think Apples is letting me run for nothing, do you?"

"Apples" — the name sounded familiar.

"There used to be a pimp around this town called Apples."

"Same one," announced the Queen. "Only he's got the town now, as far as whorehouses go. He began making his money about the time they closed up the Row. None of the madams or the girls knew exactly how to work the racket, but Apples did. He started a restaurant where girls could hang out, and took a part of whatever they made off a date. Gradually he began building up protection — first, a few dollars to the cop on the beat, and then some to the captain, and so on. When any of the girls got pinched, he furnished bond for them at high prices, and worked up quite a racket. Well, the first thing you know, he was into so many things — owning a piece of a drugstore here, a restaurant there, and all that, that he finally got into politics. Not running for office, but running a district. What he says goes. So when the Syndicate took shape, they had to put him on it or there'd have been a squawk. So he's got all the houses, sixty-five or seventy, I guess. He takes fifty per cent of the net off this place."

"And you get?"

"Well, I get fifty."

"And the girls?"

"They get fifty."

This was becoming complicated. The Queen recapitulated. When the mathematics were concluded, it resulted in this division of a "party man's" ten dollars:

Four dollars for the cabbie, who drove, incidentally, for a racket-owned company controlled by the Syndicate.

There were three dollars for the girl, less fifty cents for towels and antiseptics, less board, less lodging, less the cost of evening dresses, less the cost of any newspaper she might buy at ten cents, or a used deck of cards from a gambling joint, sold through the house, for a dollar, less tips to the maid and the housekeeper.

The Queen got a dollar and a half. The Syndicate took the rest.

"Gets me screwy, keeping track of it all," said the Queen.

Walda, the housekeeper, entered and whispered in the Queen's ear. Her Majesty nodded a negative.

"Tell her to go see Apples," the Queen answered. "That girl knows better than to go calling me up trying to get placed. I haven't got anything to do with placing girls."

Walda hurried away. The Queen, somewhat ruffled, resumed making up.

"Why the hell don't they see Apples and stop bothering me trying to get a job!" she grumbled. "Hell, half the time I don't even know the girl's names, the way they come and go."

"Times have changed," Walda laughed. "I can remember when you knew their names, and the names of some of the fellows they married out of your place, too."

The Queen laid down her mirror.

"I wonder what's become of all that?" she asked reminiscently. "You know, we used to have a saying — 'as good a wife as ever came out of a whorehouse.' No funny business about it either. Damn few of those marriages that didn't stick. Well, there was a lot of good reason for it. The fellows knew all there was to know about 'em before they ever married 'em."

She took another slug of gin. Here was a different type of woman from Cherry, in Minnesota, representative as she was of the newer generation, taking the Syndicate for granted, prattling about the business-minded mothers of seventeen-year-old prostitutes. Cherry was of the Syndicate and for the Syndicate. She never had known anything else. But the Queen had come of days in which there had been a queer, underworld respectability about being a madame, when there was prestige to the job, even if the respect did come from the corner saloon-keeper, or the police captain, who made obeisance at least to her honesty, and the cop on the beat who got no favors and asked none. She was her own mistress; not the hireling of a group of slimy Sicilians and Jewish disgraces to their race — perhaps one should apply the name which respectable Jews themselves would use: "filthy gonifs."

"Yes, there was many a girl married out of my house," mused the Queen. She paused. "That was over twenty-five years ago, wasn't it? Some miner would come in out of the West, or a cattleman from Texas or a sheepman from Wyoming, or a farmer from down in Illinois, and the first thing I knew he'd fallen in love with one of my girls. If she was just a hooker at heart, I'd try to break it up. But if she was a good girl — you know, a girl who'd had hard luck; and I don't care who it is, if a girl's pretty and if the world's been abusing her, the first thing that pops into her head is the fact that she's got a living between her legs — as I say, if she had come to me because she'd been up against it, I'd do all I could to help the match along. I wanted to see her get married; I knew she'd make a good wife for the type of man she was tying up with — honest, ignorant, and lonely. The trouble would come when some rich damn fool would fall over his head with one of them. I'd stop that sudden. My license was too valuable.

"And, sakes alive," added the Queen, reverting to a good

old Midwest expression, "if any fellow can listen to a hooker blab about herself for a couple of months, he can stand her forever. That's what gets me about these respectable women that are always fighting whores. 'Course, the reason they fight 'em is because they're afraid of 'em — jealous of 'em. Well, I used to think: some of the homes that the customers come from must be terrible places, because after a man gets to know a pleasure girl, he's stuck for more misery than any wife could ever deal out. You've heard 'em talk — they can't think of anything else except their implements. How long it takes each month, and how their sides ache, and what awful headaches they have and they wonder if they need an operation and what girl just got knocked up, and wouldn't it be better if she'd have an abortion and — God, I got sick of it myself. But — " she shook her head — "the Syndicate handles that these days. The girls don't stay in one place long enough to really get on speaking terms with anybody."

Walda, outward bound, paused at the door. "I wonder why they move 'em around so much — like shipping cattle."

"Well, new faces, for one thing. Then there's not so much chance of a girl falling in love with some guy — you know, and causing a squawk. Anyway, the hustler who's in Chicago this week is in St. Louis next, or moving around to half-dozen places in town before being sent somewhere else. And they never know where they're going until they're told."

Walda answered a bell and returned with a well-dressed, almost beautiful young woman.

"Here's Sadie," she said. The Queen half turned and held out a limp hand.

"Hello, Sadie." Then to Walda: "Bring that new girl down. What's her name?"

"Marjorie," answered the efficient Walda and returned with a bright-featured, red-haired girl of about eighteen. The Queen nodded an introduction. Sadie and Marjorie seated themselves Then Sadie said:

"They told me to come here to-night. You wanted to take some lessons?" Marjorie hesitated. Sadie, all business, brought forth her sales talk: "You'll find it very beneficial in this racket. You don't catch diseases, for one thing. Then there were so many gentlemen who went to France during the World War and learned French methods that they really don't like the American style any more. Besides, it's much quicker and you make more money and it isn't nearly the wear and tear on your system. Then again, if you've got a room-mate, another girl, and you think a great deal of each other — "

The Queen waved a hand.

"Oh, Marjorie knows what it's all about," she broke in somewhat testily. "She knows the Syndicate can't use anything but all-around girls, and she's willing to learn. So what the hell?"

Marjorie giggled. Sadie rose and departed with an arm about the newcomer. The Queen reached for another slug of gin.

"Isn't it getting to be a hell of a business?" she asked. "Now, they've got teachers to show these kids all the tricks. Hell, that's nothing. I've been waked up at eight o'clock every morning for a week by carpenters pounding. Putting in a whipping room up where old man Moneymuch used to have his gymnasium. A'that," she added somewhat thickly — her gin slugs had been growing heavier and heavier — "it's sort of appropriate; it's a kind of exercise. God, they got more tricks these days, whipping each other, stroking each other's hair, and blacking up like niggers! Hell, they aren't any more whorehouses — they're madhouses."

Walda interrupted.

"He's downstairs again," she said. The Queen whirled.

"What's he want this time?"

"The same as last. A century."

The Queen rose from her chair, all two hundred and fourteen pounds of her and plumped down again with a force which bent the legs of the fragile furniture.

"You tell that sonsabitch to get the hell out of here," she

shouted. "I gave him that money before because he pulled a hard
luck story on me and I fell for it and felt sorry for him. Now, he
turns out to be nothing but a chiseler."

"Yessum," said Walda.

The Queen continued: "You tell him he can do as he god-
damned pleases too. Tell him I don't give a damn if he's got so
many police shields on him that he can't walk for the weight of
'em. Tell him he can turn in all the squeals and beefs he feels
like to the Captain and that the only thing that'll happen is that
the Captain will turn 'em over to Apples and Apples'll tear
'em up. Tell him, if he wants to, that he can even go down in the
next block and get somebody to turn in a beef and the same
thing will happen."

"Yessum," answered Walda.

"And tell the cheap, low-down bum that he'll be damned
lucky if I don't call up Apples right now and have the sonsabitch
thrown off the force. What the hell does he think the Syndicate's
paying out its dough for? Exercise?"

Then she forgot her glass and reverted to type by turning the
gin bottle to her open lips. Walda vanished to a dark corner
of the stairway where, on the way out, the Queen's visitor saw
her talking to a man who looked strangely like a city detective.
No doubt he was. Many of them have been seen in such places,
badly afflicted by what is known as the "itching mitt."

Perhaps a visit to the Queen may be viewed only as an un-
elevating evening. It was in reality much more; it brought the
outcry of a woman of another era, who, at best, certainly has not
led a laudatory career, but who nevertheless cannot stomach the
conditions which have come about, partly through Prohibition.
Largely, through an example set by Al Capone, the racketeer
found awaiting him a form of lucrative effort all too vulnerable
to his attack. Professional reformers had succeeded thoroughly
in making criminals of prostitutes instead of a social problem.
They had driven them out of segregated districts, scattering
them hither and yon; they had made of them creatures of the

shadows instead of the red lights, eager to pursue a business as
old as civilization and willing to pay for the privilege. So gangsterism offered a haven. Gangsterism provided protection, in the
same way in which it protected bootleggers, gambling, and high-
powered criminals. Gangsterism took over prostitution, and there
are few cities in America where it does not thrive — under the
mailed fist of the Syndicate.

To-day, the Great Reverend Divine Dr. Hope would indeed
have something to preach about. Evidently, however, the subject does not appeal, since there is here so little opportunity to
describe virginity and fair white flesh, and small, half-formed
breasts and all the other things which seem to be so necessary to
any reformer's outburst on prostitution. Here would only be
stark facts — about how girls are recruited by the thousands,
promised jobs, promised pretty clothes, promised a good time;
only to become, not the white slaves of Dr. Hope's time, but a
far worse type of which it is demanded that at least seventy-five
per cent. be perverts or permit perversion.

The Syndicate-controlled house of prostitution began with
Al Capone's Four Deuces, where he first began his rise to power
and where he committed his first Chicago murder. So called
because it was located at 2222 South Wabash Avenue, the Four
Deuces was only a saloon on the first floor, with the Big Fellow's
camouflage of a furniture store near by. The second floor, reached
from the saloon by a stairway, was given to gambling. From there
one ascended another stairway, crossed a fire-escape landing into
a rambling building, built on the railroad apartment style, with
doors opening into incessant rooms. One of these was a large
affair in which the inmates were herded for purposes of solicitation.

It was a bare room, equipped only with wooden benches, lined
along the four walls. Crowded upon these benches, with so little
room that they resembled little girls sitting four in a seat designed
for three, were women of all shapes and sizes and complexions
and ages, all waving at the new arrival, all crying out their wares,

and sometimes even fighting for the possession of a patron. Rush, hurry, work — those were Capone's orders. They remain such in the houses which the Capone gang still owns and controls and protects in Chicago and its suburbs, as well as all other Syndicate houses throughout America.

Perhaps it is best to turn to the records for a glimpse at the profits into prostitution when run by Syndicate business men. During the Treasury examinations into the income of Mr. Capone, the records of a house of prostitution in Stickney, Illinois, were seized. It showed the receipts for eighteen days, on the basis of which it was computed that the annual "take" from this house alone was $129,000. There is no figure showing the number of girls required to run up this young fortune, for they were constantly being shifted from other houses in Chicago, and between the Harlem Inn and other bawdy joints such as the Shadow Inn. However, it is certain that they received little of the gross receipts.

Business was conducted upon such an efficient basis that there were printed forms for the tabulation of the intake, with percentages to be charged to the inmates. After the house had taken its fifty per cent. the girl presumably also received a like amount. However, that was only a starting point against which to charge a dozen forms of petty graft — such things as ten per cent. for towels, auto hire in Capone-owned taxicabs from downtown hotels, meals served on the premises or board and room charges, — all exorbitant, — charges for dresses which must be purchased in sufficient array to afford nightly changes. The girls worked in shifts, some coming on duty at six o'clock in the morning for the forenoon trade, others at four o'clock in the afternoon, and some being "trippers" who came in the evening and worked until morning. There were charges — all above market — for hair waving and setting, room service, maid service, bail bond insurance, doctor's fees, and every possible service — all compulsory, of course — which scheming Sicilians could devise.

All this might perhaps be regarded as a relic of the Dark Ages of the 'twenties except for one salient point. With the advent of Repeal, every controlling gang in every large city turned to prostitution as one of its new fields of endeavors. In each case, it adopted the Capone system of charge and supercharge. Many of the remaining members of the Capone organization are still in the business; at least ten Chicago houses of prostitution recently visited by private investigators quite proudly asserted that they were under Capone protection. Like gambling, present-day Syndicate management has improved on the old Capone tactics. The new style house goes in heavily for perversion, actually advertising everything from flagellation, Sapphism and Sadism to cunnilingus, through bellboys, hotel clerks, starters, bartenders, apartment house employes, tavern girls, dance hall hostesses, and taxicab drivers, all working, of course, on a percentage. It is easier to-day to reach houses of prostitution in our larger cities than it once was for a stranger to find the red-light district. However, the police in cities under Syndicate control are so strangely blinded that they rarely are able to get evidence even when public sentiment demands it, and any accusation usually results in the following newspaper headlines:

CONDITIONS DESCRIBED BY INVESTIGATOR DO NOT EXIST HERE

CITY CLEAN AS A WHISTLE
SAYS CHIEF OF POLICE

One such place is a large Eastern city where the vice squad periodically reports to the peculiar type of government which controls it that there is not an active prostitute in the whole town. Perhaps detectives go to bed early, thus being unable to discover, here and there, perfect crowds of whores, congregated at three o'clock in the morning outside cheap night clubs, scrambling for men like so many harpies, literally crying out what they are willing to do for a few dollars, pulling and hauling each other as they follow men across the street, meanwhile naming perversion after perversion into which they are willing to enter with each other for niggardly sums of money.

And, perhaps, the vice squad will be the same one regarding which I received a report from an investigator for a civic organization. It was a snowy night. Inmates were gathered in Parlor A. The madame was dilating upon how business was going to be better, now that the lawmakers were in session.

"Are you sure you haven't made one of them angry?" the investigator asked. He was posing as a business man "in town for a good time."

"Me? Listen, I've got lots of friends here," said Madame, "why should they be sore?"

"Well, somebody's sore," the investigator answered. "Because something's going to happen in a minute or two. The place is surrounded by a raiding squad."

"A raid? Here?" Madame gasped. "Listen, I'm in strong. Why, I —"

"Just the same, the place is about to be raided. This is no tip-off. You can't do anything to prevent it. Some girl here has just stayed with a man who paid her marked money — and you will avoid a lot of trouble if the girl will step forth and —"

"I'm a dirty bastard if I will!" shouted a girl, and threw a wad of bills into a corner of the room. Then police whistles sounded outside and the doorbell rang. Everybody in the house ran for the back door. There they recoiled at the *pound, pound, pound* of heavy fists and the command:

"Open up the door before we break it in!"

"Open it, girls," said Madame sadly. "It's that dirty, double-crossing sonsabitch, Detective ——."

The door was opened. A typical vice cop entered at the head of his squad. He looked as unclean as his buzzard calling should make him. He spoke genially to the landlady. He chucked the girls under the chin. Then he demanded:

"All right. Which one of you whores has got that money?

Because you're all going down if the one who pulled this stuff doesn't tell."

There was silence.

"Go on and tell me, you dirty bitches," shouted another officer.

"Yeh, or we'll tear the goddam house down."

The girl of the crumpled money sat silent and grim. The squad leader pulled forth a long-bladed knife.

"Rip the goddam furniture to pieces!" he commanded, and started forward, his knife driving deep into the upholstery of a chair. Suddenly he halted. The girl had confessed: "There it is, in the corner."

"Thanks, Baby," the vice cop said, and picked up the money, examining its serial numbers. What had happened had been this: a stool pigeon had been hired to go into this house to cohabit with one of the girls. He had paid her in marked money. Now the squad had its evidence.

They called the wagon. And up to this point, barring perhaps the coarseness of their procedure, they were justified by law. But what hardly can be regarded as good police ethics was the fact that as they waited for the wagon, two of the officers each seized a girl and pulled her down to his lap.

It seemed quite unfair to these fine gentlemen that the wagon arrived so quickly. A vice cop has so many interruptions. . . .

For instance, in a city on Lake Erie where the "town is as clean as a whistle," and where the houses of prostitution pay off through a night club owner who has protected at least fifteen of America's most dangerous public enemies, it was necessary last autumn for Federal officers to seek a widely known criminal in houses of prostitution.

Presently, in one place, the Federal men had assembled everyone for questioning, even to the maid. The doorbell rang.

"Answer that bell just like nothing had happened," commanded a Federal man. "But be sure to hold any visitors in front of this room so we can get a good look at them."

The frightened maid hurried away. She opened the door. The Federal men heard the joyous booming of voices, with the frightened one of the maid striving vainly to give the hint that all the girls were very busy. But the men came on, shouting for the landlady. She went forward. One of the quartette grabbed her and held her tight to him. Others called for favorite girls and asked what the hell they seemed so glum about. Then the four noticed the Federal men.

"All right, you," commanded a Special Agent. "Step over here and let's see who you are."

"The hell we will!" said a burly member of the quartette. "What is this, a stick-up?"

Since the quartette intimated by its actions that it carried guns, the Federal men moved swiftly. Soon the four men were lined against the walls, their coats thrown back, displaying badges of the City Police force. They were the vice squad!

No doubt there are honest men on vice squads. Certain it is that few such men of integrity care for their task. The whole business is so filthy with corruption, with bribe-taking, with double-crossing and petty extortion that clean men do not want the assignment.

In fact, when one examines the annual roll of police scandals of all sorts, one marvels at the ability of departments to maintain any sort of morale whatever. Without even seeking a nation-wide résumé, one encounters such things as the dismissal of a New York officer who could not explain either his possession of eighty-three thousand dollars or his friendship for a dealer in wholesale prostitution; one wonders why eighteen policemen beat the charges against them in a Maryland city; why there have been dismissals in Detroit; one reads of police scandals in a total of some fifty cities. It is a matter of inquiry why so many policemen refused to testify before a grand jury in San Francisco, as to what was the underlying cause of shake-ups in Minneapolis, where vice squads could not find in years what it took an alderman only one night to learn. One would query the cause of accusations against enforcement officials at Oakland, with charges of extortion and bribery; why a kidnapper should name a Minnesota detective as a fellow conspirator; why a marshal should refuse to raid an Ohio gambling house even when a woman provided proof of its illegality; why the head of a Long Island police department should be jailed on a charge of having protected the underworld. . . . On and on goes the roll call of crookedness until there are few cities in all America which can truly call themselves free of corruption, particularly in regard to the members of vice and Morals Squads.

However, it is not the province of this book to enter a court of public opinion and prove, case by case, the widely recognized indictment that police departments for one reason or another are filigreed with dishonesty. Rather this writer's job is to explain why they are crooked, and what can be done to remedy it.

There are many reasons for police crookedness. The first is political-crimester control, as explained in the story of Johnny the Guy. Certainly there were many men on the force in Johnny's city who were honest. But there were others who, seeing his protected crooks walk by, either remained quiescent through fear of their jobs or said to themselves: "What the hell? I can't get anywhere if I do arrest the fellows. I might as well take the dough — I'm not hurting anybody doing it."

From this beginning, the possible causes for police corruption may run a hundred allied channels. There is the power of the gangster — police may take his orders or accept discharge. There is the futility of arrest, such as was evidenced in the case of a bawdyhouse keeper in Philadelphia who through some magic means managed to be freed on thirty-two out of thirty-three occasions after arresting officers had persistently arrested her even in the face of threats that they would be "broken" in rank or dismissed from the force.

Again there is the constant instability of the average police force. Nobody ever is boss very long. If a chief of police remains on the job five years, he becomes known as a veteran; the usual protracted period is two years. At the end of this time, there is either a political shake-up or an election or mere dismissal "for cause." Many first-class officers absolutely refuse to become chiefs of police. In the parlance, it "puts them out in front" — subjects them to the effects of political and newspaper campaigns, often inspired by the underworld, thus wrecking a record of long and faithful service.

Again there is bitterness on the part of officers who, having seen a law infraction and having done their duty, are rewarded only by a reprimand and relegated to a beat in "the sticks" because the person they dared arrest was politically powerful. A bitter man forgets caution; the warped mind broods; insistently the temptation pounds through it: "What the hell? I get broken for doing my duty. If I'd taken dough off the guy I'd have been a swell fellow and there'd never been a squawk." So, in the future, he takes money.

Again, there is the feeling that everyone else on the force who wants it is getting money without any seeming stigma attached. To this is added the fact that a policeman's pay is about the poorest on record for persons engaged in risk-taking occupations. There are no careers in law enforcement, nothing to which a man can look forward except a poor pension, if he manages to dodge trouble long enough.

There are poor implements with which to work. There is the disillusionment of seeing wealthy or influential persons going free while poverty is sent to prison. Few cities attempt to obtain officers of education or background, and could not do so if they desired, for the simple reason that there is nothing by which to lure them. Such persons can get better jobs, and they do so. Added to this is the unusual fact that there is practically no punishment for the law enforcement man who uses any cleverness whatever in the acceptance of bribes.

In almost every city of the United States there have been recent outstanding evidences that some law enforcement official has protected crime and has been paid for it.

It has been known, for instance, that such an officer, or a set of officers, is living on a scale far above that provided by the rate of law enforcement payment. It is not unusual for a chief of police, a sheriff, or the head of a vice squad to have a home valued at from twenty-five to fifty thousand dollars, with commensurate expenses. There often is indulgence in expensive makes of cars, big parties where liquor flows by the case, the purchase of jewels, expensive furs and clothing for the women members of the family. Plus all this, there has been known association with racketeers and persons suspected of close connection with the underworld — explained by the officer as being his "source of information." Added to this is heavy partying and night-club-bing, plus, perhaps, the discovery that the officer's safe deposit box holds thousands of dollars in currency. Nevertheless, when he is finally brought up for explanation, and he gives some such silly excuse as that of having won this money by playing the numbers game, the only thing which happens to him — if any-thing at all happens — is that he loses his job. Try to remember some law enforcement officer who has been sent to prison for taking money from crooks. Then think of all the law enforce-ment officers who have been accused of at least too friendly re-lationship with crime. Perhaps by doing this, you can realize why it is that law enforcement men sometimes are corruptible. It is the same reason that accounts for all other criminality. They feel sure they can get away with it. Therefore, the con-sideration is not that law enforcement is spotted by crookedness. It is that the lethargy of the average citizen permits so many of the foregoing conditions to exist.

It also may be surprising to know that the average city does little or nothing to protect itself against being governed in its law enforcement by dyed-in-the-wool criminals. Many law enforcement officers have prison or crime records before they ever are given a star and a club. The exceptional cities which guard against such eventualities prove that rule.

The growth of fingerprint identification in America is directly due to the efforts of J. Edgar Hoover, Director of the Federal Bureau of Investigation. It was he who built up the present identification unit of the Bureau from a small affair of about eight hundred thousand prints to the largest repository in the history of the world, now containing some seven million records. With the criminal end of the unit thoroughly organized, Mr. Hoover then sought to make it function for the benefit of all good citizens. He introduced a non-criminal file in which any citizen may place his prints for purposes of identification in injury, sudden death, amnesia or catastrophe. Likewise, he became a missionary to police departments and other custodians of public trust that they might send in the prints of applicants and thus be assured of non-criminal appointees.

So far, the work has not progressed to any great extent. It cuts in too deeply upon politicians who do not care what the applicant has done, so long as he has been able to garner votes. However, the few departments which do make use of this service reveal exactly how vulnerable are the police departments of the rest of the country. From the following figures, you may judge for yourself the danger which exists in all cities where peace officers are appointed by politics or without inquiry into their past lives:

The United States Civil Service Commission submitted 6,080 sets of fingerprints of applicants. 1,001, or 16½ per cent., had records in the files.

In one month, the Police Department of Miami, Florida, sent in the fingerprint cards of two hundred and ninety-nine applicants. Fifty of these had prior fingerprint records at the Bureau. Out of the forty-three sets of applicant fingerprints received from the Cleveland, Ohio, Police Department, nine were in the files. One of the individuals in this group had been arrested ten times since 1929, including arrests for violation of the Mann Act and passing counterfeit money. The Floridian city of Miami Beach once sent in one thousand, three hundred and thirty-six cards in the same length of time. Ten per cent. had criminal records, there being one hundred and thirty-six who had been accused of everything from robbery to grand larceny. There were one hundred and twenty applicants for police jobs in one month at Kansas City, Missouri. Twenty-eight had criminal records. Omaha, Nebraska, had forty-three applicants, and eleven of them, or nearly twenty-five per cent., had committed crimes. Of eight hundred and seven who applied in Los Angeles, forty-four had criminal records.

Thus, you may sharpen your own pencil. There are 170,000 law enforcement officers in America, practically all of whom have been inducted into office without a check on their criminal records. There is nothing to prove that fewer criminals applied for law enforcement work in the past than are applying at the present time. Perhaps it would be great fun if you, wherever you live, should start a city-wide demand that every man on your police force be fingerprinted and Washington consulted as to his criminal record. It would at least separate the sheep from the goats — and in a number of cities, it might benefit the railroads considerably, especially on trains departing at night.

A job in law enforcement is the natural place to which a criminal turns. He wants some haven where he will be protected; is there any greater protection than a star and a set of brass buttons? In many cities he is absolutely safe, for the simple reason that no one seems to believe it necessary to check up on the previous record of a police applicant. Certainly, there should be statutes compelling all those who deal with the public or who are responsible for public safety — hotel clerks, bellboys, night watchmen, taxicab drivers, policemen, safety directors, servants, and private detectives, to be fingerprinted for a comparison against the criminal files in Washington.

Perhaps of this list, the private detective is one of the most important. If ever there could be a Congressional investigation which would truly and deeply delve into the lower type of private detective agency there would be so many scandals that they would cease to be news. Many of these are used for strikebreaking purposes.

There are many private detectives who are not above framing evidence — to whoever pays their fee. There are others who are immersed to their neck in such cesspool activities as assisting conspirators in the badger game and other forms of shakedown and extortion. Others are "investigators" for shysters, aiding them in their jury bribing, the subornation of perjury on the part of witnesses, the intimidation of others, the manufacture of evidence by which a criminal hopes to escape punishment for his deeds, and even to the spiriting away of material witnesses whose absence often causes the collapse of an otherwise strong prosecution.

Much of the business is steeped in the stink of divorce. I have seen narcotic addicts in the ranks of private detectives, so crazed for the drug that no report they might make possibly could adhere to facts. I have seen private agency men stationed in clean homes and so filthy with venereal disease that they threatened the health of an entire family; others who would perjure themselves for a thin dime. When Congress wants really to do a great, human service, let it get a long stick and poke it into this bottomless slime. It will not be elevating. But it will drive a lot of authority-shielded criminals back into the underworld ranks where they belong.

In fact, many of them are on a level with some vice cops, who, all too often, are merely the call-boys for the Syndicate. That it is a good business as regards money might best be gauged by a wholesale perusal of their safety deposit boxes. Until such time, however, the earnings of Syndicates must be taken as a criterion. During the recent trial of Charles (Lucky) Luciano, it was argued that the vice business of New York, with its constant shifting of women, its checking up processes, where proceeds were punched on prostitute tickets, its bail bond and other rackets, brought an estimated annual intake of $12,000,000. This seems low, when one suburban Capone house alone, back in the benighted days of 1924 when matters were not really organized, brought in $129,000 annually. A New England Syndicate, play- to a much smaller population than New York's, earned $2,500,000 annually.

There is much wonderment concerning the source of supply for such a big business as syndicate prostitution — which now is linked, city to city, throughout the United States, with suf- ficient cleverness to make wholesale Federal arrests on Mann Act charges very difficult. One of the reasons for this latter is that the Syndicate absolutely controls its girls; retribution fol- lows the one who testifies; there is no person so weak financially or morally as a prostitute. Once she has turned against her own kind, she is lost. There is no place to hide, no friend to aid. Her shadow follows her no more closely than her past; there are fine tortures which a Syndicate can devise, such as whispering in- formation about her when she has found a job, arranging her arrest by the Vice Squad if she goes on the street, then laughing at her, when, with her shoes worn through, she begs to come back into a Syndicate house. Only in rare instances are big clearing houses broken up — such as the instance of a "beauty parlor" in Chicago, the workings of which gave an insight into traffic in professional prostitutes.

In the chase of a high-powered Chicago criminal, the Federal Bureau of Investigation arrested a notorious prostitute. During the questioning, the Special Agents, always alert to the pos- sibility of uncovering Mann Act violations, queried her regarding her methods of obtaining employment. The woman replied that when she desired to be "placed" in a house, she went to a certain beauty parlor on South Michigan Avenue. The Special Agents went there also, and arrested the man who ran it, confiscating his files.

It was found that ninety per cent. of all women who entered this beauty parlor were prostitutes. A book of names, descrip- tions, and ages was found, delineating hundreds of prostitutes who were shipped to bawdyhouses in various parts of the country, the fee sometimes being paid by the girl, sometimes by the house. It was, in fact, a prostitute's employment agency; and there are many of them — not run upon as grand a scale as this, of course. The man was sent to prison. The girls turned somewhere else — to pimps and procurers, all working on commission, and the business of whoredom went cheerily along. It will continue to do so until a real effort is made toward regulation of the business, plus eradication of the crooks who now run it, plus eradication of their allies — the pimps and the procurers. In many cities, municipal judges do not even bother to send pimps to the workhouse or county jail. Their philosophy is that if a woman is damned fool enough to give a man money, that's her own business. It is this type of superficial viewpoint which is at the root of almost the entire crime problem.

It is the sort of viewpoint which allows such persons as Charles (Lucky) Luciano to rise from the position of a petty bootlegger to that of a "Vice Czar" in the City of New York, living at the Waldorf Astoria, and literally holding the power of life and death over thousands of persons.

Strangely enough, few persons ever had heard of Charlie Lucky, as he is known, until a grand jury took the bit in its teeth, cried out against racketeering and prostitution, and demanded that something be done about it. That something took the shape of Special Prosecutor Thomas E. Dewey, who, all in a few months, achieved what the New York police department had failed to accomplish in several years. In this, he had the aid of picked men assigned by Commissioner Valentine. Even then, however, a strangely rich policeman did his best, by impugning the witnesses from the stand, to throw the case for Luciano. Probably the same thing will happen again in a greater measure if Mr. Dewey ever gets his hands on the man to whom Luciano was subservient. It may be accepted as a maxim that there never yet existed a racketeer "Czar" or "King" or "Emperor" who did not pay homage and a great deal of money to some highly powerful politician who in reality was his overlord, with the result that while Charlie Lucky may have gone to prison, the organization remained, quiescent perhaps for a time, but nevertheless intact. In fact New York pimps were furnishing girls quite freely to whoever desired them even while Luciano was on trial.

Houses may depart for a time in any city, but prostitution will not cease. In the place of houses, innumerable "massage parlors" will open, where all seems to be clean and white and sanitary, but where all sorts of "services" are provided, from ordinary cohabitation to electric vibrator masturbation. Or there may be a sudden influx of Neon signs, announcing "Dancing Lessons," the best hours of the business apparently being after midnight. If the town is "hot," they exist in one neighborhood only for a few weeks at a time, then disappear, to open up in other localities, and always with a thriving trade. To the uninitiated, it might seem a tremendous task for a house of prostitution to keep its patrons informed of changes of address. It doesn't. It merely informs its "solicitors," the taxicab drivers and hotel bellboys, dance hall runners and other shillabers. The lower retail district of one of our largest cities after eleven o'clock at night is a wonderful place to observe the eagerness of runners to serve what they seemingly believe to be the uppermost thoughts of man.

It was one night last Autumn that a Federal informant strolled along the street. Rather, his walk had begun in that manner, only to be interrupted as a taxicab slid to a squealing halt beside the curbing.

"Hey, Buddie!" the driver shouted. "How about it?"

The informer continued to walk. Soon the cabby was out of his seat, leaving his motor running.

"Now listen," he announced. "I know what's on your mind, or you wouldn't be walking around like this at night. How about me showing you a bunch of swell girls? Prettiest girls in town?"

The informer really was taking a walk. The driver desisted. The man progressed a third of a block, only to halt as two taxicabs bumped fenders. The drivers were too intent upon their job even to fight about it.

"Hey!" one of them shouted. "Wait a minute. How about some girls? Want a nice girl for to-night?"

He could have been heard for a block. The other deserted his cab. The informer repulsed them and was alone again. Again and again and again — ten times within two blocks, drivers hailed him, shouting their wares, even to naming some of the perversions which they had to offer at various houses. And as the investigator stiff-armed them all, he could not help thinking of the incongruity of it.

Here were licensed taxicabs, the kind which come swinging into a station to pick up the wanderers of the world and deliver them to their hotels. They transported the business of theatres, of restaurant-going crowds, of persons intent upon marriage, innocent girls homeward-bound from an equally innocent visit to the home of a relative. They moved slowly with the crippled and agonized, returning perhaps from a hospital and not financially able to afford an ambulance. At such times these same drivers were kind, efficient, courteous, eager to serve. The young girl was safe in such cabs. The traveler got to his hotel. The injured or ill found these cabbies the epitome of gentleness. Yet they now appeared in the rôle of hawkish, predatory beings as they fought for business, bumping their cars into the curbing and even on one occasion running upon the sidewalk. All this to provide the Syndicate with its man-fodder of the whore-houses, in spite of orders to the contrary, according to the heads of the taxicab companies.

There was something about it all which aroused belligerency. When a woman accosts a man upon the street, there is at least the thought that she may be hungry, the feeling that she, at one time or another, has had to drive herself to do a thing like this. But when taxicabs run wild, their drivers shouting half across the street, when the so-called charms of prostitutes — and there are few really beautiful or brainy ones — are bartered like so many sacks of potatoes, it gets on one's nerves.

Soon the informant man was reverting to profanity. This did not halt one super-salesman.

"Now, listen," he begged. "I've got something that would interest you." This had gone on for two blocks, with his taxicab churning at the curb deep in the distance.

The unwilling listener had reached the point of sarcasm.

"Got any black and tan stuff?" he asked.

"Listen, Pal. I know the swellest black and tan joint you ever saw in your life. Right out here on South Wabash."

"Glad you've got it," came the caustic answer. "Because I don't want it. Or anything else you've got."

He started to walk on. The driver persisted.

"You're a swell guy, you know it, Pal?" he asked. "You put one over me that time. How about some nice showgirls? Right out of a night spot floor show?"

"To hell with 'em."

"All right, Pal. How about a nice Chinese girl? Eh? A chance for you to find out if it's true what they say about Chinese girls?"

"Not interested."

"Say, you been around ain't you? How about some educated cornfeds, eh? A new bunch just blew in town from down around Kansas City and Omaha and Des Moines. But they're educated up. Young too — none of 'em over twenty. But they're wise, pal — if a guy wants to do a little whipping, you know — say, they'll furnish the hairbrush. Not so far away either — just up on the near North Side."

"That's out."

"You're a guy after my own heart, Pal. I don't go for that stuff either. But I've got what you want." He named a dozen forms of perversion.

"No, for each of 'em."

"All right, Pal. I guess you've got me." He started away, suddenly to whirl. "Listen, I guess I'm licked. I only got one thing more up my sleeve. Did you ever really see a sweet, innocent girl in a whorehouse? You know, one that kind of pulls herself away from men? Well, I know where there's one. Sweetest little thing you ever saw in your life. Calls herself Juanita — you know, just a hustling name. Hell, there ain't any man that can go in and grab her like they do other girls; she won't stand for it. I guess there's more men been crazy over her — wanted her to get out of the racket and come live with 'em, be their woman. But she turns it down — she says it's bad enough seeing a man for fifteen or twenty minutes, let alone having to live with 'em. I'm not lying to you, Pal. I ain't got no right to — you're probably not even interested. Far as I can see, she'd probably be a bum lay. But it might be interesting — you know, if you ain't doing anything else. Here's a convent girl — that's straight — raised in a convent, though she ain't Catholic. And smart. Hell, she's brilliant, I mean she's got brains. Say, she does the swellest embroidery. And she don't like men. She hates 'em — I just wonder sometimes if somebody took her and pushed her into this racket."

The informer himself had been wondering. Here perhaps might be a case in which some girl had been placed in compulsory prostitution and transported across state lines.

"We'll go take a look," he said.

Juanita was in the dance hall of a typical bawdyhouse. A few minutes of conversation proved that the taxicab driver had been correct. She was excellently educated. She was pretty. Men tried to paw her; she brushed them aside.

However, the investigator noticed that the other girls pawed over her also and called her endearing names and she did not object. After a half-hour of conversation, the informer asked her a direct question. She flashed an answer with a smile in her dark eyes.

The quest of the informer for evidence by which a bawdyhouse proprietor might be prosecuted on a charge of having transported females in prostitution across state lines ended in failure. However, another and more startling discovery had been made — one which could hold no official interest for the Federal

Government; but which, nevertheless, gave a stark insight into the present-day business methods of those who promote prostitution.

Juanita had stated quite readily that she did not like men. Since she had been oversexed in youth and reared under conditions which precluded association with males, it was within possibility that her views should become rather warped.

Therefore, since she was highly educated, of good appearance, of quiet mannerisms and, as she described it, "refinement," she had been placed in this house not as an entertainer of men, whom she viewed with much revulsion, but as a companion to women of means who desired the occasional association of another female. She regarded herself as something of a pioneer, in that since she had made such a success of her business other bawdyhouse keepers were frantically seeking girls of education and "refinement" through whom they might extend their business into new and highly lucrative fields.

Thus the Syndicate reaches outward, through a new assemblage of runners: beauty shop workers, hairdressers, hotelmaids and maids. Juanita and her type, rapidly becoming more numerous, represent a new departure in prostitution. The Syndicate, ever progressive, has broken open a new gold mine.

It is Lesbianism at a price.

CHAPTER FOURTEEN

DEATH BY DESIGN

THE law enforcement official who may have pursued a devious curse has an excellent alibi beyond any one of those listed in previous chapters. It is the actions of that strange, headless, tailless, driving, yet directionless, jellyfish body known as "the Public." The attitude of the average citizen perhaps has driven more otherwise efficient men into a don't-give-a-damn attitude than any other agency.

If a murder is committed, an entire city rises up in protest, demanding action. It usually gets what it asks for; murder is one thing, provided that the killer is not an influential gangster or a millionaire, against which a police department can throw its entire efforts. Whether those efforts be well or badly directed is of no importance at this moment; it shall be taken for granted that the hunt, in this particular instance, is a successful one, that the murderer is jailed, and through the work of police, prosecutor and judge, is convicted.

Instantly, unless the culprit is beyond redemption, public sentiment changes. If he is a young man and handsome, hundreds of women decide that he is too young — and handsome — to be sent to the chair, and that he can be reformed. If the culprit is a young, pretty woman, the men perform the same task. Everybody tries the case, whether everyone knows anything about it or not, as was witnessed in the cock-eyed arguments that went on concerning whether or not Hauptmann should have been convicted on circumstantial evidence. It might be stated here, for the benefit of know-everything commentators, that, should a man walk into the White House, dropping a letter on the way in which he announced that he intended to kill the President, should he be able to accomplish the deed, should he steal the White House silver, take a memento from the President's desk, leave his fingerprints in a dozen places, write his name in blood across the forehead of his victim, photograph himself in a mirror as he stood over the body, leave behind a list of everything stolen, from marked money to personal possessions, be caught as he made his exit from the White House, gory with the blood of the dead man and with all the aforementioned articles in his pocket, plus the revolver which, through ballistics tests, could be proven to be the murder weapon — I repeat that should he do all these things, but not actually be seen committing all of them, that still would be circumstantial evidence.

The public does not take the trouble to know that about which it talks. So, if a person is convicted on the best evidence in the world, the public believes it to be all wrong. And, if the criminal can croon over the radio, or play the piano, or likes dogs, or raises canary birds, such actions are taken as evidence that, after all, he really is not a criminal and should not be executed.

The same attitude applies to sterilization, which, as a matter of fact, is looked upon by most criminals as a tremendous laugh. All it means to them is that they can cohabit with as many women as they please without spending money for contraceptives. The same desire is held by many married men. Many a youth — especially as his girl has just telephoned disturbing news — has wished for such a blessing. Nevertheless, sterilization is fought by determined old girls and sob-sister men who insist that God's will be done, and that man was made to multiply. If all the sermons which have been hammered out of pulpits decrying sterilization could be placed end to end, they would reach around the world. One sees in such ministerial objections, not so much a love of mankind as a protest against the fact that the fewer children there are born, the less money there is in it for the church. However, I agree that there should not be sterilization.

What is needed is the absolute de-sexing of a large number of the more dangerous types of offenders, and a de-sexing which will really de-sex, even to the extent of wiping out the slightest stirrings of the urge. A bull is a very vicious creature; he changes entirely after he becomes a steer. Likewise in the transformation from a stallion to a true gelding, and a boar to a hog. The same metamorphosis of the average criminal would end a tremendous amount of vicious crime.

It will not occur, however. There are too many feminine prison-workers who like to gather in front of the cells of rapists, and hear from their own lips all the horrifying details of their crimes. It is a prison axiom that rapists find it easier to obtain feminine aid in obtaining parole than any other class of prisoner. In his exposé of life as a convict, *Prison Days and Nights*, Victor F. Nelson cites a case in which one woman not only obtained the freedom of such a man, but later married him, in spite of the fact that he was rotten with syphilis.

It is time that law enforcement gave more attention to the close correlation of sex and crime. The Europeans have done it for years; practically all the literature which really goes to the roots of crime comes from Europe, and a tremendous amount has to do with sex and perversions. There have been no concerted efforts in America to learn anything about these matters. Likewise, there are few law enforcement officers who ever have read Krafft-Ebing, or studied Havelock Ellis with an idea of comparing his revelations to conditions with which they come into contact. Birnbaum on *Criminal Psychopathology* would be news to many of them; Wulffen on *Woman as a Sexual Criminal*, Nolte on *Psychology for Policemen*, Bleuler's *Manual of Psychiatry* or the application of Freud or Adler to criminal cases would only result in a haze for thousands of policemen, sheriffs and district attorneys. One great reason for this is the limited tenure in office; the law enforcement officer of to-day may have been a corporation counsel, a truck driver or a farmer yesterday; after a year or two in office he may become a criminal attorney, a bouncer for a night club or a cattle-salesman. Therefore, his primary interest is in the job itself, not what should fit him for the job. Were a career offered, conditions might be different; but what is offered is a job, so much salary, an elective or appointive office to be held until someone else takes it away from the incumbent by the same manner in which he got it. Under those conditions, it is much easier to go to the movies than to spend hours in study upon what makes the clock of criminality tick.

However, those in law enforcement have at least a smattering of practical knowledge. Those on the outside who try cases on the street corners or in pulpits often never have even been near the scene of warfare. As for digging deep into causation and pulling out the roots by which criminality grows, that seems beyond conception. Which brings me to the picture of a doddering old man, with bent shoulders, caved chest, hollow cheeks sprinkled by a white beard, his lean blue-veined hands knitting as he sat in a cell for the condemned awaiting the signal which would send him to death in the electric chair.

"This is a very sad day for me," he said in a quavering voice. Indeed it was. It should have been a sad day also for countless educators, judges, and other persons entrusted with the safety of the public. Of all these, only law enforcement stood forth blameless; six years of hard work on its part, of unremitting energy and really brilliant detective effort when at last the opportunity arose, had brought this old man to his death cell. Before that, other police officers, as well as post office inspectors, had sought to place this old fellow where he could not be a menace. Thoughtless judges had turned him loose, equally thoughtless prosecutors had looked upon him as only "an eccentric." He had been fined nominal amounts or given warnings for deeds which to a psychiatrist, or a person schooled in the workings of the perverted mind, were blazing symptoms of a mental twist which someday would result in mutilation and murder. Thus, the old man was allowed to wander about, in full possession of his sex organs and his sex impulses. How many children he lured from home, to torture, to kill, or to cut their flesh from their small bodies and possibly indulge in cannibalism, can never be determined.

His name was Albert Howard Fish, and he was the aged man who had taken ten-year-old Grace Budd from her home in New York City, lured her to a deserted house in Westchester, murdered her and hacked her to pieces. He was a degenerate of the vilest sort. In a letter to the Budd family, he boasted of his cannibalism, laying stress on the statement that he liked the soft, sweetish flesh of children.

Everyone thought it terrible that a child had so been murdered. Judges were interviewed upon the sentence of death for the old man and thereupon dilated upon the theory that crime does not pay. I wish some of these stuffed shirts who blat nothings at the slightest provocation would vary their act. It might be possible to make an excellent speech on a different phase of the crime-does-not-pay angle. Crime does not pay the victim, crime does not pay bereaved parents; it does not make up for the loss of wage-earners, it cannot pay the mother or father of a girl like Grace Budd, or fill the void left by the child's murder. Most of all it does not pay society, even though society and the type of men it puts in office are often almost directly responsible for such persons as Albert Howard Fish.

"What's the use?" a post office inspector asked me shortly after the arrest of Fish. "Everybody who had any sense knew that old fellow would some day commit a horrible sex crime. We had him in court time after time on charges of writing foully obscene letters and sending them through the mails. Half the time, the district attorneys were not eager to prosecute because they said it was just another dirty letter writer. The rest of the time the judges either fined him something like twenty-five dollars or put him on probation. He had a thirty-year record for sex offenses before he kidnapped Grace Budd.

"So what are we going to do about it? We know such men will eventually reach a point where their sexuality will demand greater sadism than the pain of whipping, or the joy derived from pinching young flesh. It will call for slashing, or perhaps the slow torture of strangling. Then it demands blood, the cutting away of piece after piece of flesh. Someone must be that victim. Usually it is a child. Then Society gasps and judges wish they could do the sentencing which sends the fellow to the chair. Well, they've probably had their chance in the past — to save the lives of a lot of kids. But they muffed it with a twenty-five dollar fine. And if you'd mention such a thing as complete emasculation of dangerous perverts, they'd run into their chambers and lock their doors. They're all afraid of what a lot of nit-wits and professional long-noses might say about cruel and unusual punishment."

When a sadist murder is committed, careful scrutiny of the background of the offender shows plainly that this case has not been merely an action of the moment. It is a culmination of something which has begun in an addiction to obscene pictures, then progressed to fetishism, or the worship of some object of feminine wearing apparel, and after that, the singling out of girls and women for the receipt of anonymous letters of putridity. This probably has continued until it has led to the rape of some girl, accompanied by beating. Finally the obsession grew to a point where nothing would satisfy but death, accompanied by mutilation of the body, possibly followed by necrophilia, or sex desire for corpses.

That such things as necrophilia exist is not even known to ninety per cent. of the law enforcement officers of America. It seems inconceivable that perversion should become so bizarre that only sexual intercourse with the dead could provide the desired excitement. Yet the perversion is ages old, and there are at least a half-dozen cases a year in which fairly strong evidence indicates that the real desire of a sex killer was not that of mere intercourse, but an eagerness for the weird contact of a live body with that of a corpse.

Even in cases which appear to be pure sadism, there is the

hint of necrophilia. In the comparatively recent murder of a California girl, the slayer did not approach her for some time following the firing of the gun which killed her. Even then, he indulged in no sadistic assaults such as might have been indicated by the fact that he had murdered her. Instead, standing over her, looking down upon her bullet-torn body, he masturbated.

There was the case of an Illinois slayer, who killed and raped a girl whom he had picked up in his automobile. This youth boasted that he had assaulted numerous women in the small town in which he lived, that he existed for the thrill of it; a sex-satiated little fiend, he had spent his nights roaming the streets in search of prey. On this particular night he had picked up a girl who was waiting for a streetcar and whom he had offered a ride home. She had resisted him. He had struck her, killing her. According to his confession, he had believed her only unconscious. However, a further confession included the fact that after some time had passed, during which time he must have been able to assure himself that life was extinct, he raped the dead.

It is a certainty that when anyone is found annoying children, he is a potential murderer. He may be lost sight of in the district where his first offenses were committed. He may escape arrest in the writing of his anonymous letters. He is certain to receive only light sentences for such infractions as exposure of his person, or being caught in a railroad toilet with some other pervert as they engage in fellatio or sodomy. In such instances the police magistrate usually commits for six months or gives the offender twenty-four hours to leave town. Or there may be such a weird miscarriage of justice as that which appeared in the case of a pervert who had served eighteen months in a reformatory for having taken indecent liberties with children, and had been paroled. For a time he apparently lived within the law. Suddenly he went wild. He caught two children, bound them, gagged them, and then criminally assaulted them while they were in their death throes. And the weird part about the case was that in rounding up suspects, another man was found who had taken one of these victims into an empty house. He was cleared of the murder, but not of the fact that he had masturbated before the unsuspecting child and given her a nickel for having watched him. The slayer was sent to prison for life, which, of course, was merely an expense upon taxpayers; he should have been executed. There is no record that anything serious happened to the masturbator. No doubt the same course was free to him which is to other sex-abnormals: that of becoming more and more vicious until he also murdered a child. A true type of destroyer was Merton Ward Goodrich, who killed a child in Detroit. She came to his door, selling punchboard tickets; he lured her into his apartment, assaulted and murdered her. When he finally was caught, it was by an astute New York policeman who was wise enough in the way of perverts to know that a man he had just noticed eying children in a Central Park wading pool was not thinking about the temperature of next winter's cold spell.

Sex killings seemingly cannot exist without a history, as exemplified in the career of Alonzo Robinson, known as the "Mississippi Cannibal," finally sentenced to death for the murder of a white man and his wife. Robinson broke into their home one night, about two years ago, crashed their skulls with an axe, injured a child, and then, seizing a double-edged knife, slashed out the woman's abdomen and womb, containing a fetus, which he laid aside. Then he bundled up the flesh in a gunnysack, took it home, cut it into strips, and salted it for eating purposes — a piece bearing his teethmarks was found on him when arrested.

It is quite possible that Robinson never would have been suspected of the crime except for the fact that a post office inspector arrived shortly after the murder to check up on filthy letters which were being sent from the little Mississippi town to women in Indianapolis. Arriving, the post office inspector

discovered that the barns and fences and outhouses of the town
were literally covered with obscene scrawls. He joined forces
with the sheriff. They learned that Alonzo had been receiving
an Indianapolis paper and that he must have obtained the
names of the women to whom he wrote from the news columns.
An arrest was made, following which the flesh and implements
of death in the double murder were revealed in the suspect's
home.

In checking back to discover why a Mississippi Negro should
subscribe to an Indiana newspaper, the officers found the very
good reason that Robinson had been paroled from an Indiana
prison after having served a part of a ten-year sentence for
having robbed a grave of the body of a young woman. Following his incarceration, the heads of four corpses had been found
in a trunk in his room.

Cases of this type, in which the sexual organs of women are
cut out and carried away, their breasts slashed off, or slices of
flesh taken from their bodies, are not unusual. A case like this
is not a primary crime but the result of a perverted life en-
compassing everything from exposure to filthy letter writing
and the practice of masturbation and sodomy with children,
plus an equally long record of fines, warnings, probation and
light sentences. The consensus gained from talks on this subject
with scientific officers, psychiatrists, and medical men of high
standing is this: —

"The person who shows sex abnormalities is potentially the
most dangerous casual criminal who exists. The fact that he
is fined or sentenced lightly is an extremely urgent reason why
judges and district attorneys should be forced to study the
progression of sex abnormalities. Above all, the common citizen
should be educated so that he should not raise the outcry of
cruel and unusual punishment when the only possible precaution is taken with such persons to insure the safety of the
public.

"The church should be made to understand that its ministers

are in effect condoning murder when they espouse the cause of sexual degenerates in demanding adherence to the Bible injunction that man was put on earth to multiply. Any minister who preaches against the desexing of perverts should be singled out for attack by all law-abiding citizens.

"Prison sentences, unless for absolute life, do nothing but turn these criminals out potentially more dangerous than ever. There is only one remedy — execution or operations of a type that may eliminate even the sex impulse. Otherwise no mother can count on absolute safety for her child, and no woman, if at all alluring, can be thoroughly free from the threat of murder by strangling, slashing, rape either before or after death, and mutilation."

In this list, however, my friends of science should have included another group of beings who need education on sex and crime. They are district attorneys, sheriffs, and police officers who often either shrug their shoulders at evidences of growing degeneracy, or fail to recognize it when practically laid before them. Again there must be the reminder that failure to prosecute is often not the law enforcement officer's fault — it is the system of American elections and political appointments which put into office men who feel sure their incumbency will not last more than a year or two at most. Beyond that is the lack of scientific equipment, of libraries on criminal topics. If a sheriff or other officer desires to read recognized authors on crime, he can buy the books at his own expense — or go without them. He hears few lectures on strange aspects of crime — often he hears none at all. All too often he has neither a crime laboratory at his disposal, nor the money with which to purchase necessary equipment.

The police department in a town of fifty thousand wanted a lie detector. It meant an outlay of several hundred dollars. The lie detector or Keeler polygraph is growing steadily in usage as a means of detecting crimes by inexperienced offenders. By recording the actions both of the heart and of respiration, it places upon a cardio-pneumograph an unalterable record of the reactions of a suspect during questioning. It is so effective, especially with amateurs of crime, that in one bank case in which a suspect was sought, the polygraph picked out seven employees and named them as liars; all confessed to various defalcations. Again when a certain member of a rich family decided about a year ago to heighten his standing as an actor and writer by pretending that he had been kidnapped, it was the lie detector which settled the matter. Members of the Federal Bureau of Investigation fastened the heart and lung reactive agents to his arm and chest. The head of the Science Laboratory asked questions, seemingly uncorrelated. Almost immediately the youth confessed.

" I knew I couldn't get away with it," he said. "That thing was inking down a record of every time I breathed hard — and the officers knew I was lying."

In such a city as Wichita, Kansas, with its highly efficient, scientific police department, under the chieftainship of O. W. Wilson, the record of the polygraph for six months in cases involving everything from larceny to murder, caused the release as not guilty of 424 persons, brought about prosecution through its clear indication of deception in 136 cases, helped to elicit 220 confessions. However, all cities are not like Wichita. The Board of Aldermen in the city to which I previously referred, announced that it did not have the money to spend on such a piece of foolery as a polygraph. On the same night, however, it appropriated $1,000 for repairs to the city park monkeyhouse. Little children go to feed the monkeys. It is possible that they may tell their parents that some nice, sweet man fixed up the house the monkeys live in. Such recommendations often make votes.

To pursue the matter of inefficient equipment: The gun manufacturers of America are now putting out a new style of weapon which can make obsolete every bit of police protective equipment in America. The Federal Bureau of Investigation has appealed to Congress to put a stop to the manufacture of the guns. Congress so far has decided to think about the matter until later. Meanwhile, there has been no concerted protest to anyone in Congress concerning the necessity of protecting our police departments against a new type revolver which shoots with the velocity and impact of a high-powered rifle, which a criminal can carry as easily as he can carry any other revolver, and which will penetrate any so-called "bulletproof vest," or hitherto bulletproof glass, car armor, or any other equipment with which police departments have supplied themselves against the onslaughts of dangerous criminality. Already, these guns have been found in the hands of lawbreakers; they will multiply as time goes on. It is certain, however, that the policemen of America will continue to carry their .38 caliber Police Positive revolvers, and to wear useless bulletproof vests, and to ride about on armored motorcycles to be shot down by criminals with mobile, manual weapons capable of killing at a distance of more than a mile. This will not happen because police departments desire it. Boards of Aldermen will be building more monkey-houses, that is all.

So perhaps there are many reasons why police often fail to make a case against a suspect. Possibly they existed in the instance of a young woman who was found murdered two years ago beneath a culvert near Monroe, Michigan, the cause of death being diagnosed as a fractured skull and hemorrhage. The body was identified as that of a former Toledo sweetheart of Pretty Boy Floyd, hence the police of that city were asked to assist in the case.

Meanwhile, the Toledo police had been receiving complaints regarding the strange actions of a man named Harry Calvin Barnett, who preyed on prostitutes. His unusual scheme was to drive his automobile along a street until he sighted a streetwalker. Then he would call her into his car, give her a ten-dollar bill, and tell her a strange story.

It would be absolutely impossible, he would announce, to go

to the prostitute's apartment. You see, he was a big New York business man and someone might observe him, thus starting a scandal. However, he did know of a roadhouse to which they might repair. The prostitute would agree. Barnett would drive her, not to a tavern, but to a spot on a lonely road, threaten her, force her to return his money, and proceed to what the complaining prostitutes coyly referred to as rape. Often he demanded sexual perversion and upon refusal beat the girls and threatened their lives, once chasing a woman with a steel bar, intent upon killing her.

The history of the man pointed to the killer type of sadistic pervert. Complaints had said that Barnett seemed to gain as much pleasure from his threats, his boasts of being a killer, his physical assaults upon the girls, as he did from the actual sex act or perversion. Toledo detectives felt sure that he was the murderer of the girl beneath the culvert. They arrested him and turned him over to the Monroe sheriff.

Barnett admitted that he had picked up the girl on the streets of Toledo and had driven her to the point where her body was found. He denied that he had killed her or had knowledge of her death, stating that while he was driving along this road at forty to fifty miles an hour, the woman had jumped from his car and, because of heavy traffic, he had not been able to turn back in time to find her; someone else must have picked her up, he said.

At the time of his arrest, it was discovered that the upholstery and floor boards of the rear end of Barnett's car had been thoroughly scrubbed, the upholstery still being wet. For this, Barnett offered no logical reason, A dark stain was visible in the back of Barnett's car, resembling blood, and there was a similar stain on the back-seat cushion.

Following the publicity attendant upon the arrest, seven women came forward to testify that Barnett had forced them into moneyless relations, beaten them and threatened their lives.

To an experienced investigator of the newer type, this case seemingly should have been an easy one. There was every possibility that some hair of the victim could have been found in the car, by the use of a vacuum cleaner, and could have been ascertained to be bloody, thus giving undeniable proof that the slaying had been accomplished in the car. Certainly chemical tests, known to up-to-date law enforcement officials, could have determined whether or not the dark stains in the car were human blood, and if so, placed the burden of proof upon Barnett to show why he had been so eager to wash the rear seats. His story that the girl had jumped out of the car at a speed of forty or fifty miles an hour, and that he could not find her when he turned back, was extremely smelly. He had admitted to being near the place where the body was found. No one saw the girl jump out of the car although Barnett insisted that the traffic was heavy. There was a past record of virtual kidnapping of prostitutes by this man; of threats, and on at least one occasion of an attempt to slay his victim. To this could have been added at least a half-dozen forms of scientific investigation which would have convicted or freed the man.

Barnett had a criminal record, involving larceny, followed by a reformatory sentence, a violated parole and escape. He also had been arrested on a charge of assault to kill, and again convicted of having morphine in his possession. In spite of all this, the sheriff was unable to build up a sufficient case against his suspect. One day the officer telephoned the Federal Bureau of Investigation and confessed his fear that there would be an acquittal if he brought Barnett to trial; the case was very weak, he said. Would the Bureau prosecute Barnett on the ground that he had taken women across a state line for immoral purposes, thus violating the Mann Act? The Bureau would and did, obtaining convictions on enough counts to send him to a Federal penitentiary for twenty years. In so doing, it probably brought about a greater punishment for this sadist than he might have obtained had he been convicted in a state court on the original accusation.

There should be no criticism of this sheriff as a lazy, dishonest or inefficient person. Certainly he displayed the ethics of a good officer when, feeling morally certain that Barnett was a murderer, he sought at least some punishment for him. However, there is a great deal of criticism for the office he held.

The business of being a sheriff to-day is largely that of being a barnacle; the job has become archaic, poorly supported by appropriations, without sufficient personnel and often unfairly filled. By that is meant the fact that the office of Sheriff is a political one, to be obtained by election. Anyone who receives the political nomination may seek it. In many counties, it is looked upon merely as a meal ticket for some deserving soul and as providing a man to serve warrants and act as warden and keeper of the county jail. In most instances, it is run on the fee system, with the incumbent getting what he can during his few years of occupation and with the certainty that at the end of this time he must return to private life in order that someone else "who needs the job" may step into his place. There are good sheriffs, excellent sheriffs, but they succeed in spite of their job, not because of it. The office should be abolished; the quicker this is done, the quicker taxes will start their long-awaited decline, with a consequent rise in the quality of law enforcement.

The good men who have succeeded as sheriffs will continue to succeed in some other branches of law enforcement. The others, who have come from the ranks of farmers, merchants, salesmen, and sometimes the town loafer, will go back to the jobs for which they are fitted, and cease to be ignorant, often too-powerful, obstacles to local law enforcement.

A Texas Sheriff visited Hollywood to pick up a murder suspect. The arrested man — rather, he was little more than a youth — was given over to the officer by the Los Angeles Police Department. He should have been started home at once.

But this sheriff wanted to see the studios. The fact that he was burdened with a murder suspect did not bother him at all. He simply put a chain around the accused youth's neck and dragged him like a dog from studio to studio. Actions like that hardly breed respect for law and order.

And when persons talk of a new day in local law enforcement, I sometimes read them a letter sent me by E. E. Kirkpatrick of Tulsa, Oklahoma. Mr. Kirkpatrick was one of the men who acted for Charles F. Urschel in taking two hundred thousand dollars of ransom money to his kidnappers, Machine-gun Kelly and Albert Bates. Following Mr. Urschel's release, there was a raid on the hideout where he had been held, known as the "Shannon Farm." A Texas Sheriff — not the one of the boy and the studios — had been asked to participate.

The invitation was given because this particular Sheriff and his deputies represented practically all the forces of law and order for the community in which the ranch was located. Had he not been invited to join the raid, there might have been the almost inevitable howl that Federal forces were "running wild" in the county "refusing to seek the coöperation of local officers."

The office of Sheriff throughout a tremendous area of America is a highly important job. In thousands of counties, such officers represent the first and last lines of defense against criminality; it is they who must arrest miscreants, track down criminals, solve murders, seek to convict offenders and guard them till they reach either penitentiary gates or the county jail, depending upon the sentence. It was this sort of job which the Texas Sheriff held, and the Federal forces were much surprised when hour upon hour passed without his appearance or even any word as to his whereabouts. At last the Federal men moved forward to the raid without this sheriff's assistance.

Sometime later, Mr. Kirkpatrick wrote the Sheriff, asking for an explanation of his nonappearance. The answer which

Mr. Kirkpatrick gave into my keeping, for this book, was such a classic that I quote it herewith: —

J. T. FAITH

SHERIFF OF WISE COUNTY.

Decatur, Texas.

Slick-Urshel oil Company

Dear Sir

i Received your letter en regard to the Shannon Kidnapping Case Wil say I never Refused to help them it was a misunderStanding they called me from Dallas i am a little hard of hearing i under Stood they wanted me to meat them on on the squar en Decatur and they come to Rhome en stead so i dont know who was rong i never did refuse to help any officer and never wil as long as i am sheriff i never had any idea wher they were going nor what they wanted so i dont see how they can accuse me a beaing a fraid when i never knew wher they wer going nor what they wanted Me and my best Dep. Set hear till Day lite and they never come as soon as i heard they wer over her i tok three of my dep. and got with en three miles of them and met them coming out from the Place they come awhile back and got a man come and went through town hear and never ask me to eaven show them the way to wher he lived its my Polittcial Enemies that is putting out that news Wil send you a sworn statement that i never new wher they were going nor what they wanted and that i never refused to help any officer to arrest any criminel since i have been en office and never expect to if you want to know anything else that i can i will furnish you gladly

Yours truly,

J. T. FAITH.

If this letter were an exception, it would not be worth printing. There are, however, hundreds of Sheriff Faiths, and it is somewhat difficult to visualize them as the modern type of sleuth, experienced in a knowledge of fingerprints, how to make a chemical analysis for human blood, what to do at the scene of a crime, how to preserve evidence for the courtroom, how to make a ballistics test, how to gather evidence, how to interrogate witnesses and the suspect and, above all, how to take the witness stand and intelligently reconstruct a murder scene before a jury. The sheriff's office, in thousands of communities, is the one to which all rural residents must turn for protection in the detection and apprehension of persons who have committed crimes in the locality.

It is also because of ignorance in office that hundreds of murders every year are not only never solved, but never suspected. I refer to poison cases.

It is difficult to convict in a poison case in almost any community. It is doubly hard for a person in a distinctly rural neighborhood to be suspected, apprehended, and properly punished for a first, second, or even third poisoning.

A man is seized with what a country doctor diagnoses as "stomach trouble." He becomes ill after meals, he has vomiting spells. One day he dies. The doctor signs the death certificate as "stomach trouble" or "stomach ulcer" or "acute indigestion" or "heart trouble," and the patient is buried while his wife gets the insurance money and a new husband. Two years pass. The second husband becomes ill, and displays exactly the same symptoms as the first. Again he is buried as a victim of heart disease, stomach ulcer, or acute indigestion. The widow gets more insurance and a third husband. When that third husband dies, the neighbors begin to talk.

Neighbors have convicted more poisoners than all the officers in the United States, especially in rural communities. In many small counties, the coroner is merely the town undertaker, or the furniture store owner who deals also in caskets and therefore feels qualified to run for a most important office, since he should stand guard against death by design. He is not able either to conduct an autopsy or, in many cases, to decide when one is necessary, nor is he even qualified to hold an intelligent inquest into a cause of death. He knows nothing of toxicology, of symptoms, of investigation. He is not a medical examiner, but merely an officeholder.

Thus it is neighborhood gossip, caused by a similarity of deaths, which finally brings about an insistent demand for investigation. The sheriff and coroner finally decide to do something about it. In rare cases there is conviction. In others, witnesses have moved away, the druggist who sold the original rat poison or toxic-bearing material has died or left town, the visitors to the house who may have seen the murderer putting something into a victim's coffee either have forgotten the event or left the vicinity, and another murderer goes free.

Even in the case of Mary Creighton, sent to the Sing Sing electric chair with her paramour for a poison murder, there was not the slightest danger of detection until the neighbors took a hand in the case. Then a letter reached the Mineola Police, which read: —

Mrs. Ada Appelgate, 12 Bryant Place, Baldwin, is dead. She didn't die of a heart attack as the doctor said. She was poisoned and you won't have to look very far for the poisoner.

In looking for that poisoner, who was Mrs. Creighton, the police also looked up her record. They found that she had been unsuccessfully tried on two murder-by-poison charges in Newark, New Jersey, accused of a third, and that she had sent food to neighbors she did not like and thereby made them ill. It was necessary to interrupt the funeral to obtain the body of the victim for an autopsy, the results of which revealed arsenic.

That was in a well-policed community. It is, therefore, easy to imagine what happens in districts where sheriffs who write illiterate letters, coroners who have graduated from casket dealers or the embalming room, and doctors of limited practice and experience are the sole safeguards against the poisoner. A prominent law enforcement official has estimated that if there are only five hundred undiscovered poison murders a year, it is an extremely low average.

Speaking of murder, one thing which seems to shock the

average person is the belief that if one knows the underworld
— particularly that part inhabited by the true gangster —
one may obtain the murder of an enemy for something like
five hundred dollars. This, of course, is in the teeming cities,
where life is held cheaply, where there is difficulty of detection,
and where the murderous gangsters are the minions of underworld powers with political or police affiliations which might
aid them to escape punishment.

It seems to me that an equal amount of horror should greet
the information that gangsterism, in demanding its union rates,
is exacting what are considered extremely high prices. During
the last two years I have looked into the financial angles of
almost every murder-for-profit which has occurred in the
United States. The results have been surprising. Once away
from the cut-and-dried killings of professionalism, one becomes
somewhat aghast at the thought of carrying even a hundred
dollars in one's pocket. Persons are murdered for so little, in
our country. It is rare that a slaying for profit ever nets the
self-appointed executioner as much as a thousand dollars. Often
the gain is closer to a hundred, and in an amazing number of
cases, the reward, either in goods, chattels or currency, runs
closer to twenty-five dollars.

That a man should plot and carry out a murder for twenty-
five dollars is almost beyond comprehension. True, anything
can happen if the killer has brooded for a long enough period,
or hated sufficiently. The murders of which I speak are not of
that kind. They are of the sort where a person wants something
and decides to kill for it or to hire a murderer. Having become
imbued with this latter desire, he starts in search of a killer or
killers. After a quest, he returns, not with some beetle-browed
gangster, not with some ex-convict made murder-crazy through
long imprisonment or bitterness, but with seemingly average
citizens who have considered the matter carefully and have set
their own price. For a hundred dollars, for fifty or even twenty-
five, they will guarantee to waylay the victim and beat him to

death. Or perhaps they will crash his head in with an axe. Or, if it seems more pleasing to their employer, they will kill him with a shotgun.

Lest preceding remarks would seem to confine the bargain murder to small communities, let me hastily make the statement that such killings know no geographical American boundaries. The big town has them as well as the small one. Basically the reason is the same; in the rural community it is often that the populace has no respect for the sheriff or other persons of law enforcement. Having lived in a small town for a great many years, I have watched the boys of the village as they followed the town constable down the street, sticking out their tongues at him, mimicking his walk, jeering at the fact that he wore a cap with "Chief" emblazoned on it when he constituted the entire police force. They called him by his nickname, as they did the county sheriff, who had been elected to this office from a lifelong occupation as a farmer. For neither of them possessed the necessary admiration and respectful fear which anyone, especially a youth, should hold for a representative of the law. Perhaps there was good reason.

The "Chief" had been a failure as a plumber. All his knowledge about law enforcement he had gained from reading detective stories. I often found him on the streets at night, wearing overalls, a bandanna around his neck and a battered old hat pulled down over his eyes; once I discovered him on crutches.

"What's the trouble, Chief?" I asked. "Get hurt?"

"Now how did you recognize me?" he queried. "I thought I was in disguise."

"For what? Expecting some big gangsters to come through town?"

"No," said the Chief, "it isn't that. But you see, I wear an awful big diamond, and I wouldn't want somebody to recognize me and steal it. Now tell me one thing — how did you get on to the fact that it was me?"

"I'll tell you, Chief," I answered. "It's really a big secret. I didn't recognize you at all. But you see, you've always got your dog with you — and you forgot to disguise him too."

Like situations may be found in hundreds of the smaller communities. Law enforcement therefore becomes a joke, and persons in contemplating murder often do not consider, until after the deed has been accomplished, that perhaps they may be brought to justice for it. Rather it is simply a matter for their own conscience; if their greed is great enough, if they need money and do not care how they get it, if they hate a person sufficiently, they will go ahead with their killing, often doing it in such a bungling manner that a small boy could track them down. In fact, there have been several instances in the last few years where youths have directed the attention of officers to persons whom they had not hitherto suspected, and thus turned what might have been a mystery into an open-and-shut case against a slayer. Hence the cause of cheap murder in rural districts is the very apparent one that the perpetrators feel sure that they can get away with it.

In cities the story is somewhat the same. Most persons can read. Most persons know from the newspapers that the rate of conviction in murder cases is surprisingly low. The horror of killing has been cheapened, beaten down, minimized. Thus the person of the big city kills for the same reason that the rural resident takes human life, because he thinks he can get away with it. The reward is surprisingly small.

As many as eight persons have been involved in a single killing which could not possibly net more than a hundred dollars apiece. In one such instance, in a suburb of Chicago, several women and five men lured a victim into a shack, beat him until his skull was crushed, cut his throat, kicked his ribs in and then set the body afire. The reward they sought was a thousand-dollar life insurance policy, from which funeral and other expenses must be deducted. Therefore, when these costs had been met, there was little more than seven hundred dollars remaining.

It costs more than four hundred dollars a year to maintain a person in prison. Therefore because eight persons thought so little of law enforcement that they believed they could get away with the crudest sort of murder, the taxpayers were forced, in addition to the costs of apprehension, detection, and conviction, to contribute thirty-two hundred dollars a year — in other words, to pension them in prison for having killed a man.

There was much excitement a few months ago on the Pacific Coast over an unusual type of murder. A man wanted to get rid of his wife so that he might spend more time in bed with his niece. Beyond this, the woman was pregnant, which also did not please him. He conceived the idea of having her bitten by a rattlesnake. To carry out this plot, he must have aid; someone must help him hold the victim while the rattlesnake did its work. He obtained that assistance in the person of a sailor. The price was twenty-five dollars.

Again, in the New York case of a man named Mike Mellory, dubbed by newspaper men "the Durable Malloy," the rewards of absolutely fiendish endeavors were so small that the plot seemed inconceivable. The office of the District Attorney in the Bronx was informed one day by a stool pigeon that there had been a murder somewhere in the vicinity. The informant did not know either the name of the victim or of his murderers; his only lead was that an undertaker had been involved. What followed was an almost superhuman job of careful, painstaking police work, which finally brought about the arrest of a tavern proprietor, two hangers-on, an undertaker, and a doctor, charged with a plot to kill Mike Mellory for industrial insurance, taken out on his life by members of the gang. A weird story developed.

They first had decided to kill another derelict who hung about the dive. They got him drunk, took him into the open, laid him on cold ground and covered his body with wet blankets, but he refused to catch pneumonia as they had hoped. They gave him contaminated sardines, spiked with pieces of chipped tin, and he thrived on them. They then spent more money on drinks, and when he was properly saturated, laid him down on a dark street and ran a taxicab back and forth across his body. He was deserted then — to be found by a passer-by who called an ambulance. From all this the first victim recovered and the gang gave him up as a bad job.

They selected a second prospect. He went through all the treatment which the first had received and also thrived upon it. He too went to a hospital after a taxicab massaging and came out of it feeling better than ever, returning immediately to his friends at the dive and there getting drunk. So, this time, they took him to a rooming house, attached a hose to a gas jet and held it in his mouth until he finally passed away.

For all of this effort, had not the stool pigeon informed upon them, they would have received $1690, the total of three insurance policies. The expenses of banging the two victims about, of getting them drunk, of feeding them and sheltering them was about $100. Added to this was the $200 which they testified they gave the doctor for signing a false death certificate. This left $1390, a split of $300 apiece. The four main conspirators were sent to the chair. The doctor was convicted of a misdemeanor based on the confessions of the other men.

However, this was big money compared to that paid by a southern planter when he desired a man and wife removed as tenants. Legal methods seemed slow, so he sought out two local youths and asked them if they desired to make twenty-five dollars apiece. They were glad to get the money, nor were they horrified when the planter told them that the job concerned the killing of an old man and his wife. Perhaps their conscience was soothed by the fact that the planter had said he would furnish the shotgun.

These young men had no criminal record. They were not

known as toughs or hoodlums. The planter, good old soul that
he was, allowed them to think the matter over for a day or
so, at the end of which time they were pleased to take the job.

They lured their first victim, the husband, into a hollow.
One of the young men literally tore off the man's head with a
shotgun charge while the other watched. Here, indeed, was a
chance for nature to revolt against greed, avarice, or even fear.
Now was the moment when a misguided youth could cry out in
terror at the sight of a bullet-torn huddle on the ground, its
spurting veins reddening the leaves of the underbrush. Instead,
he announced, according to evidence adduced at the trial:
"Now, gimme that gun and I'll go and kill the old woman
and earn my twenty-five dollars."

And he did.

On and on goes the list of the many cases in my card files;
a relative of a Supreme Court Justice killed in Detroit by a
pimp and three cheap little tarts for one hundred and thirty-
four dollars; a woman murdered on a New Mexico mesa for a
few hundred dollars; innumerable instances in which hitch-
hikers have killed car drivers merely for the use of the automobile to take them to a desired destination.

In these days it is only a super-sentimentalist or a super-idiot
who blithely picks up a hitch-hiker, no matter how well the
applicant works his thumb, or how appealing is his face. It is
the most dangerous thing that a motorist can do; furthermore
it is one of the greatest aids to crime. In at least twenty per cent.
of hold-up and robbery cases, it has been found that escape was
aided by the fact that some dumbhead saw a forlorn-looking
person standing beside a road and wiggling a thumb, whereupon he genially halted, took the crook in beside him, and
transported him out of the jurisdiction of the police, who
searched for him in vain. Murderers have thus escaped, and even
members of high-powered gangster crews who had been sepa-
rated from their companions and therefore were devoid of transportation. Until states pass adequate laws against all forms of

hitch-hiking and then sternly enforce them, the highways will remain a menace of the first order.

Turning the cards of my murder index, I find at least a dozen cases in which persons have been killed and attempts made to conceal the act by firing the home into a funeral pyre, often for as low an amount as three hundred dollars insurance money. There is the case of a farmer who killed an adopted boy by poison rather than pay him the hundred dollars which was due him. A hermit was murdered by a young man, not for the legendary wealth which is supposed to go with hermitage but because the killer knew this old man had twenty dollars.

In all these accounts, hold-ups are eliminated because such instances are grab-bag affairs; a man is gambling on the proceeds when he enters upon a stick-up. I refer to plotted murders, often consuming months in the planning, the arduous efforts, the careful surveillance and, in many instances, the actual contact with the victim for weeks before his death. There is the case of a murderer who for months went hunting with another man. Finally he decided that he wanted his partner's rifle. So he killed him and got it.

One underlying cause for such cases as the last-named is remoteness from law enforcement, and the fact that it is widely known that a sheriff of a county has an almost superhuman task on his hands in the event of a murder. It is distinctly unfair to expect decent law enforcement when there are many miles to cover and when the county in which a major crime is committed must not only furnish the man power to run down the offender but the money with which to accomplish this. There is absolutely no reason why major crimes should not be the responsibility of an entire state or of a region, with all the resources of that state or region thrown into the tracking down and punishment of the offender. As conditions exist, the officer of a poorly financed or peopled county must endure the disadvantages of inadequate assistance and practically no money with which to work — yet in that county, robbery is robbery and murder is murder with its attendant agony and suffering, just as it is robbery and murder in the rich county adjoining. Moreover, the man who plunders or kills in one county and gets away with it will do the same in another — if he doesn't like the original locale sufficiently to return for another job.

Beyond such things as poverty and poor equipment, however, is the widespread knowledge that murder doesn't amount to much in the eyes of the law. The average time spent behind bars for the crime of homicide in America — according to the figures of the Federal Bureau of Investigation — is only about forty-three months, nor is that word "months" a misprint. This, of course, includes only those who are convicted. Persons brought to trial form only about twenty-eight per cent. of the total numbers of murderers sought. And, even if culprits are sentenced to the chair, it by no means insures their feeling the tight grip of the straps or the jolt of electricity as it surges through the electrodes. By the time an execution approaches, the populace has forgotten the murder victim. It only can understand the fact that naughty jailers are going to lead to death a being who, after all, possesses the attributes of a human and has begged most strenuously for life.

Who wouldn't beg? A dog begs for a bone and loses nothing by it. A man begs for his life, and often as he does so, even from the supposedly haunted depths of the condemned cell, he has his tongue in his cheek.

It is not at all unusual for an entire state to become heated up over some unusual plea from a death cell. It never enters the non-analytical mind that here is a man fighting with every atom of shrewdness he possesses to escape the noose or chair. There seems to be no realization that this person will promise anything, accuse anybody, seek any loophole by which to get out of the doom for which he is headed. And if he is shrewd enough to think of a good catch-phrase, he is almost sure of safety: to wit, a snake of a Colorado killer named Reppin.

Here was as vile a murderer as ever existed. He killed a young

man of fine background who was working his way through
college by driving a taxicab. He lured this hard-working honest
young citizen into the outskirts of the city and deliberately
murdered him to obtain his car for another robbery. For this
he was convicted and sentenced to die.

This murderer had run with gangs. He knew the tricks of
the underworld, and he began his fight to beat the rap almost
as soon as he hit prison. One day there came a great stroke of
luck. He heard that the old gallows was to be dismantled and
a lethal gas chamber installed in its place. Inasmuch as this
method of execution was new, it gave him the opportunity for
the catch-phrase: "Don't make me an experiment!"

The suckers rolled up to that by the thousands. Petitions
were circulated. Fat-busted old pelicans who always know
everything about everybody else's business regarded this as a
"tragic error." High-powered attorneys volunteered to aid this
darling young man who objected to being put to death by new
methods; it seems that high-powered attorneys are often to be
found, battling for the underdog, when there is plenty of
publicity resultant. No one stopped to think of the fact that
if this murderer did not care to be put to death by lethal gas,
it might be possible to arrange matters legally so that a special
gallows might be erected and he be jerked to death in the good
old-fashioned way. There were appeals and what not, great
excitement, a new trial attended by mass hysteria, crowds jam-
ming the courtroom and all that. It all ended with another
conviction which again named Reppin as a slimy murderer, but
fixed the penalty at life imprisonment, which means that
Colorado will pay a minimum of four thousand dollars in tax
money because it fell for a slogan.

There is good reason for mentioning four thousand dollars.
That, of course, is not the expense of maintaining a criminal in
prison for life. It happens, however, that no convict to-day
pleads from a condemned cell for the long-dragged-out sentence of life imprisonment — and really means it.

The only ones who believe in life imprisonment are the rabbit-like beings who form the potential victims of murder. Every policeman, every judge, every district attorney, every criminal, knows that there is absolutely no such thing as a life sentence. Even while a murderer pleads that he be spared the rope and confined for the rest of his natural life, — these pleas often being made to the minister who thinks he has saved a soul, — he knows he is uttering a lie. Again the dog, with nothing to lose, begs for a bone. Often he gets it.

Everyone has read letters from the death cell to the Governor, to the newspapers, to anyone of importance whom the murderer believes can help him. (No time is wasted on persons of poverty or without influence.) These letters are heavy with conscience. Often they argue that it is greater punishment for a man to be sentenced to life imprisonment than to death, thus arousing the interest of the gullible who believe the same thing. The trick lies in the fact that the condemned man knows that, once he is free of the death threat, he has not one chance in a million of really serving the long sentence for which he pleads. As an example, I have in mind a series of letters written from the death cell of a California prison. The young man put forth every possible argument to escape the rope. He instructed his relatives and friends how to whip up popular interest in his behalf; he named persons of influence who should be persuaded to write the Governor in favor of commutation. And in one letter, a strictly private one, to his sweetheart, he told what few condemned men reveal: —

There is a small chance of my sentence being changed to life in prison. If it is, I will get out in ten years.

This thought is paramount in the mind of every convict who makes dramatic pleas from the death cell for life imprisonment. Even that length of time is a maximum.

This brings to mind a case in a southern state.

Two hitch-hikers, father and son, desired to reach a certain town. Under the pretext of hiring a youth to drive them, they inveigled him onto a lonely road, then beat him to death for the possession of his car. Rather, they killed him for a quarter of a tank of gasoline — for when that ran out, they were forced to abandon the automobile.

They were caught, tried and sentenced to death. The father was hanged. The son began to campaign from his cell, largely because the Governor's daughter had talked very pleasantly to him. Governor's daughters sometimes have a habit of sticking their noses into matters about which they are not as fully informed as they think they are. In this case, the girl's interest brought on the usual sloppy campaign to save the son's life "because he was young and could be reformed." The Governor granted stays of execution. The campaign became stronger. Finally the Governor came to the death cell and personally looked over the murderer, following which he refused clemency. The young man was hanged. Sermons were preached about it — although no sermon had been preached about the boy who had been killed by this murderer. Sentimentalists thought the whole thing a simply terrible affair; this convict was such a nice young man. He had begged so hard to be sentenced to life imprisonment; and life imprisonment is much worse than being hanged, isn't it? So the Governor, being a man of courage, sat himself down and wrote a letter to anyone who cared to read it: —

The average time served in this state by anyone sentenced to life imprisonment is only seven years. If I commute the sentence of this convict and in a few years, when he has regained his freedom, he takes the life of some other person, the blood of the victim will be on my hands. It is said that he may be reformed because he is a young man. I have no patience with this theory. A lion kitten is a lion when he grows to maturity and old age.

The planning of this murder evidently was not done by the father but mostly by this convict. People are not entitled to live who have no regard for human life and who take human life without provocation or excuse.

This indeed might be classed as an historic document. There are so few governors who write letters like this. After all, there were many votes at stake — all of whose possessors became very angry with a governor who had enough courage and common sense to do his duty.

CHAPTER FIFTEEN

A SHOT IN THE ARM

IT was after a gigantic, nation-wide raid by Treasury officers
that a Federal judge in one of the larger cities looked dis-
approvingly about him as he seated himself on his bench. The
courtroom was crowded — not with spectators, but with
prisoners. A slow coloring began to mount in the judge's
cheeks.

"What has this place become?" he inquired testily of the
Assistant United States District Attorney. "A police court?"

"If Your Honor please — " the District Attorney began.
"These men and women are all here as the result of a raid the
other night, and — "

"Police methods," snapped the judge. "Why are they here?"

"The Narcotics Division of the Treasury Department believes they are all good cases. All of them were found either
selling morphine, or heroin, or — "

"Peddlers, eh? Well, line 'em up."

"If Your Honor please — " the District Attorney began
again. "I have here the criminal records of each of these persons,
as furnished by the Identification Unit of the Federal Bureau of
Investigation. If I may suggest that you look over the record of
each accused person, it might — "

The judge brushed aside his suggestion.

"This court," he intoned, "was not conceived as a means of
dispensing justice on a police-magistrate basis. Bring the defendants to the bar for pleading." He ignored the stack of
criminal records which the District Attorney had placed be-

fore him. Then, as the dozens of defendants were lined up, he asked: "All of you who desire to plead guilty to the charges as preferred against you, raise your right hands."

There was a moment of hesitation. Then a whisper went through the crowd, begun by persons who had recognized in this announcement a holdover from the old, court-crowded days of Prohibition times. One hand went up, then another, and a third. Soon the entire assemblage stood with their right hands toward the ceiling.

The judge scowled.

"It is the decision of this court," he announced, "that you all be sentenced to six months in the county jail and be fined the sum of one hundred dollars."

Then he added a few words of extreme significance to the disappointed Narcotics Agents. Upon the payment of the fines, all these persons would be granted probation from their jail sentence, this probation dependent upon their good behavior for one year. There was shuffling compliance from the convicted group, and an attitude that was far from displeasure. There were many smiles in fact as individuals paid the required money, or shyster lawyers hurried in with the required funds. At last the courtroom was clear again, and the judge turned to matters which he deemed sufficiently important for the consideration of a Federal jurist.

In his chambers that afternoon, the judge dilated upon his actions.

"It nettles me to see men brought in like so many offenders in a police court," he announced. "A Federal court is no place for such procedure. They are the small fry, the men who merely sell a few bindles of morphine and heroin. When real offenders are brought to trial, I shall look upon them as such. But this court regards a parade of small offenders as an offense to Federal dignity."

So much for that. The other side of the story came from the head of the Narcotics Squad. It was spoken in great secrecy, for criticism of a Federal judge, among Governmental enforcement agencies, is regarded as almost akin to lese majesty.

"Well," the agent snapped, "that's what my men get for going out night after night, hanging around underworld districts, enduring cold, wet weather, unpleasant surroundings, dangers. The judge wakes up on the wrong side of the bed and our cases go out the window. As for these criminal records, he didn't even look at them.

"You see," he added with fine sarcasm, "the Government goes to considerable expense to run what is known as the Identification Unit in Washington, where all the fingerprints and criminal records of offenders are kept on file. A part of the duty of this Unit is to provide prosecuting officers with correct information about the past of a man. Naturally, that cannot be used as a means of biasing a jury or of bringing about conviction of a man who is on trial. But it is of utmost value in assisting a judge in passing a sentence.

"Now, it just happens that in the gang which showed up in court this morning, every man had a record of some sort. A number of them had been fined not once but a half-dozen times for selling narcotics. Others had records of bank robbery, assault, robbery and even murder. But the judge was offended; he said we had made his hall of justice look like a police courtroom. So he brushed aside all the information which he should have used as a guide, and fined everybody a hundred dollars."

"And a suspended sentence," it was suggested.

The agent smiled wanly.

"A slap on the wrist. Some of those prisoners were already under suspended sentence. That merely sounds good on the record and in the newspapers. More than half that crowd will be right back at the old stamping grounds by to-night, selling their wares. And, of course, this time they'll be wise to the identities of Federal men. So our job is to start at the beginning and work up our cases all over again.

"You see, we had an objective in bringing that bunch in to-day, hoping that some of them would receive at least a small sentence. Then we would have had something to work on. The chasing down of big gangsters in the narcotics racket is the one place where, above all other forms of apprehension and detection, you must depend upon informers. For instance, in a big case on the Pacific Coast, a peddler was arrested. He confessed that he had been buying from a retailer. The retailer was caught. There was another confession, naming the wholesaler. We got the wholesaler. He confessed the name of the jobber, and the jobber revealed his source of supply. That led to one of the biggest opium and morphine clean-ups in years.

"We were lucky there. Everyone seemed willing to confess. That is not the usual case. The peddler often is too fearful of reprisals to do much talking in the short time in which we are allowed to hold him; there usually is a mob of attorneys clamoring for bail or threatening *habeas corpus*. So one of our big hopes is to get a sentence and then, during the period of confinement, obtain information that will lead us on to the persons higher up.

"That is the only way in which the narcotic traffic can be attacked. The big gangsters who control it, and who import the drugs, reveal themselves to a very few jobbers. The identity of these jobbers is not widely known. It is not until the business gets down to the retailers and peddlers that there is much of a spread in the number of persons handling drugs, with the result that it is a slow and intricate process to trace a narcotics ring back to its beginning. All through the entire set-up is a reign of fear — fear that anyone who talks will be beaten by gangsters, or slashed with knives, or burned with acid, or even killed. We must work slow. We arrest men. We question them, to no avail. Once they are freed on a fine or suspended sentence, they come again under the reign of the racketeer and it is impossible to learn anything from them. So — " he spread his hands — "the whole job must be begun over again. But when we actually have a man in jail, when we can show him that we'll protect him, when we can question him and draw him out and get on

a friendly basis, then we learn things. The maximum penalty for
handling drugs is five years' imprisonment or a two-thousand-
dollar fine or both. When a man has that weighing upon him, he
may consider becoming a Government witness and telling what
he knows. But narcotics peddlers don't draw such sentences
very often. There are too many judges who merely look at the
matter from the surface standpoint, and tell us to go out and
get the fellows at the top of the racket. And I'd like to know
how to catch big fish without having small ones for bait. It's
not a happy situation," he went on; "especially when you're
dealing with a menace that is as national as narcotics — and
as elusive. Sometimes, I wonder that we're able to make any
progress at all."

Just how much of a menace lies in narcotics may be judged
by the fact that, in spite of national organizations to combat
it, the efforts of the League of Nations to uproot it, the activities of women's clubs, civic organizations, officials, border
patrols, treaties, and international spies working through Con-
sulate offices in an effort to gain information against offending
nations, the traffic continues. Ebbing and flowing in its severity, there is no surety from one day to the next whether an
apparent barrenness of offerings may mean a slackening of the
trade or merely the calm before a deluge of morphine, heroin,
and opium descends from all directions.

At times, the narcotics situation will seem to be in hand.
Peddlers will be captured and their stock in hand found to be
so heavily diluted that it amounts, in effect, to little more than a
sedative. Narcotics officials take hope. Perhaps, at last, the
traffic has been placed under control. . . .

Then suddenly, overnight, the condition changes. White pills,
which are sold in the shadowy doorways of the underworld,
and which, only twenty-four hours before, contained little
more than ten per cent. of heroin or morphine, suddenly leap
upward in narcotics content. Here, there, everywhere, dealers
are heavily supplied, as though, all in a matter of hours, emis-

saries from some central agency had made the rounds. Thus an entire problem of supply may have been changed by as slight a thing as the successful landing of one airplane. Or perhaps one Customs agent has been "reached," with the result that a few trunks have been allowed to pass over a pier without inspection. Or a big ship has docked, and numerous men of the crew, whose clothing may seem a bit bulky, have walked ashore, their bodies swathed in wrappings which conceal pound after pound of whitish substance, to be pelleted, boxed, and distributed, that gangland again may roll up the profits from the sale of illicit drugs.

Meanwhile, reports flow forth of the terrific toll in life and energy exacted by drugs; newspapers carry on campaigns; prominent citizens exhort listeners over the radio — all working toward a conformity of laws. Nevertheless, either through lethargy or through stultifying efforts on the part of men working secretly for big gangsters, numerous states have failed to pass adequate laws by which the problem of "dope" can be adequately handled from a local standpoint. Local enforcement bodies often stand idly by, regarding the job as none of their affair.

A summary of the difficulties comes in the words of Harry J. Anslinger, Commissioner: —

"In too many states the police do not go out and hunt down peddlers as a job of their own. If we ask them to assist on a raid, they do it in a minute. But they won't realize that Narcotics is as much a local problem as it is a Federal one. Out of 4,000 persons arrested on Narcotics violations, 58 per cent. had previous criminal records from petty thieveries to stick-up men, robbers, public enemies, and killers. One man had a record of 90 arrests, ranging from misdemeanors to murders. If that fellow wasn't a local problem, then I don't know one. . . .

"In the Federal courts thirty per cent. of all the probationers break their promises. Beyond this we don't get the proper coöperation from state licensing boards in cases of addiction and conviction of persons

professionally handling narcotics — doctors, druggists, and the like.
And what about the drug addict who is driving an automobile? He
endangers the public, but few states will act to revoke his license;
many states do not even require a license from anybody!"

Harry Anslinger is an outspoken man. Withal, he is only
voicing publicly what many persons of discernment in law enforcement work say privately. In other words, the Bureau of
Narcotics gets excellent aid in some places, mediocre assistance
in others, resentful or surly resistance in many additional areas,
dependent entirely upon the personal or political domination of
the enforcement agency involved.

Perhaps it is necessary to repeat, that "a lack of coöperation"
does not mean a solid block of antagonistic police departments,
all aligned against Federal agencies as against a common foe.
There is no such thing. A "lack of coöperation" in reality means
an inability to depend on diligent and efficient assistance where-
ever it may be needed. Often there is no coöperation within the
department itself even on the handling of local matters. Perhaps
the force is so disrupted through the actions of what may be
called "honest politicians," fighting among themselves for the
control of a city machine, as to be rendered useless. Perhaps the
office of Chief has had a half-dozen incumbents in as many
months; perhaps every officer on the force wonders each night
whether he will have his job on the morrow. The police departments which grit their teeth and deliberately refuse to assist
outside agencies may be counted on the fingers of the two
hands. Those who do not assist for internal reasons, who cannot assist through a lack of personnel, who fail through ignorance, mismanagement, and the disruption caused by constant
"investigations," are numerous. And of all bureaus which fail
to receive aid, the most neglected is the Federal Bureau of Narcotics.

If you ask a policeman whose job it is to keep narcotics under
control, he will, in nine cases out of ten, tell you that this is

the sole job of the United States Government through a statute called the Harrison Narcotic Act. Under this, he may inform you, the Government must catch all morphine, cocaine, and heroin peddlers, as well as those selling marihuana, and any policing that is done in the matter must be carried on by Narcotics Agents.

The reason why many officers give forth this information is because they never have been told otherwise. Every state has some sort of law under which procedure can be made against drug peddlers if there is sufficient incentive to do so. However, faith in the Harrison Act as a police measure is so great that the average police department is eager to "let the Feds have it."

Incidentally, the Harrison Narcotic Act is not a police measure. It is only a revenue measure under which prosecutions can be carried on under the taxing powers of the Government. It was devised to reach the manufacturers and big smugglers of drugs, leaving such matters as search and seizure, apprehension of street vendors, punishment or treatment of addicts, and other powers strictly to the province of the states. Many communities, however, decided it was none of their business. The result is that several states are almost wholly unprotected, others only partially so; and a number entrust such things as the garnering in of dope peddlers to provisions of pharmaceutical or poison laws. More than half of America is without comprehensive machinery to control narcotics. It may surprise some to learn that Federal courts have no jurisdiction over the illegal possession of narcotics. That is a job for the states alone. Unless it can be proved by Federal forces that the owner of drugs has sold them, manufactured them, or administered them without a license to do so, the owner of a barrel of dope can thumb his nose at the entire Bureau.

A tremendous amount of that nose-thumbing is in progress at the present time. Narcotic conditions in America are at a critical stage. Men who went to prison for bootlegging and came out to find a nation under Repeal, have gone in for selling dope. To sell, there must be a supply. This is being furnished by the bigger gangsters of Prohibition times, many of whom have learned, in their journeys abroad, how to eat rice and drink sake and what to do when one enters a Japanese home. The heavy villain of opium, morphine, cocaine, and heroin smuggling today is Japan.

Perhaps it might be wise if the average jingoistic citizen, dilating upon the possibility of war with Japan, should be forced to realize that Japan is already warring upon us, and paying for many of the sinews of Mars with opium grown upon the conquered fields of Manchukuo. Moreover, Japan is an old offender; it began the breakdown of China more than twenty-five years ago — and did it with the morphine needle.

A queer ring-around-the-rosy, the story of opium. England through its East India Company made a dope addict out of China, back in the eighteenth century. There was even a war in which clippers and gunboats from Great Britain and America fought down China's desire to break away from the poppy. At last, China got its wish and importation was halted. By 1911, the Celestial Empire was practically free from addiction. Then it was that Japan saw a great opportunity. Here was a rich country, overflowing with gold and people and, in the language of the underworld, "ripe for a trimming."

Suddenly, under Imperial Japanese Government permits, exports of opium from India and Persia began flooding into Japan, — a far greater amount than Japan itself could use in years. The reason for excessive importations lay in the fact that Japan did not intend to use this opium for its own people. It was to be manufactured into morphine and other derivatives and smuggled into the boundaries of a coveted country. White powder, plus the needle, was headed for China, and to China it went in enormous quantities. China went on the needle. Then, in 1911, revolution broke out, and the poppy came back into its own. The fact that many of the guns and much of the ammunition

which tore the Chinese Empire apart were of Japanese manufacture testifies to the statements of such men as Floyd Gib-
bons that recent troubles in the Orient were not matters of the
moment, but had been carefully planned for years.

With the Revolution came the war lord. The war lord
wanted money to carry on his fighting and to buy more guns
and shells from Japan. It was against the law to raise opium
poppies; at the same time, the war lords levied taxes which
could be paid only by poppy raising. To-day, the reports of
responsible agents in China indicate that Japan is behind a
concerted and determined narcotic policy. There is indication
that an agreement has been reached in China whereby Japan is
to have full control of the manufacture and distribution of
narcotics. Various Chinese officials are allowed opium monopoly
in a few provinces. Otherwise, in North China, Jehol, Manchuria, — or, as it is now called, Manchukuo, — Liaotung,
Kwantung, and the seaports of China, the business is thoroughly
Japanese. Practically every narcotic factory is managed by
Japanese chemists. One often finds the dispensary, hospital,
import and export firm is engaged in the smuggling of drugs.
It is common gossip among the foreign captains of the Yangtze
River that Japanese warships carry rifles and ammunition up-
stream and morphine, heroin, and opium on the downward
journey.

Even the Japanese army of occupation is engaged openly in
the traffic. Opium and heroin move in cartloads through the
military zones under the protection of Nipponese armed guards.
Many Japanese consuls in China extend judicial clemency to
any of its nationals apprehended by other nations, and turned
over for trial; the usual fine is a slap on the wrist to the extent
of about ten dollars. Seventy per cent. of the entire Japanese
population in South Manchuria derives its living from the sale
of narcotics.

Japanese drugstores have been opened even in isolated villages
of twenty-five counties or *haiens* in North China, with at least

three hundred drugstores to a *haien*, each doing an average business of eighty dollars a day through the sale of dope, making a total business of more than a half-million dollars a day derived from narcotics which are delivered to the points of sale by the Japanese Army. Those who wonder where Japan gets its money for carrying on its warlike desires may look to the profitable business in the derivatives of the poppy. China has practically been forced to pay, through its now servile subservience to narcotics, for the war through which a large portion of the nation was seized by the "little yellow men."

Beyond the activities of the Japanese are those of the war lords of every strife-torn part of China. It is they who demand that every foot of arable land under their reign pay heavy taxes — which can only be met by the raising of opium. However, opium cannot be made to pay without persons to sell it. That is done through two organizations, the methods of which should be strangely familiar to America. They are known as the *Hung-pang*, or "Prosperity Group," and the *Ching-pang* or "Purity." Translated into English, they are the Red and Green Gangs.

Perhaps there are many persons who believe that Al Capone invented gangdom. Or that perhaps it came originally from Europe with the breaking up of the Maffia organizations in Italy. In truth, it came from China.

There was the Red Gang, for instance, which originated some time in the fifteenth century, while the Green Gang was an outbranch of the Buddhist religion at about the same time. These gangs to-day are all powerful in China. Their deeds and methods of political control are exactly those of Al Capone in Chicago, except for the fact that they were invented more than five hundred years before the Big Fellow ever was born. Their methods, incidentally, were brought to this country by the various *tongs*, which are organs of the Red Gang, and from whom crooks of America learned the tricks which have made gangsterism a tremendous factor of crime.

In China everything is Red or Green. No high official can retain his position without being friendly with these gangs or belonging to them. Persons commercially prominent must be members. No wealthy family can remain in Shanghai, Tientsin, Hankow or other large cities without some kind of understanding with these gangsters, lest they be exposed to the constant danger of kidnapping, blackmailing, robbery and extortion. Big employers of labor bow to them. The privilege of running cabarets, brothels, sing-song houses or other amusements is not available to anyone who does not belong or pay tribute. It all seems quite familiar to one who knows the American underworld, for this is exactly the sort of organization which is being built up under our noses. And the connecting link between both the Japanese control of dope and the tremendous business carried on by the Red and Green gangs for the Chinese Government is the fact that there is only one big customer for their product: the United States of America. Japan, of course, is not actively in the smuggling business. It merely takes profits while doing little to prevent smuggling.

And the "junker" ships sailing from China carries its cans of narcotics, destined for America by means of smuggling from intermediate ports. They may be landed off the coast of Mexico and smuggled in by airplanes; they may be brought in by fishing smacks operating into New Orleans, Galveston, and Florida cities. They may be landed by double smuggling through Canada — or they may come straight into San Francisco or New York, by consigning what passes as merchandise through one of these ports for transshipment to another country. In the transfer from dock to dock, bribed truck drivers run the shipment into a "drop," extract the narcotics, and put real merchandise in their place. This is especially true of big Japanese shipments arranged by American gangsters.

Meanwhile, Harry Anslinger and representatives of the State Department have spoken out before the League of Nations. They have practically thrown the charge of smuggling into the teeth of Japanese and Chinese representatives. There have been protests, diplomatic letters, more or less secret reports from American emissaries which have resulted in Oriental denials — and a greater concentration on smuggling. Japan needs money for her big military programs. Every ounce of morphine she can smuggle to the white nations of the world means that many more persons weakened against yellow invasion, plus adding necessary finances to strengthen the sinews of war. (These statements are not born of imagination — they come from official documents.)

Therefore, it becomes a matter of patriotism for everyone who fears war with Japan to exhibit an equal fear of morphine and all other opium derivatives.

That the narcotics problem remains serious throughout the years is indicated by the tremendous raids which have been carried out by the Treasury Department, resulting in as many as two thousand arrests at a time. However, there will not be even a dent in the traffic until every police department in America ceases "letting the Feds have it" and itself becomes protector of its own community. That likewise goes for a growing drug menace which also began in the Orient, traveled through Mexico and now, in the United States, is reaching desperately alarming proportions. It is the use of *Cannabis Sativa* otherwise known as "marihuana."

Perhaps you have heard of hashish. The word is synonymous with the Arabic word "assassin," in deference to its deadliness. That is marihuana. Commonly, it now is being called "fu," "mezz," "mu," "moocah," "muggles," "weed," and "reefers"; but by any name at all, its ultimate effect is the same. There is only one end for the confirmed marihuana smoker, and that is insanity. Therefore, it might be of interest to know that one of the main selling places of marihuana in the United States is in the vicinity of high schools.

This is no attempt to become sensational. My facts come from the Federal Bureau of Narcotics.

The use of marihuana has spread within the last few years so rapidly as to constitute a menace which should receive the attention of every thinking parent in America. Peddlers sell it at two cigarettes for a quarter in the vicinity of schools. Apartments are run by ghoul-minded women; in such apartments high school students gather on the promise that reefer-smoking will put music in their souls and a release from all moral restraint; nothing is said about eventual insanity. Practically every major school scandal in the last few years, and several killings in which young persons have been involved, have been traced to this drug. Co-ed deaths, brought about through the use of powerful drugs or following quack abortions, had their beginnings when young men and women gathered to smoke marihuana and remained to cohabit. It is the most dangerous, the most insidious and quick-acting, harmful drug that has come to the attention of enforcement men in years.

After all, there are a great many fables about drugs. The belief that one gains marvelous dreams from smoking opium, or becomes a superman from cocaine or morphine, is erroneous. These measures represent little but surcease. The average policeman, for instance, has no more knowledge of how a morphine, cocaine, or heroin addict conducts himself under a "normal" amount of the drug than he has about the Einstein theory. Many persons believe that such persons talk wildly, that they believe themselves to be possessed of great wealth, that they see pink elephants. In nine cases out of ten, they act quite like other humans.

They have begun the use of the drug to obtain freedom from pain or mental anguish. When they are under the influence of a dose which can be properly assimilated, they seem little different from anyone else, except for such symptoms as the pin-point pupil in the eye of a morphine addict. A coward who can obtain cocaine loses his sense of inferiority and gains confidence, strength, courage, but gives little other evidence of abnormality. It is when addicts are denied the drug that their nerves become ragged, that they leap at every sound, that worms sometimes seemingly crawl in and out of their flesh, torturing them.

Therefore, the job of ordinary drugs is to induce calmness, peace, to those denied it. Marihuana is different.

I once saw a marihuana party. These participants all were addicts — all prostitutes and their men. Nevertheless, it gave an inkling of what may be happening to much of our youth — especially to those parents who insist that "my Junior is different."

They were smoking reefers. A man lit a "spiked" cigarette, rolled from a crumbly, dried-leaf substance which he poured from a tobacco tin — elongated cans used for a cheap brand of smoking tobacco are almost the inevitable container for marihuana in the bulk. Then, lighting the tube, he took a few puffs and passed it on. From one to another the cigarettes went, with no apparent effect for a time. Then suddenly a girl wanted to dance. Immediately everybody wanted to dance. It was as though the first impulse had been an imperial command.

The movements were of sensuosity. After a time, girls began to pull off their clothes. Men weaved naked over them; soon the entire room was one of the wildest sexuality. Ordinary intercourse and several forms of perversion were going on at once, girl to girl, man to man, woman to woman. Nobody seemed to care that I was there. I doubt if anyone knew it. Marihuana releases absolutely every moral barricade which exists. Through it, the old-time seducer has come into his own; there is no girl who can find the strength to resist once she has begun "to float." There is a strange type of hypnotism about it — command a true floater to do almost anything and there will be compliance. Command such a person to crawl like a snake and it will be done, to bark like a dog, to tear off one's clothes, to indulge in almost any form of perversion known and there will be obedience. Will power has disappeared.

This is one of the great reasons why girls who are little more than children are now being placed in whorehouses by members of prostitution syndicates, why young boys of otherwise straight habits suddenly join up with dangerous gangs, why there are constantly more murders committed by youth. Let us look at the record: —

A sixteen-year-old boy, caught in a Sacramento burglary was "high" on marihuana. Two California men were sent to prison for cultivating the marihuana habit among boys. There were revelations in San Francisco that an owner of a taxicab service was delivering marihuana to hotel parties. The reed was purchased by a young girl on the streets from peddlers who worked the sidewalks, hotels and beer taverns. There was an axe murder by a Florida boy who, in butchering his family while crazed by marihuana, brought about the passage of a Uniform Narcotics Drug Act. One finds the history of a crime wave in Huerfano, Colorado, including an attempt to kill the sheriff, carried on by smokers of marihuana and not broken up until the source of supply was found and destroyed.

The story goes on: the hard-working father of a family of eight was injured to the extent of a fractured skull by a marihuana addict. Dozens of marihuana peddlers were arrested in Washington, D.C., raids. Boys were found smoking marihuana in Florida; high-school students in Atlanta, soldiers at Columbus, Georgia. Then there was the high-school janitor who, conspiring with a drug peddler and four other men, ran parties for high-school children in Chicago, while in another part of town, the mother of a girl, dead as an indirect result of marihuana, announced that at least fifty of her daughter's girl and boy friends were addicts.

To these incidents should be added an estimate that of a group of four hundred and fifty young persons in a Southern city, one hundred and twenty-five were addicted to the use of reefers; that police in Baltimore were called to investigate the selling of "muggles" to high-school boys and girls; that the defense of a Maryland killer, sentenced to hang for the rape of a ten-year-old child, was that he was crazed from smoking marihuana cigarettes. On and on goes the gruesome story; the use of "reefers" has grown so swiftly that it has all but enveloped America without the average citizen even being aware of the fact.

Marihuana croons to you every night over the radio. It helps keep your feet moving on the dance floor; for it was through its widespread use by musicians, who found that the notes fairly began to dance after the smoking of a reefer, that it came into general usage. Many of the so-called "hot music" experts are not so hot without the aid of reefers. And if narcotics experts know their business, they will cool considerably with the accumulative degenerate action of the weed.

A weed it is — and a most dangerous one. It grows wild in practically every state of the Union. For the United States Government to proceed against it, under such a bill as that of the Harrison Act, it would necessitate the taxing of corn plasters, canary bird seed, and a thousand and one articles in our daily life, all of which are based on derivatives of marihuana. Practically all states have passed laws against it, with the result that hundreds of tons of it have been destroyed by police in widespread areas. Nevertheless, its use has increased. Here is a menace in narcotic form which may require the action of great bodies of people, such as Boy Scout organizations and the like, in the detection and uprooting of all growing plants of the "weed," save those cultivated under strict supervision for commercial purposes. In the West alone, there are thousands of acres of it, growing wild beside railroad tracks, or on broad prairies. As long as the widespread use of marihuana exists, as long as peddlers haunt school yards, and hideouts are run for the degradation of children — just so long will the crime statistics continue to mount in deaths by abortion, illegitimate childbirth, thefts, burglaries, hold-ups, and murder, especially among the young. The most important job that any Chief of Police can attempt is the education of his entire force in the recognition of marihuana in every possible form of growth, seed, and manufacture.

The uprooting of marihuana is almost wholly a job for the states, as this drug rarely crosses state lines. However, Federal officers work constantly to uncover marihuana cases that they may be turned over to local prosecution. Police should do the same for Federal officers with all other types of narcotics, for the highly essential reason that the selling of dope in any form traces directly back to the racketeer and the Syndicate.

Jack "Legs" Diamond was one of the pioneers in putting narcotics into gangsterism. Arnold Rothstein was another. In the office of Harry Anslinger, in Washington, is a heavy book of many pages. It is called the Black List, and it contains the pictures and criminal records of dangerous importers of narcotics. In nearly every instance, these men are affiliated with powerful gangs; Charlie Lucky's main income came, not from prostitution, but from racing and the wholesaling of narcotics.

Morphine, cocaine, or heroin, once it has been smuggled into America, can be carried from state to state with such ease that often it is intercepted only by an underworld tip. The racketeers who handle it are sufficiently powerful, sufficiently dangerous, for the average stool pigeons to refuse to inform against them — many of the gangster deaths which have followed Prohibition have been the result of discord among narcotic crews. Airplanes, belonging to smugglers, work constantly between Mexico, Honduras, the West Indies and the United States — eight tons of morphine can supply all of America for a year. It is only by following a long trail, which sometimes consumes years — such as one by which a European opium-smuggling ring was wiped out — that the main arteries can be severed. Thus the narcotics problem, when the supply is once within state borders, becomes a highly local one.

Meanwhile the growing of marihuana and the rolling of it into cigarettes goes merrily on, as does the smuggling of morphine and heroin. As yet, there is little coalition between the two types of drugs and their sellers; that, it seems, remains for the future. It is only occasionally that a peddler of the alkaloids of opium is found to have transferred his attentions to the selling of hashish.

However, a blending of the two may not be far away. The profits on morphine and heroin yet remain large enough to hold the big gangsters within that field, despite the fact that the selling of these drugs is a Federal offense. As long as smuggling remains a comparatively easy task, the two types of drugs will remain separate. But that may not always be the case.

Morphine and heroin might be described as parasitical phases of smuggling. In the days when almost every fishing smack on the Florida Coast was engaged in the running of liquor, it also indulged in two other forms of smuggling, that of aliens and that of morphine. With the death of Prohibition, the main business vanished. Then the wholesale importation of aliens from Cuba and the West Indies was cut down by agreements with the Cuban Government and through intensified activities on the part of the Coast Guard. Morphine and heroin turned to the West, as did alien-smuggling.

In one comparatively recent case, the owners of Japanese fishing smacks on the Pacific Coast were found to be engaged in the intensive smuggling of Japanese aliens. It is to be taken for granted that they also were smuggling Japanese-made morphine and heroin. Within the last few months, the United States Naturalization and Immigration Service has found it necessary to augment forces along the Southern border with fast pursuit planes, in order to cope with smuggling planes from Mexico engaged in the carriage of aliens; again it must be remembered that the man who will smuggle aliens often does so as an adjunct to a more lucrative business. The most expensive alien is worth only one thousand dollars. The same weight in morphine would be worth a hundred times that amount, and if a carrier can escape punishment in one type of smuggling, the same is true in the other type.

Negotiations have been successful with the Royal Canadian Mounted Police whereby these officers will be placed on Coast Guard boats in the Northwest, thus allowing the chasers of narcotic-runners to continue their pursuit into Canadian waters. Until now it has been possible for smugglers, moving in swift boats and picking up waterproofed bales of opium and its derivatives, dropped overboard by persons on ships inward bound from the Orient, to laugh at pursuing vessels once they strike boundary waters. The chase goes on along many fronts. But the gangsters continue to fatten, the shadowy figures of peddlers still loaf about dark doorways, and the price of morphine or heroin goes up or down, like the price of eggs or flour or bacon.

Perhaps the time will come when extraordinary efforts will shut off the supply which Japan and Japanese-affiliated sources are turning out far in excess of any possible Oriental demands. As yet, there is no indication that this will be accomplished. From China comes the word of shifting bases for supplies, the indications that the great fields of Jehol Province, where once the poppy grew for miles, are being turned to other efforts while those along the North China railway are thick with blooms. New factories are opening in Peiping, Tientsin, Kalgan, and other points along this railway, smuggling centers have moved.

However, no matter how opium may shift about, the fact remains that America continues to be regarded as the most lucrative of all exportation points. Gangland likes products which are easily received in stealth, and easily enough disposed of through agents, sub-agents, distributors, and jobbers to numerous smaller fry, to make detection or apprehension of the main offenders extremely difficult. Because of this comparative safety, they are willing even to remain in a business which constitutes a Federal offense.

However, once let there be a fortunate break for Federal officers in their efforts against opium, and there will be a concerted turn to the wholesaling of marihuana upon strict racketeer lines. There is a lure about such an occupation, in that the sale of marihuana is a local crime, with all the possibilities for local fixing and escape from punishment. Crime, as such, looks with loving eyes upon local enforcement. Under such enforcement or lack of it, gambling and prostitution, under Syndicate management, have flourished. Once the profit incentive becomes sufficiently large, the gangster will be glad to add marihuana to his list of moneymakers.

Professional crime is vastly human in that respect. All it asks is profit.

CHAPTER SIXTEEN

GOOD MORNING, JUDGE

IT should be of more than ordinary interest when any law enforcement body obtains convictions in 96.60 per cent. of all cases which it brings to the attention of a court. This was the record last year of the Federal Bureau of Investigation, which, without the use of any legerdemain or necromancy, allowed less than one man out of every twenty-five to slip through its fingers.

Because there was no magic in the accomplishment, it might behoove the average citizen to ask his police chief, his mayor, his district attorney and his judges why the same results cannot be accomplished in his own local community. There, investigation will show, a conviction record of thirty per cent. is usually looked upon as excellent. Sometimes it drops to ten and fifteen per cent. There must be a reason, even beyond fixing and politics. One possible course lies in the utterly archaic methods by which many police departments operate.

There is even a bitter battle now in progress between the advocates of old and new methods. Many law enforcement officers have recognized the worth of science as a means of detection and apprehension. Others resist it, with a tenacity equaled only by the traditional old dog who refuses to learn new tricks. Law enforcement is in the throes of revolution, with bitterness rampant. There is no scorn like that of an officer, steeped in antiquated methods, for what he sneeringly calls "the college boys." This in spite of the fact that these college boys can make more progress in a day against crime than the old-fashioned members can achieve in a month.

The battle, of course, is between the officer who believes in third degree methods, stool pigeons, and beating confessions out of prisoners with rubber hoses, against the newer type of men, brought into general knowledge through the success of the young G-men of the Federal Bureau of Investigation. The older police insist that advanced methods are merely gew-gaws. Even many members of the New York Police Department, one of the most forward-looking forces in America, held that view until it was knocked out of them by almost weird accomplishments.

Commissioner Valentine believes in new things. He actually had the temerity recently to admonish a bunch of rookies upon the necessity of politeness. He told them with vehemence that the time was past when they could look upon themselves as bullies, or herders of people. It was not clever, efficient, or good police tactics to indulge in coarse wisecracking, to treat citizens like cattle, to yell and shout and bellow at a person who had committed some infraction of city ordinances. In that he was a pioneer, and for his temerity, he should receive something better than the double-cross which, no doubt, many old-timers wished for him.

It is the province of the old-time policeman to be a roughneck. The coarser he is, the cheaper his valor, the better he thinks of himself. Polite words are not in his vocabulary. The only way in which he can interrogate a prisoner is with his fists or a rubber hose.

This type of old-timer depends almost entirely upon "getting" confessions. Newer methods depend upon working up sufficient evidence with which to convict no matter if there is no confession. That means work, enthusiasm, keen brains, thought, training, the ability to understand that the mystery of science can be turned to everyday uses. Ignorant or politically dependent officers never went into any job with such qualifications. Therefore, they feel they should contest bitterly any advancement in methods. Even where science is a pet of the

Commissioner and of most of his inspectors, as in New York, the job of progress is difficult. The department must beg for money with which to equip its laboratory properly. And not until recently did the rank and file fail to sneer openly at the idea that science could do what a burly harness-bull with a wallop in each hand might fail to accomplish.

There were great jokes about the men who worked with test-tubes and retorts instead of with a gun and club. Suddenly, however, the scoffers were amazed to learn that these science detectives had solved a case which old-time methods had failed to break.

The case hinged on the footprints of a suspect. By using a process known as "moulage," which is something like a plaster cast, without a cast's difficulty of handling, the college boys reconstructed the footprints and matched them exactly with the shoes of the suspect. The case was broken.

Then came the murder of a young woman by a rapist. Detectives of the old school worked in vain. Those of the newer order sought the Crime Laboratory, taking with them a piece of string which had been found beneath the body of the dead woman. Tests were made, all kinds of string were investigated; finally the cord was determined to be the type usually found in an upholstery shop. This particular brand was traced down to its place of manufacture and from there to the shop where the culprit worked. He was arrested, convicted, and sentenced to death.

Hardly was this over when detectives, in investigating a rumor that counterfeit bonds had been turned out in Sing Sing prison, found some ashes in a trash can and took them to the Crime Laboratory. Now the old-timers really laughed. The hopeful detectives had asked that something be done to determine from these ashes whether they were the remains of burned counterfeit bonds!

The old-timers said it could not be done. The college boys smiled and said they'd try it. Practically overnight, through intensely scientific use of photographic paraphernalia, they brought forth shadows which revealed the printing upon the ashes and showed them what the detectives sought. The rule of the old-timer was broken.

Now the New York Police Department is one which points proudly to scientifically broken cases which otherwise might have remained mysteries. But the prestige of progress over retrogression was won only after a bitter fight.

This is the story of practically every police department in the country. Even though twenty men be young, alert, eager for progress, one sour, doubting sergeant can place almost insurmountable obstacles in their way. And if the atrophied being happens to be the Chief, then indeed the case is hopeless.

Nevertheless, dependence upon science is an urgent necessity with very police department. Perhaps a bit of history from the Federal Bureau of Investigation will give an inkling as to its importance.

It was in the spring of 1933 that J. Edgar Hoover took me to a room in the old Department of Justice Building and with a proud gesture opened the door.

"Ryley," he said, "I want to show you what is potentially the biggest thing in American enforcement work. It is going to wipe out the crooked expert witness, it is going to make even the smallest police department in America as powerful as the biggest, and it is going to solve crimes that to-day are mysteries. This is the new Crime Laboratory, and its services will be free to law enforcement anywhere in America."

I looked through the door. There was one black-topped table, with a few retorts and test tubes and one man puttering about.

"You don't seem to have much business, Edgar," I answered. "But, I can see where it will grow — even to ten times this size."

He agreed. We thought it would be wonderful if the time ever came when there could be a dozen experts at work upon the scientific aspects of crime.

Both of us were wrong. To-day, less than four years since the first man went to work in that little room with its inadequate equipment, the Crime Laboratory of the Federal Bureau of Investigation is solving murders that took place as far away as Alaska. Evidence rolls in from every part of the United States — such evidence as this: —

There was a robbery. It looked like an inside job, even though entrance had been made from without by cutting through a screen with a knife. The sheriff gathered up the knives of all the suspects and sent them to the Bureau. They were placed before what is known as the "spectroscope." This is a machine which takes pictures of what might be called the insides of pieces of metal or grains of dust. On one knife had been found, by the use of a microscope, a tiny bit of metal. This was examined with the spectroscope. It was found to be of the exact texture, size and general characteristics of the metal in the screen. The report was returned to the sheriff. He questioned the owner of this particular knife — and the man confessed.

In the Alaska case, it was a matter of ballistics and blood tests. Two persons had been arrested for a murder. Each possessed a rifle of the type with which a man had been killed. One, an ex-convict, had blood on his clothing. The other suspect, an Eskimo boy, apparently was innocent.

But the Crime Laboratory proved that the blood on the clothes of the ex-convict really was animal blood, as he had insisted. His rifle did not make the same bullet markings as those found on the death slug. The Eskimo's gun tested out exactly with the lethal bullet. The finds were sent back to Alaska and the Eskimo confessed.

In this laboratory is every known machine for bringing out fingerprints. There are nearly a hundred employees where formerly there was only one. There are parallel light rays, which reveal a pencil imprint on a piece of paper, four and five sheets beneath the original field of writing. There are rays which look through boxes and packages, for use in discovering bombs.

There are comparison microscopes for use in ballistics tests, dozens of chemists, experts on code writing, experts on questioned documents — experts, in fact, on every possible phase of criminal evidence. These men crisscross each other as they move about the country, testifying in trials for which they have examined evidence.

There are violet-ray machines for testing blood and other stains. In a recent Florida case, the evidence of human blood was placed against a suspect, even after he had repeatedly washed a pair of trousers which had been splashed with it. There are machines and baths for examining the genuineness of documents. Samples of every possible tire tread, typewriter face, bullet, revolver, shotgun, and rifle are on file so that they may be compared with evidence all in a matter of moments. There is even a file of every newspaper and magazine type. This is for comparison in cases where extortioners frame their demanding letters by cutting words out of periodicals.

One finds here scales for determining the weight of the slightest particles — in case a suspect insists that the dust on his clothing came from a certain spot, while the weighing of the dust from that area shows it to be of a heavier ground substance. There are a dozen types of chemical analysis — every possible bit of paraphernalia which can be made to nail down crime is here. The only problem is that of educating the police of America in its use.

There was a murder some months ago in a Southern city. It was solved in forty-eight hours by detectives from New York City, after local authorities had devoted nearly three weeks to bungling clews, promising arrests, dragging in person after person for questioning, always intimating heavily that this was the culprit and thereby tending to fasten defamation upon these innocent victims of the law for the rest of their lives. Enforcement agencies squabbled over how the investigation should be pursued. "Sensational developments" were promised reporters from day to day, as though this inquiry was being run for the newspapers instead of in the interests of justice. Among other things, one agency decided to test the ability of the Federal Bureau of Investigation.

It sent to Washington two detectives with a hair, found in the room where the murder had been committed. The scientists only shook their heads. They could offer no aid. The detectives had stretched this hair out on a piece of cardboard, so that its tensility had been changed completely. Then to make examination impossible, they had pasted it to the card with gobs of chewing gum. There was no possibility of comparing it with a hair from the head of a suspect.

Thus the battle goes — resistance to new-time efforts, bungling work when these methods are attempted. Of the two the former is the worst, for the latter displays at least a desire to fall in step with present-day methods of detection. The power of archaic resistance is best judged through the stories of men who have attended the National Police Training School.

The Attorney General and Mr. Hoover conceived an altruistic desire. It was to give the police departments of America a chance to become familiar with science, methods of training, discipline, modes of interrogation, how to gather evidence, what is evidence, how to present it to a jury — everything which has made the G-man a super-manhunter was to be given to the police departments of America.

Naturally, it was impossible to invite everyone in law enforcement. They decided to suggest to the various departments that each select a candidate. This was done, with the result that class after class has come into Washington, there to receive the full facilities of the Department of Justice, to hear lectures by every worth-while criminologist and penologist in America — and then, diploma in hand, to return to their departments.

In many places, the schooling has resulted in quick recognition. Patrolmen have become sergeants, sergeants have been raised to captaincies and captains to chiefs. There is another body of graduates, however, which is not so fortunate. It is composed of the men who have come from politically dominated forces.

"It is a tough time I have had since I got home," a grinning young Irish sergeant told me recently. "If I'm not called a Boy Scout, then my name's the College Kid. If I dare open my mouth about scientific investigation somebody will begin to roar that I'm trying to tell them a lot of new-fangled foolishness. Catch 'em and whale hell out of 'em — that's the motto here, me boy. But," — he grinned again — "maybe there'll come a day!"

There will come a day. There must come a day. Police methods have become so outmoded, so archaic, that the average smart crook feels he can laugh at the laws. Police ideas of promotion must change — there is no reason why a good, heavy-bellied traffic cop should make a first rank detective simply because he happened to be in the track of a fleeing gang of bandits and had luck with his shooting. Yet that is the basis upon which most promotions are made.

It is done because it is often the only way which recognition can be given to heroism. A good traffic cop is ruined, and an extraordinarily bad detective is created. But men cannot work without incentive and the only way to create better pay for a man is to increase him in rank.

There must be careers in police work. There must be renewed respect. There must be an elimination of political control, with an emphasis on the education, the alertness, the enthusiasm, the ability and the good character of the applicant. It can be done. Again I quote Wichita, Kansas, because it is indicative of the newer type of police force, the one which is modeled for efficiency and for integrity and political freedom.

In this Kansas oil city, a gangster is not allowed to light. He may get off a train or out of an airplane or automobile and believe that he has reached a fertile field. But within less than a week, astute detectives have discovered his intentions and moved him upon his way. Children are encouraged, not to become cop haters, but to look upon police as big, genial, friendly fellows who can be as soft as butter and as hard as nails. Kids respect policemen in Wichita.

The Chief is young, eager for cleanliness about headquarters — the usual police station is a first cousin to an uncleaned sewer — and alert for every improvement in methods. Young college men are sought as the basis of personnel, and every effort is made to give them commensurate pay.

There are no "districts" in Wichita — no places of tumble-down, slatternly stores which tell the experienced that if he becomes slightly known he can here indulge in every kind of gambling, find any type of woman he wants, or get a shot of hop from a bindle-peddler. There are no hide-outs as such. There are no ambulance chasers, and no crooked bail bondsmen. There are no runners for shysters hanging around police headquarters, no "stoolies" loafing in an unclean detective room. There are no such innocent amusements among detectives as lighting fires under each other's chairs with discarded editions of newspapers while waiting for assignments. There are no waiting detectives, in fact; they are all working. The motto of Chief Wilson is that nobody ever caught a crook in a police station.

There are no patrolmen who wear grease-spotted, unbuttoned tunics. There is, instead, an alert, well-dressed force filled with self-respect and the necessity for maintaining it. There is two-way radio, something which many larger cities do not possess, so that prowl cars may maintain constant communication with headquarters. There is a science laboratory. There is even one on wheels.

This is a radio car, constantly on a tour of the city and in touch with headquarters at all times. It is equipped with speed-graphic and fingerprint cameras, it has dusting powders and everything else necessary for the discovery and lifting of finger-prints, and every other apparatus for the gathering of scientific evidence. Police officers in Wichita have undergone a course in knowing exactly what to do at the scene of a crime, how to rope off the area from interfering spectators, how to handle the crowds, how to seek out and interview suspects and witnesses. The scientific investigator has only one job — that of finding the things which microscope, ballistics or other tests will turn into tell-tale evidence against an accused man.

Thus it happened that the science car was sent rushing to the scene of a street accident about a year ago. There the investigator found a woman being picked up from the street by ambulance drivers; another woman already had been taken to the hospital; both were dangerously injured; one died later. It was a case of two persons having been struck by a hit-and-run driver.

No bystander had obtained the license number of the speeding machine. They thought it was a dark car of a popular make, but they were not sure. All this time, two-way radio was relaying every fact to headquarters and receiving orders in return.

Every possible movement of the two women was checked from the time they left the curbing until they were struck. A coat button was found. Then a small piece of metal which at first seemed inconsequential was discovered. On closer inspection it was discovered to be a tiny piece of what seemed to be a tip of a radiator cap ornament which evidently had been shaped like the beak of an eagle.

Then the checking began, to learn from what kind of a car this ornament could have come. It was discovered that such cap adornments had been standard equipment on late 1933 and 1934 models of a certain make of car.

The evidence was kept secret from the public, which was a terrific imposition, since the public feels it should know every clue which detectives gain, and thus be allowed to play cop-and-robber. Never a thought is given to the fact that criminals also read newspapers. Wichita police have a true gentleman's agreement with the newspapers. The fact that the ornament had been identified was not printed; in fact, nothing whatever was mentioned about the ornament.

Car lots, garages, sales agencies and parking spaces were checked without result. The whole force then was given minute descriptions and set to examining traffic. Within two days, three cars had been found, the eagle-beak of each of which had been chipped. Two were discarded as not matching with the piece of metal held by the police. The third fitted exactly. Then an examination of the car was begun.

Dents in the fenders had been straightened. Twisted headlights had been repaired. More important than anything else, the investigator found two spots of blood. Then the driver confessed to having been drunk on the day of the accident and that in driving he had felt a slight jolt and was sure he had hit a dog. But scientific tests showed these spots to be human blood. Some hairs had been found on the bumper of the hit-and-run car. The investigator compared them with hairs taken from the heads of the dead woman and her stricken companion. They matched in size, texture, weight, tensile strength and thickness. So the driver was held for trial.

That is how swiftly and how surely scientific enforcement methods can be carried on. There must come a time when every police department in America will be built upon such a basis. At the same time the office of Constable and Sheriff will have been abolished, to be supplanted by efficient, highly trained career-men in a State Police absolutely free of political domination. But even then, the battle to really corral crime will be only in its infancy. All too often, a criminal's arrest is only his first step to freedom.

For this reason, it might be highly enlightening for the average law-abiding person to change personalities and for a time adopt the viewpoint of the criminal, as against that of the pursuer. For purposes of comparison, he should forget all the viewpoints by which he maintains a law-abiding existence — the power of conscience, the Golden Rule, respect for posessions of others, lack of self-indulgence, absence of super-ego, an inability to deliberately plan for a maximum of predatory activities and a minimum of punishment.

The average person believes that a criminal goes into his act through impulse, necessity or the daring needed to risk a long prison term. That may be true of some amateurs. This book, however, is not concerned with neophytes, but with widespread professionalism. Therefore, to understand the true criminal viewpoint, the citizen must place himself in the rôle of a man who coldly and calmly figures his chances of getting something for nothing. The lawbreaker has statistics — plenty to make him believe that the chances of being punished for his misdeeds are so inconceivably small that anyone is an idiot for working. This is the reason convicts call themselves "losers," not law violators. They have entered upon a game in which the chances against them — providing they stick to local infractions — are such that only by the sheerest bad luck can they be caught, convicted and sent to prison. They do not see themselves as paying for a sin; they have no belief that they are being reformed or should be reformed. They have the same resentment against fate which is evidenced by the gambler who bets on a Man o' War against a field of scavenger cart horses, only to see his favorite fall and break his leg when he is fifty lengths ahead of the field.

The professional knows, in the first place, that he has only one chance out of five of even being arrested for his crime. That is the percentage of real arrests — not pickups on suspicion or cases in which persons are held for investigation, but arrests in which law enforcement in local cases believes it has sufficient evidence to warrant an indictment by the grand jury or for the prisoner to be bound over to a superior court after a preliminary hearing. Some police departments have a quaint habit of printing, in their annual report, the number of arrests as compared to the number of crimes, thus giving the impression that for every infraction they have gotten their man. Nothing of the sort has happened. In many cases they have made no real arrests whatever, only detentions, throwing a dragnet about pool halls, rooming houses, taverns where derelicts congregate, and bringing in the results, to be held until the victims of a

violation decide that the culprit is not among them. There are
bums and hobos in every city who are so accustomed to being
picked up on suspicion that they make ready to go to jail before
the raiding squad even suggests it. I remember one instance in
a Western city where more than a thousand men were brought
in for questioning, and every one of the thousand released.

Thus the figures representing the number of arrests as against
the number of crimes may often form a mere piece of jugglery
designed to lull citizens into believing they have an efficient
department. It is one of the oldest gags known in the making
of an annual report.

The criminal cares nothing about this. What he figures is
that he has an eighty per cent. chance to escape being suspected,
arrested and held for trial. This is only the beginning of his
chances to escape the law. The next step is the district attorney's
office. There are dozens of police departments which are unfairly stamped with the stigma of inefficiency or of crookedness.
Even if every man on the force were a reincarnated Sherlock
Holmes, even if the Chief were the greatest criminologist in all
history, all efforts would be useless unless backed up by the
work of an efficient district attorney, unhampered by politics
or dishonesty.

Here indeed is the bottleneck in the traffic of local crime. No
charge of a serious nature can reach the courtroom, or even the
grand jury, under ordinary conditions, until it has passed
through this gateway. Thus, against the entire underworld,
there stands only one man, plus his hand-picked assistants. He
can be honest, and still be defeated in his efforts by either a
negligent police department, or dishonest or politically controlled courts. He can be dishonest and thereby defeat the
eager efforts of the most diligent of police and the most honorable of judges. Beyond that, on an average of two years, he must
shunt his duties as a prosecutor into the background, and with
torch in hand, go forth into the jungle of votes, hoping to
garner enough to return him to his job.

Perhaps this will explain why a criminal looks upon the district attorney's office with such interested eyes when he contemplates the problem of whether crime can be made to pay. He need do little computing. The figures are before him, in every Uniform Crime Report of the United States Department of Justice, which reaches general circulation through the newspapers on its date of issue. In any other country, these figures would be appalling. In America, they excite little interest except among criminals, who look upon them with the same interest as that of a racing fan regarding a form sheet. These figures show that with all the thousands upon thousands of persons employed in the offices of district attorneys throughout America, with all the investigators and assistants, there is rolled up a record even worse than that of the police.

After all, the police must go and seek a suspect. The district attorneys receive him on a platter. After having been handed the cases, after having received all the information the police possess, plus all that which their investigators can unearth, they make twice as bad a record as the men of the front line. In other words, police fail to make an arrest worthy of trial in four out of five cases. Local district attorneys fail to fully convict in nine out of ten cases.

To a degree, that is a trick statement, necessary at this time, that it may be explained later. Nevertheless, the fact remains that if there are ten persons charged with first degree murder, ten more charged with armed robbery, ten more with rape, and onward throughout a list of felonies, only one man out of each group will be sent to the penitentiary for the crime he actually committed. True, there will be other convictions, but they will not be for the offense charged, and even then the entire total will amount to only one man out of every three who faces trial. There are many reasons. One is the necessity of being elected.

It is to be taken for granted that a tremendous number of district attorneys are honest. If they are also efficient, they need no further defense. If they are eager, and honest, and striving to be good officers, they should be encouraged by such laws as will give them an opportunity to become truly fearless, determined, just men. They cannot do this in the two-year term of an electoral office. It is difficult, no matter how many terms they may serve. It is absolutely essential that the district attorney become such by some other method than that of seeking votes. He should be chosen from timber which bears the recommendation of the most law-abiding of bodies — church societies, business organizations, Bar associations, educative groups, philanthropic groups. Out of a list of names submitted by such a coalition, any governor certainly can select a more capable district attorney than any political convention or primary. The same should be true for state judges. And after selection, they should be allowed to remain in office as long as their records warrant it — and no longer.

Or there is civil service, which could be made to apply to such men. Seemingly it has been a success in other fields of endeavor; it certainly is better than politics in the avenue of criminal prosecution. Or as an attorney correspondent recently put it: —

You may be familiar with the maxim, current among lawyers, that it takes two years to make a good district attorney. Let us take a typical instance:

A district attorney has been elected. He has been a good party man all his life and hence "rates" the nomination. Unfortunately, he knows nothing about criminal prosecution, which is a field in itself. In fact, he may not have had five criminal cases in his life. So, to remedy this regrettable circumstance, with the active assistance of the party boss, of course, he appoints a staff of assistants, most of whom are young and none of whom have had any criminal experience of consequence, but all of whom vote right.

The new force goes to work on the piled-up indictments. Of course, being politicians first and lawyers next, they may not be such very good lawyers. But good, bad or indifferent, they are inexperienced in prosecution work, and are opposed by shrewd, able, and practised advocates. The result is obvious.

So much for the honest man and his problems and his political difficulties.

Beyond this, however, there is the fact that no office on earth permits of as much crookedness without danger of detection as that of the district attorney. There is none which admits of so much political pressure. Nowhere is there such power to evade, to pretend, to give every evidence of integrity, and, at the same time, to double-cross honest citizenship in the interests of the criminal. There are men who have risen to much higher positions through their record as an "unremitting prosecutor," and who have paid their campaign expenses with money received for having kept criminals out of the penitentiary.

None knows this better than the man who is in the business of crime. He knows, for instance, that a district attorney may have a great name in his community and still be a crook. He may have quite a record of prosecutions. Nevertheless, he fails to bring a certain number of cases before the grand jury "because he feels he has insufficient evidence to convict." Sometimes, that attitude is honest. Sometimes he has been paid for feeling that way.

I have found that the "insufficient evidence to convict" happens in a far greater number of cases where there is professional crime, clients in the hands of law partners of the district attorney, or persons who will be defended by lawyers of a much greater legal ability than the prosecutor. There are a number of district attorneys who never take a chance. They would rather not prosecute at all, even when they know a prisoner is guilty, than to run the chance of being beaten in court, thus possibly affecting their record at election time.

Criminals also know which district attorneys are mad dogs in the courtroom and very gentle in their office, especially if what is known as "mitt-greasing" has been practised. There was a certain Los Angeles district attorney who made a wide name for himself as a fearless prosecutor. He rolled up a marvelous record, especially against the weak in purse. He was pointed to as an ideal protector of society.

Of course, there were times when he just didn't seem able to make a case. Strangely enough, these unfortunate happenings usually occurred when the client was possessed of great wealth. Finally, in the trial of a crooked oil promotion group, this district attorney worked just a little too hard to lose his case. Resultantly, there was an investigation and he went to the penitentiary to which he had sent so many other criminals.

That, however, happens seldom. With proper discretion, a district attorney can enrich himself to a degree, retain his good name, and still be a friend to criminality. He even may be known as a crusader.

Look about you in your own town. If the cases of the poor come swiftly to trial, while those of the influential are snail-like in reaching the courts, there is something wrong, either inefficiency or worse. If the district attorney seems to have a plethora of bad luck in trials which affect the rich or influential, then again something is wrong. If, every six months, he makes the announcement that gambling must stop, that crooks will be run out of town, that dance halls will be investigated to the bottom, followed by a grand jury investigation which fails to bring results in the indictment of only a few small fry, you may be sure that something is exceedingly fishy. Nor is the trouble with the grand jury. The district attorney should be made to prove that he meant what he said in his braggart statements — and that he did not in reality mean them as a warning for protected friends to cover up.

The greatest alibi of a four-flushing, inefficient, crooked, or lazy district attorney is the grand jury. This body is blamed for "whitewashing," for weaknesses that it never possessed. No grand jury can indict without evidence. Usually, when it gets that evidence, a grand jury does its duty. Often, however, the evidence has been totally lacking and for excellent reasons.

One of these has been the broadcast announcement of the district attorney long before the first session of the grand jury, thus providing a wholesale tip to the entire underworld to hide out until the session is over. With this done, the district attorney can throw dust in a dozen directions, complain of insufficient police coöperation, drag inconsequential witnesses before the jury, puff, fume, sweat and give every indication that he is working himself into a lather in an endeavor to defeat the underworld. In truth, he is putting on exactly the same grunt-and-groan performance as that of a group of wrestlers who live together, sleep together, eat together and travel together, and, each night before they enter the ring, flip a coin to decide who shall be the "winner." It is all show, blather, foaming and fussing, to deceive both the jury and the public. As a result, the jury, not having received the evidence, fails to indict. The public does not blame the district attorney. It blames the grand jury.

Again, the district attorney often controls that jury. Being laymen, they look to him for advice, receive his counsel, and act upon it.

Recently, a worn-appearing man came to the home of a grand jury foreman.

"Can I tell you my story?" he begged. He was invited within. The jury foreman asked his troubles. It was an interesting case.

"I've tried every other way to get justice," he began. "I'm wondering if you can help me. I've been trying to have a man punished for having raped my young daughter."

"Do you mean actual or statutory rape?"

The man's face grew livid.

"He caught her on the street and dragged her into an empty house and gagged her and raped her!" the complainant shouted. "I knew I couldn't get anywhere with the police, because this fellow happens to be the brother of the party boss. But I thought the district attorney would have some guts. But he hasn't. The dirty coward refuses to bring up the case — "

"Wait a minute," the foreman said. "Have you been to any-one else about this?"

"Another member of the grand jury."

"I thought so. He mentioned this case to the district attorney at our first session. The D.A. said you were crazy and to pay no attention to you."

The man rose, staring dully about him.

"Maybe I'll go crazy," he answered slowly, "trying to get something done about this. But there were witnesses — persons who saw this fellow bring my daughter out of that house and rip a handkerchief off her face, turn her loose and run. They brought her home to me. And the rat himself admitted it to a man I know — boasted about it and asked what kind of a fool I was to try to get anything done to him. Bring the people in — question them. See for yourself whether I'm crazy! Then ask that crooked district attorney how much his law partner's been getting from this dirty skunk for keeping all this covered up!"

"I'll look into it," answered the foreman.

The next day a grand jury "ran away," which is the most feared thing in the underworld. It was a runaway grand jury which brought about the upheaval in New York by which Thomas E. Dewey was appointed a special prosecutor and a dent made in the rackets for the first time in years. A grand jury truly is feared when it takes the direction away from the district attorney who has been skillfully guiding it past any-thing that would endanger "the boys," holding indictments to the poor, to those without influence, and failing to bring forth the witnesses that might cause trouble for those who are "wired in."

There was terror about town when this particular jury in-sisted on examining the witnesses in the rape case and found them truthful. Then, determined men upon a foul trail, they stuck investigative noses into everything that seemed wrong about their city. As a result more than sixty whorehouses run by a syndicate were forced to close, and the controlling racketeers

were sent to prison. The head of the Vice and Morals squad resigned under fire. Gambling was stopped and several of the
syndicate members who ran it were indicted. Confidence men
were caught. Crimesters who had used this place as a cooling-off
joint left the vicinity like blackbirds before a storm. The sooner
that grand jurors, at the slightest hint of covering up on the
part of district attorneys or judges who issue their instructions,
decide to do as they please about investigation, the sooner the
summoning of such bodies will truly mean trouble for the underworld. Otherwise, "the boys" actually gauge their vacation
periods that they may be away from home during grand jury
sessions and thus lose no time from their usual nefarious
practices.

Again, this is something which every criminal knows. Therefore if the district attorney is fixable, the grand jury often fails
to indict. If he is honest but inefficient, the case goes to trial
and the criminal still stands a three to one chance of gaining
freedom. There are so many exits from a courtroom, other than
those used for the spectators.

One great fear which possesses this writer is that he may be
accused of having written a "scolding book." Perhaps there can
be the accusation that I have not stated at frequent enough
periods that there are honest politicians, honest and efficient
policemen, honest and efficient chiefs and lawyers and doctors
and coroners and constables and district attorneys and judges
and juries. If I have been remiss, there is great eagerness to
apologize.

However, after all, this is not a book about the honest and
efficient men in crime areas. Their work is so outstanding
against the general mess as to be self-evident. I am concerned
with the large numbers of officeholders so dangerous to public
welfare that they overshadow anything which honest and
eager men may do, no matter in what field of law enforcement
that may be. In addition, it is an effort to teach persons how

to recognize the symptoms of dishonesty and inefficiency, and what to do about it. Again, as was said concerning police, if there is widespread gambling in a community, if there are slot machines under syndicate control, numerous houses of prostitution which laymen find easy to enter but against which law enforcement seems unable to get evidence, there is something wrong with the local government. If the poor, the ill-defended, the unaffiliated amateurs of crime are brought swiftly to justice and yanked away to reformatories or penitentiaries, while the influential, the crimester, and the professional seem able to miraculously escape — again, these are symptoms of a festered condition which should cause grand juries to take the reins into their own hands and, though they be able to do no more, expose the conditions which have turned a decent city into a mud-wallow of corruption.

However, there are conditions over which no one seems to have any power, unless it be a concerted movement of Public Opinion, which so seldom is concerted. These concern the majesty of the law.

A suspect is arrested. There is no dignity about that: two or more detectives, sometimes of the old school which believes in four-dent hats and illiteracy, take the man to police headquarters, where he is booked.

The desk sergeant, as a general rule, is an old man in an old room, with an old book before him; the only things older than firehouses are police stations. But at least a firehouse is clean.

The opposite is true of the average police headquarters. The platoon room is a thing of scattered newspapers, of spittle which has missed the cuspidor, crumpled paper napkins and wrappings from sandwiches which, failing to hit the wastebasket, have settled, with cigar and cigarette butts, burnt matches, and wrappings of various sorts, to the floor.

Near by is the police reporters' room, often with a dice game going in a corner, the floor, desks, and telephone booth littered with copy paper and just-read editions, the walls decorated with pencil scrawls — always a reporter in the booth, ineffectually trying to get a number and screaming in his wrath.

There is the turnkey, usually fat, tunicless, dirty. And there is the bull-pen.

You, as a citizen, should see the bull-pen. Drop in some time and ask to look at it. Spend a few moments in contemplation of the filthy toilet, out of order for these last three years, the bowl stained with iron rust and crusted with fecal matter. You might cogitate upon the written filth that fouls the walls — the knife scrapings and pencilings of degeneracy.

Then there is the washbasin, slimy with the germs of disease. It also is rusty; inevitably a faucet leaks. There is the stink of unclean bodies of the persons who inhabit the place — "holdovers," they are sometimes called: the drunks, the beggars, the flotsam and jetsam of a city, held for police court.

Upon the tattered clothing of a sleeping form on the floor, the lice crawl — white lines of them, as if in resentment against the chill of steel. There is no such thing as a delousing system — if one holdover case has lice, then all must have lice. Rats scurry about, their beady eyes gleaming in the faint, reddish glow of a single electric globe that has not been cleaned in years.

In a corner, a cocaine addict picks at his clothing, as he attempts to catch fabulous apparitions which seemingly crawl in and out of his flesh.

The cells are little better. There is steel latticework upon which to sleep, and slumgullion, served by unclean trusties. This is the city jail, the place to which you may be taken sometimes if you happen to become involved in an accident, or if you should be unfortunate enough to be a material witness to a murder. Since it has harbored many such persons as you, it might be well to visit it in advance, with the idea of doing something toward cleaning it up against the time of your arrival.

That is the prisoner's first real glimpse of the majesty of the law. His second comes during the many examinations made in an effort to gain a confession. If old-timers are making the attempt, there will be various types of the third degree, stopping far short, however, of the fabricated stories which every shyster lawyer uses for a defense when the evidence of guilt too thickly engulfs his client. In many instances, legally or illegally, prisoners deserve exactly what they get. They have jeered at their examiners, jibed them, sneered at their questions, derided them, called them foul names, until human restraint fails and a husky cop lets one go with his fist — and perhaps, had you been there, you would have done so even sooner. Nevertheless, the majesty of the law has not been aided to its pedestal by such an action.

At last, the examination is finished. The prisoner is held for trial. The district attorney files his complaint. The suspect is taken to the county jail — a usual procedure in most communities — to await the time when he will run his chances of acquittal before a jury. Now indeed does filth, inefficiency, inhumanity and downright cruelty come into its own.

The unbelievable recital of conditions which follows applies to more than forty-four per cent. of all American county jails, and among the remainder there is no such thing as perfection. Instead, the Federal Bureau of Prisons — which, under Sanford Bates, its Director, carries on an inspection service to determine whether or not county jails are fit places in which to house its prisoners — has found not one single county jail in all the United States which attains perfection in every Federal desire. There are even less than a half-dozen which come within ten per cent. of being perfect. This means that only one county jail out of every five hundred even approaches what humanitarian penologists deem necessary for the honest and just treatment of prisoners. There are more than three thousand county jails in America. Through these three thousand county jails there annually pass more than six hundred thousand men, women and children. Thousands are incarcerated in holes which are not even fit for the lowest form of animals.

Compared to the county jail at its worst, the average "hold-over" of a city jail is a palace. In the county jail disease and insanity often are housed side by side; here vermin crawl, here the rats scurry and spiders weave their webs; and to make it all the more horrible, a large number of the persons who are confined here are not even guilty of any crime!

Persons who are merely wanted for questioning often are held here for hearing. Others who have been unfortunate enough to see a major felony and thus become merely material witnesses can be incarcerated in what can only be described as hell-holes. That may be sensational language, but it will be proved by a description which should not be read either directly before or after eating.

It was a stinking place to which I was led one day by a traveling investigator. We were in a Southern state, where jails are governed by a board of County Judges, and where the county is responsible for the upkeep, while the sheriff receives what profit he can make from an average of forty-two cents per day per prisoner for their feeding. Therefore, the less money the sheriff spends, the more he makes. In this state, as in many others, every possible precaution is taken against good enforcement by a law which forbids sheriffs to succeed themselves. Their income comes from the fee system; anything which they spend for humanitarian purposes cuts into the total which they hope to carry away with them at the end of their incumbency. This jail which we were about to visit was a monument to official greed.

It was frightfully overcrowded. The penitentiary in this state had no more room for prisoners, so they were being held in various jails. One man had served two years in this madhouse, another had been here for five years. That he was still sane is a miracle. The jail had a capacity for nearly two hundred prisoners, and housed half again that number. Only a reincarnation of the most horrible days of the Middle Ages could equal what was observed there.

A Kangaroo Court ran this jail. To return for a moment to

the professional criminal who has figured on escaping punishment, it must be taken for granted that if he did reach a jail such as this, he would immediately be granted a judgeship in the Kangaroo Court.

Average citizens look upon a Kangaroo Court as some sort of a funny game, wherein persons are tried for imaginary offenses, not allowed to plead in their own defense, and given idiotic sentences. That is the parlor interpretation. The jail version is a vastly different thing: ghastly, cruel, unbelievable.

The system began two hundred years ago; it functions to-day as it functioned then. The most desperate criminals become its judges. Before them, every other prisoner is herded, to be tried without appeal, and to be subjected to any forfeiture, any degrading punishment that the Court may decide upon. The charge is usually some senseless thing like that of having broken into jail without the use of dynamite. It is a form of piracy, by which experienced, hardened criminals prey upon the weak, stealing under the pretext of fines what money and other valuables they may have been allowed to bring into jail with them; seizing upon the best cells, forcing other prisoners to become their servants; demanding, under pain of physical violence, that objectionable prisoners, such as syphilitics or the insane, remain away from them.

Thus, the professional finds comfort even in such a hogpen as the one we visited. An ancient, rambling building, built at least fifty years ago, with seepage from roof-leaks apparent at a dozen places, with tiny windows, and almost a total lack of ventilation or sanitary equipment, this was the sort of jail into which Oscar Wilde might have been cast. Rub my eyes though I might, slap my cheeks, pinch my flesh as much as I pleased to assure myself that I was awake, it still remained a ghoulish nightmare, peopled by such human beings as one could imagine rotting in the fetid cells of a prison ship of ages gone, or dungeons dug into the dripping rocks beneath the Château d'If.

Perhaps the professional crimester would not even have been forced to occupy a cell here, for there were two large rooms in this jail which were comparatively cleanly. They were called "the hospital," but they were occupied by men in the best of health — the Big Shots of the criminal population, who either had used bribery or other influential means to segregate themselves from the common herd. Having thus viewed the haven of the affluent, we shall descend into hell.

The cell blocks teemed with humanity of all ages and stages. Cockroaches scurried almost beneath our feet as we walked along. The scabby, unclean mass of humanity which jammed the cells — all but the first seven in each block which were reserved for Their Worships of Kangaroo Courts — scratched and dug at scabby skin diseases or to rid themselves of the itch of vermin. My friend entered an open cell, and jerked at the bedding. The action disturbed a perfect army of lice and bedbugs and roaches; a few rats scurried into the half-shadows and crouched there, surveying us with shoe-button eyes.

Suddenly the investigator asked of a fifteen-year-old boy, his face cratered by deep scars of disease sores: "Syphilis?"

"Yes, sir," answered the boy. "I've shore had a right smart dose of it."

The investigator turned to the sheriff.

"Why do you keep this syphilitic in here?"

"Hell," answered the official. "He's all cured up."

"The tertiary stage of syphilis doesn't cure up that easily. Besides, he's in an adult block!"

"By God, that's right! Well, we'll get him out of here — move him out of the damn jail. Send him to the juvenile home."

So a boy in the final stages of syphilis — the time when the disease even attacks the bones — was taken out of the jail and sent to mingle with hundreds of other boys, in a place called a juvenile "home." The investigator could only say under his breath:

"What should really happen is to put the officials in here instead of the prisoners. They're the real criminals."

This place stunk like a charnel house. Seven of the eighteen cells in a single block being occupied by the pirates of the Kangaroo Court, the remaining eleven were jammed with a heterogeneous collection of forty-five human beings, some staring, some cursing, some singing with that strange, haunting melody of beings in durance — and some screaming with insanity.

For the crazed were here also. There was one syphilitic so devoured by the disease that his reason had vanished; gaping, gibbering, he lay there in filth.

"You see," the sheriff explained, "I'd send him to a hospital, except that hospitals around here don't want insane patients, and there isn't any county institution for 'em, and the state hospitals are full."

"Then there are insane patients incarcerated here simply because they have mental disease?"

"Sure."

"They have committed no other crime than to be unfortunate enough to lose control of their mental faculties?"

"Well, if you want to put it that way. They're crazy, aren't they? They've got to be locked up. Where else are we going to put them?"

So here they were, the insane and the sane, jumbled together, with active cases of syphilis and running gonorrhea. In fact, gonorrhea was so general as to be hardly worth mentioning, one prisoner said.

"How about the baths?" asked the investigator. A grim-faced man leered at him.

"What the hell, take a bath? You only shake up the seam squirrels and maybe get a dose of syph off the towels. It's bad enough takin' your chances on the dishes you eat off of."

Yes, the sheriff admitted, there was some danger of that, since, after all, syphilis germs can be carried from one person to another by towels and eating utensils. And there really wasn't any way to tell who had previously eaten from a dish, a healthy person or one with syphilis.

In one cell, a tubercular hacked and spat upon the floor, his spittle to dry into dust there and waft its death message to whoever inhaled this horrible air. His cell mate groaned with a case of epididymitis, or inflammation of the testicles, resultant from gonorrhea. In another cell lay a man, his sexual organs so swollen from disease that he was actually a hospital case. Nobody bothered about him.

This, I must repeat, was not something from the Dark Ages. Nor was it a part of a dream, a play, a book of fiction. This is going on to-day — in the last months of 1936, as this book is being written. Healthy men are celled with syphilitics whose open sores drip the virus of one of the most dreadful diseases known; crazed persons scream and laugh and shriek; the ill groan as they are dragged before a gang of ruffians who call themselves the Kangaroo Court — a body countenanced by the sheriff because he believes they help "keep discipline" with their beatings, their robbery, their lashings, and the filthy, degrading duties which they inflict upon weaker prisoners. All this goes on right now, to-day, with rats scurrying about, and vermin literally covering the bodies of those who strive to sleep, and with each mealtime a glory hour for disease germs as platters are handed about between sick and well with no thought of segregation.

If some of the enormous sums being spent presumably for the welfare of our population were used to improve prison conditions, we might have less crime and less disease, for both of which we now pay a heavy bill.

Of course, there is the alibi that all this happened in just one jail. So we shall go to another, where a man lay in a cell where there was no toilet — rather, his slatterned, filthy bed was made up so that it covered the toilet and he therefore used the cell floor. He had done this month on month, until the excrement was dried like the manure heap of a barnyard, and until it was nearly as high as his bed. There he lived, something that once had been a human being, but now only a caged animal living with his own dung.

And we shall walk into six hundred and eleven jails where there is no attempt to separate juveniles from adults, and where there also is practically no effort to afford segregation of the sick from the diseased. We shall go into two thousand, two hundred and four county jails that never, in all their existence, have been inspected by local boards of health or any other sanitary organization; where the sheriff is responsible to no one for his treatment of prisoners — and where conditions such as the following, from an official report, are to be found: —

The sewage system has been out of commission for some time. The septic tank overflows not far from the jail kitchen, causing bad odors and a great menace to health; also causing most of the sanitary facilities to be stopped up. Since the windows have neither heavy screens or fly screens, great swarms of flies to-day were seen all over the food the prisoners were eating.

These flies had come to feast upon the food provided for twenty-eight human beings, the diseased and the well, the guilty and the innocent, and even the person held as a witness. They had swarmed about, moved from dish to dish, covered the faces and the hands of inmates and their food; they had nipped at sores or chewed at the rawness of scabby flesh — and they had swarmed in here to the smell of food directly from the jail cess-pool.

If this is not enough, it might be possible to step into female wards where the food and other wants of woman are attended to by jail trusties or deputy sheriffs, and where any innocent woman or witness, though she be from the best of homes, and with the best of breeding, is practically at the mercy of Negroes or slatternly whites, or "stir-crazy" ex-convicts, depending upon the vigilance or lethargy of the sheriff. There are hundreds of jails which have no matrons. There are others where the sheriff's wife is the woman in charge, no matter whether or not she knows anything about the handling of prisoners. There are other places of incarceration where the keys to the jail are actually carried by "paid-up" inmates or by trusties who have it within their power to unlock the female ward to the ingress of whatever prisoner desires to force himself upon an incarcerated woman.

During the last Federal check-up to determine which jails the United States Government deemed fit for human housing, it was found that more than half of all the jails in America were either so low in caliber as to admit of emergency use only by the Federal Government, or so rotten in filth, vermin, and management as to be viewed as unfair and unjust places in which to incarcerate human beings. In fact, of nearly two thousand jails more than twelve hundred were condemned as being utterly unfitted to humanitarian requirements. Nevertheless, they were filled with local prisoners, living among the rats, the vermin, the offal, and fetidity. Remember again that there are more than six hundred thousand persons annually imprisoned in our county jails, — the guilty and the innocent and the insane, — a total equal to one person out of every two hundred and fifty of our total population.

To repeat: it is the poor, the innocent, the weak, the unprotected, the unaffiliated, and the amateur who suffers from such abuses. The expert crimester gets his place in the hospital ward — like Joey Ray, the gangster, unearthed by a courageous Commissioner of Correction, living in grandeur on old Welfare Island, enjoying the association of a police dog. There are jails in America where favored prisoners even live in the sheriff's house and eat at his table.

For that matter, it is on the official records that "paid-up members" often leave jail as they please, to go to baseball and football games, to mingle with women, to ride about town in their automobiles, returning only for sufficient time to maintain a pretense of being incarcerated. Others have attended race tracks, gone to county fairs, and in one instance at least been spectators at a World's Series. In another jail, the women were taken out to work as waitresses in a tearoom owned by the sheriff. In another, a local preacher, hoping to bring something of cheer, entered the stinking place to preach a sermon. Suddenly he straightened, as with a great shock. The sheriff laughed at that. So did favored prisoners, a number of whom were drunk, and carrying whisky on their hip. Drugs and liquor enter a county jail as easily as the cockroaches. Sometimes the sheriff does the selling. At one jail, an inmate who carried the keys to the place left the jail three times in one evening, and, going to his home, became intoxicated and created a disturbance. Twice the sheriff took him back to jail. This did not impress the prisoner. He stepped out again, and this time raised so much hell that it was necessary for him to be re-arrested by the local police. It is possible to buy almost any favor, from better food to a whore. There are fire hazards. In many jails there is no running water. But, of course, in many such cases, professional criminals are given "preferred accommodation."

Thus, in computing his chances to avoid punishment, the true crimester figures on all these elements. And having endured with a minimum of inconvenience what to others would be a degrading existence, he finally walks into court for his trial.

It has been my duty at various times to cover some two hundred murder trials, many of great importance. In only a few, and those in Federal court, have I ever found the dignity commensurate to what should happen when a human being faces the tribunal which can cause the loss of his liberty or his life.

A man lies buried, dead at the hand of a murderer. The power of the Commonwealth has been assembled to weigh the innocence or guilt of a person accused of having taken from this world a human being, with human attributes, be they good, bad, or indifferent. Someone's hand has brought the ghastly majesty of death into a home. Now, he must stand in judgment with, theoretically at least, the same majestic shadow above him which he is accused of having visited upon the dead. But where is the majesty?

All too often, the courtroom is dingy, dirty, and with grimy windows. In flagrant instances the bailiffs are political hangers-on, given their jobs because of their usefulness on election day. The judge sometimes sits in his shirt sleeves, chewing tobacco, and spitting at random. Crowds push and haul and shove, especially if this be a sex case. They laugh at every sally at the attorneys, who often play to the gallery like vaudeville performers on Saturday night. In the jury box are twelve men, selected not for their knowledge of law and jurisprudence and court procedure and justice, but for their ignorance. I remember having been examined as a prospective juror in a case involving a notorious gangster. I was asked no questions by the defense which challenged.

"What's eating you?" I queried of the defense attorney, widely known for his "shrewd" ability to win murder cases. "Am I poison? Why did you challenge me?"

"Why?" he asked. "Me let a guy like you on a jury — a fellow who knows all the tricks? Christ, give a fellow a break. I've got to beat this case."

So, you see, a trial is not a trial. It is a game, a rough-and-tumble affair, in which it is deemed brilliant play if a defense shyster can frighten away a witness, or so tear down the reputation of a complainant through inference or deduction as to forever blast his reputation. It is not a majestic judging of the facts; it is a hurly-burly, with the judge sitting as a referee, and, if he is crooked, aiding the district attorney in so filling the record with error as to make a Supreme Court reversal almost mandatory. It is cheap, tawdry, filled with tricks and legerdemain. Sometimes it is worse than that.

I have seen the judge, the prosecutor, the bailiffs, the defendant, and the defendant's attorney all drunk during trial hours. I have seen drunken reporters, during a murder trial, take the uniform from a drunken bailiff and parade up and down the aisles, in an inebriated attempt to keep order. I have seen juries go absolutely unguarded while the bailiffs who were supposed to watch them congregated in a separate room and got bilged to the eyebrows. I have been recipient of an offer from a prosecutor's office to engage in the blackmailing of numerous witnesses, through material worked up by the district attorney's investigation.

Then there was the Hauptmann trial, where, in addition to other circus features, a woman reporter boasted that she had sufficient influence to cause certain witnesses to be put on the stand in the morning hours, so that she could play up "human interest" angles for her afternoon papers. That is not all. She always seemed to have the story she wanted.

Thus the true criminal, knowing all the angles, takes his chance — three to one for acquittal. He depends on many things. First of all, there is the virtual certainty that his lawyer is a better attorney than the elected prosecutor. Secondly, he has the advantage of a private check-up on the jurors, often with information as to which will convict and which will acquit — money sometimes having passed to assure the latter. He has the advantage of professional alibi perjurers — perjury has become so common that in New York the penalty has been lowered in the hope that more persons can be convicted of lying in court. It seems to a person on the sidelines that if the court itself, through earnest work by bar associations, judges, and others, could assume some of the true majesty which it is alleged to possess, laymen might gain a respect which would demand the truth. To-day, there are thousands of witnesses annually who take an oath upon the Bible and then lie themselves black in the face, for no other reason than that somebody has asked them to do so. Fifty dollars, according to shyster lawyers who should know, is a high price for perjury witnesses in a criminal case, especially concerning alibis. Many have been bought for ten.

Even with all these things in his favor, however, the professional criminal and his lawyer may see that there is a preponderance of evidence for conviction. Then the crook is going to lose in this game which he has pursued from the beginning — this extra-long chance that he will not be made to pay commensurately for his crimes.

Thus there is a sudden conference between defense and prosecution. The defense may use any one of a dozen forms of argument — threats, cajolery, flattery, the old gag of saving money for the State through a plea of guilty, the certainty of another conviction to which the State's attorney can point with pride at election time, or the passage of bribe money. This is what is known as copping a plea, and the abuse has become so widespread, so indicative of corruption, that in at least one state recent laws make it incumbent upon district attorneys to file written and specified reports in every case in which a "copped plea" has been accepted.

All this means that the criminal does not plead guilty to the charge against him, but to a lesser one. If he has been accused of first degree murder, he pleads to second degree or manslaughter. If the charge is armed robbery, he admits to breaking and entering. If it is actual rape, he pleads to the statutory sort, which is an entirely different thing. Thus he wins even when he loses. Even though he goes to prison — he has not received the punishment he has deserved.

Of the seventy-odd thousand persons in our American prisons, there are forty-nine thousand who are serving sentences for a smaller offense than the one with which they were charged.

Nor is this the end. There are few prisons in America which insist that even a third of the sentence be served before a man is eligible for parole. All this, when the small risk of detection is considered, plus loopholes by which indictments may be evaded, and the inability of juries to convict, means that a criminal has a fifty-to-one chance to dodge punishment for the crime he committed, and then often serves less than one third of even the lesser sentence he has received. It is because of such conditions that more and more people, viewing law violation as an occupation, cannot for the life of them understand what theorists mean when they say that crime "cannot be made to pay."

CHAPTER SEVENTEEN

PRISONER'S PROGRESS

A PERSON who writes a book on crime, especially one such as this, inevitably finds himself in a decidedly unpleasant position. For pages and reams and chapters he has been demanding that lawbreakers receive what they deserve for having offended against society. Nevertheless, when a prisoner of the professional sort reaches the gates of a penitentiary, there, theoretically at least, to be shut in, for what is a partial recompense to the law, what has happened? If one is honest, one must admit that under present conditions, little has been achieved for the betterment of humanity.

An exceedingly dangerous circle has been completed. Its existence, however, as a detrimental factor, has not ceased. The circling will continue — leading in and out of prison, whirling from weak beginnings to vortex-like rapidity, creating whirlpools into which the young, the inexperienced, the amateurs and casuals are sucked, there to be turned and twisted and warped in their viewpoints until they also become professionals and act as examples to other amateurs, in practical lessons on how to beat the law.

Perhaps, therefore, it might be enlightening to dig into the life of the professional criminal who now is being bathed, barbered, deloused and dressed, in the teeming place of his incarceration. Who is he? Whence did he come? Was he always a professional crimester? Did he always possess this sneering, vicious attitude which governs his every action? Were his thoughts ever against the law? Or did society itself thus mold him — the same society which I have been writing about for hundreds of pages, in a demand that it be protected?

At the present moment, with guards about him, perhaps grimly remarking that he is back to visit them again, the professional criminal finds himself in a muddled state of mind. He has won, yet he has lost. In the estimation of society, he has beaten the barrier. Perhaps he has reckoned upon this as a portion of his profit and loss, even as a merchant would compute the gains or deficits of his business. Continuing the comparison, he is well-fortified against this reverse; experience has taught him ways and means by which to escape the rigors which once he knew in institutions such as this.

If he has gained his schooling in any one but a very few of our prisons, he will not be merely a shuffling nonentity in gray. He will be a big shot; revered by moronic subjects, accepted by the other big shots who, instead of the warden, all too often virtually control the inside workings of a penitentiary.

At this point, there must be an interruption to explain that in this statement Federal institutions are excluded. There was a time when they had little to recommend them above other institutions, but that time is gone; the reasons will be told later. The matter of the moment is the type of State penal system which exists too frequently. Any body or group of institutions which admits of numerous scandals is fundamentally wrong. There are frequent upheavals in our State prison systems — which, incidentally, have changed little since the Wickersham Committee issued the following indictment: —

We conclude that the present prison system is antiquated and inefficient. It does not reform the criminal. It fails to protect society. There is reason to believe that it contributes to the increase of crime by hardening the prisoner. We are convinced that a new type of penal institution must be developed, one that is new in spirit, in method and objective.

The Federal Government has tried to answer that challenge. The various states have had investigations, committees, meetings, and all sorts of things — including the ever-present changing of wardens with almost every election. The result is that, except in at most a dozen commonwealths, the professional criminal upon entering prison for his cut-rate sentence will find conditions exactly as he left them years before.

Incidentally, by the time this prisoner has reached his cell, he may have forgotten that he made a bet which was all in his favor, and lost; or he may perhaps be more bitter over his fate, due to the fact that the odds were so greatly against defeat. Or he may be philosophical. Whatever feelings he may have, there is one certainty: he is going to look out for himself. Thus he becomes a member of a pirate crew. If there are guards who can be bribed for any purpose whatever, he will know and use them, because he is a big shot. If he wants the food of the next man at the mess table, he will take it; he is a big shot. If he wants an easy job and the prison is run upon the loose lines of so many institutions, he will work at whatever he desires; or if he chooses, he will not work at all.

He will not suffer for women, for he will have his substitute — a man, of course, but serving as a female, either orally or through sodomy. The big shot obtains this person, simply by taking him, like a caveman. He will have money, either smuggled to him from friends on the outside, working through approachable guards, or brought to him by other means.

Perhaps he will have his own radio and his newspaper and a hundred other conveniences. But all these will not suffice. There is one quality which demands fulfillment greater than anything he has yet found: that is the gratification of the ego upon which his criminal impulses have fed throughout the years, the ego which has been developed since the first day he ever stepped into a penal institution and there had pointed out to him the reigning monarch, perhaps a murderer. Thus, through the strange anti-reform atmosphere which permeates places of "reform" an idol had been created. Now that the professional is himself a big shot, he wants the adulation of such persons as once he was when he was an amateur, a nobody. He joins the parade of other desperadoes who strut before weaklings. He condescends to talk to the "fresh fish." He dilates upon his life of crime. He sneers at whatever ideas they may have toward reformation. In a college of crime, he is one of its most eager professors, subconsciously retaliating upon society because he has lost a fifty-to-one bet. Perhaps, therefore, that the futility of present day manhandling of offenders be properly set forth, it is necessary to turn time backward into the childhood of this strutting big shot, and review his climb to what is to him — and thousands of moronic disciples — a status of fame.

It is necessary that his beginnings should not be attended by plenitude. The instances in which the rich boy becomes a professional offender are so few that they are not worth considering. This is not because there is holiness about riches. Rather, it is because incentive vanishes to a certain degree when plenty takes the place of poverty — plus, of course, the fact that you cannot convict a million dollars.

One night last spring, I strolled with one of the most widely known of motion picture stars on the smooth lawn of a widely known country eating-place near Washington. We had been talking of his rôles in the pictures, incessantly those of gangsters, or hard-hitting fighters of the tenements. I asked him if he liked them. He shrugged.

"Pictures throw you to a type," he answered. Young, exceptionally vibrant in the films, he is offstage a person of quiet philosophies, of deep thought, of great interest in psychology. "You see, I came from Tenth Avenue. They won't let me forget it."

"Would you like to?"

He smiled.

"Does a fish swim?" Then, after a time: "You know, I wonder why everybody blames a person who commits a crime. I wonder why they don't blame the parents, or conditions, or society. You see, I was lucky. The boys in my family got ex-

actly the sort of advice that other boys got — but our mother
told it to us in a different way. Our mother spoke to us about
honest endeavor, about hard work, about never losing sight of
our ambitions to be somebody, to amount to something.

"But the mothers of the fellows I played with didn't think
like mine. Maybe she had a better brain. The whole thought
in the minds of other mothers in that underfed tenement district
was that their children shouldn't grow up to fight life like they
had done, and live four or five in a room, with only one bathroom for the whole floor of the building and it out of order
most of the time. They didn't want their kids to live in fire-
traps, and to play in grime and dirt with every day an even
bet as to whether a motor truck would hit one of 'em while
he was out there in the street with his eyes on a game instead of
the traffic.

"So they'd pound at them — not like my mother did, with
a purpose — but without any idea of how it was going to happen,
and not much caring.

" 'Don't end up like your father and mother, living down here
in this smelly neighborhood. Don't end up poor. Go out and get
the money — any way at all to get it. Look at the rich. They've
got plenty to eat. They've got clothes on their backs. They've
got swell places to live in. They went out and got it. You do the
same. Other people have gotten it. Now you get it!' "

There was a long silence as we strolled under the elms. At last
he said: —

"Well, I saw 'em go get it. The very fellows I played with.
Some of them are in prison now — they turned into gangsters.
Others have gone to the electric chair. Everybody blamed the
kids. Nobody thought of blaming the mothers who told them
what to do. And I guess it would be crazy to blame the conditions that made the mothers say what they did."

Sooner or later, however, those conditions must be blamed, as
well as the conditions which followed those boys of the tenements
step by step along a tough road. They were the same conditions

which follow a country boy from parents of moderate circumstances, the boy from the small town. In fact it is a great tribute
to the slums that, with such a tremendous group of incentives
to make persons hate the law, there are so many who travel the
straight path. Tenements furnish racketeers of the parasitical
sort, thieves, gangsters who gather about a leader if one develops. But the strata just above the slums and even extending
into the lower middle classes of cities and of small towns are
equally fertile contributors.

The public enemies of the last five years, for instance, with
very few exceptions, came from the village, the small town, or
the "typically American city." With the exception of Alvin
Karpis and a half-dozen others, they were of supposedly clear
American stock. Many of them had been reared in an atmosphere
supposedly the best of all — that of the little community, and
even of the farm.

One after another you may count them off and check them
into rural or minor-urban surroundings. John Dillinger came
from a farm background. The Barrow Boys and Bonnie Parker,
their murderous companion, were from a Texas city. Mrs. Barker,
designated by J. Edgar Hoover as the most dangerous woman
criminal of the last twenty-five years, was at one time a psalm-
singing country girl, while her brood of four criminal sons was
reared either in the country or in small cities. Pretty Boy Floyd
originated in rural surroundings. Alvin Karpis was reared in a
Kansas town. The kidnappers of George Weyerhaeuser came
from villages. Frank Nash, the super-bank-robber, killed in what
is known as the "Kansas City Massacre," when Verne Miller and
Pretty Boy Floyd attempted to machine-gun the officers who
were taking Nash to prison, originated in an Oklahoma community, while Miller began in the same sort of place in South
Dakota. Eddie Bentz was the son of a farmer. Harvey Bailey,
a genius at robbery, kidnapping and prison escapes, came from
a Missouri farm. Machine-gun Kelly was reared in Memphis.

The list goes on indefinitely, as does that of the gun molls who trailed with these desperadoes. In every instance, their geographical beginnings were of that portion of America commonly looked upon as good, clean, and God-fearing.

However, even though there be a difference of geography, there is little division of causation. For some there was a background of a home broken by divorce. For others there was the pound of poverty — the grime of tiny mining towns, lack of outlook, of opportunity.

The motivation of many public enemies into whose histories I have inquired within the last few years has been either absence of discipline, lack of guidance, and the lackadaisical or bad example set by their parents. Moreover, their criminal career usually has begun in childhood, at a time when proper parental control could have either saved them from their first contact with the law, or at least made an effort to prevent its recurrence. To the contrary, however: it has been from the parents, with their almost animal-like antagonism toward authority, that some of these children learned their first lessons in defiance of the law.

Perhaps the acme of the instances in which parents were thoroughly unaware of what was happening to their brood was that revealed through a New York case in which the police, following a complaint by the Society for the Prevention of Cruelty to Children, advised the Federal Bureau of Investigation of a strange series of infractions. They announced they were holding a man on a charge of sodomy and rape, the victims being children ranging in age from nine to fifteen years.

The pivotal case had involved two girls, thirteen and fourteen years old, who had been picked up one Sunday by this man in Central Park and invited by him to go swimming. They had agreed. He had taken them to a secluded and wooded part of New Jersey, where he had induced them to become the participants in both sexual intercourse and sodomy. Returning, he had given them a dollar apiece, cautioned them to tell no one of their adventure, and asked them to meet him the next Sunday.

The week had passed and the children had awaited him. The

same program had been gone through. Then, looking for variety, he had asked them if they had any young friends who also would like to make some money. Thus the children had been made procurers, bringing with them, at various times, other victims. The procedure was to use the man's automobile as the place of intercourse with one child, while another was placed on a near-by rock to be on the lookout for passers-by. Then the first victim of sodomy or rape would become the guard and the other child be engaged in the automobile.

Two of the girls became hospital cases. One was found to be pregnant, heightening the feeling against the arrested man until it was learned that she had become so as the result of previous contact with another man.

The prisoner was diagnosed as an "infantile schizoid type of personality," and subconscious phallic worship being what it is, the offender was sent to prison for fifteen years, without the castration so necessary in all such cases. There his story ends — until he is freed and perhaps strangles a few children or cuts out their bowels.

However, there remains another and exceedingly vital angle of this case which is unsolved. This concerns the types of homes from which these victims came — the parental ideas of super-vision, the concern or lack of concern about the methods of amusement in which these children indulged, where they went, whom they met, and what they thought about. I greatly doubt if, in a single instance, there was self-blame on the part of any parents. There rarely is, the entire subject being summed up in a sigh, a shrug of the shoulders, hands folded upon the stomach, and a martyred expression, together with the self-absolving statement: "Oh, dear, these children! You never know what they're up to."

In this regard, there will be a tremendous advance in the mental and moral aspect of this country when the incessant propaganda regarding the glories of motherhood gives place to a public admission of what everyone privately knows — which is that pregnancies, especially among the ignorant and poverty-stricken, are more often accidental than desired. If more politicians had the moral fiber to aid in the honest prevention of undesired and, therefore, handicapped additions to the population, instead of seeking votes by kissing babies, there would be less misfortune, less poverty, less sorrow, less hunger — and less crime.

Therefore, when one finds a professional criminal, it is to be supposed that parentage, for any one of numerous reasons, has, in a degree failed. This having happened, the natural sequence of events, in early life, has led to a punishable infraction. If the offender had been a rich boy, the patrolman would have taken him to his parents. In this case, however, he has gone to the juvenile court.

There he may have met a kindly man, eager to do all in his power to help youth. Or the judge may have represented a certain type who indulges in quite theatrical exhibitions of love for children — the kind who is not averse to being photographed for the newspapers as he hands out lollipops and wisdom to wayward children, the subjects not knowing, of course, that they are being publicly labeled as delinquents for the personal gratification of a politician. Or the craftiness may have had even a wider scope, which takes shape in a juvenile political machine, the sort which induces unfortunate childhood to go from door to door at election-time telling its story — that it was bad and wayward, that kindly Judge Blank has been generous and helpful, and would the lady of the house vote for Judge Blank so he might remain on the juvenile bench and continue doing wonderful things for little neglected children?

It has happened in some of our best cities. But — bad judge, good judge, mediocre judge — one thing has been sure to happen. The potential professional has been placed "on probation," therein theoretically being given every possible chance to redeem himself — which means that he has been largely replaced in the hands of his parents.

In thousands of cases, a brush with the law is an awakening influence to parents who, whether they realize it or not, recast their views of their responsibility, and thereby themselves undergo a reformation. For others the true realization of offense has been sufficient to overcome what, in reality, has been more of a dereliction than an infraction. For the remainder, where parental control fails and where the child himself does not possess the ability to reconstruct himself, there has remained the probation officer.

Perhaps this official has been kindly, full of common sense, devoted to the task in hand. There are such probation officers and many of them, facing a superhuman task in which a common handicap is lack of funds and personnel. There also is another type — the type which has worked hard before election, which always has stood by the Party, and which deserves some reward, even though he or she doesn't seem to fit into any sort of a position demanding responsibility. All too often a harried political boss, tired of seeing the same faces day after day in his outer office, has commanded his lieutenant: "For Christ's sake, take a run down to the courthouse. See the judges. Ask 'em to do me a favor and appoint these pests out here to some sort of a job, anything to get rid of them."

Thus men and women, without training and without ability, have found themselves the mentors of young lives. They are the bulwarks upon whom future manhood and womanhood all too often lean. They may be lazy. They may be ill-tempered. They may be devoid of common sense. They may imagine themselves to be officers in the punitive sense instead of in a friendly one. Soon they are objects of contempt or hate. Either suffices.

It is to be supposed that the embryo professional has had bad luck with probation. In his teens, he has faced a superior court.

Perhaps the ward boss now has been forced to take over the job of assuring the family vote by "speaking to the judge," thereby entering the future professional criminal upon another era of probation, which, since there has been another political hanger-on to do the work, results only in the budding of an idea in the youth's brain — that there is something wrong about all these lectures he has received in court to the effect that crime "cannot be made to pay."

The mind of youth is quick to sense hypocrisy. Naturally closer to the animal, where life itself is dependent upon both the ability to camouflage and the super-ability to detect it, youth is essentially realistic. Its unfolding career is built upon the resistance of natural instincts to the bulwarks by which society attempts to protect itself, and which, to the every teaching of the animal, are false. Animals take what they desire, or fight for it. The motto of civilization is that one should take only what one is permitted to have. That creates quite a gulf.

So, the growing professional has gone before a "big judge." He has heard the same old rote that he received in the juvenile court, or from the probation officer, who may have learned it word for word from a book of instructions. The same story has come from the captain of police, who has questioned him after his first robbery, and from the jailer, who may have been taking money from a dozen criminals and salved his conscience by delivering a lecture to that punk in Cell 14. Therefore, after the scene in court and the successful plea "not to make a felon out of this boy, but to return him to his saddened mother," the juvenile mind, direct, realistic, free from sham, has been inclined to sum it all up in one word — usually before an admiring gang of younger kids on the corner: —

"Hooey!"

Sooner or later he has come back in court; then again; and for a third time. The probation officer has done his best as he knows it. The judge, from his chambers, has telephoned the ward leader: —

"Listen, Joe, this boy's back again. It's a serious charge this time. Two or three really influential people are kicking about him getting off too easy. I'll just have to do something about him."

To which has come the answer: —

"All right, send him up for a stretch. I was just fronting for him because his folks asked me to."

Thus another piece of criminal fodder has gone to a "reformatory," which is supposed to be "a correctional institution for the rehabilitation of youthful offenders," but which, all too often, is a poorly run slip-shod place, where boys, youths, and men are indiscriminately herded, often unclassified, rarely segregated. Even in what is called a fine type of state reformatory, investigators found that boys whose troubles truly had resulted from a lack of proper training and discipline were the co-prisoners of men up to twenty-five years of age who had committed such crimes as robbery with a gun, and who possessed previous records of servitude.

Moreover, it was revealed that this reformatory — remember that its standing is exceptionally high — had been a haven for the feeble-minded, the psychopathic, epileptics, the near-insane and the sexual perverts.

Only 41 per cent. were of a fit type for a reformatory routine; 7.5 per cent. should have been sent to a home for the feeble-minded, and the balance to a state prison or mental hospital.

It was further learned that 5 per cent. of the inmates showed symptoms of tuberculosis. There were 8 per cent. who suffered from syphilis in its various stages, while 12.5 per cent. had gonorrhea. Moreover, it was developed that, even though the institution had the power to hold these prisoners until the end of their maximum sentence in order to cure these diseases, inmates were turned loose upon society at the end of short minimum sentences and their promise "to take treatments." Mind you, this is an institution which rates highly. The conditions are not wholly those of administration, as is the fact in other states. From the comparatively high standards of places like this institution — if there can be high standards in places where there are such conditions — the status of reformatories goes steadily downward, reaching in some states a degraded level little above that of a poorly conducted county jail. Only the most strong-willed and self-reformed youth can depart from one of these lower fester-spots without a tremendous amount of bitterness and a thorough education in the possibilities of crime.

Certainly if a boy, at an impressionable age, can associate day after day with sex perverts and himself remain clean, he needs but little outside discipline. If a boy or youth can overcome the natural hero-worship heritage of the young, and refrain from looking with admiration upon his fellow prisoner who shot a cop, then indeed is he above the average. If he can evade the constant talk of filth, of braggadocio from the older members, of plans hatched by persons who, for this plane at least, are big shots, he certainly can be his own reformatory and needs no institutional "assistance."

Thus the reformatory as it exists in many states is not a reformatory. It is a crawling mass of criminal education, fostered by a thorough lack of proper administration and segregation. There have been numerous instances where hardened criminals of middle age have been sent to such places. Youth looks to the more adult mind, be it in a college or a correctional institution. It is an unusual youngster who can find the arguments with which to repel the advice of an old-timer: —

"Take it easy. Pretend to obey all the rules and like 'em. Pretend you're going to go straight from now on — that's the first thing to learn. Stay out of the hole, but don't be a stoolie. Pretend you don't know anything. Get to be a trusty; that's a soft job and you can make dough smuggling out letters or bringing in a bottle of booze now and then. And if anybody asks you if you're reformed, say 'Sure, this joint's done a lot for me.' "

That is the first lesson in playing at parole, a game found exceptionally beneficial by practically every one of America's recent public enemies, who went free in this manner not only once but, in some cases, more than a half-dozen times.

It is to be expected that the growing professional whose past record we are reconstructing thus has ended his first sentence in a "correctional institution designed for the rehabilitation of

youthful offenders." He has been graduated from a common
school of crime.

This is not the place to talk about parole, except to say that
the parole conditions upon which he has left have been ideally
conceived, and administered as well as excellent, good, mediocre,
inefficient, lazy, politically-minded or frightfully undermanned
staffs could accomplish. The youth already has learned from other
youths, returned for violation of their paroles, just what to do to
fool the parole officer. He has learned the names of the friendly
ones, the sensible ones, the fools and the lazy. He may even have
been told that there is not a parole board in the United States,
except that of the Federal Parole system, which has sufficient
men or sufficient money with which to carry out the true theory
of parole.

So, the youth who is destined to be a professional crimester
has done largely as he has pleased, practised a dozen forms of
deception, finally to be discovered in a violation and sent back
for a post-graduate course in criminality. This time he has found
himself somewhat exalted above the average inmate. Completion
of the term has made him a high-school graduate with a lot of
knowledge imparted to him by fellows who once looked down
upon him as "just a punk."

It seems so strange, so unjust, so heartlessly cruel that there
are so few successes which come from reform schools, and so
many which result from the quiet, kindly, and highly efficient
methods of private institutions backed by public-minded citizens. When one reads grand jury reports demanding action in
cleaning up our reformatories, transcripts of evidence from investigations, the excuses of wardens ousted for one reason or
another, one wishes for the miracle that could wipe out reformatories entirely. One wishes that there might be such places everywhere as adaptations of Father Flanagan's Boys' Home, in Boys
Town, just outside Omaha, Nebraska, which, while it is in truth
a home, not for unregenerate, but for homeless boys, gives a faint
idea what private work may accomplish. In this place only a
handful of supervising adults guide the activities of children, who

otherwise govern themselves. More than four thousand boys have been given an understanding of how to seek out the green lights on a straight path ahead. The same sincerity of planning, of freedom from statutory red tape, from political interference might achieve the same results for errant boys.

One has only to spend an evening at the Boys' Brotherhood Republic, in the heart of the Chicago or New York slums, to understand that there is something better than the average "correctional institution for the youthful offender." The job here is to keep the boy off the teeming streets and away from formative gangs. There are experience meetings in which the "citizens" tell what the organization has done for them and why. There is no pretense about it — they have come here voluntarily; some have even joined against the jeers and threats of playmates who are potential gangsters. Then, in the cause of better living, these same boys have become missionaries to the very fellows who jeered at them and threatened them — and brought them into the organization, likewise to become disciples.

There is nothing mysterious about it. There is only the constant example that a clean life can give a fellow more fun than a crooked one. There is no preaching, as such. Good sportsmanship is taught in the boxing ring, good thoughts are provided in a library where an overseer possesses enough knowledge of youthful psychology to interest boys in reading books that are good for them — without their realizing that they have been led into it. Beginning with almost nothing, it now has one thousand citizens in Chicago; and in New York it has taken over an entire building, after a comparatively recent beginning of only eight boys. The kid from this organization who becomes a self-made missionary does not talk in any such platitudes as "crime does not pay" when he argues with a former street-gang friend. He merely announces: —

"Don't be a sap. What's it get you? Duckin' de cops. What for? To get what you want? Listen, I'll show you where they teach you how to do it and have fun at the same time."

Although there are many boys in the club who already have

brushed with the police or who have belonged to gangs, there is not a single instance of arrest since those boys have joined the club.

Nor can one help wondering why the P.A.L. — or Police Athletic League organization, a sideline of police departments, devoted to the prevention of crime — has so many members, sneering at fellows who instinctively shy from the police.

"Duck de cops?" they ask. "Who wants to duck de cops? There's a couple of 'em umpirin' our baseball game. Why should we duck 'em?"

However, there has been no such history for the average professional. That is especially true if his case has included a parole violation. Then indeed, upon his release, he may become a braggart before the other kids of the neighborhood. He has felt he must speak of himself in crook terms and as "a two-time loser." He now retails the filth he learned about onanisms, fetishism, sodomy. To further parade his status before awe-struck kids, he has pictured himself as a young man of desperation, a cop hater. Sooner or later, there has been an effort to prove how bad he has become. As a result, there has been a sentence to prison.

For purposes of verification there must again be cited the record of practically all public enemies who have been captured or killed within the last few years. They have, almost without exception, followed such a trail, and, upon coming forth from the reformatory school of crime, traveled on to higher education.

Sadly enough that is about all the judge's words in pronouncing a penitentiary sentence has meant for the budding professional. Already he had been taught to look upon the vicious offender as a person to be emulated. And instead of eradicating that idea, the average State Prison has fostered it.

Here his cell-mate may have been a gangster of the worst sort — or he may have been celled with two or three of them; there are prisons where the overcrowding is so terrible that even five men are assigned to a cell. Here he has seen the big shots, watched them

in action as they pirated their way to possessions they desired —
crowding about another prisoner, for instance, and stabbing him
with knives made under the very noses of the guards in the prison
machine-shops. During this first prison sentence he has almost
surely been taught subjection to greatness. His tutors have
sneered at everything which society sets up as a theoretical protection. His cell-mates have lived, thought, and talked of little
but the crimes to be committed upon release or escape — except
perhaps the necessity for the simulation of good behavior and
good intentions, by which to keep clear their records in hope of
an early parole. Not that parole is given for good conduct;
nevertheless, insubordination against prison rules easily may work
against it.

Here he has learned the mysteries of the prison "grapevine" —
which is not a mystery at all, but merely a testimonial to the
laxness with which so many prisons are conducted. There is no
fiction-book signaling, no weird telegraph, when information
sweeps through a prison. It comes from contact during recreation
hours when the majority of prisoners come together in the big
yard. It arrives through information imparted by prisoners engaged in clerical and other types of work in the warden's office,
the record room, and the deputy warden's office. These prisoners
usually have a recreation hour different from that of the main
body of men, where they mingle and exchange the news of the
institution, much of which has been information supposedly
confidential and only for the administration. These prisoners
sleep in the cell-blocks — it is only necessary to whisper their
news in jerky sentences to one other convict for it to sweep the
prison. Friendly guards are not tight-lipped. Others may be
bribed. Trusties who are engaged in work outside the walls smuggle letters and information in and out — they sleep in cells like
any other prisoner. Attorneys and friends pass along information
during visiting hours which may be designed for another convict
than the one to whom they are talking. Almost any prison is a
teeming mass of plot and counterplot, hunger for information

concerning possible criminal activities, and escape — constant intrigue.

The embryo professional has occupied a place in his prison corresponding to that of a freshman in his college. The old-timers, the desperadoes, have been the seniors; and they not only have inflicted their will, but their viewpoint. The place of in-carceration, for instance, may have possessed such an atmosphere as that accredited for years to San Quentin, where gangs ruled the prison yards, where there were outbreaks and escapes, where homemade guns were manufactured in the machine shops, where there were plots to destroy the buildings by dynamite, others to create havoc through poison which could be obtained within prison walls, and where, as a climax, a counterfeiting plant was set up by convicts in the photo-engraving department. Secret service agents, in tracing down ten-dollar bills which had been passed all the way from San Francisco to Seattle, finally nailed the passers as ex-convicts from San Quentin. The trail which be-gan here led inside the prison walls and to the photo-engraving plant — where fake money was being manufactured, and enough poisonous chemicals, necessary in photography, were on hand to kill off the entire executive staff. It was after this recent discovery that the warden resigned and a new regime began.

Or perhaps the newcomer may have fallen into such a place as Joliet was alleged to be, the sort of place any prison must be under strictly political domination.

It was in Joliet that Henry "Midget" Fernekes, gangster, rob-ber, and multiple murderer, was incarcerated; and from this place he escaped, ostensibly by growing a mustache under a piece of courtplaster and by changing his convict's uniform to civilian clothes. One wonders, naturally, why there was no investigation into his story that he had cut his lip while shaving. And where does one get civilian clothing inside a penitentiary?

If the budding professional has been in such a place as Joliet was before recent investigations, he may have learned the truth of charges that convicts played poker for high stakes and that money was smuggled to inmates, on a percentage basis, by guards who made a racket of such a business. Prisoners testified that liquor was to be had by whoever possessed the money to buy it. The same was allegedly true of drug addiction — the usual price for a shot in the arm being one dollar. There were even stories that favorite prisoners were permitted to wear entirely different garb from other men — even to white shirts and flannel trousers.

Or our professional could have been in a prison like the Southwestern one in which murder after murder occurred only a short time ago — or perhaps in the one in which a search of the place revealed an entire bushel-basket full of guns, knives, and other weapons. There are so many evidences of lax prison administration that it is difficult to keep track of them. For instance, there are the conditions which brought about the killing of Dickie Loeb in an Illinois prison and for the first time revealed the truth about what prisons really can be.

Here was an institution in which money seemed to rule. At the hearings which followed the killing of this particular convict, it was testified that on at least one occasion, a prisoner and a guard went out on a grand drunk together. There were stories that convicts were allowed — provided they had the money — unlimited spending allowances at the prison commissary. There was evidence that the place was partially controlled by Nathan Leopold and Dickie Loeb, who, in case you do not remember, were the "joint insanity" homosexuals who killed Bobbie Franks in Chicago. Following this, they were saved from the execution they deserved by the legal efforts of a great defender of the weak and oppressed.

This alleged control was largely a blind for an entirely different sort of existence from that promised by the judge, who after exceedingly heavy deliberation had sentenced them to life imprisonment at hard labor, plus ninety-nine years for kidnapping.

Sentimentalists often talk of the embitterment caused prisoners by punishment. Rather, the bitterness is brought about by lax and inefficient methods which punish some, while allowing others to have privileges denied those without influence or the prestige given by money. Among the things of which certain prison wardens were accused in this case was the fact that they allowed Leopold and Loeb to be together as much as they chose, in spite of orders to the contrary since they had been proved by the great attorney to be insane while in each other's company. Leopold's "hard labor" consisted of working in the greenhouse, where, other convicts said, he received as many visitors as he chose and refrained from wearing such stultifying garments as a convict's uniform. Dickie Loeb also disliked prison clothes, inmates insisted, so was garbed as befitted a man of money, even in prison. More than that, he and Leopold ran a correspondence school for convicts, an activity pointed out by various officials as something of high moral import, but referred to by other inmates as a gag by which they might obtain easy jobs for their favorites — especially the favorites of Dickie Loeb. There were even charges that one of the pair possessed a pass which allowed him to go outside prison walls at any time during the day. There were other accusations: that they ate at the officers' mess instead of with the main body of convicts, or in their cells if they chose; and that they were allowed to choose their cell-mates, this being particularly true of Loeb. And the killing of Dickie Loeb was not brought about by a mere prison quarrel, or by the stifling life of punishment, but by the fact that he wanted another and new favorite — another male woman, if you will.

The sooner the problem of homosexuality in prison is brought into the open, the sooner a growing menace to American morals will be properly studied and eliminated. There was a time when homosexuality was sufficiently rare and sufficiently abhorrent to be classed with subjects not to be mentioned in polite conversation. To-day everything is different.

Cocktail-time gossip usually, sooner or later, turns upon the subject of "fairies," "pansies," "nances," "fags." In the larger cities, there are even annual celebrations, in which thousands of homosexuals gather at tremendous dances, called "drags," where most of them are dressed as women. It is not unusual, in cities like Chicago or New York, to see them in clusters on street corners, parading the fact that they are "queer," and even ogling men they desire. There are "queer" night clubs, "queer" taverns, "queer" tearooms, where the clientele is composed almost wholly of homosexuals. Their prevalence has become so great in certain congested districts of larger cities that it is not at all unusual for male passers-by to be solicited.

It is upon the modern American prison system, in the most advanced nation of the earth, that the blame for homosexuality and a large amount of other perversions is to be placed. The tremendous increase in recent years is helped by the fact that reformatories, prisons, and other penal institutions became grossly overcrowded in the Prohibition era, and overcrowding breeds homosexuality, almost inevitably.

There are few state prisons which do not have their complement of wolves, or predatory homosexuals. Usually they are prisoners who have attained influence — either through money, or through their reputation for desperation, or for fierceness. One reads with some wonderment of prison fights, knife duels, murders; and one may meditate upon the intrigue of prison life which brings about a battle to the death. It rarely occurs to the average citizen that here may be a stark drama of which the facts have been concealed — the clash of two humans who have become worse than beasts, fighting each other as cavemen might have fought, not for the possession of a female, but of a man who shall serve them as a woman. Fellatio and sodomy are the curses of prison. Lax administration in many instances has allowed groups of wolves to band together until, mincing and primping with the acquired psychology of the "queer," they form a half-man monarchy which literally controls the institution. It was this sort of thing which is said to have occurred at Stateville.

Every newcomer, especially if he were young and good-looking, became a potential mate for Dickie Loeb. He had the run of the prison. He had what amounted to his private office and his private bathroom. Boy after boy came under his control, to serve him in whatever manners of perversion Dickie Loeb desired. At last he fixed upon a youth and fell in love with him.

That happens in prison — a man may fall as deeply in love with another man as ever one fell in love with a girl. There are the same intensity of affection, the same flatteries, the same blandishments, and the same fierceness when they are denied. Dickie Loeb made love to this youth for more than a year. The young fellow repulsed him. Then one day, desperate, Loeb met him in the shower and sought with a razor to threaten him into the action which Loeb desired, which according to evidence, was fellatio. A fight resulted. The youth got the razor away from Loeb and hacked him to death. He was tried for murder and was acquitted.

There are wolves scattered here, there, everywhere, in state penal institutions. Day by day they are turning more youths into homosexuals. To proceed upon their course they must enjoy a certain amount of laxity in prison discipline, or the unsanitary, unmoral conditions brought about by overcrowding. Beyond this is the fact that they are the breeders, the mainsprings, of the tremendous fairy and pansy population which is growing greater in every city. Such population, in its majority, comes from the cell-block.

Officials variously estimate that from fifty to seventy-five per cent. of all men who spend more than a minor term in prison there engage in some sort of perversion, and that if they remain long enough, they come forth confirmed homosexuals. It is a condition of the social set-up which deserves far more attention than it has received. Fairies are not funny, as most persons believe them to be. They are not "unusual." They are not, in many instances, "born that way." In too horrible a percentage they are the sins of our prisons, sent back to society to mock and jeer at the thought that persons can be placed in four walls and so many

blocks of steel and there forgotten in a mass of politics and political corruption.

Conditions like these which have just been described have
been a part of the professional criminal's education during his
first prison sentence. He may have been forced to become a fag's
"girl-boy" and because of him become steeped in homosexuality.
Certainly he has learned that all guards are not honest, that all
are underpaid, that all are grossly tempted. He has learned how to
write secret letters, even though they pass under the very eyes
of the warden — simply by eating starchy foods and writing
between the lines of his regular letter with his saliva instead of
ink. The aspirin tablet he has received from the prison hospital
for his "headache," or even urine, will suffice to create words
invisible on the paper until "brought out" by chemical action
when the letter reaches its recipient. The writing appears mysteriously on the paper when touched lightly with a weak solution
of iodine. And when the convict receives a letter in return,
he merely cuts his finger, is bandaged and doused with iodine
by a hospital trusty who knows what it is all about, and uses that
bandage as a swab with which to bring out the details as sent by
his moll concerning the outside arrangements for a possible
escape.

He has learned that the bigger a criminal, the better he fares
in the average prison. He has been taught a thousand and one
angles of crime by mingling with a thousand and one convicts,
many of whom have done little but talk over the infractions they
will commit upon leaving prison. He has learned to follow the
reformatory technique concerning parole.

And then he has been paroled.

Thus has come about a station in life in which, no matter
whether crime pays or not, the professional must regard it as his
"business." He has learned all its fine points; he has gone to its
colleges, he has studied under its professors, with all of whom
there has been only one ambition, that of beating the law. So he
has gone into it with the same determination with which another

man has become an artist, an architect, a builder, a merchant. They have their reverses; the same has applied to him.

Therefore, now that the fifty-to-one shot has once more returned him to servitude, it is asking too much to expect him to think of reform. Only one thought is possible as he struts about the recreation yard. His ears are attuned for only one sound — the whispering of two near-by "fish," perhaps newly arrived: —

"That's Laramie Red. He's a big shot. They say he's killed ten men and robbed fifty banks."

It is inevitable that Laramie Red should turn. Ego flares. He is a big shot. He amounts to something. In all this teeming mass of gray, crowded in the recreation yard, he stands forth, a man apart; a man of accomplishments, a man who has done something in life.

"Listen, fish," he announces through an almost ventriloquistic slit in the side of his mouth: "I'll put you guys wise to something. Don't let 'em slip you this blah that you can't make crime pay. Say, listen, I got more bonds stached away, I got more dough in the old tin box, than you ever laid eyes on. And listen — " he looks quickly about him, for he has longed to find two fish who might be willing to die to aid a big shot — "if you two guys have got any guts, I know a way we can blow out of this stir. Get me? Over the wall, see. There's two guys that's got to go ahead — you get me — Nothin' to it — the guards are fixed."

Perhaps the next week, there may be a flash from the prison that two young convicts were killed in a dash for liberty. (That made little difference to Laramie Red. He'd told them they'd have to have guts.) So Laramie reads his paper, and listens to his radio, and slips a friendly guard a five-buck note to get a bottle of whisky for his girl-boy. . . .

He's a big shot.

CHAPTER EIGHTEEN

GREEN LIGHTS

PERHAPS this chapter is the place to put illustration into reverse and prove the case against the penal attitude of many of our backward states by setting forth some achievements in humanity accomplished by the United States Government. This is not meant as an attempt to place the Government upon a pedestal. It is done merely to show, as in the work of apprehension and detection, that there is no miracle-working about efficiency. All that is needed is honest desire, honest effort, freedom from interference, and the intelligence necessary to point out to legislatures the crucial demand existing for better means by which to combat crime. Nor shall there be any attempt to prove that the Federal system is a perfect one. However, it is, by far, the best penal system we have and as such deserves serious consideration, both for its excellent points and for what may be classed as its bad ones.

For years, the United States penal system had suffered through indigence, as other agencies had suffered. But the Government, though scattered across thousands of miles, is far more of an integer than the average state. Perhaps, therefore, conditions were sensed by it with more rapidity. Perhaps, also, by the time a man becomes Congressman or Senator, he is more imbued with a sense of responsibility than when he is State Legislator. And certainly a President has more power and more fearlessness, more ability to control instead of being controlled, than the average Governor. It also is to be hoped that he has more intelligence than the run-of-the-mill fellow who sometimes rattles about in the big chair in the biggest office of the State Capitol.

There was one man in particular who had foreseen the possibility of such an indictment as that of the Wickersham Committee. That person was then President of the United States. He sent into Massachusetts for a man who had made quite a reputation as a penologist. His name was Sanford Bates; and his job, when in 1929 he was made superintendent of the Federal Bureau of Prisons, was that of remolding many punitive practices, which through the years had been accepted as fundamental. Since that time, there has been a tremendous upheaval in the manner in which Federal prisoners are handled, with a view toward both reformation and punishment.

There seems to be no cure-all for crime. There also seems to be no way in which all offenders can be made to conform to the picture which the average citizen paints of them — beetle-browed, slope-shouldered, evil-eyed and evil-featured. One man may be a moron. Another may be instinctively against the law. A third may be a victim of circumstances. A fourth may have offended only technically, while other members of the crowd with whom he was found guilty were the real culprits. To pour all these components into a common boiling-pot can result only in a product which, though it may be different, will contain one central ingredient: a conviction that law was made to be hated. This, sadly enough, is the program followed by many states. It was the one which had largely obtained in Federal prisons.

Strange practices, many of them the holdovers of years, were accepted in many places of incarceration as proper prison routine. However, this was to be a new day, a revolution in an attempt at both deserved punishment and deserved rehabilitation. Prisons and reformatories, to a large extent, were doing neither — just as the prisons and reformatories of many of the more backward states are to-day accomplishing nothing but the breeding of more crime.

A new day is quite a task for even a rising sun to bring about; the task of rebuilding the prison system of the Federal Government had somewhat the same dimensions. It must be conceded that in no integer was the Federal prison system nearly so filthy as many state institutions to-day. But it was of the old order, and needed decisive action in many quarters. Here and there, scattered throughout the system, were men of vision, of common sense, of excellent executive abilities. This meant a nucleus about which to mold general practice. From that much good was wrought.

All this change did not come about in one Administration. It is to the credit of both Parties that the work of moving forward toward both the rehabilitation of offenders and the protection of society, by the removal of mad dogs, has been accomplished under Republican and Democratic regimes alike, with a minimum of interference and a maximum of progress. In fact, the first job to be done was that of assuring the prison employee, of integrity and ability that he now would have not only a job, but a chance for a career without fear of politics.

Careers are usually the last thing that a person considers when he gets a prison job — at least under a state regime. A new governor has come into office. The old warden thereupon clears out his desk and prepares to go back to the farm, to his business or law office, or to the political headquarters whence he came, many of his personnel departing at the same time. Meanwhile, from a farm, a law office, a business concern or political headquarters, a new guardian of wrecked or thwarted or twisted lives moves into a two or four-year tenure of incumbency for which he is ill equipped. There is little future; there is less pay, for himself or his men. The tower guard, with his rifle, stuck on top of a wall with his food coming up to him in a tin bucket on the end of a rope, is in some places expected to kill escaping men for a thousand dollars a year. The sentry guards, pacing their posts in fair weather or foul, are supposed to be exempt from temptation — when their jobs may end any day, and when it is worth more than a year's salary to them to look the other way for only five minutes while a desperate man goes over the wall. The cell-block guards, the inside and outside ones, with wives and families and hopes and ambitions and greed and avarice and all other things which compose human nature, allegedly are magically transformed into untouchable angels by the presence of an ill-fitting uniform and the taking of an oath. The warden somehow is believed to have somewhere absorbed a knowledge of psychology, psychiatry, sex-impulses, criminal viewpoint. He is supposed to possess incisiveness, courage, common sense, clarity of thought, coolness in times of danger, diplomacy, impeccability of character, ability to command men, humanity without sentimentality, discipline without cruelty, and business acumen, simply because a governor, who until a few days before may have been a successful cattle buyer, has shaken him by the hand and said: "I now appoint you Warden of the State Penitentiary."

However, in the set-up of the Federal system there were men of more firmly molded abilities. Their ranks have been augmented by others who, in the mass of state inefficiency, have stood forth as preëminent penologists. Guards of the old, bullying, bribe-taking type were fired, to be supplanted by a different type, many college graduates and all either professionally trained or amenable to training. With the exception of seven inspectors attached to the central office, there is not a subordinate, an employee, or an official who is not under Civil Service. A man's job cannot be yanked from under his feet by the political friend of a gangster in Cell Block 2, because he wouldn't provide that individual with a turkey at Thanksgiving and a bottle of gin. Moreover, his job is his as long as he deserves it — which is a supreme aid against temptation when Laramie Red asks him to put cotton in his ears while a bunch of the boys saw out of cells. Many prison escapes have been that ridiculous. There ever will remain that classic of the "escape-proof" Dallas jail, when the night jailer actually went out and bought the hacksaws with which a prisoner cut his way to freedom.

There is no official of the Federal prison system who is not either a college graduate, a Number One man or a Number

Two man on the Civil Service list, or an outstanding veteran of from five to forty years in prison service. All have had training in the care and guarding of prisoners. They know every trick that a convict may concoct. There is professionalism about the entire service, in the training of all officers, the promotional examinations, the rewards for meritorious conduct, and in the actions of the special court which tries officers charged with malfeasance or neglect. The justice that descends upon a renegade guard in Federal service resembles vastly the justice of a Federal court, deliberate, unfailing, inflexible. There is morale about this organization. Men who handle prisoners do not look upon themselves as "screws" or "bulls" or "convict busters."

They are in a profession, where they may rise through the ranks or be promoted by examination. They have a future. They have ideals. They know their business.

The result of this is that there has not been a true escape from a walled Federal prison since 1931, when many of the old conditions still remained, when agitators and big shots exerted their influence and when there yet were holdovers of a time when it was not considered necessary for a guard to know much more than how to write a letter to his Senator or Representative and thus hope to receive a job.

During this time, of course, there have been walk-aways, from camps and such, designated as technical escapes. But there has been no such thing as the Leavenworth crush-out of 1931, in which desperate men smuggled dynamite into a prison, threatened guards with death, kidnapped and wounded the warden and embarked upon a career of terror which ended in death for several of the plotters.

The Federal prison system deems its minor employees underpaid; they receive nearly twice as much as many in state service, and in some instances three times the amount which guards and jailers in county institutions get for supposedly watching over men who have, at various times, offered as high as twenty-five thousand dollars for the privilege of escape.

To begin his career, he must qualify in such specifications as the following:

He is graded on his intelligence and capacity to learn, on his alertness, his punctuality, his accuracy, neatness and orderliness. His poise and deportment become a part of his record, as well as his diligence, his judgment and his common sense. He must have initiative, resourcefulness, coöperativeness, administrative ability, courage, and a properly balanced attitude toward prisoners. He must be honest, sober, of excellent character and fitness. Unless the applicant shows these qualities by the end of his first training course, he does not even go on probation duty. And if the qualities do appear, there is a year of trial employment, followed by more training. Not until then does a new employee receive his certificate of graduation as a full-fledged member of a Federal prison personnel.

Against such a Federal record, there are state and county guards who can neither read nor write. There are others who themselves possess criminal records. There are examples who, like their prisoners, are sex degenerates — one instance exists of a Kangaroo Court which operated upon perversion principles in a county jail and where all new arrivals were sentenced to become the "women" of the corsairs who performed their acts of perversion with the full knowledge and ofttime assistance of jailers. No such thing can happen in a Federal institution.

With the new regime, the medical staff was placed by legislation under the United States Public Health Service. Every prison has a staff of officers and nurses provided by that institution, plus a psychiatrist and a psychologist. Prisoners rotten with syphilis or gonorrhea or other communicable diseases do not mingle with others whom they may infect. There are no soft berths in hospitals for convicts with "drags," for there are no drags. Sexual perverts do not fight over their "women" because they are segregated and watched with the alertness which such cases demand.

Moreover, the Federal Bureau of Prisons has recognized the

fact that mentalities and characters are like faces — there are many differences. Therefore there is prison grouping; a man who deserves to go to Chillicothe Reformatory does not find himself in Alcatraz, nor an Alcatraz prisoner in Chillicothe.

There are types of prisons for types of prisoners. There is McNeil's Island, for instance, in Puget Sound, a prison without walls. It is the hope of the Attorney General that some day the United States may own this entire island, and that this prison which was developed as a place of incarceration for nine hundred members of a milder type of inmate may become the center of a farming and dairying community, peopled by convicts, all working, all living in fresh air and character-building surroundings. To provide work is the greatest endeavor of Federal prisons, work which will not interfere with outside labor: erection of prison buildings, the manufacture of supplies to be used in Government departments, the building of roads on Government land, the growing of crops for the feeding of prisoners in institutions which have no such facilities. For this work a prisoner receives a small wage; it tends to build self-respect in making him able to contribute to the support of the true sufferers of crime, his wife or family.

There are such institutions as the Chillicothe, Ohio, reformatory, where it has been possible to build a high standard of honor in the minds of the inmates. Chillicothe's prisoners form a vigilance committee for the protection of the institution in which they are incarcerated. Here the youth who is returned from having violated a parole is viewed as he should be viewed in any prison or reformatory — as an enemy to the hopes and chances of other inmates. There have been actual cases in which released prisoners have forced escaping ones to return and knock at the door of the institution, asking that they may be re-admitted. Chillicothe houses true first offenders; young men who never before have committed a felony. The discipline is built upon a flexible system which takes into account the strength or weakness of each prisoner. There are self-govern-ing inmate committees, built upon something of the same principles which prevail in the Boys' Brotherhood Republic and Father Flanagan's Boys' Home. There are clean, fireproof buildings. There are farming activities; shop programs, including brick-making, laundry, and maintenance shops; education in a school of letters to the sixth grade, vocational training and a library which functions, not under some high-powered convict who has fixed himself for an easy job, but under a trained librarian. The hospital is manned as the prisons are manned, by the United States Public Health Service. The discipline is that of a military school, variable to the degree which the subject can assimilate. There is no indiscriminate mixing of inmates; upon arrival they are held for thirty days in quarantine, tested for communicable diseases and for mental rating, inoculated and interrogated thoroughly that a true case history may be obtained. In other words, here are individuals who are deemed worthy of every effort at rebuilding, remolding, education, rehabilitation, and separation from conditions which may have made them accidentals or casuals of crime. Infractions of the rules are punished after a hearing by a board at which a psychiatrist is present. Privileges must be earned, and membership in an honor group is attained only when, in the judgment of the inmates themselves, this promotion is deserved.

May I remind you at this time of the findings of a grand jury previously quoted, regarding a state reformatory of high rank, wherein there was prevalence of disease, the mixing of old offenders with new, the power of the big shot, the lack of proper concern for inmates and their future. Regarding this institution, the jury said: —

On account of the improper type of prisoners sent there, the class of parolees is among the most troublesome and potentially dangerous of all released criminals.

By comparison I quote remarks from an impartial report on Chillicothe: —

Business men in this city regard the parolee from Chillicothe as an exceptionally good risk. We have found that the boy who comes from this institution does so with an inculcated sense of honor, a considerable amount of ambition and the desire to be a good citizen.

In that paragraph is the answer to every honest prison man's prayer. This is what the law, so far as it concerns the first offender, the casual, the accidental, is supposed to accomplish.

Thus, the idea of progression in reformation, or of punishment, travels onward in the Federal system, to such penitentiaries as Lewisburg, where there are few cells, but nevertheless a walled enclosure with guards, automatic gun detectors, and the necessary protections which must be maintained against offenders who may have within them the dangerous elements necessary to the planning of a concerted escape. There are cell-clocks, and cell-rooms, and dormitories; just as there are incarcerated men who deserve to be in cells, others who should be in cell-rooms, and still others who, for the mental upheaval which in their particular case has been the cause of crime, might better be treated through the comparative freedom of a dormitory. Here again is the constant idea that if a person is to gain anything out of life, he must work for it, he must deserve it. Perhaps it is an adaptation of the old slogan that crime does not pay — at least it is told in language which enables persons, often of limited intelligence, to understand how to live that they may make more of a success of an honest existence than of a criminal one.

By way of contrast, there are the old stand-bys, such as Leavenworth and Atlanta, which might not possess their present heavy inmate list had there been a different penal viewpoint in olden days.

It is in the handling of prisoners at such places as Atlanta and Leavenworth that the Federal Prison system comes in for its worst criticism. Many law enforcement officials believe that these places should be more sternly devoted to punishment than they appear to be, what with radios, magazines and newspapers, name plates on cells instead of numbers, dungarees instead of numbered uniforms, and cell-blocks brightened by tremendous paintings, the gift of an ex-convict. They insist that, for prisoners of the type for which these two penitentiaries are intended, there is too much effort at reform and not enough of punishment.

They point out that peon Mexicans, returning to their homes, brag of the swell time they had in prison and the wonderful food they received, even to pancakes and sausages for breakfast, and other meals in accordance, eaten to music furnished by an eighteen-piece orchestra. Hillbillies from the Ozarks of Missouri, Kansas, and Arkansas also insist that they have been exceedingly well entertained, their only punishment that of being detained under discipline. The answer of the Prison Director is that as long as a man falls short of absolute incorrigibility he should be regarded as material worthy of being partially if not completely remolded, and that a prison where there is strict discipline, lack of favoritism, lack of graft and personal aggrandizement, should be gauged by what it accomplishes in a lack of recidivists, not by what prisoners from the lowest possible stratum of life may think of it. That is wholly a matter of differing opinion; Sanford Bates has swept out several cells for me during our many arguments on this score. And after all, he is the most successful prison administrator in many years. Therefore, one day, in a moment of truce, I asked: —

"What is the biggest job in running a prison?"

He answered quickly: —

"The wiping out of special privilege."

Whereupon he refused to tell me a story which I knew he possessed. So I went out and got it elsewhere, and print it here.

One of the most difficult tasks of all in building a new day for Federal prisons was the elimination of what was known as the "commissary racket." A tremendous portion of that difficulty was caused by persons who called themselves good, clean, honest American citizens.

There is nothing which can so disrupt a prison as a commissary run for prisoners who have money in plenty. The first thing, therefore, was to eliminate money. Heretofore, it had flowed into prison with something of regularity. Hard-working wives of prisoners, instead of spending their few dollars upon themselves, saved for their husbands. Big shots got cash in plenty. Eventually, most of it traveled into the prison commissary run "for the benefit of prisoners."

Already the establishment of the classification system had eliminated the power of single officers to reward their favorites — again a matter of the temptation of money. Then the money itself became taboo. Instantly, there was a roar from the merchants of prison cities.

They had been fattening upon this commissary, where oranges cost three to five times their worth, where other delicacies cost in proportion, where the meager offerings of what amounted to a prison-run merchandise store came from the merchants of the town at extraordinarily high prices. There were letters to Senators. There were insinuations of favoritism — why, nobody knows. There were threats of retaliation, because citizens had been deprived of profiteering. Perhaps that is why cynical criminologists sometimes give vent to their feelings in a paraphrase: —

"The more you see of so-called honesty, the more you wonder who's the crook, the fellow inside or the one who's out."

Out the commissary went as a convict-run racket. The money departed except for minor amounts to be spent according to rigid rules. Special food for privileged convicts was abolished — as well as the privileges. Then trusty-ships began to vanish, except as appointed by a committee of nine, instead of merely by the warden, as so often happens in state institutions. I have visited in the homes of state wardens, where the service resembled that of a hotel. There were convict chefs, convict gardeners, convict men-of-all-work, convict butlers, convict chauffeurs, convict caretakers, convict mowers of lawns. There were so many convict workers, all laboring in the warden's vineyard, that one almost had to pick his way between them. There are no such things in to-day's Federal prisons. If the warden needs a chauffeur, he obtains one from regular channels, not from the list of inmates; the same is true of other servants. It is almost an inviolable rule that any prison which has a great body of trusties is a place of danger. A prison official once clearly explained the reason.

He did this during the period in which newspapermen waited in Trenton for Governor Harold G. Hoffman to deplete the varied avenues of investigation by which he hoped to save the life of the kidnapper-murderer, Bruno Richard Hauptmann. I had grown sick of listening to the versions of why all this was being done, why half-baked investigators were flying here and there seeking evidence which, it had long ago been determined, leaked like a sieve, why discredited and discharged state troopers suddenly had been lifted to a status wherein they strove to set aside the findings of a jury which managed to keep its head in the midst of the greatest circus-trial ever exhibited under one canvas. I had wearied of striving to follow the mental wanderings of a favored gubernatorial investigator who, for two hours one night, had jammed me into a corner at the Stacy-Trent Hotel and then dilated upon his reasons for thinking that Hauptmann had not kidnapped and murdered the Lindbergh baby. It is only fair that his great piece of reasoning be passed on to the world. It will give a faint idea of the weird atmosphere in which one was forced to labor during that jumbled week when newspapermen and radio commentators blew up scheme after scheme to save this murderer. A crazy week, in which we worked without sleep or rest for nearly six straight days — to force, through the power of public opinion, an execution which we honestly believed necessary to the continuance of a respect for justice. Anyone who could decipher what this investigator had in mind, was fit to be crowned Queen of the May.

It seemed that this delver had discovered that the Lindbergh baby had been shot in the head. Able medical examiners refuted this by insisting that what he called a bullet wound was in truth a common fracture, but the investigator knew better. As he informed me during that two-hour session, he was young as a criminologist and if he could get a lot of publicity on this case it might make him a great deal of money. I, therefore, should assist as much as possible.

To prove that the child had been shot, he had procured the bodies of eight babies. He had laid them all in a row, more or less. Of course the babies were dead. Then he went from one to another, putting bullets in their mouth. Into one mouth he put a certain caliber pellet. Another he dosed with still a larger caliber, and so on. Then he placed them all in a crematory and incinerated them. After this, he conducted chemical analyses, and by so doing proved that the Lindbergh baby had been shot with a certain caliber gun. Following which, he said, he had broken the news to the prosecution.

"But," he told me as I weaved uncertainly in a haze of dead babies, bullets, chemical analyses and all that, "they told me that if this information were given to a jury, it would blow up the whole case for the prosecution. So, of course, I just kept quiet."

Therefore, if a man had kept quiet when a human being was on trial, and following the trial had gone to work for someone who believed in the defense, at a salary of course, when he could have created a grand slam for justice by proving a man innocent at the proper time, if he had done all these things — well, you figure it out. I never have been able to make head or tail of it, just as I never have been able to come to a truly sensible realization of what all that mad week was about. It doesn't make sense, even now.

While it all was happening, it seemed even more chimerical. One became blurred, hazy; one felt one's head and asked oneself if the whole world had gone crazy. For surcease I often went out to the Trenton State Prison. There, at least, was an entirely sane man. His name was Colonel Mark O. Kimberling, the Principal Keeper.

Whatever inanities there may have been during the last days of Bruno Richard Hauptmann, there were none from Colonel Kimberling, now head of the New Jersey State Police. He was genial without overdoing it. Himself believing Hauptmann innocent, he did not attempt to force his views upon others, but proceeded to his duty quietly and efficiently, because it was his duty. In all the mad scramble of that night of klieg lights, roaring crowds, shouting newspapermen as they fought their way to their typewriters to tell the story of a murderer's death, he remained a balanced figure of dignity. There was no ballyhoo from this man who had believed a man innocent, yet had been sufficiently endowed with a sense of his job to see him die. There had been no evading of his task, no play for the first page by a grandstand statement that he could not bear to see an innocent man electrocuted.

As we waited in the center hall of the ancient prison, awaiting the order to march to the death chamber, it was this man who in a paragraph returned solemnity to what had been travesty: —

"I am the Principal Keeper of this prison. I am in command. There shall be no demonstration when the prisoner is brought to the electric chair, none when he is strapped into place, none when he is dying, and none when he is dead. I shall expect my commands to be obeyed. There shall be no attempt to interrogate him, or interview him, or photograph him, or otherwise interfere with the solemn process of this execution. You will now begin the march to the death chamber."

It was a great relief to be able to chat with such a man when all the world seemingly was in turmoil. I was greedy for the opportunity. I was often beside his desk. One day I remarked:

"Warden, I've been watching the activities around this prison. It looks like a good institution."

"Thanks. I've had good luck. After all, it's quite a job. You see, a part of this prison is more than a hundred years old.

There are other ancient sections. It isn't built according to all the modern specifications. Yes," he smiled, "I've had good luck."

"Or good administration." Suddenly I said, "That reminds me, I haven't yet seen a trusty."

The warden laughed.

"Maybe that's the secret of my good luck. I have a theory that there is no such thing as an honest trusty." Quickly he added: "That may sound unfair. I have not meant it to be so. A trusty does not have it in his power to be honest." He continued: —

"Suppose you were a trusty in a prison. You might desire to be as honest as the day was long. I'm talking now of trusties who run in and out, who work around the executive offices or in the warden's home or some such place where they can get information, act as smugglers, or take part in the plans for prison intrigues or prison breaks.

"Suppose, as I say, you were as honest as a statue of Integrity. Suppose you wanted to do the right thing. Suppose you tried to keep your ears and eyes closed to things which should not concern you. Suppose you rebelled against the thought of smuggling in dope, or of smuggling out letters, or of knowing what conversations came over the prison telephone. You might try. You might make the fight of your life. But there would be one factor to make you dishonest in spite of yourself. When night came, you would be forced, under the prison rules, to go back there in the block, be checked into your cell, and, ceasing to be a trusty for the night, become a member of the convict population."

He shook his head.

"Those two ingredients don't mix. There is no man who can stand the pressure, the drive, drive, drive of the convict body, demanding to know whether you intend to follow the code of the underworld or whether you intend to be a snitch and a stoolie. In the next cell, someone sits all night long, working upon a piece of steel which he has smuggled from the machine shop and whetting it into a razor-edged knife. He mutters to himself, between clinched teeth:

"So that stoolie in the next cell wants to turn down his pals, eh? He wants to be a pidge for the warden, eh? He wants to suck in! Well, he'll either play with the gang he belongs to or he'll get this chiv in his guts."

Suddenly he asked: "What would you do?"

"I wouldn't take the chiv in my guts, that's what I wouldn't do; I know that."

"Neither does any other trusty," came the quiet answer of the Colonel.

Perhaps if other wardens had that same insight into criminal psychology, there would be fewer temptations placed in the paths of men attempting to be honest, fewer prison escapes, fewer guards murdered and fewer citizens endangered by convicts running wild after a crush-out. Instead, however, there is this indictment of state institutions by Leonard D. White, United States Civil Service Commissioner: —

"Patronage has put men on the walls of our prison because they carried their precinct in the last election. Politics has made men wardens of jails and prisons because for many years they faithfully served their party organization. . . .

"A man wins votes by giving favors and ingratiating himself with his constituency. The man who carries his precinct must be a hail-fellow-well-met, must be willing to go out of his way to please people, must be ready to do favors, even sometimes on the edge of the shadowy side of the law. He is expected to have influence and use it.

"If there is any type of institution or agency in the public service in which the hail-fellow-well-met who gets ahead by using influence is a liability, it is in the prison service."

It might be believed that with the elimination of such troubles as indicated in Commissioner White's indictment, plus curtailed special privilege, lack of outside trusties, and other disbarred dangers, the goal set by the Federal system of making equal all men within prison walls should have been accomplished with ease. On the contrary, there remained an element of failure.

From the beginning there had been a studied desire to bring about one important measure — the elimination of the big shot. What Babe Ruth was to baseball, the arch criminal is to the all-too-often moronic main body of a prison population.

Privilege after privilege was shorn from these men. Conditions which had been permitted in other days were dispensed with. Nevertheless, big shots continued to remain big shots. The hero-worship of the convict population insisted on so regarding them; their very presence was sufficient incentive to create the desire to imitate.

In Atlanta, there was Al Capone, who remained Al Capone in spite of his number, in spite of his sentence. Whatever Al Capone thought was the ultimate to other convicts. How he looked when he appeared in the mess hall, how he acted, what he said out of a corner of his mouth, how much food he ate, how he winked at someone as he passed — these were vital factors of convict news. The Atlanta world revolved about Al Capone. He was the man who had been able to make crime pay. Everybody knew he had money hidden away somewhere; what if he did have to spend a few years behind bars? He'd get out, and he'd live in riches forever. It was a lucky fellow who could be an Al Capone.

There were others of his ilk in Atlanta: agitators, breeders of hatred, of intrigue, of plots. There were many more in Leavenworth — some of the toughest men in all America. They had plundered, they had murdered, they had escaped and been recaptured only after officers had taken desperate risks. The convict population regarded them as supermen of crime. No rules could prevent this adulation, nor could rules prevent the danger that some day these men might band together and by their mere command bring about a general uprising on the part of admiring fools.

So Homer Cummings, Attorney General of the United States, laid aside his glasses — he always does so when he desires to see something close at hand — and, raising his lean form from his desk, strolled over to a much-beloved chart which he kept with its face to the wall. It was his course of action, outlined early in his days as Attorney General — a plan for proper laws by which to protect Federal officers from assault and murder, a plan for the tightening-up of what was known as the "Twilight Zone of Crime," wherein criminals so often escaped by not being exactly guilty of either a state offense or a Federal one; a plan for extension of kidnapping statutes and other laws which he has brought about and which have coördinated state and Federal enforcement activity as it has not been done in years. On this chart was a piece of unfinished business. It pertained to an island in San Francisco Bay, upon which was built an aged, fortress-like affair formerly used as a military disciplinary barracks. It was called Alcatraz Island.

"There is a tremendous need for a prison for men who display neither the ability nor the desire to be reformed," he said in his drawling manner. "Alcatraz Island is the proper place to build such an institution."

Thus, there came into being a fortress, impregnable to attack from within and without, except to those studied ones made by certain San Francisco business men who believe it bad publicity to have such an institution in the neighborhood. Some business men are delightfully quaint; they believe so thoroughly in the protection of society — especially if it does not entail any effort on their part, or any lessening of the tourist trade. Perhaps when they learn that, in a recent trip of many thousands of miles, I met many persons who wanted to visit San Francisco that they might gain a glimpse of Alcatraz Island more than for any other reason, it might be cheering. And there may be a lessening of the incessant propaganda which has issued from the Pacific Coast, designed to paint this prison as a chamber of horrors. The truth is that Alcatraz Prison has only one punishment. It brings the ego of so-called criminal big shots down to sea level.

Otherwise, it is everything which a true prison built for the inescapable incarceration of human mad dogs should be. It has no cruelty — unless one calls it cruelty to maintain a place of absolute cleanliness, quiet but inflexible discipline, humane but nevertheless rigid supervision against rebellion by more than two hundred of the worst thugs in the history of America. For years these men ran wild, kidnapping our citizens and children, blowing out prison walls, holding up trains, murdering policemen, sheriffs, Federal officers, and effecting what, in a small way, amounted to armed insurrection against the commonwealths upon which they preyed. Such men cannot be confined in a bird cage. They have proved over and over that they cannot even be confined in state institutions where sentimentalists are allowed to weep over such gentle manifestations as exhibited by convicts who raise canary birds in their cells.

If there has been one convict who has won early parole or quick pardon by the raising of canary birds, so that their dulcet notes might cheer the inmates of the cell-block, there have been two dozen. It is necessary that a canary bird be fed a certain type of seed for it to remain at top singing form, and able to hit High C with every effort. Any convict so filled with love of the gentle little creatures as to desire them in his cell, as a memento of God's beautiful outdoors, deserves to be allowed to feed his canary the proper sort of seed.

Therefore in the last year, there have been two instances in which such gentle-hearted convicts have passed over a portion of this particular birdseed to scheming trusties. The trusties in turn have surreptitiously planted this seed, either in the prison garden or the one maintained by the warden. Therefrom grew tall plants which the trusties garnered carefully and as surreptitiously brought back to the cell-blocks where they were dried and crumpled. Then at night there was much happiness in prison. Girl-boys found themselves tightly enclosed in the arms of their perverted mates. There was music in the air, soft humming, and a pervading atmosphere of geniality. For, to make a canary bird really sing, it is necessary to feed it that ingredient upon which so many hot musicians depend for their interpolations. The particular seed which makes canary birds sing their best is marihuana.

There are no canary birds in Alcatraz. There are no pet rabbits or white mice or toads or bullfrogs. There is, however, a program of quiet amusement sufficient for a man's needs. There is single-celling to prevent sexuality. And there is protection for society.

It was in the latter part of 1933 that the Department of Justice took over by transfer this twelve acres of rock in San Francisco. Plans were immediately made to build an escape-proof prison.

The six hundred old soft-steel cell fronts of military times were removed. Tool-proof steel with automatic locking devices replaced them. Tool-proof steel bars were installed in the windows. Tear gas outlets were provided; and a special group of trained, experienced guards were recruited from the other Federal penitentiaries. A zone in the water was marked out with buoys into which boats were forbidden to enter. Automatic gun detectors, called "bugs" by the convicts, were placed at the dock and in the doorways to the cell-blocks. These record the presence of any secreted metal on the person of any individual who passes. New guard towers were erected, floodlights put in place, and additional barriers built around the seventy-five-foot cliffs of the little island. Gun galleries at each end of cell-blocks controlled the interior of the buildings, while the island could be surveyed by a system of towers connected by overhead walks.

So that is Alcatraz, and perhaps the story of the transfer of the dangerous gangsters who inhabit it may give an insight into the viewpoint which the Federal Government takes toward them and their potential viciousness.

It was necessary that special cars be constructed to carry these men across the country. Windows were barred. There were double entrances to each car, especially the diner. These prisoners were so deadly that they could not even be trusted with china platters or metal knives and forks for feeding; paper plates and picnic eating utensils were used.

In addition to the window bars there were metal screens, so that no lurking group of gangsters, hiding in a railroad yard, might throw guns to their friends and thereby aid an attempt at escape. The regular locks were removed from car doors and special ones substituted. They could be manipulated only from the outside.

For each coach there was an inside guard. On each platform there was a guard at the outside door, fully armed. The dining car was under surveillance at each end. And for each car there was a mobile officer armed with a machine gun and tear gas.

In front of the forward prison coach — there were two prison coaches for Atlanta prisoners, with a diner between — there was a sleeper where the guards might rest while they were relieved by reserves. The same was true at the rear, with special provisions made for attack from the outside. Conditions in gangland were such at the time of this movement that it was necessary that every precaution be taken against an underworld attempt at rescue. After all, here was a gathering of the most feared criminals in all America. Almost every one had been the leader of a desperate gang. Practically every man had been the instrument of from one to ten murders. Life meant nothing to them — escape everything.

There were conferences and meetings with railroad executives along the lines to be used. Secret orders covered as much as possible the movement of the trains — there were two shipments, one from Atlanta, one from Leavenworth. Every railroad man along the route worked under pain of losing his job — if word leaked out, if an order became public, if newspapers could flash ahead the news of the schedule, it might mean wholesale escape or wholesale death. This was serious business.

On the first train, to guard this mad-dog crew, the personnel consisted of the Warden of Atlanta Prison, a prison doctor, Special Agents of the Federal Bureau of Investigation and twenty guards. They carried two machine guns, ten sawed-off shotguns, eight revolvers, besides numerous gas grenades, and even then were tense with apprehension throughout the days and nights in which this train of potential death seemed to crawl across America, in spite of excellent railroading which brought it in ahead of schedule.

There were extra leg-irons, extra handcuffs, in readiness for any emergency. These prisoners were so fierce, so brooding with eagerness to escape, so powerful as super-crimesters, that officials could not even risk placing them side by side. They were cross-shackled, the right leg of one chained to the right leg of the other, and they were seated opposite each other, so that should there be a concerted effort to rise in revolt, the movement would throw one man against another and break up the movement long enough for the guards to swing into action.

Cars were switched into prison walls, secretly, after dark. They moved out before daybreak in the morning. There was not a public stop anywhere on the journey across the country. Servicing of these trains was carried on far out in railroad yards with only the most trusted of employees assigned to the task. On the last night before reaching Alcatraz, not a guard, not an official slept. There was no relaxation, no cessation of caution.

The trip which carried the convicts from Leavenworth was even more tense. Here were even more dangerous enemies than had come from Atlanta. This time, there were three prison cars, two diners and one hundred and three prisoners, all of whom, had they received the punishment merited for their crimes would have been executed years ago. Upon this trip, there came an underworld tip that a delivery was to be attempted.

The information had come from Kansas City, the place which had witnessed the attempt of Verne Miller and Pretty Boy Floyd to release Miller's friend, Frank Nash, by shooting down the officers who surrounded him.

This had happened only recently. Therefore, the news that there would be an attempt to hold up the Leavenworth Prison train was to be regarded as serious. The plotters had agreed that if they could obtain six hours' notice of the progress of the train they could accomplish their purpose. Ten gangsters would be used, all armed with machine guns and all experts. The plan called for the closing of a block signal, thus forcing the train to slow its speed. Thus a group of determined officers planned for the worst. A guard who lived through the hell of those nights between Kansas and San Francisco Bay gave me the details: —

"It was watch, watch, watch every minute, night and day, but especially at night. Even when we were relieved by the reserves and went to our berths in the sleeper, we didn't dare take off our clothes. Our guns were at our fingertips. We may have dozed, but we didn't sleep.

"We couldn't sleep. We had the pictures of the fellows in those coaches constantly before us: Machine-gun Kelly, the kidnapper, scowling at the man to whom he was shackled . . . Grover Durrell, the train-robber, itching for a chance at freedom. . . . There was Tom Holden and Francis Keating, who had engineered that dynamite break at Leavenworth; they'd have chanced their lives in a minute. Everywhere you looked, there were men who loved the feel of a gun, who had killed and plundered until they believed there was no law or no power in the world that could stop them.

"Harvey Bailey, one of the most dangerous of them all, swayed in his seat, seething hatred. How did we know what messages he had sent to the members of his old gangs? That's what was in our minds — did the underworld know we were coming? Had the schedule leaked out? Had some railroad man

forgotten his promises? Had some prison guard gone false and
tipped off friends of desperadoes?

"It was moonlight one night — the night we felt sure the
delivery would be attempted. We were on the plains, the shadows
of the train black against the fields. Every time a block signal
winked past me, I counted it as one more goal passed, only to
worry about the next one. Hour after hour it went on — with
the world out there beautiful in the moonlight, little houses
with lights shining in their windows, and people sitting inside,
believing themselves secure, happy. And me standing there on
that steel-lined deck, a machine gun sweating in my hands,
wondering as each minute passed if this was the place where
they'd throw the block against us, me standing there hoping
that if the attack did come, I could get at least one man before
they got me. Once I thought the train was slowing its speed.
I remember muttering between gritted teeth: 'If this thing happens, if they get away with it, if they turn these crime-crazed
mad dogs loose — *God help America!*'"

However, secrets remained secrets. Every man who had been
trusted with information was faithful. The train rolled into
Point Richmond on San Francisco Bay without interruption, at
6 o'clock in the morning. By seven the cars had been barged
across the foggy bay. The complete check and dress-in for this
murderous crew was completed before noon, and the beginning
of a wholesale deflation in criminal ego had begun.

Perhaps the story of that downfall best can be described
by using Al Capone as an illustration.

It started in Atlanta. One by one the prisoners were being
called from their cells, to be taken to isolation wards, where they
were stripped of their old uniforms, bathed, and dressed in new
garb. Then they were shod in carpet slippers — it was dangerous to give them shoes, lest someone kick a guard in the groin,
and with the aid of others, stamp him to death. They were
handcuffed in pairs and taken to the train, where they were

shackled leg to leg. In preparation for all this, a member of the prison staff approached the Big Fellow's cell.

"All right, Capone," he ordered. "If you've any trinkets or keepsakes you want to take with you, gather them up so they can be inspected. You're going out."

Capone leered.

"Out where?"

"Alcatraz."

Capone scowled.

"What the hell are you taking me there for? That's only for tough guys. You haven't got any right to put my name on that list!"

It was the big shot speaking, the man who had ordered death with a mild wave of his fat hand, the King who had commanded his executioners to step into a garage on St. Valentine's Day and shoot seven men in the back. Such was the man of whom a rival gangster had gasped: "Seven men dead? Shot in the back? Only Capone kills like that!"

So now, snarling in his cell, rebellious, defiant, he insisted that his name was not on the Alcatraz list. The official replied grimly: "I said your name was on the list and I meant it. And if it's anything to you, it's the first one on the list. Get your things and come along."

The Continent had been crossed. The deadly crew of crimesters was being checked into Alcatraz, the place where they would cease to be swaggering examples that crime can be made to pay. A deputy warden, who had seen every one of these prisoners each day throughout their incarceration, sat at a table, his case file before him. Now identities had ceased. Personages of the underworld would no longer be men of criminal affairs. They would be numbers, nonentities — the worst punishment that any super-gangster can know.

The deputy warden, his face immobile, his expression that of a man who never before had seen this murderous crew, commanded that they form in line and step forward to be checked in. One after another of the criminals had come before him, stated his name and received his number. Capone was next in line. The official eyed him.

"Name?" he demanded.

"Capone," the Great One replied. There was only one Capone. Everybody knew Capone. Books had been written about him. Once upon a time gawking crowds had gathered, as if for a parade, to see him ride down Michigan Boulevard in his armored car. He, the Great Capone, had even been on a reception committee to great transoceanic fliers. Newspapers had fought for his latest pictures. He was the only Capone —

The official's eyes were emotionless.

"First name?" he asked.

Capone gulped. He shuffled uneasily in his felt slippers.

"Alphonse," he answered weakly.

That is the spirit and the job of Alcatraz: to reduce Capones to Alphonses. Had there been a properly run Alcatraz in regional districts, maintained efficiently by states, there would have been no need for this one on the Rock. Every one of these men first had been a state problem, and the states had failed; with the result that the United States Government was forced to take the job and to point the way. It is not the only part of criminal procedure in which the Federal system has been a guidepost, pointing to green lights — if only those in power could see.

There is parole, for instance.

One hears little objection to Federal administration of parole. One hears of few cases in which parole is violated. Certainly there is a very small percentage of released inmates who insist upon further criminality. There is no mystery about how this result is reached. The Federal system believes not only in the theory of parole, but in its proper and just administration. That solves the entire problem of how to prevent a parole system from becoming a parole scandal.

There are no secrets in the formula. First of all, the parole board consists of able men. They cannot be influenced by politics or pressure. They follow exactly the formula that has been outlined by parole conferences for use by the states. They are simple rules, any child can understand them; any group of honest men, freed of influence and given the proper and sufficient personnel by which to enforce them, can comply with every demand that —

The minimum and maximum of indeterminate sentences should be compatible with adequate punishment, rehabilitation, and public welfare and protection.

Paroles should be granted only by a full-time salaried board of qualified persons.

Full information should be available and sought for the use of the board as to the prisoners' records, habits, environment, family and prospects.

The names of all persons endorsing a prisoner for parole should be made public on request of the press or any responsible person or organization.

No parole should be granted except where adequate employment and rigid supervision are provided.

One parole officer should not be expected to supervise more than a number to which he can give adequate attention.

No political or other improper influence shall be tolerated.

Machinery should be provided for the prompt revocation of any parole when continuance at liberty is not in the public interest.

That is the entire story. Therefore, why should there be scandal after scandal in our various states? Why should conditions in Florida reach a point, for instance, where all of the one thousand inmates of an institution — regardless of how long they had been incarcerated — could apply for freedom? And why should it be necessary for a vigilant newspaper campaign, plus practically every thinking citizen, to come into aroused action, thus bringing about a final announcement from the board that no parole should be granted until a prisoner had served at least a third of his sentence?

Why should there be so few states exempt from parole scandals that it was necessary for the Attorney General of the United States to use Relief white-collar workers in a general survey to determine, in each community, what underlay existing faults?

Why, for instance, should it be possible for a man to take the witness stand in court, and, in an alibi defense, state that on the day he was accused of being in one portion of the state, he was in reality at the Capitol, with two hundred and fifty dollars to spend, on a parole? But, he explained, the Governor wasn't in, so he came away. Or why should the charge be made and not denied that, in another state, shyster attorneys gather like starved dogs outside the doors of certain prisons there to denude paroled convicts of their ten-dollar release money in payment of fees for having obtained their release; that hundreds of crimester murderers have been arrested for new offenses, and their records found thick with repeated paroles? That John Dillinger and every other public enemy was a parolee? That Bill Mahan — the man who helped to kidnap George Weyerhaeuser of Tacoma, to drag him around the country in the trunk of an automobile, to chain him to posts in holes in the ground, to handcuff him to trees, to hold him captive for days in a stifling closet — should have been paroled in spite of the fact that other states wanted him for previous crimes and also despite a record of insubordination which caused him to be classified as one of the most dangerous men ever incarcerated in this particular prison? And why did the warden retire a few days after Bill Mahan got out?

Why, why, why — the query rises constantly when one has before one a private report which already has been made on the parole situation, and which reveals almost unbelievable conditions. It is impossible to quote this report even in summary; it consumes one thousand, eight hundred single-spaced typewritten pages of scandal from practically every commonwealth in America. It tells of communities which "deport" their parolees into other states that a pretense may be made of a low violation record. It shows that others have orders on file with the Federal Bureau of Investigation to forgo notification on fugitive parolees captured beyond state lines, since the state does not care to pay the expense of returning them, no matter what crime they may have committed. It reveals that in another state there are 579 parolees on the board's books as in good standing, while there are noted 1096 men who have been listed as violators, but who have not even been returned to prison. In another state more than half the entire prison population consists of men who have been paroled and who have been arrested as recidivists. On and on goes the unbelievable record of graft and inefficiency, even to such a revolting instance as that of an almost chimerical person known as Rufe Persfal.

Rufe was a product of the Ozark hills. Lank, keen of eye, a hunter all the years of his liberty, he was known to be such an expert with the rifle that he could kill a crow on the wing.

This fellow began his criminal career when he was seventeen years old, by the murder and robbery of an aged man. For this he was sentenced to fifteen years in prison on a "copped plea" of second degree murder. Thus, even in the beginning, he beat the barrier.

In the particular state in which this man was incarcerated, the entire paid penal staff consists of less than a dozen persons. Newspapers have alleged that as many as twenty-five thousand paroled convicts, and others who have received clemency, roam the state. The place in which Persfal was incarcerated was a prison farm. There, owing to the shortage of paid man-power, much of the guarding was done by trusty convicts. There were trusty line-guards, who remained close to the workers in the fields, and there were outriders, called "high-powers," who, mounted on horses, patrolled outlying regions, armed with high-velocity rifles. It has been charged that these "high-powers" on more than one occasion induced men to attempt escape. The incentive seems to have been an unwritten law that should a "high-power" wound or kill an escape, he was entitled to a parole.

Rufe Persfal won a parole. He received it almost directly after he had shot and killed a prisoner, who he said was attempting to flee.

Thus, the young man faced the world for a new try at life. Here was his opportunity to show the powers of clemency that he could live an upright, clean existence and recast himself into a better mold. So he went forth into his new world — and shot a woman in the back with a shotgun.

This is not fiction. It is no concoction of dreams or gossip. It comes from the official files of the United States Department of Justice. Back to the prison farm they brought Rufe Persfal, the desperado who had killed an old man, who had slain a fellow convict, and who had shot a woman in the back. There he was again made a "high-power."

He did not long remain in this position. Soon again he was free, once more facing the world with his shoulders back and his head held high as befits a man who has received his second parole. Rufe Persfal had killed another "escaping" prisoner.

It was not long until he had been caught and convicted of robbery with firearms. He was returned to the prison farm. Nor did much time elapse before again he was on his horse, with his murderous rifle under his arm, his keen eyes alert for the sight of a man he might shoot down. The opportunity this time arrived en masse. Rufe shot four convicts, killing one and permanently crippling three others. For this he received his third parole and for a third time displayed his gratitude and desire to reform by once more committing a major crime.

But they got him. They laid the hand of the law on his shoulder. They brought him back to the prison farm; and they gave him his horse again and his rifle and sent him forth, to ride, to watch, and for the fourth time to take human life. Likewise for the fourth time they sent him out to freedom.

This time Rufe Persfal expanded his efforts. In the process

of two robberies, he helped to kidnap five persons and transport them across state lines — which put the Federal Bureau of Investigation upon his trail and brought him, upon conviction, into the province of the Federal Bureau of Prisons.

Rufe Persfal now serves a long term in a Federal Penitentiary. He is not allowed to be a high-power and carry a rifle. From there he shall not be paroled for having slain his fellow beings. From there he may not be paroled at all.

Men like Rufe Persfal must serve their sentence in Federal institutions for the plain reason that a sensible, non-political board regards them as menaces who should be removed from society. No shyster lawyers appear before the Federal board. No men are turned loose without supervision. No men are released without jobs. No prisoners go free with absolutely no provision for learning whether or not they observe or violate their promises to live straight, refrain from bad companionship, work and seek to become decent members of society.

There should be a plain understanding of what is the real objection to parole, as it exists in so many states. It is not to the theory of parole. There is absolutely no objection to the underlying principle that humanity, an arm about the shoulders, is better than cruelty and continued incarceration.

The antagonism of thinking persons is to the fact that in many states no attention whatever is paid to either the type of convict who is released or what afterward becomes of him. The accusation cannot be denied that parole in too many states is in political hands and that in many there has been the stain of graft. Public opinion instinctively rebels against indiscriminate release. When commonwealths realize that they must protect society and at the same time aid the unfortunate in a business-like, humane, common sense manner, then objection to parole will vanish. It cannot cease, however, until states refrain from releasing hardened convicts, until state boards are no longer subject to the whims or politics or the use of money, until sufficient man power of the properly trained type is available to give assurance that released inmates have jobs, that they live as they have promised to live, and that they have not merely made use of an easy exit from imprisonment by the use of graft, bribery, fakery, chicanery or political pressure.

The practice of parole as it exists in so many states to-day is the worst travesty on justice that could be devised. Parole was designed to help the fellow who needs a chance, not the man who takes one. Every time a confirmed, a professional, or an incorrigible prisoner is released, to go his way without supervision, to brag about the fact that he could have done his stretch standing on his head, that law enforcement is a joke, it defeats the very purpose for which parole was founded. It makes good folks boil to see a political big shot walk free while a man who has stolen the traditional loaf of bread perhaps serves a long term. It makes honest men of law enforcement white with rage to read that the brutal professional killer with a record two decades long has, all in a year, been esteemed redeemable by a political pardon board and freed with hardly a care as to what he does once he has passed beyond the shadow of the prison.

All such things breed crime. They help to paint a slogan in letters ten feet high, glowing with the announcement that crime does pay — if one can become a sufficiently big criminal. Such examples are conducive to more robberies, more assaults, more rapes, more murders. Beyond this, they are in violation of all honest viewpoints of decent law enforcement and penology. This is especially so when there is an apparent example of sensible law enforcement, sensible administration, sensible prison and parole systems as practised by the United States Government to display clearly the green lights ahead by which progress can be made against the advance of criminality.

CHAPTER NINETEEN

PATHS AHEAD

IT would be fortunate if, with this narrative of crime completed, the writer could escape further responsibility. That, however, seems impossible. When one essays to detail conditions, the natural assumption is that there exists an equal amount of knowledge concerning preventives and remedies. Any diagnostician ultimately finds himself in a difficult position. If he segregates symptoms, it seemingly follows that he should know the cure. But any man who could prescribe a panacea for crime, all in a few pages, would be a genius. This writer pretends to be little more than a seasoned reporter. However, certain things are self-evident: —

There should be a persistent campaign, not only to restore the majesty of the law, but to reëstablish the contumely and stigma which should attach itself to one who has offended against the law. There has been a flood of propaganda, ever since the days of Thomas Mott Osborne, for the acceptance of the ex-convict as a brother, to be restored to the status which he once occupied. The theory is splendid, the practice exceedingly poor.

Because of an abuse of this theory, the disgrace of having been a convict has largely disappeared. And what with loosely administered penitentiaries where convicts are given the run of the buildings, where there are conveniences and luxuries which often never existed in the prior life of the inmate, the average felon emerges with few deterrent results from his incarceration. This writer is not a believer in the old idea that a prison should be wholly punitive. However, the subsequent case histories of men who roam about freely after prison sentences force one to

believe that their penitentiary sentences failed entirely to en-
gender any fear of the law.

There should be a remolding of public opinion, not especially
against the convict, but certainly for the victim. Certain shrewd
purveyors of propaganda have set up such a sympathetic reac-
tion toward the man caught by the law that all sight has been
lost of the fact that for every criminal there must be an innocent sufferer, and it is a three to one chance that this person may
be you provided you fulfill your normal span of life. Civic
organizations, good government leagues, and the like should
insist that wardens, judges, and all who deal with criminals must
not forget the victim of crime or the suffering of his family,
but rather should make that consideration paramount to the
sympathy-evoking appeals by which crooks hope to evade punishment.

Publicity; the topic of crime as a continuous subject of discussion by civic organizations and women's clubs; demands for
better protection: all these efforts must be continued until the
cry penetrates the usually deaf ears of state and national representatives. As a body, our law-makers are little more than lazy
messenger boys who can hear only the insistent ringing of the
bell of reëlection. It is necessary to make them obedient, to hold
over them the pickaxe of political defeat unless their actions look
to the good of the Commonwealth.

If a National Board of Inquiry is the means by which attention
can be centralized and worth-while results obtained, it is necessary that the ground be constantly spaded in order that this
come into being. There should be constant hounding for common-sense prison conditions instead of the dissemination of
widely variant viewpoints which run all the way from inhuman
brutality to milk-sop coddling. If the entire community would
remain away from the grandstand when some publicity-loving
warden brings his football team of arsonists, rapers and murderers to play against the local police force, it might enter official
heads that the community doesn't like such a show. And if the

entire community should begin work at once to cause the dismissal of police officers who sanctioned such a show, you may be sure it would not occur again.

In this work of remolding public opinion, there should be education for parents, through example. It should be the duty of law enforcement and probation officials to dig into the home conditions and past of every juvenile offender, learn what has or has not been done by his parents to prevent his dip into crime, discover what he has been taught which accounts for an antisocial attitude. Then appropriate action should be taken through judicial censure, which will place the true causes of this child's delinquency in the public eye. Many a mother who weepingly declares she cannot understand why her boy has gone wrong has herself been responsible for this delinquency by her fierce, animal-like spirit of protectiveness which sees no wrong in any of his actions. "Ma" Barker, killed at Oklawaha, Florida, as a kidnapper, in company with her four murdering sons, was such a woman. There are thousands of minor "Ma" Barkers, hundreds of thousands of potential ones. Fully half the convicts who people our cell blocks have little cause to celebrate Mother's Day. If Mother had been more judicious, if she had shown kindly sternness instead of maudlin indulgence, — if she had guided, instead of throwing wide the gates, — if she had accepted the duty imposed upon her, when, as in a majority of such cases, an accident of ignorance or laziness caused a new heart to beat and a new being to take form, — the inmate might not be where he is.

Plainly, there is a job for every citizen in bettering conditions surrounding crime prevention. This book has been dedicated largely to the results of crime, since the writer felt that through the depiction of the effect, attention might be brought to the cause. We are supposed to be a nation of education. Education about crime should be made a part of all schooling. First, there should be primary education to the effect that a person who is not honest is not worthy. Whenever the name of a desperate criminal flashes across the front pages, it should be the duty of any earnest educator to obtain the information by which this culprit can be stripped down to his truly filthy standards. The fact that there is no romance in crime should be pounded into the schoolboy and schoolgirl until it becomes an ever-present conviction.

There should be the building of a missionary spirit among youth; this writer has only to remember his own boyhood to realize the tremendous power of child-revulsion. A campaign was then waged among children for a more humane attitude toward dumb animals. Brutality was villainized; and as a result, a tremendous reform was brought about: the person of to-day who is a brute toward animals is looked upon as a brute toward humanity. The same tactics can be used to eradicate crime and criminals.

It is not sufficient to place emphasis on athletics, playgrounds and the like as a cure-all for crime in youth. All these are highly necessary, just as slum clearance is mandatory, but there are other elements of much deeper significance. There is the necessity for the building of a psychology that crime is a sucker's game and that there is nothing heroic or glamorous about it. There should be courses in law enforcement in every college, a large part of which should be devoted to the study of crime-prevention, especially that part of it which can be reached through an appeal to the psychology of youth.

Business clubs and civic organizations should study the same courses, with an eye toward the young of the community.

Corporations have reduced the accident rate tremendously through "safety-first" campaigns. Let them now embark upon anti-criminal campaigns (using the parent as a means of educating youth), and thus build better communities, employ happier and safer workers, root out agitators who have criminal records, and save themselves much sabotage.

We know that three out of every four persons are potential victims of the criminal. Since every one of us is thus thrown into a dangerous grab-bag, the remedy must become a personal effort to slash at crime in its early stages — for youth under twenty-one now commits seventeen per cent. of our infractions.

This personal effort requires the constant hammering at youth of the fact that crime is filthy and rotten. No boy can believe that crime does not pay when newspapers tell him that a gang got $12,000 here, $35,000 in another town, $60,000 from a bank robbery and $200,000 from a kidnapping. The boy knows nothing of the hundred and one pay-offs which a criminal must make. He believes that all these sums go only into the pockets of a few men. Considering this, one could argue forever that crime does not pay, and talk only to deaf ears. But those ears will listen to the true story of filth, degradation and pay-offs. Youth will lose respect for a Dillinger who is painted in his true colors as a cowardly, beer-swilling bully. Youth also will lose interest in him upon the de-moting of his gun molls to cheap, ignorant little narcotic-fiend tarts instead of glamorous beauties.

The "romance" of extra-legal activities will rapidly disappear when our youngsters are brought face to face with the insanity statistics on marihuana victims. And the same salutary horror can be engendered by motion pictures and lectures regarding syphilis and gonorrhea. Some educators may view this as a subject to be barred; yet such a lecture certainly is no franker than prevalent lectures which teach girls and boys how frogs become papas and rabbits have young. Youth, if it is to have one part of knowledge, should have all beneficial parts of it. Above all, youth should be confronted with the results of folly: a few technicolor motion pictures of syphilitics in the tertiary stage will make the disease one to be constantly guarded against. Weak-minded mammas may protest, but the time has come when weak-minded mammas should be revealed as a great contributing factor to contempt on the part of their children — and subsequent contempt of the law. The same goes for weak-minded papas. They have hidden too long behind the protective cloak of sacred parenthood. They should be dragged into the open and

shown for what they are: a huge group of duty-evading simpletons.

No less important than education in any reform program is the
ousting of dishonest and inefficient officials. The writer hopes he
has proved that much of major crime could not exist without
malfeasance or nonfeasance on the part of the agents of law
enforcement. When the careers of such men as Count Lustig-
Miller, Baby Face Nelson, John Dillinger, Pretty Boy Floyd and
all the rest of the scaly crew who aspired to leadership in crime
are found to be worm-holed with official protection, it naturally
follows that they could not have existed as menaces to society
without the active or passive assistance of so-called "protectors"
of public welfare. When one realizes that the absolute minimum
of actual crooks engaged in law enforcement numbers thousands,
it stands to reason that if honest men could replace them, a good
deal of progress in our crusade would be made. To assist in
achieving this end, it should here be reëmphasized that one of
the prime requisites for the safety of society is the immediate
fingerprinting, for submission to the Identification Unit of the
Federal Bureaus at Washington, of absolutely every person who
is in the slightest degree concerned with law enforcement.

This requirement should be laid upon every constable, every
justice of the peace, every judge and district attorney. It should
encompass the police departments of every city in the United
States, no matter how large or how small. It should extend to
court bailiffs, clerks of courts, jailers, keepers and guards in
reformatories, prisons, and penitentiaries. It should include taxicab drivers, doctors, and certainly any lawyer with a criminal
practice. Moreover, it should reach out to ambulance chasers,
runners for shyster lawyers, bail bondsmen, and bond-makers —
especially those who deal in "quick service," hurrying to the
police station with bonds for well-known criminals even before
newspapers are aware of their arrest.

Certainly, private detectives should be fingerprinted; and private detective agencies should be forced to make public the number of ex-convicts whom they employ to pry into the affairs of private citizens, shadow persons in divorce suits, treat with the underworld in stolen-property cases, engage strikebreakers to travel from state to state, or aid and abet labor racketeers in bringing about violence and bloodshed.

Tavern keepers should be fingerprinted. Certainly hotel employees should be on record. Within the last year, there has been a minimum of six murders in which hotel employees have been implicated. The laxity in inquiring into the past of persons employed in many hotels is utterly appalling; bellboys, for instance, are often hired without any attempt to learn whether they have a good reputation or bad. No doubt the fingerprinting of many such individuals would fail to reveal a criminal record, in spite of possible infractions. It would, however, exert a salutary influence upon future operations. Our soldiers and sailors are fingerprinted, not only for purposes of identification in time of accident or death, but to provide a deterrent against desertion. Certainly the scum of that vast army of persons who hang about the fringe of police or public work have far less right to anonymity than our military and naval forces.

There should be compulsory fingerprinting of all persons engaged in probation, pardon, and parole work, and an extremely diligent examination into their qualifications before ever they are given such jobs. In many states, one inspector is required to guard over the good behavior of as many as two hundred parolees. What might happen if he too should prove to be an ex-convict is too obvious for discussion.

Attention should be given to judges of all sorts, especially the country justice of the peace — often a mere grafter subsisting on fees in trumped-up charges. The job of justice of the peace is, alas, conducive to the temptation of fraud and deceit. It must be remembered also that a justice of the peace can become a circuit or district judge and that if he has been a grafter in one place he will be a grafter in another. It sometimes happens that our most ferocious judges, those looked upon by a community as most ardent enemies of crime, can be our biggest deceivers. The man who roars and bellows at the defense, apparently eager to convict by allowing glaringly inadmissible evidence to be put over by the prosecution, and prone to give extraordinarily severe sentences, may be a crook of a dozen colors. By exhibiting a prejudicial attitude from the bench, he lays the case wide open to reversal by a superior court; by his severe sentences he causes a revulsion on the part of jurors against conviction. Naturally, these jurors do not know that the apparent severity may be a device known to the underworld as a "gimmick" or a "gaff." Palm-itching judges have often imposed severe sentences with one thought in mind: money from crooks who depend upon the parole board for shortening over-severe sentences. Judges of this sort should be exposed. They should be unearthed by shrewd investigators. The district attorney who has accepted numerous "copped pleas" under circumstances which will not bear publicity, should be named, and his record plastered in places of public view. The judge who has a record of continuous reversals should be forced to give an explanation of his ignorance, his bias, or the suspicion of monetary influence.

Along with such miscreants, the persons who live on the fringes of crime should know that they are under investigation. Bar Associations could install competent vigilance committees to seek out and shame the shysters of the profession, whether in or out of the Association. The same should hold true in the Medical Associations.

And what is to be done about the maladministration of liquor? Through inadequate laws, civic corruption, and high pressure sales methods by liquor purveyors, the ghost of Prohibition has already begun to stir in its grave. This has been evidenced by a growth of local option elections. Some stringent recommendations should be adopted by which idiotic and greedy operators may be prevented from killing the goose which now is laying golden eggs in restored personal liberty, increased employment, more rentals and tax revenue. This writer was one

of the first to contribute to the fight for Repeal. He would contribute again. Therefore, as a man who believes in liquor, who
believes in personal freedom, who believes that Prohibition breeds
hypocrisy and crime, he feels that he has a right to protest against
unbridled and senseless abuse of a great privilege. Liquor dealers
were given no mandate to encourage drunkenness by incessant
and fake advertising to the effect that whiskies contain no headache or hangover; they were not licensed to dispense the propaganda of overindulgence; they were not encouraged to lock arms
with crime by employing thousands of ex-bootleggers and rum
runners as salesmen, sales managers and distributors. It was not
believed possible that soda squirts, college boys, inexperienced
youths possessing no mature knowledge of human nature, should
be put behind hotel bars and in positions where they, theoretically at least, become guardians of appetite. The bartender of
to-day who knows when diplomatically to convince a patron
that the limit of drinking has been reached is rare indeed. Beyond this, the only disgrace that is worse than the unrestricted
and prevalent selling of drinks to minors is the widespread use
of persons under age, especially girls, in the promotion of alcohol. Perhaps all this is not a matter for a Board of Inquiry to
consider. Perhaps it will not need such consideration. There
can be only one answer to such conditions, unless the men vitally
concerned with liquor use strenuous efforts to combat it. That
is: a steady and swift growth of local option, followed by a
new battle for Prohibition; and there will then be no need for
a National Board of Inquiry to delve into the matter, for the
very abuses which ended Prohibition will bring it back again —
and Crime will come with it, on the gallop.

Corrupt officials and maladministration of liquor bring us
inevitably to the consideration of that malfeasance and nonfeasance which result from corruption in office. Everywhere,
there should be a wider latitude of inquiry and prosecution. The
crime of officially aiding criminality cannot be eliminated as
long as no deterrent is placed upon it. Why should an officer of

any sort worry about being fined if he already has feathered his nest to the extent of hundreds of thousands of dollars? Why should a warden or prison guard worry about the contumely heaped upon him by an inquiry board if the penalty is nothing more than dismissal? This latter is frequently the utmost limit of punishment visited upon crooked or inefficient officers in all branches of enforcement. There should be actual prosecution — swift, stern, unrelenting, and with a double penalty for any officer who betrays his trust. If the officers who betray their communities held some real fear of reprisal, there would not be as much scandal in public office. But there is no fear; except that of the honest guardian of the peace who constantly shakes in his shoes lest he accidentally arrest a person of political or monetary influence and thereby lose his job!

Whenever the executive of a state or a parole board decides to open prison doors for persons who have shown themselves, through a multiplicity of arrests, to be enemies of society, that executive or that parole board should be forced to accept responsibility — the kind with teeth in it — for such an action. It is upon this decision that a dangerous criminal has been foisted upon an unwilling society. It should be the responsibility of such officials that criminals live up to parole or pardon promises. In case of subsequent unlawful activities, there should be prosecution, not simply of the offenders, but of the man or men who, through criminal alliances, or criminal negligence, have brought about a condition of plunder, pillage or murder. If such boards or governors with clemency powers were thus forced to accept responsibility for their cell-clearing actions, there would be fewer states where the known price of parole runs as low as two hundred and fifty dollars. There would be fewer governors extending leaves of absence or Christmas furloughs to dear boys of the cell block.

As for the prisoners themselves, the estoppage of crime is not brought closer by the luxuries of "sob-sister" prisons. A favorite excuse of convict-coddlers is that something must be done to occupy a prisoner's mind, both to save his sanity and to prevent rebellion against incarceration. To this belief, all the over-abundance of amusement in certain prisons can be traced; in other words, many wardens are incapable of the discipline necessary to handle their prisoners, or of sufficient resourcefulness to provide work, and so they resort to cajolery to hold their idle charges in contentment. They say they cannot keep their men occupied.

This is idiotic. If a man is sentenced to servitude at hard labor, he should serve a sentence at hard labor. Otherwise, there should be a change in the language of the courts so that the public knows that the offender is going to a life of sun-baths, radio, and first-run motion pictures. Visit such a penitentiary sometime. Listen to the warden's plaint that he has no work for his men. Then look about the place. You will find that the workshops "where there is not enough work to go round" are filled with *labor-saving devices*. In one prison where "there is not enough work to go round" a big part of the labor program is in the shoeshop. Here can be found every sort of latest patented machinery for the production of shoes. A prison is the last place in the world where industry should be attempted on a production-line basis. Hand-made shoes would almost create a "labor shortage" in this institution. The same is true of other places where machinery does the work of ten men, while the nine men unemployed loll about their cells, reading the latest magazines, plotting new crimes. There should be work in prisons. The average warden who says that his greatest job is to provide work, insists that labor union legislation will not permit the manufacture of many articles. Then, the legislation should be altered! And it is up to us to alter it.

Federal investigations may not be unanimously successful, but they are at least a step in the right direction. Certainly there could be no more enlightening investigation than a national in-

quiry into gambling. With billions being poured into the hands
of the underworld, with local corruption rearing protective barriers about places which are little more than hide-outs, quick
action should be taken to negative such activities. Betting is not
the chief business of such places; they too often constitute an
area where crime thrives in safety. If the Federal Government
can prosecute under the Mann Act, under the Stolen Property
Act, under the Dyer Act and under other laws prohibiting
interstate criminal activities, it can prohibit the interstate movement of slot machines, gambling devices, lottery tickets and
gaming paraphernalia. This, in itself, would provide a weapon
with which to cripple the syndicates which control gambling
from one end of America to the other. It would hamstring the
makers of slot machines, roulette wheels, and other devices. It
would confine the personnel of a slimy crew to areas where,
at least, the community would be responsible to itself for its misdeeds.

One adjunct of gambling is the hostess, protected in all her
forms of predatory activity by the fact that her boss "has the
town." The same element which bribes officials, or contributes
heavily to the campaign funds of a "favorable" administration,
owns night clubs, taverns where women are employed as "come-
ons," or halls where sex-in-clothes is an attraction. Investigations
by a National Board of Inquiry would, I feel sure, make startling
revelations in this respect, even in small towns. Every person who
engages in the hostess "profession" should be fingerprinted and
there should be stringent regulations defining her activities. There
is a crying need for this; too many thousands of harpies are
robbers, blackmailers, suborners of good government. Some are
out-and-out whores; others on the fringe. They should be
recorded for what they are, not foisted upon the public as
"hostesses."

As a further protection against such activities, this writer
hopes that he is not crying in the wilderness when he urges the
establishment of the proper type of segregated district, rigidly

run, rigidly policed. There are many people who actually believe that whoredom has been done away with; that there is no "Row," no red light district, no surface evidence. But whoredom cannot be eliminated by law. It is among the most persistent of infractions, and it cannot be hidden without a sequel of bribery, disease, destruction of fealty to office, and blackmail. It cannot be coped with by viewing the prostitute as a criminal problem instead of what she is — a social one, to be adjusted upon a basis of understanding and a certain amount of sympathy. Persons of discernment and of highly anti-Communistic sentiments who have toured Russia under conditions which allow them to see beneath the surface, report one phase of life with which they are in accord with the Stalin government: Prostitution, they say, had been reduced by the comparatively simple method of providing work and remuneration for those who entered the life because of economic reasons.

However, in spite of work, in spite of everything, there will remain a certain number of women who are congenitally inclined toward prostitution. The efforts of the entire world could not change their outlook or their desires. For them there is a definite niche while human nature remains as it is. For such women there should be the segregated district, honestly and rigidly supervised by a Board of Public Health and Morals, with fingerprinting, registration cards, blood tests and other medical examination. There should be clean living conditions, and freedom from excessive percentages, which, under to-day's system, cut a prostitute's income to practically nothing. There should be inflexible rules for closing time, efficient police supervision, and the stricture that no men be allowed to live off the profits of the business.

This writer has received reports from several cities which have had the temerity to open segregated districts. They are not model ones by any means — merely an honest attempt to combat a social evil with the best weapons at hand. In one of these, there are no madams; each prostitute has her small apartment for which she pays nominal rent; and no carrion-feeding syndicate extorts the major part of her earnings. She can remain there as long or as short a time as she pleases. There is a restaurant, commissary, police guard. Drunken men are turned back at the gates. Undue soliciting is forbidden. Medical examination is strict. The history of every woman is recorded, with her fingerprints. She must have no pimp. Inside the district she is free to pursue her chosen trade. Once outside, her actions must be most decorous; otherwise she faces heavy penalties. There are no "party girls" in this town — they go to jail if caught. There are no "call-houses" or prostitutes sneaking in and out of hotels. The tourist camps are really tourist camps instead of assignation houses. If school-kids desire to engage in parked-car intercourse, they must go outside the county lines to do so — and even then there is danger that parents will be notified. A pimp is thrown into jail and sent to highway work or rock pile. And this city believes that, by doing all these things, it has decreased its crime bill by a tremendous amount.

And here we come to crime-contributors whom society can easily chase down. Society must give more attention to the pimp and procurer — regarding him for what he is: a direct menace not only to the girl upon whose earnings he feeds but to the community. He is the man who, through constant promises of better days just as "soon as they get a little money ahead" inveigles women into prostitution. He finds arguments to keep her in business; he seeks out syndicate owners and makes a deal whereby, as long as he receives a portion of her earnings, she will remain in debt to the syndicate and become a virtual slave. He "frames" her with police if she tries to quit him. There are no printable adjectives by which to describe his degradation.

Many states have no penalty for the pimp. Other commonwealths regard him as a petty offender. But the man who adopts this life is degraded, dangerous, and a first aid to crime. There should be statutes to deal with him, statutes which bite like a steel trap. If more rats of his type were sent to prison and there segregated and treated with the scorn and stern punishment which their calling deserves, there would be fewer women walking the streets in search of paying bedfellows. These men possess no sense of moral obligation. They should be given the most menial tasks that a warden can invent. All efforts should be made at true punishment without a thought of reform, for it is only through the inculcation of fear that the pimp can be curbed. One cannot build morals where morals have been totally destroyed. It accomplishes nothing to punish the whore; after all, she is an effect. The cause is her pimp, and when he learns that the law is determined to eradicate him by the most punitive of methods, he will cease to become a bloodsucker of society — not before.

We must track down all contributing factors to crime. Particularly should there be an increase of public interest as to what becomes of the fruits of crime, and a persistent heckling of police departments looking toward the eradication of fences. To this end, a few rough words might be addressed to the district attorney and to legislators who, through devious laws, have made the fence particularly contemptuous of the law. No robber can exist without a fence to whom he can sell his stolen gains; that is self-evident. Your protection from robbery therefore depends upon how vigorously you insist that law enforcement drive continuously against the man who makes the robber possible.

The same applies to the sellers of morphine, cocaine, heroin, marihuana and other drugs. There is absolutely no reason why every police department in America should not be alert to these infractions. That "the Feds should have the job" is simply a cheap alibi. After all, your police department is your first line of offense and defense against criminal invasion. There should be a "dope detail" on every police department, composed of high-caliber men, especially trained for coöperation with Federal Narcotics officers.

Many of the foregoing suggestions are items into which a National Board of Inquiry of sufficient and able personnel, with adequate appropriations, could and should inquire. However, in none of this writer's references to such an Inquiry is the duty of the citizen forgotten. After all, he is the real sufferer; likewise, he should be the prime protagonist. It is only through his vociferous and insistent demand that such an Inquiry is likely to be set up. Yet the army of more than 600,000 or more persons who annually pass through our prisons and county jails, plus the millions of victims, is entitled to direct and immediate consideration. It seems only just, only decent, that a permanent Board of Inquiry be appointed, with the consent of the states, and be permitted to study all phases of the crime problem, including those of penology and reform. Such a Board, after deep study, should be able to issue something more than a Report. Its recommendations should be common-sense, judicial *decisions*, backed by public opinion of sufficient strength to force their adoption. Let it be a really formidable body — appointed by the President of the United States, from nominations made by civic organizations, the Bar Association, the Attorney General, the American Prison Association, the International Association of Chiefs of Police, the Federal Board of Investigation — with every nominee's qualifications rigidly examined. Members should be paid salaries commensurate with the terrific task, and should be given an unstinted appropriation. The United States Government eagerly sets aside millions for flood relief, drought relief, cinch-bug relief, boll-weevil relief, and every other type of relief affecting relatively small numbers of people. The Government surely owes similar consideration for the relief of crime, which directly concerns three quarters of our population, and indirectly affects every man, woman, and child in America!

Such a Board should have the power to formulate a guide which is now highly necessary in America — a simple set of rules by which law enforcement, penology, parole, and so forth may be administered. Above all else, it should have the power to take the maze of ineffectual, archaic, overlapping, and idiotic laws which exist upon so many of our statute books and throw them overboard. This done, it could then begin upon that best friend of the crook — the statutes and contradictory criminal procedure of our various states! Then would come the greatest undertaking of all: to unify our laws.

Many offenders go to prison because of ignorance. What is permissible in one state is a felony in another. There is no attempt at unification of penalty; a crime which draws two years here brings twenty somewhere else, and is no offense whatever in another community.

One of the principal avenues of escape from punishment is the faulty indictment. Just why a person who is accused of murdering John Jones should not be brought to trial on the simple statement that he has murdered John Jones always has been beyond this writer's comprehension. Nevertheless, in many states, the charge must needs be so long, so involved, so expertly constructed that the district attorney who can draw an indictment which will not result in a demurrer by a shrewd defense attorney is akin to a genius!

When laws are being considered, it should be the duty of any investigating committee to look behind numerous statutes designed ostensibly for the "protection of the innocent man" and seek the ulterior motives which, in many cases, prompted their enactment. Our legislatures, after all, are not only law-making bodies but *lawyer* bodies. Any profession is concerned with its own money-making welfare; excessively clannish, always eager to do a good turn for a brother barrister, the lawyer-legislatures of America have been concerned for decades with the formulation of tangled technicalities, particularly regarding crime, which will result to the benefit, not of the commonwealth, but of the legal profession. In addition to seemingly studied efforts to leave loopholes for criminals under the guise of protecting the innocent, there has also been great neglect in the repealing of conflicting, confusing, or misleading statutes. An excellent example exists in one state, widely press-agented as a model of justice, where a statute is so worded that a person making a dying declaration as to the identity of his murderer must also affirm his belief in God; otherwise the statement is useless. There is an actual case on record in which a murder victim named his three assailants, described them, furnished the motives and every other necessity for conviction. The defendants went free, because the officials taking the statement had not obtained the victim's affirmation of a belief in the Deity!

Such criminally idiotic examples represent the thousands of outlets upon our statute books, familiar to criminal attorneys, but often quite unknown to politically appointed district attorneys who have never before concerned themselves with criminal jurisprudence.

Unification of statutes, clarity of the documentary process of criminal procedure, plus a reduction to a common plane of penalty, are among the urgent needs of criminal procedure to-day. To this should be added a unification and purification of trial methods, by which more of the British system might be brought into the American courtroom. Through the tireless efforts of crime promoters, the functions of a judge have been reduced to a plane almost equal to that of a baseball umpire. Beyond all else, a judge should be allowed to interject himself into a case; he should be able to comment to a jury upon the evidence and the character of the witnesses as he views them. Laws should be amended so that, in these comments, the judge should be allowed to refer to the past record of a man on trial; under most statutes he and the jury are forced to remain deaf, dumb, and blind to the criminal history of a defendant. If a man consistently used a *modus operandi* recognizable in a certain crime for which he is arraigned, it is entirely just that this observation be made. Defense attorneys and sob sisters will wail loudly that this is prejudicial to the defendant. Such protests can be assessed at their true valuation — a part of a persistent campaign for easy escape for the guilty.

It is true that a slightly different technique can be pursued with the first offender from that observed with the hardened criminal. The theory of rehabilitation as expressed by the over-sympathetic might be an excellent means of assistance to the first offender. However, in many states it is almost impossible to differentiate between the neophyte and the confirmed criminal. Many persons technically classed as first offenders have records extending back for years; they have been in juvenile courts, in jails, in places of incarceration designed for youthful offenders; they may even have committed felonies and escaped punishment therefor by "copping pleas" to misdemeanors. They may have a record of as many as twenty arrests — but still, until they are convicted of a major offense bringing a conviction on a felony charge, they remain first offenders in the eyes of the law. Therefore, to regard these subjects as rehabilitation material, to be reformed by kind words, sweet music, and enfoldment in the bosom of society, is to subject that society to the constant danger of depredation by hardened and vicious enemies.

Because of this state of affairs, laws should be changed, so that first offenders be first offenders in reality, and not technically. To true unfortunates the hand of fellowship should be extended. But convict-coddlers have so imposed upon society that now little stigma attaches to persons of even recidivistic tendencies.

A true first offender, no doubt, may be cured by what might be called mental hospitalization. It is ridiculous, however, to assume that hardened criminals are likely to respond to such measures.

There is a civic, national, and industrial responsibility in the eradication of slum conditions. In the factory community, this is largely a duty of the corporation. There are many reasons why hatred exists among corporation employees: the drab lives which workers must lead; the grimy filth of factory smoke in which they must dwell; the sunless days of industry-clouded skies, the lack of wholesome amusement, of playgrounds, of interest on the part of employers in what goes on after labor hours

— all this is conducive to rebellion. The suggestion that these conditions be alleviated is not socialistic; it arises from the observations of many years spent in covering crime waves in such communities, in viewing the hopelessness everywhere manifest, in watching girls go down the streets, easy meat for any procurer who will paint a sufficiently luring picture to the spiritually starved individual.

Corporations are, to a degree, parents. Human parents are ofttimes the victims of ingratitude, therefore it is not unnatural that corporation parents should receive something of the same treatment, such as was evidenced in the Kohler case. But perhaps some of this would disappear if all industry instead of a few concerns planned its towns with more thought toward cleanliness, smoke-free skies, clean streets, gardens, garden clubs, recreation centers, playgrounds, kindly aides who would be something more human than mere "social workers." Perhaps it would require a decade for enmities and hatreds to fade; but the cost would be cheap if such a millennium could be established in that time.

Law enforcement would have an easier job if these elementary conditions in slum and school and factory and court were corrected. But all of law enforcement, in its every root, branch, flower, and seed, should attain a career status. Crime in many of its ramifications has become a highly specialized "profession." It can be combated only by careers in law enforcement. There should be State Departments of Justice, built upon the non-magical formula of the Federal Bureau of Investigation. There should be tremendous enlargement in the scope, personnel, requirements, and authority of the State Police, which should take over the duties of such offices as those of Sheriff and Constable and small-town police officer. There should be earnest attention to the badly administered system by which undertakers and casket-sellers are now enabled to become county coroners. Why is this not a part of the functions of a State Police, with

regional medical examiners? Prisons should be swept clean of all
human scum in official capacities, with the personnel replaced
with merit men trained to their tasks and assured of jobs and
advancement *so long as they deserve it*. District attorneys and all
assistants and investigators should be career men.

There is no reason why there should not be a State Department
of Defense applicable to all. A prisoner does not choose his prosecutor; if he likewise could not choose his defender, fewer poor
persons and more rich ones would go to prison and everyone
would be given the backing of a state's resources in proving
either innocence or guilt. One of the reasons why the Federal
Bureau of Investigation obtains a percentage of 96.6 in convictions is because the Bureau acts as both defense and prosecution,
before arrest. The case is carefully sifted; evidence for the suspected man is weighed as heavily as evidence against him. By the
time the guilt of a man is decided upon, practically every defense argument which can be brought up in court already has
been considered in his behalf and ticketed as false.   Therefore,
when the Bureau finally presents its case in court, the evidence
is well-nigh incontrovertible. Any law enforcement agency,
given the right type of personnel and direction, and freedom to
proceed, can do the same thing. Also, any rich man, deprived of
the power to bribe, to hire powerful attorneys and "friendly experts," and to overwhelm the prosecution by his wealth, will be
exceedingly chary of committing crimes. Such a condition of
course entails emancipation from politics and influence. This is
true of all law enforcement, including that of penology and so-
called "reform" as exemplified by the actions of parole boards.
Hardly a parole administrator but is affiliated with politics.
No Governor should have the power of life and death. If he is
a good Governor, he has not the time to inquire personally into
cases; he must depend upon the reports of others. If he is a
bad one, he can be swayed by political currents, by personal appeals to his sympathy, or he can even be reached through his
pocketbook. For these reasons, no politician or pet of politicians

should have any place on a parole board or on probationary groups.

It may seem impossible to divorce law enforcement from politics. This writer believes that it is not at all impossible, but highly possible. There is needed, of course, a crushing weight of public opinion; and, above all, concentrated effort. The campaign of a minority few brought about Prohibition, even when the main body of citizens emphatically did not want it. This was done by pinning down candidates to definite promises, promises obtained through the threat of adverse balloting. The same method can be used for the worthy cause of crime prevention: a concerted demand that all candidates for legislatures must promise to work and vote for utter divorcement of politics from all branches of law enforcement.

Candidates hate the questionnaire, particularly if it represents heavy blocks of votes from cohesive groups such as civic clubs, churches, women's clubs, luncheon organizations, business men, etc. They dodge and squirm and lie and evade before they sign on the dotted line. But Prohibition made them sign! Citizens who want decent law enforcement can make them sign too. Fire fights fire. The same weapons, if used intelligently, can defeat the forces which now foster corruption.

Of course there will be candidates who will prove false to promises; that is inevitable and human. There will be others, however, who will live up to suggested ideals. The time will come when there will be efficient and politically free law enforcement — provided that large groups possessing sufficient vision work steadily for the future through many disappointments.

There is no weapon on earth so powerful as the ballot when properly and consistently used as a means of reward or reprisal. This weapon has been unfailing over a period of many years. It is yours in the interest of a crime-free America —

If you will only use it.

THE END